Better Homes and Gardens®

BIGGEST BOOK OF GRILLING

★

MEREDITH® BOOKS

DES MOINES, IOWA

Better Homes and Gardens® Books
An imprint of Meredith® Books

BIGGEST BOOK OF GRILLING

Editor: Carrie E. Holcomb
Senior Associate Design Director: John Eric Seid
Contributing Editors: Spectrum Communication Services, Inc., Winifred Moranville
Contributing Designer: Joyce DeWitt
Cover Design and Illustration: Daniel Pelavin
Copy Chief: Terri Fredrickson
Copy and Production Editor: Victoria Forlini
Editorial Operations Manager: Karen Schirm
Managers, Book Production: Pam Kvitne, Marjorie J. Schenkelberg, Rick Vonholdt
Contributing Copy Editor: Susan Fagan
Contributing Proofreaders: Susan Brown, Gretchen Kauffman, Jim Roberts
Indexer: Elizabeth Parson
Editorial and Design Assistants: Karen McFadden, Mary Lee Gavin
Test Kitchen Director: Lynn Blanchard
Test Kitchen Product Supervisor: Marilyn Cornelius
Test Kitchen Home Economists: Juliana Hale; Laura Harms, R.D.; Jennifer Kalanowski, R.D.;
Maryellen Krantz; Jill Moberly; Colleen Weeden; Lori Wilson

Meredith® Books
Editor in Chief: Linda Raglan Cunningham
Design Director: Matt Strelecki
Executive Editor, Food and Crafts: Jennifer Dorland Darling

Publisher: James D. Blume
Executive Director, Marketing: Jeffrey Meyers
Executive Director, New Business Development: Todd M. Davis
Executive Director, Sales: Ken Zagor
Director, Operations: George A. Susral
Director, Production: Douglas M. Johnston
Business Director: Jim Leonard

Vice President and General Manager: Douglas J. Guendel

Better Homes and Gardens® Magazine
Editor in Chief: Karol DeWulf Nickell
Deputy Editor, Food and Entertaining: Nancy Hopkins

Meredith Publishing Group
President, Publishing Group: Stephen M. Lacy
Vice President-Publishing Director: Bob Mate

Meredith Corporation
Chairman and Chief Executive Officer: William T. Kerr

In Memoriam: E. T. Meredith III (1933-2003)

All of us at Better Homes and Gardens® Books are dedicated to providing you with the information and ideas
you need to create delicious foods. We welcome your comments and suggestions. Write to us at:
Better Homes and Gardens Books, Cookbook Editorial Department, 1716 Locust St., Des Moines, IA 50309-3023.

If you would like to purchase any of our cooking, crafts, gardening, home improvement, or home decorating
and design books, check wherever quality books are sold. Or visit us at: bhgbooks.com

Our Better Homes and Gardens® Test Kitchen seal on the back cover of this book assures you
that every recipe in the *Biggest Book of Grilling* has been tested in the Better Homes and Gardens®
Test Kitchen. This means that each recipe is practical and reliable, and meets our high
standards of taste appeal. We guarantee your satisfaction with
this book for as long as you own it.

BIGGEST BOOK OF GRILLING

TABLE of CONTENTS

"LET'S GRILL"

is the perfect answer to the question "What's for dinner?" With nearly 450 recipes *Better Homes and Gardens® Biggest Book of Grilling* offers you a wide selection of entrées, side dishes, and desserts to fit your fancy—and your timetable. And to accommodate either charcoal or gas grills, the recipes include dual directions.

BUILD YOUR MEAL around grilled steaks, chops, chicken, fish, seafood, burgers, sandwiches, or even pizza. Take advantage of the grill's heat to cook a side dish or dessert alongside the entrée and you have a whole meal hot off the grill.

GRILLING OVER WOOD adds a distinctively delicious flavor to all types of dishes. To try your hand at smoke cooking, turn page 331 and discover a chapter full of recipes that use a grill and wood chips or a water smoker and wood chunks.

ON THOSE DAYS WHEN STAYING INDOORS seems preferable, use the Indoor Grilling chapter. Here you'll find 25 recipes tailored to indoor electric grills. And with timings for both covered and uncovered indoor grills, you can be sure that these recipes will work on your appliance.

SO FIRE UP THE GRILL AND ENJOY A DELECTABLE MEAL ANY— OR EVERY—NIGHT OF THE WEEK!

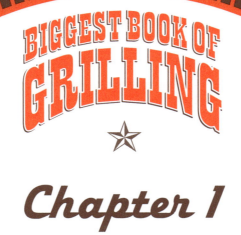

Chapter 1

MEAT

Peppered Rib Roast

A simple, five-ingredient rub adds outstanding flavor to a beef rib roast.

PREP: 10 MINUTES **GRILL:** 2¼ HOURS **STAND:** 15 MINUTES **MAKES:** 10 TO 12 SERVINGS

1 6-pound beef rib roast

2 tablespoons finely chopped shallots

4 teaspoons coarsely ground black pepper

1 teaspoon coarse salt

1 teaspoon dried basil, crushed

1 teaspoon dried thyme, crushed

1 tablespoon olive oil

1 Trim fat from roast. For rub, in a small bowl combine shallots, pepper, salt, basil, and thyme. Brush meat with oil. Sprinkle rub evenly over roast; rub in with your fingers.

2 For a charcoal grill, arrange medium coals around drip pan. Test for medium-low heat above pan. Place roast, bone side down, on grill rack over pan. Cover and grill until desired doneness. Allow 2¼ to 2¾ hours for medium-rare doneness (135°F) or 2¾ to 3¼ hours for medium doneness (150°F). Add coals as necessary to maintain heat. (For a gas grill, preheat grill. Reduce heat to medium-low. Adjust for indirect cooking. Place roast on rack in roasting pan, place on grill rack, and grill as above.)

3 Remove meat from grill. Cover with foil; let stand for 15 minutes before carving. The meat's temperature after standing should be 145°F for medium-rare or 160°F for medium.

NUTRITION FACTS PER SERVING: 310 cal., 18 g total fat (7 g sat. fat), 100 mg chol., 305 mg sodium, 1 g carbo., 0 g fiber, 34 g pro.

Crab-Stuffed Tenderloin

It's hard to improve grilled beef tenderloin, but this recipe does. Then again, what wouldn't sweet and delicate crab, artichoke hearts, and garlic-herb goat cheese improve?

PREP: 20 MINUTES   **GRILL:** 8 MINUTES + 35 MINUTES   **STAND:** 15 MINUTES
MAKES: 6 TO 8 SERVINGS

4 ounces cooked crabmeat

½ of a 14-ounce can artichoke hearts, drained and chopped

¼ of a 5-ounce container semisoft goat cheese with garlic and herb

2 tablespoons thinly sliced green onion

1 2-pound center-cut beef tenderloin

1 tablespoon coarsely ground black pepper

1 For filling, in a small bowl combine crabmeat, artichoke hearts, cheese, and green onion.

2 Trim fat from beef. Split tenderloin lengthwise, cutting to but not through the opposite side. Spread meat open. Place knife in the "V" of the first cut. Cut away from the first cut and parallel to the cut surface to within ½ inch of the other side of the meat. Repeat on opposite side of "V." Spread these sections open. Gently pound meat to ¾-inch thickness. Spoon filling over meat. Starting from a short side, roll up meat. Tie with 100%-cotton kitchen string at 1-inch intervals. Sprinkle pepper evenly over meat; rub in with your fingers.

3 For a charcoal grill, arrange hot coals around a drip pan. Test for medium-hot heat above the pan. Place meat on grill rack directly over coals. Grill for 8 to 10 minutes or until meat is browned, turning frequently. Place meat over drip pan. Cover and grill for 35 to 50 minutes or until medium-rare doneness (135°F). (For a gas grill, preheat grill. Reduce heat to medium-hot. Adjust for indirect cooking. Grill as above, except place meat on a rack in a roasting pan after browning.)

4 Remove meat from grill. Cover with foil; let stand for 15 minutes before slicing. The meat's temperature after standing should be 145°F.

NUTRITION FACTS PER SERVING: 260 cal., 12 g total fat (5 g sat. fat), 110 mg chol., 135 mg sodium, 3 g carbo., 1 g fiber, 34 g pro.

Three-Pepper Beef Tenderloin Roast

*Fork-tender beef tenderloin, seasoned with a trio of peppers,
will make guests feel you've gone the extra mile for them.*

PREP: 15 MINUTES **GRILL:** 1 HOUR **STAND:** 15 MINUTES **MAKES:** 9 OR 10 SERVINGS

1 3- to 3½-pound beef tenderloin roast

1 teaspoon salt

1 teaspoon dried oregano, crushed

1 teaspoon dried thyme, crushed

1 teaspoon paprika

½ teaspoon garlic powder

½ teaspoon onion powder

½ teaspoon ground white pepper

½ teaspoon freshly ground black pepper

¼ teaspoon cayenne pepper

1 Trim the fat from roast. For rub, in a small bowl combine salt, oregano, thyme, paprika, garlic powder, onion powder, white pepper, black pepper, and cayenne pepper. Sprinkle rub evenly over roast; rub in with your fingers.

2 For a charcoal grill, arrange hot coals around a drip pan. Test for medium-hot heat above the pan. Place meat on grill rack over drip pan. Cover and grill for 1 to 1¼ hours or until medium-rare doneness (135°F). Add coals as necessary to maintain heat. (For a gas grill, preheat grill. Reduce heat to medium. Adjust for indirect cooking. Place meat on a rack in a roasting pan, place on grill rack, and grill as above.)

3 Transfer meat to a cutting board; tent meat with foil and let stand for 15 minutes before carving into ¼- to ½-inch-thick slices. The meat's temperature after standing should be 145°F.

NUTRITION FACTS PER SERVING: 253 cal., 13 g total fat (5 g sat. fat), 93 mg chol., 328 mg sodium, 1 g carbo., 0 g fiber, 32 g pro.

Chilled Thai Tenderloin and Pasta with Tons of Basil

Make this recipe two days in advance of a party. Tying the tenderloin butcher-style helps it keep its shape during cooking. Thai peanut sauce is available at most grocery stores.

PREP: 30 MINUTES **GRILL:** 1 HOUR **STAND:** 10 MINUTES **CHILL:** 8 HOURS TO 2 DAYS

MAKES: 10 SERVINGS

1 3-pound center-cut beef tenderloin
   Freshly ground black pepper
½ cup purchased Thai peanut sauce
3 cups packed fresh purple or opal basil sprigs
   (do not remove leaves from stems)
2 pounds dried angel hair pasta, cooked according
   to package directions
2 cups fennel cut into strips
1½ cups purchased Thai peanut sauce
1 cup slivered fresh purple or opal basil
2 tablespoons olive oil

1 Butcher-tie the beef tenderloin (or ask the butcher to do this for you).* Season the beef with pepper. Spread the ½ cup peanut sauce over the beef until coated. Tuck the basil sprigs under the string "cage," covering as much of the beef as possible. For a charcoal grill, arrange hot coals around a drip pan. Test for medium-hot heat above pan. Place beef on grill rack over drip pan. Cover and grill until desired doneness. Allow 1 to 1¼ hours for medium-rare doneness (135°F) or 1¼ to 1½ hours for medium doneness (150°F). Add coals as necessary to maintain heat. (For a gas grill, preheat grill. Reduce heat to medium-hot. Adjust for indirect cooking. Place beef on a rack in a roasting pan, place on grill rack, and grill as above.) Remove beef from grill; cover with foil and let stand for 10 minutes. The meat's temperature after standing should be 145°F for medium-rare or 160°F for medium. Place beef in a food storage container; cover and chill in the refrigerator for at least 8 hours or up to 2 days.

2 In a very large bowl, toss cooked angel hair pasta with fennel and the 1½ cups peanut sauce. Add slivered basil; toss to mix. Cover and chill for at least 2 hours or up to 8 hours.

3 To serve, toss pasta mixture with olive oil; arrange on serving platter. Remove beef from refrigerator. Cut string and remove basil sprigs; discard basil. Slice tenderloin into ¼-inch-thick slices. Arrange beef alongside pasta.

NUTRITION FACTS PER SERVING: 670 cal., 19 g total fat (5 g sat. fat), 62 mg chol., 828 mg sodium, 83 g carbo., 7 g fiber; 37 g pro.

*NOTE: To butcher-tie the tenderloin, place beef tenderloin on a cutting board or a tray. Using an 8-foot piece of 100%-cotton kitchen string, slide the string under the tenderloin crosswise about 2 inches from one end. Pull string up and around the top; make a knot, keeping one end of the string short. Do not cut the long end of the string. Using the long end, pull the string toward the other end of tenderloin. About 2 inches from the first tie, hold string and loop underneath tenderloin, bringing it up and around; insert the long end of the string under the top string to secure, pulling to tighten the loop. Repeat, making a loop about every 2 inches until you reach the end of the tenderloin. Bring the string around the tenderloin and back to the starting point. Knot it around the initial loop. Cut the string.

Tri-Tip with Jambalaya Rice

Tri-tip beef roasts are popular on the West Coast.
If you can't find this cut in your area, substitute beef sirloin steak.

PREP: 25 MINUTES **GRILL:** 35 MINUTES **STAND:** 10 MINUTES **MAKES:** 6 SERVINGS

¼ **cup soy sauce**

2 **tablespoons finely chopped onion**

2 **tablespoons granulated sugar**

2 **tablespoons brown sugar**

2 **tablespoons lemon juice**

1 **tablespoon vinegar**

½ **teaspoon chili powder**

1 **1½- to 2-pound boneless beef bottom sirloin roast (tri-tip) or boneless beef sirloin steak, cut 1½ to 2 inches thick**

4 **ounces bulk hot Italian sausage**

2 **stalks celery, sliced**

1 **small red sweet pepper, chopped**

1 **small yellow sweet pepper, chopped**

⅓ **cup chopped onion**

½ **teaspoon bottled minced garlic (1 clove)**

¾ **cup uncooked long grain rice**

¼ **teaspoon cayenne pepper**

¼ **teaspoon paprika**

1 **10½-ounce can condensed cream of mushroom or cream of chicken soup**

1¼ **cups water**

1 For brush-on, in a small bowl stir together soy sauce, the 2 tablespoons onion, the granulated sugar, brown sugar, lemon juice, vinegar, and chili powder; set aside.

2 For a charcoal grill, arrange medium-hot coals around a drip pan. Test for medium heat above pan. Place roast or steak on grill rack over pan. Cover and grill until desired doneness, turning once halfway through grilling and brushing often with soy sauce mixture during last 10 minutes of grilling. Allow 35 to 40 minutes for medium-rare doneness (140°F) or 40 to 45 minutes for medium doneness (155°F). (For a gas grill, preheat grill. Reduce heat to medium. Adjust for indirect cooking. Place roast or steak on a rack in a roasting pan, place on grill rack, and grill as above.)

3 Remove roast or steak from grill. Cover with foil and let stand 10 minutes before slicing. The meat's temperature after standing should be 145°F for medium-rare or 160°F for medium doneness.

4 Meanwhile, in large saucepan cook Italian sausage until browned. Add celery, sweet peppers, the ⅓ cup onion, and the garlic. Cook and stir for 5 minutes. Add uncooked rice, cayenne pepper, and paprika; cook and stir for 2 minutes more. Add soup and the water. Bring just to boiling; reduce heat. Cover and simmer for 15 to 20 minutes or until rice is tender, stirring occasionally. To serve, slice roast or steak. Serve rice mixture with meat.

NUTRITION FACTS PER SERVING: 387 cal., 14 g total fat (5 g sat. fat), 80 mg chol., 1,204 mg sodium, 34 g carbo., 2 g fiber, 30 g pro.

Sage-Brushed Cowboy Steak

Using a homemade sage "brush" to slather on the butter mixture adds more fresh sage flavor to the steak.

PREP: 40 MINUTES   GRILL: 11 MINUTES   MAKES: 4 SERVINGS

3 cups fresh-cut corn kernels

1 tablespoon olive oil

¼ teaspoon salt

2 beef T-bone or porterhouse steaks, cut 1 inch thick

Salt (optional)

Ground black pepper (optional)

1 small red or yellow sweet pepper, halved and seeded

¼ cup snipped fresh sage

2 tablespoons butter or margarine, melted

3 or 4 large fresh sage leaves (optional)

⅓ cup crumbled queso fresco or farmer cheese

1 In a large skillet cook corn in hot oil over medium-hot heat about 10 minutes or until corn is tender and golden brown, stirring often. Stir in the ¼ teaspoon salt. Remove from heat. Cover; keep warm.

2 If desired, sprinkle the steaks with additional salt and pepper. For a charcoal grill, grill the steaks and sweet pepper halves on the rack of an uncovered grill directly over medium coals until steak is desired doneness and sweet peppers are tender; turning once halfway through grilling. For steaks, allow 11 to 14 minutes for medium-rare doneness (145°F) or 13 to 16 minutes for medium doneness (160°F). For sweet peppers, allow 8 to 10 minutes; remove when tender. (For a gas grill, preheat grill. Reduce heat to medium. Place steaks and sweet pepper halves on grill rack over heat. Cover and grill as above.)

3 Meanwhile, stir 2 tablespoons of the snipped fresh sage into the melted butter. If desired, make a sage "brush" by tying the fresh sage leaves together at the base of the leaves; tie again closer to the leaves to make a sturdier brush. After turning steaks, brush with butter mixture using sage brush (or a pastry brush). Discard any remaining butter mixture.

4 Chop grilled sweet peppers. Stir chopped sweet peppers and remaining 2 tablespoons snipped sage into corn. Just before serving, sprinkle corn mixture with crumbled cheese. Serve corn mixture with steaks.

NUTRITION FACTS PER SERVING: 483 cal., 22 g total fat (9 g sat. fat), 111 mg chol., 317 mg sodium, 29 g carbo., 4 g fiber, 44 g pro.

Steak with Sweet-Pepper Mustard

Here are steaks with a Gallic touch—a Dijon sauce enlivened by grilled sweet peppers and a rub featuring a French favorite—thyme.

PREP: 30 MINUTES **GRILL:** 10 MINUTES + 8 MINUTES **MAKES:** 4 SERVINGS

2 medium red sweet peppers, quartered lengthwise

Olive oil

2 tablespoons snipped fresh thyme or 2 teaspoons dried thyme, crushed

1 tablespoon Dijon-style mustard

1½ teaspoons bottled minced garlic (3 cloves)

2 beef T-bone steaks, cut 1 inch thick (1¾ to 2 pounds total)

¼ teaspoon salt

¼ teaspoon ground black pepper

1 Brush sweet peppers with olive oil. For a charcoal grill, grill peppers, cut sides up, on the rack of an uncovered grill directly over medium-hot coals about 10 minutes or until pepper skins are blistered and dark. (For a gas grill, preheat grill. Reduce heat to medium-hot. Place peppers, cut sides up, on grill rack over heat. Cover and grill as above.)

2 Wrap peppers in foil and let stand for 20 minutes. Remove pepper skins; discard skins. Cut 2 pepper pieces lengthwise into thin strips; set aside. In a blender container or food processor bowl combine the remaining pepper pieces, 1 tablespoon of the fresh thyme or 1 teaspoon of the dried thyme, the Dijon mustard, and ½ teaspoon of the garlic. Cover and blend or process until smooth.

3 Meanwhile, trim fat from steaks. For rub, in a small bowl combine the remaining 1 tablespoon fresh thyme or 1 teaspoon dried thyme, the remaining 1 teaspoon garlic, the salt, and black pepper. Sprinkle rub evenly over both sides of each steak; rub in with your fingers. Add steaks to grill. Grill until desired doneness, turning once halfway through grilling. Allow 8 to 12 minutes for medium-rare doneness (145°F) or 12 to 15 minutes for medium doneness (160°F).

4 To serve, cut each steak in half. Top the steaks with the grilled pepper strips. Serve with the mustard mixture.

NUTRITION FACTS PER SERVING: 216 cal., 8 g total fat (3 g sat. fat), 66 mg chol., 299 mg sodium, 5 g carbo., 1 g fiber, 29 g pro.

Teriyaki T-Bone Steaks

The tangy-sweet taste of teriyaki flavors these T-bones. Serve them with steamed rice tossed with toasted macadamia nuts and thinly sliced green onions.

PREP: 15 MINUTES **MARINATE:** 4 TO 6 HOURS **GRILL:** 11 MINUTES **MAKES:** 4 SERVINGS

2   beef T-bone steaks, cut 1 inch thick (1¾ to 2 pounds total)

⅓   cup bottled teriyaki sauce

2   tablespoons sliced green onion

1   tablespoon honey

1   tablespoon lemon juice or rice vinegar

1   tablespoon finely chopped fresh ginger

1   teaspoon toasted sesame oil

½   teaspoon bottled minced garlic (1 clove)

¼   teaspoon coarsely ground black pepper

1   small fresh pineapple, cut into wedges and cored

2   or 4 1-inch-thick slices tomato or sweet pepper

1   tablespoon cooking oil

1 Trim fat from steaks. Place steaks in a resealable plastic bag set in a shallow dish. For marinade, in a small bowl combine teriyaki sauce, green onion, honey, lemon juice or rice vinegar, fresh ginger, sesame oil, garlic, and black pepper. Pour marinade over steaks. Seal bag; turn to coat steaks. Marinate in the refrigerator for at least 4 hours or up to 6 hours, turning bag occasionally.

2 Drain steaks, reserving marinade. For a charcoal grill, grill steaks on the rack of an uncovered grill directly over medium coals until desired doneness, turning and bushing once with reserved marinade halfway through grilling. Allow 11 to 14 minutes for medium-rare doneness (145°F) or 13 to 16 minutes for medium doneness (160°F). Discard any remaining marinade.

3 While the steaks are grilling, brush pineapple wedges and tomato or sweet pepper slices with cooking oil; add pineapple and tomato or sweet pepper to grill. Grill for 6 to 8 minutes or until slightly charred, turning once halfway through grilling. (For a gas grill, preheat grill. Reduce heat to medium. Place steaks, then pineapple and tomato or sweet pepper slices on grill rack over heat. Cover and grill as above.)

4 To serve, cut each steak in half. Serve with pineapple and tomato or sweet pepper slices.

NUTRITION FACTS PER SERVING: 296 cal., 12 g total fat (4 g sat. fat), 66 mg chol., 586 mg sodium, 16 g carbo., 1 g fiber, 29 g pro.

Beef Tenderloin Fillets with Horseradish Chili

A bold dry rub seals in the flavor of these thick and juicy steaks.
The horseradish chili is a surefire wake-up call for your palate.

PREP: 25 MINUTES   GRILL: 13 MINUTES   MAKES: 4 SERVINGS

2 teaspoons snipped fresh sage or ½ teaspoon dried sage, crushed

¼ to 1 teaspoon coarsely ground white or black pepper

¼ teaspoon salt

4 beef tenderloin steaks, cut 1¼ inches thick (about 1½ pounds total)

2 teaspoons cooking oil

1 cup coarsely chopped tomatoes

2 tablespoons chili seasoning mix

1 teaspoon bottled minced garlic (2 cloves)

½ cup drained canned red beans, rinsed

¼ to ½ cup grated fresh horseradish root

Fresh sage leaves (optional)

Steamed vegetables (optional)

1 For rub, in a small bowl combine snipped or dried sage, pepper, and salt. Sprinkle rub evenly over both sides of each steak; rub in with your fingers. In a heavy small skillet heat oil over medium-hot heat. Add tomatoes, chili seasoning, and garlic to skillet; cook for 1 to 2 minutes or just until tomatoes start to soften. Reduce heat to medium-low. Add beans and horseradish. Cook and stir for 2 minutes more. Loosely cover bean mixture; keep warm.

2 For charcoal grill, grill steaks on the rack of an uncovered grill directly over medium coals until desired doneness. Allow 13 to 17 minutes for medium-rare doneness (145°F) or 16 to 21 minutes for medium doneness (160°F). (For a gas grill, preheat grill. Reduce heat to medium. Place steaks on grill rack over heat. Cover and grill as above.) To serve, place steaks on dinner plates; spoon warm chili sauce over steaks. If desired, garnish with sage leaves and serve with steamed vegetables.

NUTRITION FACTS PER SERVING: 347 cal., 14 g total fat (5 g sat. fat), 96 mg chol., 759 mg sodium, 18 g carbo., 1 g fiber, 37 g pro.

14

Filet Mignon with Portobello Sauce

Just a splash of Madeira or port wine makes this buttery, meltingly tender steak and mushroom dish simply marvelous. Madeira and port are slightly sweet Spanish wines flavored with a bit of brandy.

PREP: 15 MINUTES   GRILL: 11 MINUTES   MAKES: 4 SERVINGS

4 beef tenderloin steaks, cut 1 inch thick (about 1¼ pounds total)

1 teaspoon olive oil

¼ teaspoon ground black pepper

2 large portobello mushrooms, halved and sliced

8 green onions, cut into 1-inch pieces

1 tablespoon butter or margarine

⅓ cup beef broth

2 tablespoons Madeira or port wine

1 Trim fat from steaks. Rub both sides of each steak with oil and pepper. For charcoal grill, grill steaks on the rack of an uncovered grill directly over medium coals until desired doneness, turning once halfway through grilling. Allow 11 to 15 minutes for medium-rare doneness (145°F) or 14 to 18 minutes for medium doneness (160°F). (For a gas grill, preheat grill. Reduce heat to medium. Place steaks on grill rack over heat. Cover and grill as above.)

2 Meanwhile, for sauce, in a large skillet cook and stir mushrooms and green onions in hot butter over medium heat about 5 minutes or until vegetables are tender. Stir in broth and wine. Bring to boiling. Remove from heat. Thinly slice steaks diagonally and serve with sauce.

NUTRITION FACTS PER SERVING: 260 cal., 13 g total fat (5 g sat. fat), 88 mg chol., 160 mg sodium, 4 g carbo., 1 g fiber, 29 g pro.

Chipotle Tenderloin Steak with Potatoes

These steaks have all the attributes of a classic Mexican dish—chile peppers, cilantro, garlic, and lime. Enjoy a margarita while dinner grills.

PREP: 15 MINUTES **GRILL:** 20 MINUTES **MAKES:** 4 SERVINGS

4 beef tenderloin or ribeye steaks, cut 1 to 1¼ inches thick

2 to 4 tablespoons finely chopped, drained chipotle chile peppers in adobo sauce

2 tablespoons snipped fresh cilantro

1 tablespoon lime juice

2 teaspoons bottled minced garlic (4 cloves)

½ teaspoon salt

3 medium potatoes, each cut lengthwise into 8 wedges

2 teaspoons olive oil

1 teaspoon coarse salt or kosher salt

1 lime, cut into wedges

1 Trim fat from steaks. In a small bowl stir together chipotle peppers, cilantro, lime juice, garlic, and salt. Brush mixture onto both sides of each steak. Brush potato wedges with olive oil; sprinkle with salt.

2 For a charcoal grill, place potatoes on the rack of a grill with a cover directly over medium coals. Cover and grill for 20 to 25 minutes or until potatoes are tender and brown, turning once halfway through grilling. While the potatoes are grilling, add steaks to grill. Cover and grill until steaks are desired doneness, turning once halfway through grilling. Allow 11 to 15 minutes for medium-rare doneness (145°F) or 14 to 18 minutes for medium doneness (160°F). (For a gas grill, preheat grill. Reduce heat to medium. Place potatoes, then steaks on grill rack over heat. Cover and grill as above.) To serve, pass lime wedges with steaks.

NUTRITION FACTS PER SERVING: 385 cal., 13 g total fat (4 g sat. fat), 96 mg chol., 959 mg sodium, 30 g carbo., 1 g fiber, 35 g pro.

Mustard-Wine Sauced Beef Tenderloins

Serve these elegant steaks with mashed potatoes
subtly seasoned with crumbled blue cheese.

PREP: 25 MINUTES   COOK: 43 MINUTES   GRILL: 14 MINUTES   MAKES: 8 SERVINGS

¼ ounce dried mushrooms (morels or chanterelles) (⅓ cup)

3 tablespoons butter

1 cup chopped red onion

1 tablespoon whole green peppercorns in brine, drained

2 teaspoons cracked black pepper

1 cup dry Marsala or dry red wine

2 cups whipping cream

½ cup condensed beef broth

   Salt

8 beef tenderloin steaks, cut 1¼ inches thick

❶ For sauce, in a small bowl cover the dried mushrooms with hot water. Let stand for 20 minutes. Rinse under warm running water; squeeze out the excess moisture. Chop mushrooms.

❷ In large skillet melt the butter over medium heat. Add the mushrooms, onion, drained green peppercorns, and cracked black pepper. Cook, uncovered, over medium-low heat for 15 minutes, stirring frequently.

❸ Add Marsala. Bring to boiling; reduce heat. Simmer, uncovered, for 8 to 10 minutes or until wine is reduced by about half and mushroom mixture is slightly thickened, stirring occasionally.

❹ Add whipping cream and condensed beef broth. Cook over medium heat just until tiny bubbles form around the edge; reduce heat. Cook over medium-low heat, stirring occasionally with a wooden spoon, for 20 to 25 minutes or until mixture thickens to desired consistency. Season to taste with salt; set aside.

❺ Trim fat from steaks. For a charcoal grill, grill steaks on the rack of an uncovered grill directly over medium coals until desired doneness, turning once halfway through grilling. Allow 14 to 18 minutes for medium-rare doneness (145°F) or 17 to 21 minutes for medium doneness (160°F). (For a gas grill, preheat grill. Reduce heat to medium. Place steaks on grill rack over heat. Cover and grill as above.)

❻ To serve, reheat the sauce; transfer sauce to a serving bowl and pass with the grilled steaks.

NUTRITION FACTS PER SERVING: 843 cal., 55 g total fat (28 g sat. fat), 303 mg chol., 391 mg sodium, 6 g carbo., 1 g fiber, 73 g pro.

BLT Steak

The makings of the classic summer sandwich deliciously top this belt-busting steak.

PREP: 15 MINUTES GRILL: 14 MINUTES MAKES: 4 SERVINGS

2 12-ounce beef top loin steaks, cut 1¼ inches thick

8 slices bacon

½ cup bottled balsamic vinaigrette salad dressing

12 red and/or yellow tomato slices

2 cups torn mixed salad greens

1 For charcoal grill, grill steaks on the rack of an uncovered grill directly over medium coals until desired doneness, turning once halfway through grilling. Allow 14 to 18 minutes for medium-rare doneness (145°F) or 17 to 21 minutes for medium doneness (160°F). (For a gas grill, preheat grill. Reduce heat to medium. Place steaks on grill rack over heat. Cover and grill as above.)

2 Meanwhile, in a skillet cook bacon until crisp. Drain bacon on paper towels, reserving 1 tablespoon drippings in skillet. Add balsamic vinaigrette salad dressing to the drippings in skillet. Cook and stir for 1 minute, scraping up any browned bits. Halve the steaks. Top steaks with tomato slices, bacon, mixed greens, and dressing mixture.

NUTRITION FACTS PER SERVING: 556 cal., 42 g total fat (14 g sat. fat), 122 mg chol., 636 mg sodium, 5 g carbo., 1 g fiber, 38 g pro.

Beef Steaks with Tomato-Garlic Butter

Beef steaks take kindly to the enhancement of butter, especially this tangy, garlic-infused blend. Double the butter recipe if you want to spread it on warm bread.

PREP: 12 MINUTES **GRILL:** 11 MINUTES **MAKES:** 4 SERVINGS

½ cup butter, softened

1 tablespoon snipped oil-packed dried tomatoes

1 tablespoon chopped kalamata olives

1 tablespoon finely chopped green onion

½ teaspoon bottled minced garlic (1 clove)

4 boneless beef top loin steaks, cut 1 inch thick (about 1½ pounds total)

Salt (optional)

Ground black pepper (optional)

1 For flavored butter, in a small bowl stir together butter, dried tomatoes, kalamata olives, green onion, and garlic. Set aside. Trim fat from steaks.

2 For a charcoal grill, grill steaks on the rack of an uncovered grill directly over medium coals until desired doneness, turning once halfway through grilling. Allow 11 to 15 minutes for medium-rare doneness (145°F) or 14 to 18 minutes for medium doneness (160°F). (For a gas grill, preheat grill. Reduce heat to medium. Place steaks on grill rack over heat. Cover and grill as above.)

3 If desired, sprinkle steaks with salt and pepper. To serve, spread 1 tablespoon of the butter mixture over each steak. Cover and chill the remaining butter mixture for another time (also can be used as a spread for bread).

NUTRITION FACTS PER SERVING: 383 cal., 22 g total fat (11 g sat. fat), 161 mg chol., 227 mg sodium, 0 g carbo., 0 g fiber, 45 g pro.

Garlic Steaks with Nectarine-Onion Relish

What's better than the smell of steak on the grill in the summertime? The aroma of garlic-studded beef on the grill. The mint-scented relish features one of summer's favorite fruits. Serve this steak with some crusty bread to soak up the delicious juices.

PREP: 25 MINUTES   STAND: 20 MINUTES   GRILL: 11 MINUTES   MAKES: 4 SERVINGS

4   boneless beef top loin steaks, cut 1 inch thick (1½ to 2 pounds total)

6   cloves garlic, thinly sliced

Salt

Ground black pepper

2   medium onions, coarsely chopped

1   teaspoon olive oil

2   tablespoons cider vinegar

1   tablespoon honey

1   medium nectarine, chopped

2   teaspoons snipped fresh applemint, pineapplemint, or spearmint

Fresh applemint, pineapplemint, or spearmint sprigs (optional)

1 Trim fat from steaks. With the point of a paring knife, make small slits in steaks. Insert half of the garlic into slits. Wrap steaks in plastic wrap; let stand at room temperature up to 20 minutes. (For more intense flavor, refrigerate up to 8 hours.) Sprinkle with salt and pepper.

2 Meanwhile, for relish, in a large nonstick skillet cook onions and remaining garlic in hot oil over medium heat about 10 minutes or until onions are a deep golden color (but not brown), stirring occasionally. Stir in vinegar and honey. Stir in nectarine and the snipped mint; heat through.

3 For charcoal grill, grill steaks on the rack of an uncovered grill directly over medium coals until desired doneness, turning once halfway through grilling. Allow 11 to 15 minutes for medium-rare doneness (145°F) or 14 to 18 minutes for medium doneness (160°F). (For a gas grill, preheat grill. Reduce heat to medium. Place steaks on grill rack over heat. Cover and grill as above.) Serve the relish with steaks. If desired, garnish with mint sprigs.

NUTRITION FACTS PER SERVING: 272 cal., 9 g total fat (3 g sat. fat), 97 mg chol., 108 mg sodium, 13 g carbo., 1 g fiber, 34 g pro.

Garlic-Barbecued Steaks

Who has the best barbecue? You do—whether you're in Kansas City, Memphis, Houston, or Kalamazoo—with these garlic-studded steaks smothered in a sweet, easy sauce.

PREP: 20 MINUTES **GRILL:** 11 MINUTES **MAKES:** 4 SERVINGS

2 boneless beef top loin or ribeye steaks, cut 1 inch thick (about 1½ pounds total)

2 large cloves garlic, thinly sliced

1 tablespoon olive oil

Salt

Ground black pepper

¾ to 1 cup bottled barbecue sauce

1 tablespoon yellow mustard

1 tablespoon cider vinegar

1 tablespoon honey or brown sugar

1 teaspoon dried thyme, crushed

1 Trim fat from steaks. With the point of a paring knife, make small slits in steaks. Insert garlic slices into slits. Rub steaks with oil and sprinkle with salt and pepper.

2 For sauce, in a small bowl stir together barbecue sauce, mustard, vinegar, honey or brown sugar, and thyme.

3 For a charcoal grill, grill steaks on the rack of an uncovered grill directly over medium coals until desired doneness, turning and brushing once with sauce halfway through grilling. Allow 11 to 15 minutes for medium-rare doneness (145°F) or 14 to 18 minutes for medium doneness (160°F). (For a gas grill, preheat grill. Reduce heat to medium. Place steaks on the grill rack directly over heat. Cover and grill as above.)

4 In a small saucepan bring the remaining sauce to boiling. Boil gently, uncovered, for 1 minute. To serve, cut each steak in half. Pass the sauce with the steaks.

NUTRITION FACTS PER SERVING: 301 cal., 12 g total fat (3 g sat. fat), 98 mg chol., 648 mg sodium, 11 g carbo., 1 g fiber, 34 g pro.

Here's-the-Beef Steak and Onions

The sweet mustard topper transforms grilled steak and onions into extraordinary fare.

PREP: 10 MINUTES GRILL: 11 MINUTES MAKES: 4 SERVINGS

¼ cup Dijon-style, brown, or yellow mustard

1 tablespoon honey

1½ teaspoons snipped fresh thyme or ½ teaspoon dried thyme, crushed

½ teaspoon bottled minced garlic (1 clove)

⅛ teaspoon ground black pepper

2 boneless beef top loin steaks, cut 1 inch thick (about 12 ounces total)

2 medium onions, cut into ½-inch-thick slices

1 For glaze, in a small bowl stir together mustard, honey, thyme, garlic, and pepper. Set aside. Trim fat from steaks.

2 For charcoal grill, grill steaks and onion slices on the rack of an uncovered grill directly over medium coals until steaks are desired doneness and onions are tender, turning and generously brushing steaks and onions once with glaze halfway through grilling. Allow 11 to 15 minutes for medium-rare doneness (145°F) or 14 to 18 minutes for medium doneness (160°F). (For a gas grill, preheat grill. Reduce heat to medium. Place steaks and onion slices on grill rack over heat. Cover and grill as above.) Discard any remaining glaze.

3 To serve, thinly slice the steaks and arrange with the onion slices on 4 dinner plates.

NUTRITION FACTS PER SERVING: 158 cal., 4 g total fat (1 g sat. fat), 50 mg chol., 389 mg sodium, 8 g carbo., 1 g fiber, 19 g pro.

Kansas City Strip Steaks

Cuts other than strip steaks will benefit from this peppy seasoning.
Rub the mixture on T-bone or sirloin steaks too. Halve the mixture for fewer steaks.

PREP: 10 MINUTES   CHILL: 1 HOUR   GRILL: 11 MINUTES   MAKES: 8 SERVINGS

- **2** tablespoons prepared horseradish
- **2** tablespoons lemon juice
- **4** teaspoons sugar
- **2** teaspoons paprika
- **2** teaspoons bottled minced garlic (4 cloves)
- **1** teaspoon salt
- **1** teaspoon ground black pepper
- **½** teaspoon instant beef bouillon granules
- **4** 8-ounce beef top loin steaks, cut 1 inch thick

1 In a small bowl combine horseradish, lemon juice, sugar, paprika, garlic, salt, pepper, and beef bouillon granules. Trim fat from meat. Rub mixture on both sides of each steak. Cover; refrigerate steaks for 1 hour.

2 For charcoal grill, grill steaks on the rack of an uncovered grill directly over medium coals until desired doneness, turning once halfway through grilling. Allow 11 to 15 minutes for medium-rare doneness (145°F) or 14 to 18 minutes for medium doneness (160°F). (For a gas grill, preheat grill. Reduce heat to medium. Place steaks on grill rack over heat. Cover and grill as above.)

NUTRITION FACTS PER SERVING: 276 cal., 19 g total fat (8 g sat. fat), 74 mg chol., 400 mg sodium, 8 g carbo., 0 g fiber, 22 g pro.

Rosemary Beef with Sweet Pepper Relish

The onion-and-pepper relish conveniently cooks in a foil pack along with the rosemary-rubbed juicy steaks.

PREP: 25 MINUTES GRILL: 11 MINUTES MAKES: 4 SERVINGS

1 medium onion, thinly sliced

1 red or yellow sweet pepper, cut into strips

1 tablespoon red wine vinegar

1 tablespoon olive oil

⅛ teaspoon ground black pepper

2 teaspoons snipped fresh rosemary

2 teaspoons bottled minced garlic (4 cloves)

4 boneless beef top loin steaks, cut 1 inch thick (about 1 pound total)

1 tablespoon prepared horseradish

1 For relish, fold a 24×18-inch piece of heavy foil in half to make a 12×18-inch rectangle. Place onion and sweet pepper in center of foil. Drizzle vinegar and 2 teaspoons of the oil over vegetables; sprinkle with black pepper. Bring up 2 opposite edges of foil; seal with a double fold. Fold remaining ends to completely enclose vegetables, leaving space for steam to build. Set aside.

2 In a small bowl combine remaining 1 teaspoon oil, the rosemary, and garlic. Trim fat from steaks. Rub steaks with rosemary mixture. Spread one side of each steak with horseradish.

3 For a charcoal grill, grill steaks and relish packet on the rack of an uncovered grill directly over medium coals until steaks are desired doneness, turning steaks and relish packet once halfway through grilling. Allow 11 to 15 minutes for medium-rare doneness (145°F) or 14 to 18 minutes for medium doneness (160°F). (For a gas grill, preheat grill. Reduce heat to medium. Place steak and relish packet on grill rack over heat. Cover and grill as above.) To serve, spoon the relish over steaks.

NUTRITION FACTS PER SERVING: 198 cal., 9 g total fat (2 g sat. fat), 65 mg chol., 92 mg sodium, 7 g carbo., 1 g fiber, 23 g pro.

Steak Lover's Platter

If all the food won't fit on your grill at once, cook it in two batches, vegetables first. If the vegetables get too cool, warm them on the grill while you slice the meat.

PREP: 30 MINUTES MARINATE: 4 TO 6 HOURS GRILL: 20 MINUTES MAKES: 6 SERVINGS

½	cup cider vinegar
¼	cup dark beer or dark or amber nonalcoholic beer
5	tablespoons snipped fresh marjoram or 1 tablespoon dried marjoram, crushed
2	tablespoons olive oil or cooking oil
½	teaspoon salt
½	teaspoon ground black pepper
½	teaspoon bottled minced garlic (1 clove)
1	2-pound boneless beef top sirloin steak, cut 1½ inches thick
3	medium baking potatoes, each cut lengthwise into 8 wedges (about 1 pound)
4	small zucchini, halved lengthwise (about 1 pound)
3	medium yellow, orange, green, or red sweet peppers, seeded and cut into 1-inch-wide rings
2	tablespoons olive oil or cooking oil
¼	teaspoon salt
¼	teaspoon ground black pepper
1	recipe Onion Sauce

1 For marinade, in a small bowl combine vinegar, beer, 2 tablespoons of the fresh marjoram or 2 teaspoons of the dried marjoram, 2 tablespoons oil, the ½ teaspoon salt, the ½ teaspoon black pepper, and the garlic. Place steak in a resealable plastic bag set in a shallow dish. Pour marinade over steak. Seal bag; turn to coat steak. Marinate in the refrigerator for at least 4 hours or up to 6 hours, turning bag occasionally.

2 In a covered medium saucepan cook potato wedges in a large amount of boiling water for 4 minutes; drain. In a large bowl stir together potatoes, zucchini, and sweet peppers. In a small bowl stir together 1 tablespoon of the remaining fresh marjoram or remaining 1 teaspoon dried marjoram, 2 tablespoons oil, the ¼ teaspoon salt, and the ¼ teaspoon black pepper; sprinkle over vegetables. Toss to coat.

3 Drain meat, discarding marinade. For a charcoal grill, grill meat, potatoes, zucchini, and sweet peppers on the greased rack of an uncovered grill directly over medium coals until meat is desired doneness and vegetables are tender. Allow 20 to 24 minutes for medium-rare doneness (145°F) or 24 to 28 minutes for medium doneness (160°F), turning meat and vegetables once halfway through grilling. (For a gas grill, preheat grill. Reduce heat to medium. Place meat, potatoes, zucchini, and sweet peppers on grill rack over heat. Cover and grill as above.)

4 Carve beef across grain into ¼-inch-thick slices. Arrange beef, potatoes, zucchini, and peppers on serving platter.

5 Drizzle with half of the Onion Sauce; pass remaining sauce. Sprinkle with remaining fresh marjoram, if using.

Onion Sauce: In a small saucepan cook 1 cup chopped onion and ½ teaspoon bottled minced garlic (1 clove) in 1 tablespoon hot butter or margarine over medium heat for 4 minutes or until onions are tender. In a small bowl gradually stir ½ cup dark beer or dark or amber nonalcoholic beer, ½ cup beef broth, and 1 tablespoon Worcestershire sauce into 1 tablespoon cornstarch. Add to saucepan. Cook and stir over medium heat until thickened and bubbly. Cook and stir for 2 minutes more.

NUTRITION FACTS PER SERVING: 510 cal., 23 g total fat (7 g sat. fat), 106 mg chol., 445 mg sodium, 34 g carbo., 2 g fiber, 39 g pro.

Marinated Steak with Blue Cheese

*Plain steak becomes a showstopper when it's marinated
and served with a chunky blue cheese topper.*

PREP: 20 MINUTES **MARINATE:** 6 TO 24 HOURS **GRILL:** 14 MINUTES **MAKES:** 4 SERVINGS

1 pound boneless beef top sirloin steak, cut 1 inch thick

¼ cup olive oil

¼ cup dry red wine

1 teaspoon coarsely ground black pepper

1 teaspoon bottled minced garlic (2 cloves)

½ teaspoon salt

½ teaspoon Dijon-style mustard

¼ cup thinly sliced green onions

¼ cup crumbled blue cheese (1 ounce)

2 tablespoons soft goat cheese (chèvre)

½ teaspoon bottled minced garlic (1 clove)

1 Trim fat from steak. Place steak in a resealable plastic bag set in a shallow dish. For marinade, in a small bowl stir together olive oil, red wine, pepper, the 1 teaspoon minced garlic, the salt, and mustard. Pour marinade over steak. Seal bag; turn to coat steak. Marinate in the refrigerator for at least 6 hours or up to 24 hours, turning bag occasionally.

2 Drain steak, discarding marinade. For a charcoal grill, grill steak on the rack of an uncovered grill directly over medium coals until desired doneness, turning once halfway through. Allow 14 to 18 minutes for medium-rare doneness (145°F) or 18 to 22 minutes for medium doneness (160°F). (For a gas grill, preheat grill. Reduce heat to medium. Place steak on grill rack over heat. Cover and grill as above.)

3 Meanwhile, in a small bowl combine green onions, blue cheese, goat cheese, and the ½ teaspoon garlic. Transfer meat to serving platter. Dollop some of the blue cheese mixture over steak. To serve, thinly slice meat across the grain. Pass remaining blue cheese mixture.

NUTRITION FACTS PER SERVING: 315 cal., 21 g total fat (7 g sat. fat), 89 mg chol., 345 mg sodium, 1 g carbo., 0 g fiber, 29 g pro.

Lettuce-Wrapped Vietnamese Beef

Vietnamese cuisine is increasingly popular, and this fresh, flavorful dish makes it easy to see why. The marinade is key here, giving strips of sirloin an enticing lightness. To serve, wrap the lettuce leaves around the beef slices and eat out-of-hand.

PREP: 15 MINUTES **MARINATE:** 2 TO 24 HOURS **GRILL:** 14 MINUTES **MAKES:** 4 SERVINGS

1   pound beef top sirloin steak, cut 1 inch thick

¼   cup chopped green onions

2   stalks lemongrass, chopped

2   tablespoons sugar

2   tablespoons lime juice

2   tablespoons bottled fish sauce

1½   teaspoons bottled minced garlic (3 cloves)

8   large lettuce leaves

Assorted toppings (such as shredded carrot, fresh cilantro leaves, shredded fresh mint leaves, and/or chopped peanuts)

1   recipe Rice Vinegar Sauce

1 Trim fat from steak. Place steak in a resealable plastic bag set in a shallow dish. For marinade, in a small bowl combine the green onions, lemongrass, sugar, lime juice, fish sauce, and garlic. Pour marinade over steak. Seal bag; turn to coat steak. Marinate in the refrigerator for at least 2 hours or up to 24 hours, turning bag occasionally.

2 Drain steak, discarding marinade. For a charcoal grill, grill steak on the rack of an uncovered grill directly over medium coals until desired doneness, turning once halfway through grilling. Allow 14 to 18 minutes for medium-rare doneness (145°F) or 18 to 22 minutes for medium doneness (160°F). (For a gas grill, preheat grill. Reduce heat to medium. Place steaks on grill rack over heat. Cover and grill as above.)

3 To serve, overlap 2 lettuce leaves on each of 4 dinner plates. Thinly slice steak. Arrange steak slices on lettuce leaves. Add the desired toppings; drizzle with Rice Vinegar Sauce. Roll lettuce leaves around meat.

Rice Vinegar Sauce: In a small bowl combine ¼ cup sugar, ¼ cup rice vinegar, 2 tablespoons lime juice, 2 tablespoons bottled fish sauce, 1 teaspoon bottled minced garlic (2 cloves), and dash cayenne pepper.

NUTRITION FACTS PER SERVING: 348 cal., 13 g total fat (5 g sat. fat), 76 mg chol., 671 mg sodium, 30 g carbo., 1 g fiber, 29 g pro.

Basil-Stuffed Steak

A parsley rub and a basil stuffing make this steak a masterpiece.

PREP: 25 MINUTES **GRILL:** 32 MINUTES **STAND:** 5 MINUTES **MAKES:** 6 SERVINGS

1	2- to 2½-pound boneless beef top sirloin steak, cut 1½ inches thick
½	teaspoon salt
¼	teaspoon ground black pepper
¼	teaspoon dried parsley flakes
1	cup lightly packed fresh basil leaves, coarsely snipped
¼	cup finely chopped onion
2	teaspoons bottled minced garlic (4 cloves)
1½	teaspoons finely snipped fresh rosemary or ½ teaspoon dried rosemary, crushed
⅛	teaspoon finely snipped fresh thyme or dried thyme, crushed
1	teaspoon olive oil

1 With sharp knife, make 5 lengthwise slits three-quarters of the way through the steak. For rub, in a small bowl combine the salt, pepper, and parsley flakes. Sprinkle rub evenly over both sides of steak; rub in with your fingers.

2 In a small bowl combine basil, onion, garlic, rosemary, and thyme. Press basil mixture into slits in steak. Using 100%-cotton kitchen string, tie steak loosely at 2-inch intervals to close the slits and hold in the stuffing. Drizzle with oil.

3 For a charcoal grill, arrange medium-hot coals around a drip pan. Test for medium heat above the pan. Place steak on grill rack over drip pan. Cover and grill to desired doneness, turning once halfway through grilling. Allow 32 to 36 minutes for medium-rare doneness (145°F) or 36 to 40 minutes for medium doneness (160°F). (For a gas grill, preheat grill. Reduce heat to medium. Adjust for indirect cooking. Grill as above.)

4 Transfer steak to a carving board; remove strings. Cover with foil; let stand for 5 minutes before carving. Cut into ½-inch-thick slices.

NUTRITION FACTS PER SERVING: 201 cal., 6 g total fat (2 g sat. fat), 71 mg chol., 275 mg sodium, 2 g carbo., 0 g fiber, 33 g pro.

Cilantro-Pepper Steak

Marinating the meat overnight in an aromatic mélange of fresh ingredients makes this steak doubly good: It intensifies the delicious flavors and the dish can be ready to eat in a flash on a weeknight. Serve it with cilantro-flecked rice or warm flour tortillas.

PREP: 20 MINUTES   **MARINATE:** 6 TO 24 HOURS   **GRILL:** 20 MINUTES   **MAKES:** 4 SERVINGS

1	pound boneless beef top sirloin steak, cut 1½ inches thick
1	medium onion, chopped
⅓	cup lime juice
¼	cup snipped fresh cilantro
3	fresh jalapeño chile peppers, seeded and finely chopped*
3	tablespoons water
2	tablespoons cooking oil
1	teaspoon ground cumin
1	teaspoon bottled minced garlic (2 cloves)
½	teaspoon cayenne pepper
¼	teaspoon salt
	Snipped fresh cilantro (optional)
	Hot cooked rice (optional)

1 Trim fat from steak. Place steak in a resealable plastic bag set in a shallow dish. For marinade, in a medium bowl combine onion, lime juice, 2 tablespoons of the cilantro, the jalapeño peppers, the water, oil, cumin, garlic, cayenne pepper, and salt. Pour marinade over steak. Seal bag; turn to coat steak. Marinate in refrigerator for at least 6 hours or up to 24 hours, turning bag occasionally.

2 Drain steak, reserving marinade. For a charcoal grill, grill steak on the rack of an uncovered grill directly over medium coals to desired doneness, turning once and brushing occasionally with reserved marinade up to the last 5 minutes of grilling. Allow 20 to 24 minutes for medium-rare doneness (145°F) or 24 to 28 minutes for medium doneness (160°F). (For a gas grill, preheat grill. Reduce heat to medium. Place steak on grill rack over heat. Cover and grill as above.) Discard any remaining marinade. Sprinkle steak with the remaining 2 tablespoons cilantro. If desired, stir additional cilantro into cooked rice and serve with steak.

NUTRITION FACTS PER SERVING: 256 cal., 15 g total fat (5 g sat. fat), 76 mg chol., 148 mg sodium, 3 g carbo., 0 g fiber, 26 g pro.

***NOTE:** Because chile peppers contain volatile oils that can burn your skin and eyes, avoid direct contact with them as much as possible. When working with chile peppers, wear plastic or rubber gloves. If your bare hands do touch the chile peppers, wash your hands and nails well with soap and warm water.

Steak with Roasted Garlic and Herbs

When roasted, garlic turns mild and sweet—ideal for spreading on grilled steak or your favorite bread or crackers.

PREP: 15 MINUTES **GRILL:** 30 MINUTES **MAKES:** 6 SERVINGS

1	or 2 whole bulb(s) garlic
3	to 4 teaspoons snipped fresh basil or 1 teaspoon dried basil, crushed
1	tablespoon snipped fresh rosemary or 1 teaspoon dried rosemary, crushed
2	tablespoons olive oil or cooking oil
1	to 2 teaspoons cracked black pepper
½	teaspoon salt
1	1½-pound boneless beef top sirloin steak, cut 1 inch thick, or 1½ pounds beef ribeye steaks, cut 1 inch thick
	Fresh rosemary sprigs (optional)

1 Remove papery outer layers from garlic bulb(s), leaving individual cloves attached to bulb(s). Cut off about ½ inch from top of bulb(s) and discard. Tear off a 20×10-inch piece of heavy foil. Fold in half to make a double thickness of foil that measures 10×10 inches. Place garlic in center of foil. Bring foil up around garlic to form a shallow bowl. Sprinkle garlic with basil and snipped or dried rosemary; drizzle with oil.

2 Completely enclose garlic in foil, twisting ends of foil on top. For a charcoal grill, grill foil packet on the rack of an uncovered grill directly over medium coals about 30 minutes or until garlic cloves are soft. Remove bulb(s) from foil packet, reserving herb-oil mixture. Let cool slightly.

3 Meanwhile, for rub, in a small bowl combine pepper and salt. Sprinkle rub evenly over both sides of steak; rub in with your fingers. Grill steak alongside the garlic packet until desired doneness, turning steak once halfway through grilling. For sirloin steak, allow 14 to 18 minutes for medium-rare doneness (145°F) or 18 to 22 minutes for medium doneness (160°F). For ribeye steaks, allow 11 to 15 minutes for medium-rare doneness (145°F) or 14 to 18 minutes for medium doneness (160°F). (For a gas grill, preheat grill. Reduce heat to medium. Place foil packet, then steaks on grill rack over heat. Cover and grill as above.)

4 To serve, cut steak into serving-size pieces. Carefully squeeze the pulp from the garlic cloves onto the steak pieces. Mash pulp slightly with a fork and spread over steak pieces. Drizzle steaks with the reserved herb-oil mixture. If desired, garnish with rosemary sprigs.

NUTRITION FACTS PER SERVING: 251 cal., 15 g total fat (5 g sat. fat), 76 mg chol., 235 mg sodium, 2 g carbo., 0 g fiber, 26 g pro.

Salsa-Topped Rosemary Ribeyes

The simple treatment of rubbing steaks with a blend of herbs and seasonings brings bursts of flavor once grilled.

PREP: 15 MINUTES **GRILL:** 11 MINUTES **MAKES:** 4 SERVINGS

1 tablespoon snipped fresh rosemary or 1 teaspoon dried rosemary, crushed

1 teaspoon snipped fresh thyme or ¼ teaspoon dried thyme, crushed

¼ teaspoon salt

⅛ teaspoon ground black pepper

2 12-ounce beef ribeye steaks, cut 1 inch thick

1 medium tomato, seeded and chopped

¼ cup chopped red onion

¼ cup chopped yellow and/or green sweet pepper

½ teaspoon bottled minced garlic (1 clove)

Dash salt

Dash ground black pepper

Dash bottled hot pepper sauce

1 For rub, in a small bowl combine rosemary, thyme, the ¼ teaspoon salt, and the ⅛ teaspoon black pepper. Sprinkle rub evenly over both sides of each steak; rub in with your fingers.

2 For a charcoal grill, grill steaks on the rack of an uncovered grill directly over medium coals until desired doneness, turning once halfway through grilling. Allow 11 to 15 minutes for medium-rare doneness (145°F) or 14 to 18 minutes for medium doneness (160°F). (For a gas grill, preheat grill. Reduce heat to medium. Place steaks on grill rack over heat. Cover and grill as above.)

3 Meanwhile, for salsa, in a medium bowl stir together the tomato, onion, sweet pepper, garlic, the dash salt, the dash black pepper, and the hot pepper sauce. Serve the salsa with steaks.

NUTRITION FACTS PER SERVING: 309 cal., 17 g total fat (7 g sat. fat), 100 mg chol., 262 mg sodium, 3 g carbo., 1 g fiber, 34 g pro.

Chili-Rubbed Steaks

Down in the Rio Grande Valley, the aromatic spice cumin is called comino and longtime residents put it on everything but their breakfast cereal. There's no question—cumin in the rub makes these steaks great.

PREP: 10 MINUTES **MARINATE:** 1 TO 2 HOURS **GRILL:** 11 MINUTES **MAKES:** 4 SERVINGS

2 12-ounce beef ribeye steaks, cut 1 inch thick
1 tablespoon chili powder
1 tablespoon olive oil
1½ teaspoons dried oregano, crushed
½ teaspoon salt
½ teaspoon ground cumin

1 Trim fat from steaks. Place steaks in a single layer in a shallow dish. For rub, in a small bowl combine the chili powder, oil, oregano, salt, and cumin. Spoon mixture evenly over steaks; rub in with your fingers. Cover and marinate in the refrigerator for at least 1 hour or up to 2 hours.

2 For a charcoal grill, grill steaks on the rack of an uncovered grill directly over medium coals until desired doneness, turning once halfway through grilling. Allow 11 to 15 minutes for medium-rare doneness (145°F) or 14 to 18 minutes for medium doneness (160°F). (For a gas grill, preheat grill. Reduce heat to medium. Place steaks on grill rack over heat. Cover and grill as above.)

3 To serve, cut each steak in half.

NUTRITION FACTS PER SERVING: 323 cal., 16 g total fat (5 g sat. fat), 92 mg chol., 376 mg sodium, 1 g carbo., 1 g fiber, 42 g pro.

Beef Steak with Avocado Sauce

Latin America was the inspiration for a chili powder rub for the steak and a creamy gravy made from avocado and tomatillos.

PREP: 25 MINUTES **STAND:** 30 MINUTES **GRILL:** 14 MINUTES **MAKES:** 4 TO 6 SERVINGS

2 12-ounce beef ribeye steaks or top loin steaks, cut 1¼ to 1½ inches thick

1 tablespoon brown sugar

1 teaspoon chili powder

½ teaspoon garlic salt

½ teaspoon ground black pepper

8 ounces fresh tomatillos, husked and quartered (6 medium)

¼ cup water

2 ounces cream cheese

1 avocado, halved, seeded, peeled, and cut up

¼ cup sliced green onions

½ teaspoon salt

8 to 12 green onions, trimmed to 6-inch lengths

4 to 6 fresh jalapeño chile peppers*

Cooking oil (optional)

1 large tomato, chopped

1 Trim fat from around the edges of the steaks. For rub, in a small bowl combine the brown sugar, chili powder, garlic salt, and black pepper. Sprinkle rub evenly over both sides of each steak; rub in with your fingers. Let steaks stand at room temperature for 30 minutes.

2 Meanwhile, for sauce, in a small saucepan combine the quartered tomatillos and the water. Bring to boiling; reduce heat. Cover and simmer for 5 to 7 minutes or until soft. Stir the cream cheese into tomatillo mixture until melted; cool mixture slightly.

3 In a food processor bowl or blender container combine tomatillo mixture, avocado, sliced green onions, and salt. Cover and process or blend until smooth. Transfer sauce to a serving bowl.

4 For a charcoal grill, grill steaks on the rack of an uncovered grill directly over medium coals until desired doneness, turning once halfway through grilling. Allow 14 to 19 minutes for medium-rare doneness (145°F) or 17 to 23 minutes for medium doneness (160°F). If desired, brush the whole green onions and jalapeños lightly with oil; grill jalapeños alongside steaks about 10 minutes and green onions about 5 minutes or until soft and lightly charred, turning occasionally. (For a gas grill, preheat grill. Reduce heat to medium. Place steaks, then jalapeños and green onions on grill rack over heat. Cover and grill as above.)

5 To serve, slice steaks. Serve with sauce and grilled jalapeños and green onions. Sprinkle with tomato.

NUTRITION FACTS PER SERVING: 415 cal., 24 g total fat (8 g sat. fat), 96 mg chol., 559 mg sodium, 11 g carbo., 4 g fiber, 40 g pro.

*NOTE: Because chile peppers contain volatile oils that can burn your skin and eyes, avoid direct contact with them as much as possible. When working with chile peppers, wear plastic or rubber gloves. If your bare hands do touch the chile peppers, wash your hands and nails well with soap and warm water.

Flank Steak on Tap

Hearty pub food like this beer-marinated beef steak is always in style for good reason—it's warm and welcoming. On a cool fall evening, enjoy it outdoors with the seasonal colors, an Oktoberfest brew, and, of course, lots of good conversation.

PREP: 20 MINUTES   **MARINATE:** 4 TO 24 HOURS   **GRILL:** 17 MINUTES   **MAKES:** 4 SERVINGS

1	large onion, thinly sliced
¾	cup beer
3	tablespoons Worcestershire sauce
2	tablespoons brown sugar
1½	teaspoons bottled minced garlic (3 cloves)
1	bay leaf
¼	teaspoon coarsely ground black pepper
1	1¼- to 1½-pound beef flank steak
¼	teaspoon salt
2	teaspoons cornstarch
	Snipped fresh parsley (optional)
	Coarsely ground black pepper (optional)

1 For marinade, in a small saucepan combine onion, beer, Worcestershire sauce, brown sugar, garlic, bay leaf, and the ¼ teaspoon pepper. Bring to boiling; reduce heat. Simmer, uncovered, for 4 to 5 minutes or until brown sugar is dissolved and onion and garlic begin to soften. Cool marinade to room temperature.

2 Score steak on both sides in a diamond pattern by cutting diagonally at 1-inch intervals. Place the steak in a resealable plastic bag set in a shallow dish. Pour marinade over steak. Seal bag; turn to coat steak. Marinate in refrigerator for at least 4 hours or up to 24 hours, turning bag occasionally.

3 Drain steak, reserving marinade. Discard bay leaf. Season steak with salt. For charcoal grill, grill steak on the rack of an uncovered grill directly over medium coals for 17 to 21 minutes or until medium doneness (160°F). (For a gas grill, preheat grill. Reduce heat to medium. Place steak on grill rack over heat. Cover and grill as above.)

4 Meanwhile, for sauce, in a small saucepan combine reserved marinade and cornstarch. Cook and stir over medium heat until the sauce is thickened and bubbly. Cook and stir for 2 minutes more. To serve, cut steak across the grain into ⅛- to ¼-inch-thick slices; spoon sauce over steak. If desired, sprinkle with parsley and additional pepper.

NUTRITION FACTS PER SERVING: 185 cal., 7 g total fat (3 g sat. fat), 44 mg chol., 221 mg sodium, 10 g carbo., 1 g fiber, 17 g pro.

Flank Steak Spirals

*When summer rolls around, serve this delectable hot-off-the-grill creation.
Perfect companions to this light and elegant dinner
are a fresh spinach salad and crusty Italian or French bread.*

PREP: 30 MINUTES **MARINATE:** 4 TO 24 HOURS **GRILL:** 10 MINUTES **MAKES:** 4 SERVINGS

1	1¼-pound beef flank steak
1	cup dry red wine
¼	cup finely chopped green onions
1	bay leaf
1½	teaspoons Worcestershire sauce
½	teaspoon bottled minced garlic (1 clove)
½	teaspoon salt
¼	teaspoon coarsely ground black pepper
6	slices bacon
¼	cup finely chopped onion
2	tablespoons snipped fresh parsley
1	teaspoon bottled minced garlic (2 cloves)
½	teaspoon coarsely ground black pepper
¼	teaspoon salt

1 Score steak on both sides in a diamond pattern by making shallow diagonal cuts at 1-inch intervals.

2 Place meat between 2 pieces of plastic wrap. Working from center to edges, use flat side of a meat mallet to pound steak into a 12×8-inch rectangle. Remove plastic wrap. Place meat in a resealable plastic bag set in a shallow dish.

3 For marinade, in a medium bowl stir together wine, green onions, bay leaf, Worcestershire sauce, the ½ teaspoon minced garlic, the ½ teaspoon salt, and the ¼ teaspoon pepper. Pour marinade over steak. Seal bag; turn to coat steak. Marinate in refrigerator for at least 4 hours or up to 24 hours, turning bag occasionally.

4 Meanwhile, in a large skillet cook bacon just until done, but not crisp. Drain on paper towels. In a small bowl combine onion, parsley, the 1 teaspoon minced garlic, the ½ teaspoon pepper, and the ¼ teaspoon salt.

5 Drain steak, reserving marinade. Sprinkle one side of the steak with parsley mixture. Lay bacon strips lengthwise on steak. Roll up from a short side. Secure with wooden toothpicks at 1-inch intervals, starting ½ inch from one end. Cut between the toothpicks into eight 1-inch-thick slices.

6 For charcoal grill, grill steak slices, cut sides down, on the rack of an uncovered grill directly over medium coals for 10 to 12 minutes, turning and brushing once with reserved marinade halfway through the grilling. (For a gas grill, preheat grill. Reduce heat to medium. Place steak slices, cut sides down, on grill rack over heat. Cover and grill as above.) Discard any remaining marinade.

NUTRITION FACTS PER SERVING: 324 cal., 16 g total fat (6 g sat. fat), 67 mg chol., 575 mg sodium, 3 g carbo., 0 g fiber, 35 g pro.

Jerk London Broil

A Scotch bonnet pepper adds extra sizzle to this jerk-marinated steak.

PREP: 10 MINUTES **MARINATE:** 4 TO 24 HOURS **GRILL:** 17 MINUTES **MAKES:** 6 SERVINGS

4	green onions
¼	cup lime juice
1	1-inch piece fresh ginger, sliced
1	Scotch bonnet chile pepper, seeded and finely chopped (optional)*
2	tablespoons cooking oil
3	cloves garlic
2	teaspoons Jamaican jerk seasoning
1	1¼- to 1½-pound beef flank steak

1 For jerk marinade, in a blender container combine green onions, lime juice, ginger, Scotch bonnet pepper (if desired), oil, garlic, and jerk seasoning; cover and blend until smooth. Score both sides of the steak in a diamond pattern by making shallow diagonal cuts at 1-inch intervals. Place the steak in a glass dish; spread the jerk marinade over the steak. Cover dish with plastic wrap and marinate in the refrigerator for at least 4 hours or up to 24 hours.

2 Drain steak, discarding marinade. For charcoal grill, grill steak on the rack of an uncovered grill directly over medium coals for 17 to 21 minutes or until medium doneness (160°F), turning once halfway through grilling. (For a gas grill, preheat grill. Reduce heat to medium. Place steak on grill rack over heat. Cover and grill as above.)

3 Transfer steak to a cutting board; cut steak across the grain into ⅛- to ¼-inch-thick slices.

NUTRITION FACTS PER SERVING: 187 cal., 11 g total fat (3 g sat. fat), 44 mg chol., 117 mg sodium, 2 g carbo., 0 g fiber, 18 g pro.

*NOTE: Because chile peppers contain volatile oils that can burn your skin and eyes, avoid direct contact with them as much as possible. When working with chile peppers, wear plastic or rubber gloves. If your bare hands do touch the chile peppers, wash your hands and nails well with soap and warm water.

Mexican Fiesta Flank Steak

Warm the tortillas in a foil packet during the last few minutes of grilling.

PREP: 15 MINUTES **MARINATE:** 12 TO 24 HOURS **GRILL:** 17 MINUTES **MAKES:** 6 SERVINGS

1   1½- to 2-pound beef flank steak or skirt steak

½   cup finely chopped onion

½   cup snipped fresh cilantro

¼   cup lime juice or lemon juice

3   tablespoons olive oil

½   teaspoon salt

½   teaspoon ground cumin

½   teaspoon dried oregano, crushed

¼   to ½ teaspoon cayenne pepper or 1 fresh or pickled jalapeño chile pepper, chopped*

3   medium red, yellow, and/or green sweet peppers, quartered

6   flour tortillas

1   tomato, cut into thin wedges

1 Trim fat from steak. Score both sides of steak in a diamond pattern by making shallow diagonal cuts at 1-inch intervals. Place steak in a resealable plastic bag set in a shallow dish.

2 For marinade, in a small bowl combine onion, cilantro, lime juice, 2 tablespoons of the olive oil, the salt, cumin, oregano, and cayenne pepper or jalapeño pepper. Pour marinade over steak. Seal bag; turn to coat steak. Marinate in the refrigerator for at least 12 hours or up to 24 hours, turning bag occasionally.

3 Drain steak, discarding marinade. For a charcoal grill, grill steak on the rack of an uncovered grill directly over medium coals for 17 to 21 minutes or until medium doneness (160°F), turning once halfway through grilling. While steak is grilling, brush sweet peppers with the remaining 1 tablespoon olive oil; add sweet peppers to grill alongside steak. Grill for 8 to 10 minutes or until tender and slightly charred, turning once halfway through grilling. (For a gas grill, preheat grill. Reduce heat to medium. Place steak, then sweet peppers on grill rack over heat. Cover and grill as above.)

4 Thinly slice steak across the grain. Slice sweet peppers into strips. Serve the steak and peppers with tortillas and tomato wedges.

NUTRITION FACTS PER SERVING: 334 cal., 15 g total fat (4 g sat. fat), 45 mg chol., 314 mg sodium, 22 g carbo., 2 g fiber, 28 g pro.

*****NOTE:** Because chile peppers contain volatile oils that can burn your skin and eyes, avoid direct contact with them as much as possible. When working with chile peppers, wear plastic or rubber gloves. If your bare hands do touch the chile peppers, wash your hands and nails well with soap and warm water.

Soy Flank Steak

A zesty ginger mixture does double duty as a marinade for the steak and a dressing for the Chinese cabbage slaw.

PREP: 20 MINUTES MARINATE: 2 HOURS GRILL: 17 MINUTES MAKES: 6 SERVINGS

- **3** tablespoons rice vinegar
- **2** tablespoons thinly sliced green onion
- **2** tablespoons sesame seeds, toasted
- **2** tablespoons reduced-sodium soy sauce
- **2** tablespoons grated fresh ginger
- **2** teaspoons brown sugar
- **⅓** cup peanut oil
- **1** tablespoon toasted sesame oil
- **1** 1¼-pound beef flank steak
- **6** cups shredded Chinese cabbage
- **1** cup coarsely shredded carrots
- **2** tablespoons snipped fresh cilantro

1 For dressing, in a small bowl combine vinegar, green onion, sesame seeds, soy sauce, ginger, and brown sugar; stir until sugar dissolves. Slowly whisk in peanut oil and sesame oil.

2 Trim fat from steak. Place steak in a resealable plastic bag set in a shallow dish. Pour half of dressing over steak. Seal bag; turn to coat steak. Marinate in refrigerator for 2 hours, turning bag occasionally.

3 Meanwhile, for slaw, in a large bowl combine cabbage, carrots, cilantro, and remaining dressing; toss to coat. Cover; chill until serving time.

4 Drain steak, discarding marinade. For a charcoal grill, grill steak on the rack of an uncovered grill directly over medium coals for 17 to 21 minutes or until medium doneness (160°F), turning once halfway through grilling. (For a gas grill, preheat grill. Reduce heat to medium. Place steak on grill rack over heat. Cover and grill as above.) Thinly slice steak across grain. Serve steak with the slaw.

NUTRITION FACTS PER SERVING: 292 cal., 20 g total fat (5 g sat. fat), 44 mg chol., 217 mg sodium, 9 g carbo., 2 g fiber, 20 g pro.

Beer-Braised Beef Short Ribs

If you enjoy ribs with a touch of fire, add the bottled hot pepper sauce to the subtly sweet molasses basting mixture.

PREP: 30 MINUTES **BAKE:** 2 HOURS **GRILL:** 10 MINUTES **MAKES:** 4 TO 6 SERVINGS

5	**pounds beef chuck short ribs**
2	**12-ounce cans dark beer**
1	**14-ounce can beef broth**
1	**medium onion, sliced**
1	**teaspoon dried thyme, crushed**
½	**teaspoon salt**
¼	**cup molasses**
2	**tablespoons balsamic vinegar**
½	**to 1 teaspoon bottled hot pepper sauce (optional)**

1 Place short ribs in a 6- to 7-quart Dutch oven. Add beer, broth, onion, ½ teaspoon of the thyme, and ¼ teaspoon of the salt. Bring to boiling; remove from heat. Cover and bake in a 350°F oven about 2 hours or until ribs are very tender.

2 Remove from oven; cool slightly. Remove short ribs from cooking liquid. (If desired, cover and store short ribs in the refrigerator up to 24 hours or until ready to grill.) Spoon fat from surface of cooking liquid;* discard fat. Strain cooking liquid, reserving ¼ cup; discard remaining cooking liquid and solids. Stir molasses, balsamic vinegar, hot pepper sauce (if desired), the remaining ½ teaspoon thyme, and the remaining ¼ teaspoon salt into reserved ¼ cup cooking liquid.

3 For a charcoal grill, grill short ribs, bone sides down, on the rack of an uncovered grill directly over medium coals for 10 to 15 minutes or until short ribs are crisp and heated through, turning and brushing frequently with molasses mixture. (For a gas grill, preheat grill. Reduce heat to medium. Place short ribs on grill rack over heat. Cover and grill as above.)

NUTRITION FACTS PER SERVING: 371 cal., 15 g total fat (6 g sat. fat), 85 mg chol., 466 mg sodium, 17 g carbo., 0 g fiber, 37 g pro.

*NOTE: To easily remove fat from the cooking liquid, pour the liquid into a bowl. Set the bowl inside a larger bowl filled with ice cubes. Cover and refrigerate about 1 hour or until fat is solidified. (Or cover and refrigerate cooking liquid overnight.) Remove and discard fat.

Molasses and Mustard Barbecued Short Ribs

Ordinary bottled barbecue sauce gets a flavor boost from molasses, mustard, balsamic vinegar, and hot pepper sauce in this sure-to-please recipe.

PREP: 15 MINUTES **BAKE:** 1½ HOURS **CHILL:** 4 TO 24 HOURS **GRILL:** 10 MINUTES
MAKES: 6 SERVINGS

5 pounds beef chuck short ribs

2 tablespoons freshly ground multicolored peppercorns or regular peppercorns

2 tablespoons bottled minced garlic (12 cloves)

2 teaspoons dried thyme, crushed

1 12-ounce bottle dark beer

1 medium onion, coarsely chopped

3 bay leaves

1 cup bottled barbecue sauce

¼ cup stone-ground mustard

¼ cup molasses

2 tablespoons balsamic vinegar or cider vinegar

2 teaspoons bottled hot pepper sauce

1. Trim fat from short ribs. For rub, in a small bowl stir together the ground peppercorns, garlic, and thyme. Sprinkle rub evenly over short ribs; rub in with your fingers.

2. In an ovenproof Dutch oven or kettle combine beer, onion, and bay leaves. Add short ribs. Cover and bake in a 350°F oven about 1½ hours or until meat is very tender.

3. Remove from oven; cool slightly. Remove short ribs from cooking liquid. Place short ribs and cooking liquid in separate storage containers; cover and chill in the refrigerator for at least 4 hours or up to 24 hours.

4. Spoon fat from surface of cooking liquid; discard fat. Reserve 1 cup of the cooking liquid; discard remaining cooking liquid and bay leaves. In a medium bowl stir together reserved cooking liquid, barbecue sauce, mustard, molasses, balsamic vinegar, and hot pepper sauce.

5. For a charcoal grill, grill short ribs, bone sides down, on the rack of an uncovered grill directly over medium coals about 10 minutes or until crisp and heated through, turning and basting frequently with molasses mixture. (For a gas grill, preheat grill. Reduce heat to medium. Place short ribs, bone sides down, on grill rack over heat. Cover and grill as above.)

6. In a small saucepan heat remaining molasses mixture until bubbly; pass with short ribs.

NUTRITION FACTS PER SERVING: 522 cal., 18 g total fat (6 g sat. fat), 127 mg chol., 657 mg sodium, 24 g carbo., 2 g fiber, 59 g pro.

Beef Fajitas

Mexican cowboys first created beef fajitas when they began tinkering with the lowly skirt steak. They started by marinating the tough cut to tenderize it and then cooked it over a hot wood fire to bring out its robust flavor.

PREP: 20 MINUTES   **MARINATE:** 6 TO 24 HOURS   **GRILL:** 17 MINUTES   **MAKES:** 6 SERVINGS

1   1½-pound beef skirt steak or flank steak

½   cup bottled salsa

⅓   cup bottled Italian salad dressing

3   fresh serrano chile peppers, seeded (if desired) and finely chopped*

1   teaspoon bottled minced garlic (2 cloves)

¼   teaspoon ground black pepper

6   7- to 8-inch flour tortillas, warmed**

Sweet pepper strips (optional)

Shredded cheddar cheese (optional)

Bottled salsa

1 Trim fat from meat. Place meat in a resealable plastic bag set in a shallow dish. For marinade, in a small bowl stir together the ½ cup salsa, the Italian dressing, serrano chile peppers, garlic, and black pepper. Pour marinade over meat. Seal bag; turn to coat meat. Marinate in the refrigerator for at least 6 hours or up to 24 hours, turning bag occasionally.

2 Drain meat, discarding marinade. For a charcoal grill, grill meat on the rack of an uncovered grill directly over medium coals for 17 to 21 minutes or until medium doneness (160°F), turning once halfway through grilling. (For a gas grill, preheat grill. Reduce heat to medium. Place meat on grill rack over heat. Cover and grill as above.)

3 Transfer meat to a cutting board. Thinly slice across the grain. Divide the sliced meat among warm tortillas. If desired, top with sweet pepper strips, cheese, and additional salsa. Fold tortillas.

NUTRITION FACTS PER SERVING: 341 cal., 14 g total fat (5 g sat. fat), 45 mg chol., 350 mg sodium, 24 g carbo., 1 g fiber, 28 g pro.

*NOTE: Because chile peppers contain volatile oils that can burn your skin and eyes, avoid direct contact with them as much as possible. When working with chile peppers, wear plastic or rubber gloves. If your bare hands do touch the chile peppers, wash your hands and nails well with soap and warm water.

**NOTE: To heat the tortillas on the grill, wrap them in foil. Place on the grill rack next to the meat; heat about 10 minutes or until warm, turning once.

Beef Satay

Five-spice powder jazzes up flank steaks. This seasoning blend, often used in Chinese cooking, mixes cinnamon, cloves, fennel seeds, star anise, and Szechwan peppercorns.

PREP: 10 MINUTES   **MARINATE:** 2 TO 4 HOURS   **GRILL:** 8 MINUTES   **MAKES:** 6 SERVINGS

1	pound beef flank steak, cut across the grain into ¼-inch-thick strips
¼	cup sweet rice cooking wine*
¼	cup bottled tamari sauce* or soy sauce
2	tablespoons bottled oyster sauce* (optional)
1	teaspoon grated fresh ginger or ⅛ teaspoon ground ginger
1	teaspoon bottled minced garlic (2 cloves)
¼	teaspoon ground black pepper
¼	teaspoon five-spice powder*
6	10- to 12-inch wooden skewers

1 Place steak strips in a resealable plastic bag. For marinade, in a small bowl combine cooking wine, tamari sauce or soy sauce, oyster sauce (if desired), ginger, garlic, pepper, and five-spice powder. Pour marinade over meat. Seal bag; turn to coat meat. Marinate in the refrigerator for at least 2 hours or up to 4 hours, turning bag occasionally. Meanwhile, soak the wooden skewers in water for 1 hour.

2 Drain meat, reserving marinade. Thread meat (accordion-style) on wooden skewers. For a charcoal grill, grill skewers on the rack of an uncovered grill directly over medium coals for 8 to 12 minutes or until desired doneness, turning and brushing once with reserved marinade halfway through grilling. (For a gas grill, preheat grill. Reduce heat to medium. Place skewers on grill rack over heat. Cover and grill as above.) Discard any remaining marinade.

NUTRITION FACTS PER SERVING: 140 cal., 5 g total fat (2 g sat. fat), 30 mg chol., 711 mg sodium, 2 g carbo., 0 g fiber, 18 g pro.

*NOTE: Look for sweet rice cooking wine, tamari sauce, oyster sauce, and five-spice powder in the Asian foods section of large supermarkets or at an Asian grocery store.

Beef Brochettes Tamarind

Look for the distinctively tart tamarind concentrate at a market that has East Indian or Middle Eastern food products.

PREP: 30 MINUTES **MARINATE:** 2 TO 24 HOURS **GRILL:** 12 MINUTES **MAKES:** 6 SERVINGS

1½ pounds boneless beef sirloin steak

¼ cup honey

¼ cup water

1 to 2 tablespoons grated fresh ginger

1 tablespoon tamarind concentrate
   (no water added)

¾ teaspoon salt

2 cups assorted fresh vegetables (such as whole
   mushrooms, ½-inch-thick slices zucchini or
   yellow summer squash, and/or 1-inch pieces
   sweet pepper)

1 Trim fat from steak. Cut steak into 1½-inch cubes. Place steak cubes in a resealable plastic bag set in a shallow dish. For marinade, in a small bowl stir together honey, the water, ginger, tamarind concentrate, and salt. Pour marinade over steak. Seal bag; turn to coat steak cubes. Marinate in the refrigerator for at least 2 hours or up to 24 hours, turning bag occasionally.

2 Drain steak, reserving marinade. On six 10- to 12-inch metal skewers, alternately thread steak cubes and vegetables, leaving ¼-inch space between pieces.

3 For a charcoal grill, grill kabobs on the rack of an uncovered grill directly over medium coals for 12 to 15 minutes or until desired doneness, turning once and brushing occasionally with the reserved marinade during the first 7 minutes of grilling. (For a gas grill, preheat grill. Reduce heat to medium. Place kabobs on grill rack over heat. Cover and grill as above.) Discard any remaining marinade. To serve, remove meat and vegetables from skewers.

NUTRITION FACTS PER SERVING: 257 cal., 10 g total fat (4 g sat. fat), 76 mg chol., 424 mg sodium, 14 g carbo., 1 g fiber, 26 g pro.

Meat and Vegetable Kabobs

Start with your favorite barbecue sauce and add a medley of seasonings for a flavorful sauce that complements beef, chicken, and vegetables.

PREP: 25 MINUTES **MARINATE:** 6 TO 24 HOURS **GRILL:** 8 MINUTES **MAKES:** 4 OR 5 SERVINGS

½ cup bottled barbecue sauce

¼ cup water

1 to 2 teaspoons bottled minced garlic (2 to 4 cloves)

2 tablespoons dried minced onion

2 tablespoons sugar

2 tablespoons bottled steak sauce

2 tablespoons vinegar

2 tablespoons Worcestershire sauce

2 tablespoons cooking oil

½ teaspoon salt

1½ pounds beef sirloin steak, cut 1 inch thick, and/or skinless, boneless chicken breasts and/or thighs

2 medium onions, each cut into 8 wedges

10 to 12 fresh mushrooms, stems removed

1 medium zucchini, halved and cut into ½-inch-thick slices

1 large red or green sweet pepper, cut into 1-inch pieces

Fresh herb sprigs (optional)

1 For marinade, in a small saucepan combine barbecue sauce, the water, garlic, dried onion, sugar, steak sauce, vinegar, Worcestershire sauce, oil, and salt. Bring just to boiling. Cool.

2 Cut steak into 1-inch cubes or cut chicken into 1-inch pieces. Place steak and/or chicken in a resealable plastic bag set in a deep bowl. Pour marinade over steak and/or chicken. Seal bag; turn to coat steak and/or chicken. Marinate in the refrigerator for at least 6 hours or up to 24 hours, turning bag occasionally.

3 In a covered medium saucepan cook onions in a small amount of boiling water for 3 minutes. Add mushrooms; cook for 1 minute more. Drain.

4 Drain meat, reserving marinade. On metal skewers, alternately thread vegetables and steak and/or chicken, leaving ¼-inch space between pieces. For a charcoal grill, grill kabobs on rack of an uncovered grill directly over medium coals for 8 to 14 minutes or until done, turning once halfway through grilling and brushing once with reserved marinade after 3 minutes of grilling. (For a gas grill, preheat grill. Reduce heat to medium. Place kabobs on grill rack over heat. Cover and grill as above.)

5 In a small saucepan heat remaining marinade to boiling; serve warmed marinade with kabobs. If desired, garnish with fresh herb sprigs.

NUTRITION FACTS PER SERVING: 381 cal., 14 g total fat (3 g sat. fat), 103 mg chol., 849 mg sodium, 24 g carbo., 3 g fiber, 40 g pro.

44

Beef and Avocado Tacos

In Mexican cuisine, carne asada (grilled meat) is a popular choice for tacos and burritos.

PREP: 20 MINUTES **GRILL:** 10 MINUTES **MAKES:** 4 SERVINGS

2   tablespoons lemon juice

1   avocado, pitted, peeled, and cut into
    ½-inch cubes

1   pound boneless beef sirloin steak or
    eye round steak, cut 1 inch thick

1   medium onion, cut into wedges

2   fresh Anaheim or poblano chile peppers,
    cut into 1-inch squares*

1   tablespoon olive oil

½   cup bottled picante sauce

2   cups shredded lettuce

4   7- to 8-inch flour tortillas

    Bottled picante sauce (optional)

1 Drizzle lemon juice over avocado; toss gently to coat. Set aside.

2 Cut steak into 2×1-inch strips. On four 12-inch metal skewers, thread steak strips (accordion-style). On four additional 12-inch metal skewers, alternately thread onion wedges and pepper squares. Brush vegetables with olive oil.

3 For a charcoal grill, grill skewers on the rack of an uncovered grill directly over medium coals for 10 to 12 minutes or until steak is done, turning kabobs once halfway through grilling and brushing occasionally with the ½ cup picante sauce during the first 5 minutes of grilling. (For a gas grill, preheat grill. Reduce heat to medium. Place skewers on grill rack over heat. Cover and grill as above.) Discard remainder of the ½ cup picante sauce.

4 To serve, divide the steak, onion, peppers, avocado, and lettuce among the flour tortillas. Fold tortillas over filling. If desired, serve with additional picante sauce.

NUTRITION FACTS PER SERVING: 425 cal., 24 g total fat (6 g sat. fat), 76 mg chol., 403 mg sodium, 24 g carbo., 3 g fiber, 30 g pro.

*NOTE: Because chile peppers contain volatile oils that can burn your skin and eyes, avoid direct contact with them as much as possible. When working with chile peppers, wear plastic or rubber gloves. If your bare hands do touch the chile peppers, wash your hands and nails well with soap and warm water.

Asian Salad with Beef

Many Vietnamese restaurants are famous for pho, noodle soup served in monster-size bowls. This beefy fusilli salad is inspired by the other side of the menu, where cool salads made of enticing blends of noodles, meat, herbs, and vegetables are found.

PREP: 15 MINUTES **MARINATE:** 1 TO 8 HOURS **GRILL:** 17 MINUTES **MAKES:** 6 SERVINGS

1	1¼- to 1½-pound beef flank steak
½	cup red wine vinegar
3	tablespoons sugar
3	tablespoons cooking oil
1	tablespoon toasted sesame oil
1	tablespoon bottled fish sauce or soy sauce
2	teaspoons bottled minced garlic (4 cloves)
2	teaspoons grated fresh ginger
½	teaspoon salt
½	teaspoon crushed red pepper
12	ounces dried fusilli
2	medium carrots, thinly bias-sliced
1	medium red or yellow sweet pepper, cut into cubes or thin strips
⅓	cup snipped fresh mint or cilantro

1 Trim fat from steak. Score both sides of steak in a diamond pattern by making shallow diagonal cuts at 1-inch intervals. Place in a resealable plastic bag set in a shallow dish.

2 In a screw-top jar combine vinegar, sugar, cooking oil, sesame oil, fish sauce or soy sauce, garlic, ginger, salt, and crushed red pepper; cover and shake well. Pour ⅓ cup of the vinegar mixture over steak. Seal bag; turn to coat steak. Marinate in the refrigerator for at least 1 hour or up to 8 hours, turning bag occasionally. Cover and chill the remaining vinegar mixture until needed.

3 In a Dutch oven cook pasta in lightly salted boiling water for 10 to 15 minutes or until tender but still firm, adding carrots to pasta for the last 1 minute of cooking. Drain pasta and carrots in colander. Rinse with cold water; drain well. Transfer to a large bowl; drizzle with the remaining chilled vinegar mixture. Add sweet pepper and mint or cilantro; toss gently to coat.

4 Meanwhile, drain steak, discarding marinade. For a charcoal grill, grill steak on the rack of an uncovered grill directly over medium coals for 17 to 21 minutes or until medium doneness (160°F), turning once halfway through grilling. (For a gas grill, preheat grill. Reduce heat to medium. Place steak on grill rack over heat. Cover and grill as above.)

5 To serve, thinly slice steak diagonally across the grain. Add to the pasta mixture; toss gently to coat.

NUTRITION FACTS PER SERVING: 474 cal., 16 g total fat (4 g sat. fat), 45 mg chol., 311 mg sodium, 56 g carbo., 3 g fiber, 26 g pro.

Beef and Fruit Salad

Choose whatever fruits are in season for this refreshing main-dish salad.

PREP: 20 MINUTES **MARINATE:** 30 MINUTES TO 8 HOURS **GRILL:** 14 MINUTES
MAKES: 4 SERVINGS

12 ounces boneless beef top sirloin steak, cut 1 inch thick

⅓ cup reduced-sodium bottled teriyaki sauce or soy sauce

¼ cup lemon juice

¼ cup water

2 teaspoons toasted sesame oil

⅛ teaspoon bottled hot pepper sauce

3 cups shredded napa cabbage

1 cup torn or shredded fresh sorrel or spinach

2 cups fresh fruit (such as sliced plums, nectarines, or kiwifruit; halved seedless grapes or strawberries; raspberries; and/or blueberries)

1 Trim fat from steak. Place steak in a resealable plastic bag set in a shallow dish. In a small bowl combine teriyaki sauce, lemon juice, the water, sesame oil, and hot pepper sauce. Reserve ⅓ cup for dressing; cover and chill. Pour remaining teriyaki mixture over steak. Seal bag; turn to coat steak. Marinate in refrigerator for at least 30 minutes or up to 8 hours, turning bag occasionally.

2 Drain steak, reserving marinade. For charcoal grill, grill steak on the rack of an uncovered grill directly over medium coals until desired doneness, turning once and brushing occasionally with marinade up to the last 5 minutes of grilling. Allow 14 to 18 minutes for medium-rare doneness (145°F) or 18 to 22 minutes for medium doneness (160°F). (For a gas grill, preheat grill. Reduce heat to medium. Place steaks on grill rack over heat. Cover and grill as above.) Discard any remaining marinade.

3 To serve, divide cabbage and sorrel or spinach among 4 dinner plates. Thinly slice steak diagonally. Arrange steak and fruit on top of greens. Drizzle with the ⅓ cup chilled teriyaki mixture.

NUTRITION FACTS PER SERVING: 248 cal., 10 g total fat (3 g sat. fat), 57 mg chol., 307 mg sodium, 19 g carbo., 2 g fiber, 22 g pro.

Grilled Beef, Red Onion, and Blue Cheese Salad

The natural sweetness of red onions is intensified when the onions are brushed with a balsamic vinaigrette and grilled alongside sirloin steak. Aromatic grilled herb bread makes a perfect go-along with this crisp and hearty main-dish salad.

PREP: 15 MINUTES   GRILL: 14 MINUTES   MAKES: 4 SERVINGS

- **2** tablespoons olive oil
- **3** tablespoons balsamic vinegar
- **½** teaspoon bottled minced garlic (1 clove)
- **½** teaspoon salt
- **½** teaspoon ground black pepper
- **1** boneless beef top sirloin steak, cut 1 inch thick (about 12 ounces)
- **1** tablespoon snipped fresh thyme
- **2** teaspoons snipped fresh rosemary
- **4** ¼-inch-thick slices red onion
- **6** cups lightly packed mesclun or torn mixed salad greens
- **2** tablespoons crumbled blue cheese
- **8** yellow and/or red pear tomatoes, halved

1 For vinaigrette, in a screw-top jar combine oil, balsamic vinegar, garlic, salt, and pepper; cover and shake well. Trim fat from steak. Remove 1 tablespoon of the vinaigrette from jar and brush evenly onto both sides of steak. Press thyme and rosemary onto both sides of the steak. Brush both sides of onion slices with some of the remaining vinaigrette, reserving the rest; set aside.

2 For charcoal grill, grill steak on rack of an uncovered grill directly over medium coals until desired doneness, turning once halfway through grilling. Allow 14 to 18 minutes for medium-rare doneness (145°F) or 18 to 22 minutes for medium doneness (160°F). For last 10 minutes of grilling, place onions on grill rack alongside meat. Grill onions until tender, turning once. (For a gas grill, preheat grill. Reduce heat to medium. Place steaks, then onions on the grill rack over heat. Cover and grill as above.)

3 Divide mesclun or mixed salad greens among 4 dinner plates. To serve, thinly slice the steak across the grain. Separate onion slices into rings. Arrange warm steak and onions on greens. Drizzle with the reserved vinaigrette. Top with cheese and tomatoes.

NUTRITION FACTS PER SERVING: 266 cal., 16 g total fat (5 g sat. fat), 59 mg chol., 373 mg sodium, 9 g carbo., 2 g fiber, 22 g pro.

Sizzling Beef Salad

Pungent red chile paste and hoisin sauce add an Asian accent to beef.

PREP: 20 MINUTES **STAND:** 30 MINUTES **GRILL:** 14 MINUTES **MAKES:** 4 SERVINGS

12 ounces boneless beef top sirloin steak, cut 1 inch thick

Salt

1 to 2 tablespoons purchased red chile paste (sambal)

⅓ cup lime juice

3 tablespoons cooking oil

2 tablespoons bottled hoisin sauce

6 cups shredded romaine

1 medium fresh papaya, seeded, peeled, and sliced

2 tablespoons chopped honey-roasted peanuts

1 Sprinkle both sides of meat lightly with salt. Spread one or both sides of steak with chile paste. Place in a resealable plastic bag set in a shallow dish. Seal bag. Let stand at room temperature for 30 minutes. (Or refrigerate for at least 4 hours or up to 24 hours.)

2 For a charcoal grill, grill steak on the rack of an uncovered grill directly over medium coals until desired doneness, turning once halfway through grilling. Allow 14 to 18 minutes for medium-rare doneness (145°F) or 18 to 22 minutes for medium doneness (160°F). (For a gas grill, preheat grill. Reduce heat to medium. Place steaks on grill rack over heat. Cover and grill as above.)

3 Meanwhile, for dressing, in a screw-top jar combine lime juice, oil, and hoisin sauce. Cover and shake well. Arrange romaine on 4 chilled dinner plates. To serve, thinly slice steak. Arrange steak slices on shredded romaine; add papaya slices. Drizzle with dressing; sprinkle with peanuts.

NUTRITION FACTS PER SERVING: 369 cal., 20 g total fat (5 g sat. fat), 57 mg chol., 259 mg sodium, 25 g carbo., 4 g fiber, 22 g pro.

Garlic-Studded Veal Chops and Asparagus

The grilled asparagus also pairs well with grilled chicken or pork.

PREP: 15 MINUTES   **STAND:** 30 MINUTES   **GRILL:** 11 MINUTES + 3 MINUTES

MAKES: 4 SERVINGS

- **1** pound fresh asparagus spears
- **2** tablespoons dry sherry
- **2** tablespoons olive oil
- **½** teaspoon bottled minced garlic (1 clove)
- **4** boneless veal top loin chops, cut ¾ inch thick
- **3** or 4 cloves garlic, cut into thin slivers
- **1** tablespoon snipped fresh thyme or 1 teaspoon dried thyme, crushed
- **⅛** teaspoon salt
- **⅛** teaspoon ground black pepper

1 Snap off and discard woody stems from asparagus spears. In a medium skillet bring a small amount of water to boiling; add asparagus. Cover and simmer about 3 minutes or until crisp-tender; drain. Place asparagus in a resealable plastic bag; add sherry, 1 tablespoon of the olive oil, and the minced garlic. Let stand at room temperature for 30 minutes.

2 Meanwhile, trim fat from chops. With the tip of a sharp knife, make a few small slits in each veal chop; insert garlic slivers in slits. In a small bowl combine the remaining 1 tablespoon olive oil, the thyme, salt, and pepper; brush over chops.

3 For a charcoal grill, grill chops on the rack of an uncovered grill directly over medium coals for 11 to 13 minutes or until medium doneness (160°F), turning once halfway through grilling.

4 Add asparagus spears to grill (lay spears perpendicular to wires on grill rack so they won't fall into coals). Grill for 3 to 4 minutes or until crisp-tender and lightly browned, turning occasionally. (For a gas grill, preheat the grill. Reduce heat to medium. Place chops, then asparagus on grill rack over heat. Cover and grill as above.) Serve asparagus with chops.

NUTRITION FACTS PER SERVING: 237 cal., 11 g total fat (3 g sat. fat), 92 mg chol., 131 mg sodium, 5 g carbo., 2 g fiber, 27 g pro.

Stuffed Veal Chops with Gorgonzola

Grill these unmistakably autumnal chops—with their stuffing of leeks, apples, and fresh sage—on a crisp fall day. Crumble blue cheese over each chop and serve the chops with your favorite chilled white wine.

PREP: 15 MINUTES   GRILL: 11 MINUTES   MAKES: 4 SERVINGS

½   cup finely chopped tart apple

½   cup finely chopped leek

½   teaspoon snipped fresh sage

¼   teaspoon salt

¼   teaspoon ground black pepper

4   boneless veal top loin chops, cut ¾ inch thick (about 1¼ pounds total)

1   tablespoon olive oil

     Salt

     Ground black pepper

½   cup crumbled blue cheese (2 ounces)

1 For stuffing, in a small bowl combine the chopped apple, leek, sage, the ¼ teaspoon salt, and the ¼ teaspoon pepper.

2 Trim fat from veal chops. Make a pocket in each veal chop by cutting horizontally from the fat side almost to, but not through, the opposite side. Divide stuffing among pockets in chops. If necessary, secure with wooden toothpicks. Brush chops with olive oil; sprinkle lightly with additional salt and additional pepper.

3 For a charcoal grill, grill veal chops on the rack of an uncovered grill directly over medium coals for 11 to 13 minutes or until medium doneness (160°F), turning once halfway through grilling. (For a gas grill, preheat grill. Reduce heat to medium. Place veal chops on grill rack over heat. Cover and grill as above.)

4 If using toothpicks, remove them. To serve, sprinkle crumbled blue cheese over veal chops.

NUTRITION FACTS PER SERVING: 260 cal., 14 g total fat (5 g sat. fat), 105 mg chol., 422 mg sodium, 6 g carbo., 2 g fiber, 27 g pro.

Sweet and Sour Veal Chops

Orange juice and vinegar, with the flavorful additions of ginger and cinnamon, become the perfect marinade for these veal chops. Toasted sesame oil, either drizzled or brushed over the chops after grilling, adds a delicious finishing touch.

PREP: 15 MINUTES   MARINATE: 2 HOURS   GRILL: 12 MINUTES   MAKES: 4 SERVINGS

4   veal loin chops, cut 1 inch thick
    (about 2 pounds total)

½   cup frozen orange juice concentrate, thawed

½   cup rice vinegar or cider vinegar

3   tablespoons olive oil or peanut oil

2   tablespoons soy sauce

2   tablespoons grated fresh ginger

2   teaspoons bottled minced garlic (4 cloves)

¼   teaspoon ground cinnamon

½   teaspoon toasted sesame oil

    Freshly ground black pepper

1 Trim fat from veal chops. Place veal chops in a resealable plastic bag set in a shallow dish. For marinade, in a small bowl combine orange juice concentrate, vinegar, oil, soy sauce, ginger, garlic, and cinnamon. Pour marinade over veal chops. Seal bag; turn to coat veal chops. Marinate in the refrigerator for 2 hours, turning bag occasionally.

2 Drain veal chops, reserving marinade. For a charcoal grill, grill veal chops on the rack of an uncovered grill directly over medium coals for 12 to 15 minutes or until juices run clear (160°F), turning once and brushing occasionally with reserved marinade during the first 15 minutes of grilling. (For a gas grill, preheat grill. Reduce heat to medium. Place veal chops on grill rack over heat. Cover and grill as above.) Discard any remaining marinade.

3 To serve, brush veal chops with sesame oil and sprinkle with freshly ground black pepper.

NUTRITION FACTS PER SERVING: 345 cal., 17 g total fat (4 g sat. fat), 135 mg chol., 511 mg sodium, 13 g carbo., 0 g fiber, 35 g pro.

Veal Chops with Pesto-Stuffed Mushrooms

For maximum flavor, marinate the chops in the white wine and sage mixture for 24 hours.

PREP: 10 MINUTES **MARINATE: 30 MINUTES TO 24 HOURS** **GRILL: 11 MINUTES**

MAKES: 4 SERVINGS

¼ cup dry white wine

1 tablespoon snipped fresh sage or snipped fresh thyme

1 tablespoon white wine Worcestershire sauce

1 tablespoon olive oil

1½ teaspoons bottled minced garlic (3 cloves)

4 veal loin chops, cut ¾ inch thick (about 1¼ pounds total)

Ground black pepper

8 large fresh mushrooms (2 to 2½ inches in diameter)

2 to 3 tablespoons purchased pesto

Hot cooked rice (optional)

1 For marinade, in a small bowl combine wine, the sage or thyme, the Worcestershire sauce, oil, and garlic. Place chops in a resealable plastic bag set in a shallow dish. Pour marinade over chops. Seal bag; turn to coat chops. Marinate in refrigerator for at least 30 minutes or up to 24 hours, turning bag occasionally.

2 Drain chops, reserving marinade. Sprinkle chops with pepper. For a charcoal grill, grill chops on the rack of an uncovered grill directly over medium coals for 11 to 13 minutes or until juices run clear (160°F), turning once halfway through grilling and brushing with reserved marinade during the first 5 minutes of grilling.

3 Meanwhile, carefully remove stems from mushrooms; chop stems for another use or discard. Brush mushroom caps with reserved marinade. Discard any remaining marinade. Place mushrooms, stem sides down, on grill rack. Grill for 4 minutes. Turn stem sides up; spoon some pesto into each. Grill about 4 minutes more or until heated through. (For a gas grill, preheat grill. Reduce heat to medium. Place chops, then mushrooms on grill rack over heat. Cover and grill as above.) Serve mushrooms with chops. If desired, serve with hot cooked rice.

NUTRITION FACTS PER SERVING: 285 cal., 16 g total fat (2 g sat. fat), 100 mg chol., 157 mg sodium, 4 g carbo., 1 g fiber, 28 g pro.

Mediterranean Veal Brochettes

Brochette is French for skewer. Serve these tender veal brochettes over a Caesar salad or on top of cooked broken spaghetti tossed with snipped fresh tarragon, olive oil, and sliced grilled vegetables.

PREP: 20 MINUTES **MARINATE:** 1 TO 4 HOURS **GRILL:** 10 MINUTES **MAKES:** 6 SERVINGS

1½ pounds boneless veal or beef tenderloin, trimmed and cut into 1½-inch cubes

3 green onions, sliced

¼ cup olive oil

3 tablespoons lemon juice

2 teaspoons dried tarragon, crushed

1½ teaspoons bottled minced garlic (3 cloves)

½ teaspoon dried oregano, crushed

¼ teaspoon freshly ground black pepper

1 Place meat cubes in a resealable plastic bag set in a shallow dish. For marinade, in a small bowl combine green onions, olive oil, lemon juice, tarragon, garlic, oregano, and pepper. Pour marinade over meat. Seal bag; turn to coat meat. Marinate in the refrigerator for at least 1 hour or up to 4 hours, turning bag occasionally.

2 Drain meat, discarding marinade. On six 12-inch metal skewers, thread meat, leaving ¼-inch space between cubes. For a charcoal grill, grill skewers on rack of an uncovered grill directly over medium coals for 10 to 12 minutes or until meat is done, turning occasionally. (For gas grill, preheat grill. Reduce heat to medium. Place skewers on grill rack over heat. Cover and grill as above.)

NUTRITION FACTS PER SERVING: 164 cal., 6 g total fat (1 g sat. fat), 88 mg chol., 62 mg sodium, 1 g carbo., 0 g fiber, 24 g pro.

Bacon-Tarragon Veal Skewers

Be sure to cook the bacon just until brown so it is still pliable enough to thread on the skewers.

PREP: 15 MINUTES   MARINATE: 2 HOURS   GRILL: 12 MINUTES   MAKES: 4 TO 6 SERVINGS

- **2** pounds boneless veal
- **3** tablespoons dry white wine
- **2** tablespoons snipped fresh tarragon
- **2** tablespoons olive oil
- **2** tablespoons lemon juice
- **½** teaspoon salt
- **½** teaspoon ground black pepper
- **8** slices bacon

1 Trim fat from meat. Cut meat into 1-inch cubes. Place meat in a resealable plastic bag set in a shallow dish. For marinade, combine wine, tarragon, oil, lemon juice, salt, and pepper. Pour marinade over meat. Seal bag; turn to coat meat. Marinate in the refrigerator for 2 hours, turning bag occasionally.

2 Drain meat, reserving marinade. In a large skillet cook bacon over medium heat just until brown, but still limp. Drain on paper towels. On 10- to 12-inch metal skewers, alternately thread meat and bacon, weaving bacon between and around meat in an "S" shape.

3 For a charcoal grill, place kabobs on the rack of an uncovered grill directly over medium coals for 12 to 14 minutes or until meat is done, turning once and brushing occasionally with reserved marinade for the first 7 minutes of grilling. (For a gas grill, preheat grill. Reduce heat to medium. Place kabobs on grill rack over heat. Cover and grill as above.) Discard any remaining marinade.

NUTRITION FACTS PER SERVING: 429 cal., 21 g total fat (6 g sat. fat), 195 mg chol., 591 mg sodium, 1 g carbo., 0 g fiber, 54 g pro.

Spicy Maple-Glazed Pork Loin

Chipotle peppers add just the right amount of spiciness to the flavorful glaze that features beer, peanut butter, and maple-flavored syrup.

PREP: 35 MINUTES   GRILL: 2 HOURS   STAND: 10 MINUTES   MAKES: 8 SERVINGS

¾   cup beer (½ of a 12-ounce can)

¼   cup maple-flavored syrup or mild-flavored molasses

1   to 2 canned chipotle chile peppers in adobo sauce, finely chopped*

2   tablespoons creamy peanut butter

1   tablespoon Worcestershire sauce

2   teaspoons Dijon-style mustard

1   teaspoon bottled minced garlic (2 cloves)

½   teaspoon ground cinnamon

1   4- to 5-pound pork loin center rib roast (backbone loosened)**

¼   teaspoon salt

¼   teaspoon ground black pepper

1 For glaze, in a small saucepan combine beer, syrup or molasses, chipotle peppers, peanut butter, Worcestershire sauce, mustard, garlic, and cinnamon. Bring to boiling; reduce heat. Simmer, uncovered, for 20 to 30 minutes or until desired consistency, stirring occasionally. Set aside.

2 Meanwhile, trim fat from meat. Sprinkle meat with salt and pepper.

3 For a charcoal grill, arrange medium coals around edge of grill with a cover. Test for medium-low heat above center of grill (not over coals). Place meat on rack in a roasting pan. Place pan over center of grill (not over coals). Cover and grill for 2 to 2¾ hours or until meat juices run clear (155°F), brushing meat with glaze during the last 20 minutes of grilling. Add coals as necessary to maintain heat. (For a gas grill, preheat grill. Reduce heat to medium-low. Adjust for indirect cooking. Grill as above.)

4 Remove meat from grill. Cover meat and let stand for 10 minutes. The meat's temperature after standing should be 160°F. Slice meat.

NUTRITION FACTS PER SERVING: 378 cal., 13 g total fat (4 g sat. fat), 142 mg chol., 264 mg sodium, 10 g carbo., 0 g fiber, 51 g pro.

*NOTE: Because chile peppers contain volatile oils that can burn your skin and eyes, avoid direct contact with them as much as possible. When working with chile peppers, wear plastic or rubber gloves. If your bare hands do touch the chile peppers, wash your hands and nails well with soap and warm water.

**NOTE: Ask your butcher to loosen the backbone for you.

Herb-Cured Pork Platter

Black beans and pineapple give this herbed pork a tropical flair.

PREP: 15 MINUTES **CHILL:** 24 HOURS **GRILL:** 1 HOUR **STAND:** 15 MINUTES
MAKES: 6 TO 8 SERVINGS

1 tablespoon snipped fresh thyme or ¾ teaspoon dried thyme, crushed

1 tablespoon snipped fresh sage or ¾ teaspoon dried sage, crushed

1 tablespoon snipped fresh rosemary or ¾ teaspoon dried rosemary, crushed

1½ teaspoons coarsely ground black pepper

1 to 1½ teaspoons coarse salt

1 teaspoon bottled minced garlic (2 cloves)

½ teaspoon crushed red pepper

1 2- to 3-pound boneless pork top loin roast (single loin)

1 large fresh pineapple

1 tablespoon cooking oil

1 recipe Savory Black Beans

1 For rub, in a small bowl combine thyme, sage, rosemary, black pepper, salt, garlic, and crushed red pepper. Sprinkle rub evenly over roast; rub in with your fingers. Place roast in a baking dish. Cover tightly with plastic wrap; chill in the refrigerator for 24 hours.

2 For charcoal grill, arrange medium coals around a drip pan. Test for medium-low heat above pan. Place roast on grill rack over pan. Cover and grill for 1 to 1½ hours or until meat juices run clear (155°F). Add coals as necessary to maintain heat. Cover; let stand for 15 minutes before slicing. The meat's temperature after standing should be 160°F. (For a gas grill, preheat grill. Reduce heat to medium-low. Adjust for indirect cooking. Place meat on a rack in a roasting pan, place on grill rack, and grill as above.)

3 To prepare pineapple, cut pineapple lengthwise into 6 to 8 wedges, leaving leaves on fruit. Cut away center core. Brush pineapple with oil. Grill directly over coals for the last 15 minutes of grilling roast, turning occasionally.

4 To serve, loosen pineapple peel by cutting between peel and fruit. Slice roast. Arrange pork slices on platter with pineapple and Savory Black Beans.

Savory Black Beans: Drain and rinse one 15-ounce can black beans. In a medium saucepan combine the drained beans; one 15-ounce can black beans, undrained; 1 teaspoon ground cumin; and ½ teaspoon bottled minced garlic (1 clove). Heat through, stirring occasionally, being careful not to mash beans. Just before serving, place bean mixture in a serving bowl. Sprinkle bean mixture with 1 medium avocado, halved, seeded, peeled, and cubed; ½ cup crumbled feta cheese or shredded Monterey Jack cheese (2 ounces); and 1 small tomato, seeded and chopped.

NUTRITION FACTS PER SERVING: 407 cal., 21 g total fat (5 g sat. fat), 76 mg chol., 646 mg sodium, 32 g carbo., 7 g fiber, 30 g pro.

Herb-and-Garlic Pork

Marinating meat in a resealable plastic bag assures that the marinade surrounds the meat. It also helps avoid spills and minimize cleanup.

PREP: 15 MINUTES   MARINATE: 2 TO 24 HOURS   GRILL: 1½ HOURS   STAND: 15 MINUTES
MAKES: 12 SERVINGS

1	3- to 4-pound boneless pork top loin roast (double loin, tied)
¼	cup olive oil
2	tablespoons snipped fresh basil
2	tablespoons snipped fresh chives or chopped green onion
1	tablespoon bottled minced garlic (6 cloves)
2	teaspoons chili powder or ¼ teaspoon cayenne pepper
1	teaspoon snipped fresh sage or oregano
1	teaspoon salt
½	teaspoon ground black pepper

1 Place meat in a resealable plastic bag set in a shallow dish. For marinade, in a small bowl combine oil, basil, chives or green onion, garlic, chili powder or cayenne pepper, sage or oregano, salt, and black pepper. Pour marinade over meat. Seal bag; turn to coat meat. Marinate in the refrigerator for at least 2 hours or up to 24 hours, turning bag occasionally.

2 Drain meat, discarding marinade. For a charcoal grill, arrange medium coals around drip pan. Test for medium-low heat above pan. Place meat on grill rack over drip pan. Cover and grill for 1½ to 2¼ hours or until meat juices run clear (155°F). Add coals as necessary to maintain heat. (For a gas grill, preheat grill. Reduce heat to medium-low. Adjust for indirect cooking. Place meat on a rack in a roasting pan, place on grill rack, and grill as above.) Remove roast from grill. Cover with foil; let stand for 15 minutes before slicing. The meat's temperature after standing should be 160°F.

3 To serve, remove strings and slice meat.

NUTRITION FACTS PER SERVING: 201 cal., 10 g total fat (3 g sat. fat), 62 mg chol., 239 mg sodium, 1 g carbo., 0 g fiber, 25 g pro.

Paradise Pork Roast

Orange marmalade, spiked with dry mustard and ginger, glazes this company-special pork top loin roast.

PREP: 15 MINUTES   GRILL: 1 HOUR + 30 MINUTES   STAND: 15 MINUTES   MAKES: 12 SERVINGS

- **1** 3- to 4-pound boneless pork top loin roast (double loin, tied)
- **1** teaspoon salt
- **1** teaspoon dry mustard
- **½** teaspoon ground white pepper
- **½** teaspoon ground ginger
- **1** cup orange marmalade
- **¼** cup light-colored corn syrup
- **2** tablespoons lemon juice
- **½** teaspoon dry mustard
- **½** teaspoon ground ginger

1 Trim fat from roast. For rub, in a small bowl combine salt, the 1 teaspoon mustard, the white pepper, and ½ teaspoon ginger. Sprinkle the rub evenly onto all sides of roast; rub in with your fingers.

2 For a charcoal grill, arrange medium coals around a drip pan. Test for medium-low heat above the pan. Place roast on the grill rack over drip pan. Cover and grill for 1 hour.

3 Meanwhile, for glaze, in a medium saucepan combine orange marmalade, corn syrup, lemon juice, the ½ teaspoon mustard, and ½ teaspoon ginger. Cook over medium heat for 5 minutes, stirring frequently. Set aside half of the glaze mixture to serve with the pork roast.

4 Continue grilling roast for 30 minutes to 1 hour more or until meat juices run clear (155°F), brushing with some of the remaining glaze every 10 minutes. Add coals as necessary to maintain heat. Remove roast from grill. Cover with foil; let stand for 15 minutes before carving. The meat's temperature after standing should be 160°F. (For a gas grill, preheat grill. Reduce heat to medium-low. Adjust for indirect cooking. Place meat on rack in a roasting pan, place on grill rack, and grill as above.)

5 Discard remainder of the glaze used as brush-on. Reheat the reserved glaze; pass it with roast.

NUTRITION FACTS PER SERVING: 244 cal., 6 g total fat (2 g sat. fat), 62 mg chol., 258 mg sodium, 23 g carbo., 0 g fiber, 25 g pro.

Pork Loin Stuffed with Dried Fruit and Gorgonzola

*Savory, slightly pungent Gorgonzola cheese complements
the pork and the pear-and-walnut stuffing.*

PREP: 30 MINUTES   GRILL: 1½ HOURS   STAND: 15 MINUTES   MAKES: 10 TO 14 SERVINGS

⅓   cup chopped onion

2   tablespoons butter or margarine

1½   cups snipped dried pears or dried apples

1   tablespoon balsamic vinegar

½   cup chopped walnuts, toasted

¼   cup crumbled Gorgonzola cheese (1 ounce)

1   3- to 4-pound boneless pork top loin roast (double loin, tied)

1   tablespoon snipped fresh rosemary

1   teaspoon bottled minced garlic (2 cloves)

½   teaspoon coarsely ground black pepper

1 For stuffing, in a large skillet cook onion in hot butter over medium heat until tender. Stir in pears or apples and vinegar. Remove from heat; stir in walnuts and Gorgonzola cheese.

2 Untie roast; trim fat from meat. Spoon stuffing on flat side of one loin. Replace second loin and retie roast. For rub, in a small bowl stir together rosemary, garlic, and pepper. Sprinkle rub evenly over meat; rub in with your fingers.

3 For a charcoal grill, arrange medium coals around a drip pan. Test for medium-low heat above pan. Place meat on grill rack over drip pan. Cover and grill for 1½ to 2¼ hours or until meat juices run clear (155°F). Add coals as necessary to maintain heat. (For a gas grill, preheat grill. Reduce heat to medium-low. Adjust for indirect grilling. Place meat on rack in a roasting pan, place on grill rack, and grill as above.)

4 Remove meat from grill. Cover with foil; let stand for 15 minutes before carving. The meat's temperature after standing should be 160°F.

NUTRITION FACTS PER SERVING: 306 cal., 16 g total fat (5 g sat. fat), 70 mg chol., 112 mg sodium, 21 g carbo., 2 g fiber, 21 g pro.

Country Boy Pork Tenderloins

Instead of serving grilled pork with applesauce, make a marinade of apple butter that sweetly coats every slice of the meat.

PREP: 10 MINUTES **MARINATE:** 2 TO 8 HOURS **GRILL:** 40 MINUTES **MAKES:** 6 TO 8 SERVINGS

1	cup apple butter
½	cup white vinegar
1	tablespoon sugar
1	tablespoon Worcestershire sauce
1	tablespoon brandy
1	tablespoon soy sauce
½	teaspoon dry mustard
½	teaspoon salt
¼	teaspoon ground black pepper
¼	teaspoon paprika
	Few dashes bottled hot pepper sauce
2	1-pound pork tenderloins

1 In a medium bowl stir together apple butter, vinegar, sugar, Worcestershire sauce, brandy, soy sauce, mustard, salt, black pepper, paprika, and bottled hot pepper sauce.

2 Place the tenderloins in a resealable plastic bag set in a shallow dish. Pour the apple butter mixture over meat. Seal bag; turn to coat tenderloin. Marinate in the refrigerator for at least 2 hours or up to 8 hours. Drain meat, reserving marinade.

3 For a charcoal grill, arrange hot coals around a drip pan. Test for medium-hot heat above the pan. Place tenderloins on grill rack over drip pan. Cover and grill for 40 to 50 minutes or until meat juices run clear (160°F), brushing occasionally with marinade during the first 20 minutes of grilling. (For a gas grill, preheat grill. Reduce heat to medium-hot. Adjust for indirect cooking. Place tenderloins on rack in a roasting pan, place on grill rack, and grill as above.) Discard any remaining marinade.

NUTRITION FACTS PER SERVING: 459 cal., 3 g total fat (1 g sat. fat), 89 mg chol., 442 mg sodium, 64 g carbo., 2 g fiber, 37 g pro.

Grilled Mustard-Glazed Pork

Start the tenderloins marinating; then put your feet up and relax until it's time to grill.

PREP: 10 MINUTES   **MARINATE:** 30 MINUTES   **GRILL:** 40 MINUTES   **MAKES:** 6 SERVINGS

2	pork tenderloins (about 1½ pounds total)
½	cup apple juice or apple cider
2	large shallots, minced
¼	cup cider vinegar
¼	cup coarse-grain brown mustard
2	tablespoons olive oil
1	tablespoon brown sugar
1½	teaspoons soy sauce
	Dash ground black pepper
	Snipped fresh chives (optional)

1 Place tenderloins in a resealable plastic bag set in a shallow dish. For marinade, in a small bowl combine the apple juice, shallots, vinegar, mustard, oil, brown sugar, soy sauce, and pepper. Pour over tenderloins. Seal bag; turn to coat tenderloins. Marinate in the refrigerator for 30 minutes, turning bag occasionally.

2 Drain meat, reserving marinade. For charcoal grill, arrange hot coals around a drip pan. Test for medium-hot heat above pan. Place tenderloins on grill rack over pan. Cover and grill for 40 to 50 minutes or until meat juices run clear (160°F), turning once halfway through grilling. (For a gas grill, preheat grill. Reduce heat to medium-hot. Adjust for indirect cooking. Place tenderloins on a rack in a roasting pan, place on grill rack, and grill as above.)

3 Meanwhile, for sauce, pour reserved marinade into a medium saucepan. Bring to boiling; reduce heat. Simmer, uncovered, about 8 minutes or until reduced to ⅔ cup. Slice tenderloins across the grain. Serve with the sauce. If desired, sprinkle with chives.

NUTRITION FACTS PER SERVING: 215 cal., 9 g total fat (2 g sat. fat), 81 mg chol., 280 mg sodium, 7 g carbo., 0 g fiber, 26 g pro.

Jalapeño-Stuffed Pork Tenderloin

This spunky grilled roast starts with a sprinkling of jalapeño peppers,
tomato, and cilantro, and ends with a sassy butter brush-on.

PREP: 30 MINUTES   **MARINATE:** 8 TO 24 HOURS   **GRILL:** 30 MINUTES   **STAND:** 10 MINUTES

MAKES: 4 TO 6 SERVINGS

1	1- to 1¼-pound pork tenderloin
6	fresh jalapeño chile peppers, seeded and chopped*
1	plum tomato, chopped
2	tablespoons snipped fresh cilantro
2	tablespoons lime juice
2½	teaspoons bottled minced garlic (5 cloves)
½	teaspoon salt
¼	cup butter, melted
	Ground black pepper
	Salt

1 Trim fat from meat. Split tenderloin lengthwise, cutting to but not through the opposite side. Spread meat open. Cover with plastic wrap. Working from the center to the edges, pound with the flat side of a meat mallet to about ½-inch thickness. Remove plastic wrap.

2 In a small bowl combine half of the jalapeño peppers, the tomato, cilantro, lime juice, garlic, and ¼ teaspoon of the salt. Sprinkle over meat. Starting from a long side, roll up into a spiral, tucking in ends. Tie at 1-inch intervals with 100%-cotton kitchen string; place in a shallow dish. Cover and chill in the refrigerator for at least 8 hours or up to 24 hours. Cover and refrigerate the remaining 3 chopped jalapeño peppers.

3 In a small bowl combine melted butter, the remaining jalapeño peppers, and the remaining ¼ teaspoon salt. For a charcoal grill, arrange medium-hot coals around a drip pan. Test for medium heat above the pan. Place meat on grill rack over drip pan. Cover and grill for 30 to 45 minutes or until meat juices run clear (160°F), brushing occasionally with butter mixture during the first 20 minutes of grilling. (For a gas grill, preheat grill. Reduce heat to medium. Adjust for indirect cooking. Place meat on a rack in a roasting pan, place on the grill rack, and grill as above.) Discard any remaining butter mixture.

4 Remove meat from grill. Cover with foil; let stand for 10 minutes. Remove string from meat. Slice meat. Sprinkle with black pepper and additional salt.

NUTRITION FACTS PER SERVING: 260 cal., 16 g total fat (9 g sat. fat), 106 mg chol., 543 mg sodium, 4 g carbo., 1 g fiber, 25 g pro.

*NOTE: Because chile peppers contain volatile oils that can burn your skin and eyes, avoid direct contact with them as much as possible. When working with chile peppers, wear plastic or rubber gloves. If your bare hands do touch the chile peppers, wash your hands and nails well with soap and warm water.

Pork Tenderloin with Green Olive Tapenade

The Provence region of France proudly claims the mixture of olives, capers, anchovies, and seasonings known as tapenade.

PREP: 20 MINUTES **GRILL:** 1 HOUR **STAND:** 10 MINUTES **MAKES:** 6 SERVINGS

1 cup pitted green olives, drained

1 tablespoon capers, drained

1 tablespoon Dijon-style mustard

1 tablespoon olive oil

1 tablespoon lemon juice

2 teaspoons anchovy paste

1 teaspoon snipped fresh thyme

½ teaspoon bottled minced garlic (1 clove)

2 12-ounce pork tenderloins

1 For tapenade, in a food processor bowl combine olives, capers, mustard, oil, lemon juice, anchovy paste, thyme, and garlic. Cover; process until smooth, scraping side as necessary. Cover and chill up to 24 hours.

2 Trim fat from meat. Split each tenderloin lengthwise, cutting to but not through the opposite side. Spread meat open. Place meat between 2 pieces of plastic wrap overlapping one long side of each tenderloin about 2 inches. Working from the center to the edges, use the flat side of a meat mallet to pound meat into a 12×10-inch rectangle. Remove plastic wrap. Spread tapenade over meat rectangle to within 1 inch of edges. Fold in long sides just to cover edge of stuffing. Starting at one of the short sides, roll up into a spiral. Tie with 100%-cotton kitchen string at 1-inch intervals.

3 For a charcoal grill, arrange medium-hot coals around a drip pan. Test for medium heat above the pan. Place meat on grill rack over drip pan. Cover and grill for 1 to 1¼ hours or until meat juices run clear (160°F). Add coals as necessary to maintain heat. (For a gas grill, preheat grill. Reduce heat to medium. Adjust for indirect cooking. Place meat on rack in a roasting pan, place on grill rack, and grill as above.)

4 Remove meat from grill. Cover with foil; let stand for 10 minutes. Remove string from meat. Slice meat.

NUTRITION FACTS PER SERVING: 201 cal., 10 g total fat (2 g sat. fat), 83 mg chol., 347 mg sodium, 1 g carbo., 0 g fiber, 27 g pro.

Pork Tenderloin with Mango, Mint, and Basil

Tropical tamarind has a wonderful sweet-sour flavor, which is enhanced here with honey and ginger to become both marinade and sauce for pork tenderloin. Tamarind pulp, which usually contains seeds, is readily available in Asian and Latin food stores.

PREP: 30 MINUTES   MARINATE: 1 TO 3 HOURS   GRILL: 20 MINUTES   MAKES: 6 SERVINGS

⅓ cup tamarind pulp (about 2 ounces)

1 cup boiling water

2 tablespoons honey

1 tablespoon grated fresh ginger

¼ teaspoon salt

2 12-ounce pork tenderloins

2 firm ripe mangoes, seeded, peeled, and cut into 1- to 1½-inch slices or cubes

¼ cup finely shredded fresh basil

¼ cup finely shredded fresh mint

Coarsely cracked black pepper

1 For marinade, break the tamarind pulp into small pieces. In a medium bowl combine tamarind pulp, boiling water, and honey, stirring and mashing until cool. Strain through a medium sieve, forcing pulp through and scraping bottom of sieve. Discard seeds. Stir in ginger and salt. Set aside ½ cup of the marinade to drizzle over grilled meat; cover and chill. Pour remaining marinade into a resealable plastic bag set in a deep bowl.

2 Prick tenderloins all over about 30 times with the tip of a paring knife. Place tenderloins in bag. Seal bag; turn to coat tenderloins. Marinate in the refrigerator for at least 1 hour or up to 3 hours, turning bag occasionally.

3 Drain tenderloins, discarding marinade. For a charcoal grill, grill tenderloins on the rack of an uncovered grill directly over medium coals about 20 minutes or until meat juices run clear (160°F), turning once halfway through grilling. (For a gas grill, preheat grill. Reduce heat to medium. Place tenderloin on grill rack over heat. Cover and grill as above.)

4 Cut tenderloin across grain into ½-inch-thick slices. Arrange pork on platter with mangoes. Drizzle the reserved chilled marinade over meat. Sprinkle with basil, mint, and cracked black pepper.

NUTRITION FACTS PER SERVING: 216 cal., 3 g total fat (1 g sat. fat), 73 mg chol., 147 mg sodium, 22 g carbo., 2 g fiber, 24 g pro.

Sassy Mojo Pork

The word "mojo" (moe-hoe) comes from a Spanish word, mojado, which means wet. Found predominantly in Spanish and Cuban cuisine, mojos are used as sauces or marinades.

PREP: 20 MINUTES **MARINATE:** 2 HOURS **GRILL:** 40 MINUTES **MAKES:** 6 SERVINGS

2	12- to 16-ounce pork tenderloins
4	canned chipotle chile peppers in adobo sauce, rinsed and drained (2 ounces)
½	cup orange juice
¼	cup coarsely chopped onion
2	tablespoons snipped fresh oregano or 2 teaspoons dried oregano, crushed
2	tablespoons lime juice
1	tablespoon honey
1	tablespoon cooking oil
1½	teaspoons bottled minced garlic (3 cloves)
½	teaspoon salt

1 Place meat in a resealable plastic bag set in a shallow dish. For marinade, in a food processor bowl or blender container combine chipotle peppers, orange juice, onion, oregano, lime juice, honey, oil, garlic, and salt. Cover; process or blend until nearly smooth. Pour marinade over meat. Seal bag; turn to coat meat. Marinate in refrigerator for 2 hours. (Do not marinate more than 2 hours because the citrus juices will cause the meat to become too tender and mushy.)

2 Drain meat, discarding marinade. For a charcoal grill, arrange hot coals around edge of grill. Test for medium-hot heat over center of grill (not over coals). Place the meat on a rack in a roasting pan. Place on the grill rack (not over coals). Cover and grill for 40 to 50 minutes or until meat juices run clear (160°F). (For a gas grill, preheat grill. Reduce heat to medium-hot. Adjust for indirect cooking. Grill as above.)

NUTRITION FACTS PER SERVING: 164 cal., 5 g total fat (2 g sat. fat), 81 mg chol., 153 mg sodium, 3 g carbo., 0 g fiber, 25 g pro.

Smoky Chipotle Tenderloin

This fiery tenderloin takes its inspiration from Southwestern cuisine.

PREP: 15 MINUTES **MARINATE:** 1 TO 4 HOURS **GRILL:** 40 MINUTES **MAKES:** 6 TO 8 SERVINGS

1 tablespoon bottled minced garlic (6 cloves)

1 teaspoon ground cumin

1 teaspoon dried oregano, crushed

¼ teaspoon ground cinnamon

1 tablespoon cooking oil

1 8-ounce can tomato sauce

½ cup water

¼ cup cider vinegar

2 teaspoons sugar

½ teaspoon salt

2 12- to 16-ounce pork tenderloins

3 to 5 canned chipotle peppers in adobo sauce

① For marinade, in a medium skillet cook garlic, cumin, oregano, and cinnamon in hot oil for 1 minute. Stir in tomato sauce, the water, vinegar, sugar, and salt. Bring to boiling. Remove skillet from heat; cool slightly.

② Meanwhile, trim fat from meat. Place meat in a resealable plastic bag set in a shallow dish. Set aside. In a food processor bowl or blender container combine tomato sauce mixture and chipotle peppers. Cover and process or blend until smooth. Pour over meat in bag. Seal bag; turn to coat meat. Marinate in the refrigerator for at least 1 hour or up to 4 hours, turning bag occasionally.

③ Drain, reserving marinade. For a charcoal grill, arrange hot coals around a drip pan. Test for medium-hot heat above the pan. Place meat on grill rack over drip pan. Cover and grill for 40 to 50 minutes or until meat juices run clear (160°F), brushing occasionally with reserved marinade during the first 20 minutes of grilling. (For a gas grill, preheat grill. Reduce heat to medium-hot. Adjust for indirect cooking. Place meat on a rack in a roasting pan, place on grill rack, and grill as above.) Discard any remaining marinade.

NUTRITION FACTS PER SERVING: 198 cal., 7 g total fat (2 g sat. fat), 81 mg chol., 545 mg sodium, 8 g carbo., 1 g fiber, 26 g pro.

Adobo Pork Chops

For an extra hit of heat, add the cayenne pepper to the marinade mixture.

PREP: 15 MINUTES **MARINATE:** 2 TO 24 HOURS **GRILL:** 12 MINUTES **MAKES:** 6 SERVINGS

6   boneless pork loin chops, cut ¾ inch thick

2   tablespoons brown sugar

2   tablespoons olive oil

2   tablespoons orange juice

2   tablespoons snipped fresh cilantro

1   tablespoon red wine vinegar or cider vinegar

2   teaspoons hot chili powder

1   teaspoon ground cumin

1   teaspoon dried oregano, crushed

½   teaspoon salt

¼   teaspoon cayenne pepper (optional)

¼   teaspoon ground cinnamon

1½   teaspoons bottled minced garlic (3 cloves)

1 Trim fat from chops. Place pork chops in a resealable plastic bag set in a shallow dish. For marinade, in a small bowl combine brown sugar, oil, orange juice, cilantro, vinegar, chili powder, cumin, oregano, salt, cayenne pepper (if desired), cinnamon, and garlic. Pour over pork chops. Seal bag; turn to coat pork chops. Marinate in the refrigerator for at least 2 hours or up to 24 hours, turning bag occasionally. Drain pork chops, discarding marinade.

2 For a charcoal grill, grill pork chops on the rack of an uncovered grill directly over medium coals for 12 to 15 minutes or until meat juices run clear (160°F), turning once halfway through grilling. (For a gas grill, preheat grill. Reduce heat to medium. Place pork chops on grill rack over heat. Cover and grill as above.)

NUTRITION FACTS PER SERVING: 180 cal., 11 g total fat (3 g sat. fat), 51 mg chol., 166 mg sodium, 4 g carbo., 0 g fiber, 16 g pro.

Apple-Glazed Stuffed Pork Chops

*If you prefer, substitute a large onion for the sliced leeks—
just halve the onion lengthwise and slice it.*

PREP: 15 MINUTES **GRILL:** 20 MINUTES **MAKES:** 4 SERVINGS

6 slices bacon, chopped

1 cup sliced leeks

¼ cup dry white wine or apple juice

2 teaspoons snipped fresh thyme or
½ teaspoon dried thyme, crushed

⅛ teaspoon salt

⅛ teaspoon ground black pepper

¼ cup apple jelly

1 teaspoon Dijon-style mustard

4 boneless pork top loin chops, cut
1 to 1¼ inches thick

Salt

Ground black pepper

1 For stuffing, in a large skillet cook bacon over medium-hot heat until crisp. Remove with a slotted spoon and drain on paper towels. Reserve 2 teaspoons of the bacon drippings in skillet. Cook leeks in reserved bacon drippings for 3 to 4 minutes or until almost tender. Add the wine or apple juice, thyme, the ⅛ teaspoon salt, and the ⅛ teaspoon pepper. Cook and stir until liquid is evaporated. Remove from heat. Stir in cooked bacon.

2 For glaze, in a small bowl stir together apple jelly and mustard; set aside. Trim fat from chops. Make a pocket in each chop by cutting horizontally from fat side almost to, but not through, the opposite side. Divide stuffing among pockets in chops. If necessary, secure with wooden toothpicks. Sprinkle with additional salt and additional pepper.

3 For a charcoal grill, grill pork chops on the rack of an uncovered grill directly over medium coals about 20 minutes or until meat juices run clear (160°F), turning once and brushing frequently with glaze during the last 5 minutes of grilling. (For a gas grill, preheat grill. Reduce heat to medium. Place pork chops on grill rack over heat. Cover and grill as above.) Remove toothpicks before serving.

NUTRITION FACTS PER SERVING: 409 cal., 15 g total fat (5 g sat. fat), 124 mg chol., 334 mg sodium, 17 g carbo., 1 g fiber, 46 g pro.

Maple Barbecue Glazed Pork Chops

This sweet-tangy glaze also goes well with beef or chicken.

PREP: 20 MINUTES **GRILL:** 30 MINUTES **MAKES:** 4 SERVINGS

¾ cup pure maple syrup

2 tablespoons bottled chili sauce

2 tablespoons cider vinegar

1 tablespoon Worcestershire sauce

1½ teaspoons finely chopped onion

1 teaspoon salt

½ teaspoon dry mustard

½ teaspoon ground black pepper

4 pork loin chops or boneless pork loin chops, cut 1¼ inches thick

1 For maple glaze, in a medium saucepan combine maple syrup, chili sauce, vinegar, Worcestershire sauce, onion, salt, dry mustard, and pepper. Bring to boiling; reduce heat. Simmer, uncovered, about 5 minutes or until slightly thickened. Set aside half (about ⅓ cup) of the maple glaze.

2 For a charcoal grill, arrange medium-hot coals around a drip pan. Test for medium heat above the drip pan. Place pork chops on grill rack over drip pan. Cover and grill for 30 to 40 minutes or until meat juices run clear (160°F), turning once and brushing with the maple glaze during the last 10 minutes of grilling. (For a gas grill, preheat grill. Reduce heat to medium. Adjust for indirect cooking. Grill as above.) Serve the remaining glaze with the pork chops.

NUTRITION FACTS PER SERVING: 418 cal., 9 g total fat (3 g sat. fat), 92 mg chol., 805 mg sodium, 44 g carbo., 1 g fiber, 38 g pro.

Peppery Pork Chops

*Marinating these peppery chops the night before you plan
to serve them makes quick work of a great dinner.
Get some fried rice to go at your favorite Chinese spot, and dinner is done.*

PREP: 15 MINUTES   **MARINATE:** 6 TO 24 HOURS   **GRILL:** 20 MINUTES   **MAKES:** 4 SERVINGS

4   boneless pork loin chops, cut 1 inch thick

¼   cup dry sherry

2   tablespoons soy sauce

2   tablespoons cooking oil

2   tablespoons grated fresh ginger

1   tablespoon sugar

1   tablespoon rice vinegar or lemon juice

¾   teaspoon coarsely ground black pepper

½   teaspoon bottled minced garlic (1 clove)

8   green onions (optional)

2   teaspoons cooking oil (optional)

Steamed or fried rice (optional)

1 Trim fat from chops. Place chops in a resealable plastic bag set in a shallow dish. For marinade, in a small bowl combine sherry, soy sauce, the 2 tablespoons cooking oil, the ginger, sugar, rice vinegar or lemon juice, pepper, and garlic. Pour marinade over chops. Seal bag; turn to coat chops. Marinate in the refrigerator for at least 6 hours or up to 24 hours, turning bag occasionally.

2 Drain chops, discarding marinade. For a charcoal grill, arrange medium-hot coals around a drip pan. Test for medium heat above pan. Place chops on grill rack over drip pan. Cover and grill for 20 to 24 minutes or until meat juices run clear (160°F). (For a gas grill, preheat grill. Reduce heat to medium. Adjust for indirect cooking. Grill as above.)

3 While the chops are grilling, if using green onions, brush onions with the 2 teaspoons oil; add green onions to grill. Cover and grill about 2 minutes or until tender. If desired, serve the chops with the green onions and rice.

NUTRITION FACTS PER SERVING: 255 cal., 11 g total fat (4 g sat. fat), 93 mg chol., 183 mg sodium, 1 g carbo., 0 g fiber, 35 g pro.

Pork Chops with Grilled Vegetables

Season the chops with your choice of lemon-pepper seasoning or garlic-pepper seasoning.

PREP: 20 MINUTES   GRILL: 35 MINUTES   MAKES: 4 SERVINGS

4   pork loin chops, cut 1¼ inches thick

2   teaspoons olive oil

1   teaspoon lemon-pepper seasoning or garlic-pepper seasoning

⅓   cup plain low-fat yogurt

1¼   teaspoons snipped fresh thyme or rosemary

¼   teaspoon salt

¼   teaspoon ground black pepper

1   medium Vidalia or other sweet onion, cut into ½-inch-thick slices

1   green or yellow sweet pepper, seeded and cut into quarters

4   plum tomatoes, halved lengthwise

1   tablespoon balsamic vinegar

1   tablespoon olive oil

1 Trim fat from chops. Brush chops on both sides with the 2 teaspoons oil; sprinkle with lemon-pepper or garlic-pepper seasoning. In a small bowl combine yogurt, ¾ teaspoon of the thyme or rosemary, ⅛ teaspoon of the salt, and ⅛ teaspoon of the black pepper. Cover and chill yogurt mixture.

2 For a charcoal grill, arrange medium-hot coals around a drip pan. Test for medium heat above pan. Place chops on grill rack over drip pan. Cover and grill for 35 to 40 minutes or until meat juices run clear (160°F). Place onions on grill rack directly over coals for the last 15 minutes of grilling or until crisp-tender, turning once. Place sweet peppers and tomatoes directly over coals for the last 5 to 8 minutes of grilling or until peppers are crisp-tender and tomatoes begin to soften, turning once. (For a gas grill, preheat grill. Reduce heat to medium. Adjust for indirect cooking. Grill chops, onion, and peppers as above.)

3 Meanwhile, in a large bowl combine vinegar, the 1 tablespoon olive oil, the remaining ½ teaspoon thyme, the remaining ⅛ teaspoon salt, and the remaining ⅛ teaspoon black pepper. Add onions, sweet peppers, and tomatoes; toss gently to coat. To serve, spoon vegetables over chops. Serve with yogurt mixture.

NUTRITION FACTS PER SERVING: 225 cal., 13 g total fat (4 g sat. fat), 64 mg chol., 353 mg sodium, 2 g carbo., 1 g fiber, 22 g pro.

Pork Chops with Savory Mushroom Stuffing

There's a surprise inside the pocket of these quick-cooking boneless pork chops —a mouthwatering mushroom stuffing. Instead of white button mushrooms, try using brown crimini mushrooms for even more mushroom flavor.

PREP: 15 MINUTES   GRILL: 20 MINUTES   MAKES: 4 SERVINGS

2 teaspoons olive oil

2 tablespoons thinly sliced green onion

1 8-ounce package fresh mushrooms, coarsely chopped

2 teaspoons snipped fresh rosemary or oregano

⅛ teaspoon salt

⅛ teaspoon ground black pepper

4 boneless pork loin chops, cut 1 inch thick

2 teaspoons Worcestershire sauce

Salt

Ground black pepper

1 For stuffing, in a large skillet heat oil over medium heat. Add green onion and cook for 1 minute. Stir in mushrooms, rosemary or oregano, the ⅛ teaspoon salt, and the ⅛ teaspoon pepper. Cook and stir for 2 to 3 minutes more or until mushrooms are tender. Remove from heat.

2 Trim fat from pork chops. Make a pocket in each pork chop by cutting horizontally from the fat side almost to, but not through, the opposite side. Divide stuffing among pockets in pork chops. If necessary, secure with wooden toothpicks.

3 Brush chops with Worcestershire sauce. Sprinkle chops lightly with additional salt and pepper. For a charcoal grill, grill chops on the rack of an uncovered grill directly over medium heat about 20 minutes or until meat juices run clear (160°F), turning once halfway through grilling. (For a gas grill, preheat grill. Reduce heat to medium. Place chops on grill rack over heat. Cover and grill as above.) To serve, remove wooden toothpicks.

NUTRITION FACTS PER SERVING: 241 cal., 14 g total fat (4 g sat. fat), 77 mg chol., 218 mg sodium, 4 g carbo., 1 g fiber, 25 g pro.

South Carolina Barbecued Chops

Even from region to region within a state, the way meat is barbecued is different—and so are the sauces. True to form, this South Carolina-style sauce is sweet, mustardy, and the color of sunshine.

PREP: 20 MINUTES **GRILL:** 25 MINUTES **MAKES:** 4 SERVINGS

4	boneless pork top loin chops, cut 1 to 1¼ inches thick
⅓	cup yellow mustard
⅓	cup red wine vinegar
4	teaspoons brown sugar
1	tablespoon butter or margarine
1	teaspoon Worcestershire sauce
½	teaspoon freshly ground black pepper
¼	to ½ teaspoon bottled hot pepper sauce

1 Trim fat from pork chops; set chops aside. For sauce, in a small saucepan whisk together mustard, vinegar, brown sugar, butter, Worcestershire sauce, black pepper, and hot pepper sauce. Bring to boiling; reduce heat. Simmer, uncovered, for 5 minutes; remove from heat. Cool slightly. Set aside half of the sauce to serve with chops.

2 For charcoal grill, arrange medium-hot coals around drip pan. Test for medium heat above the pan. Place chops on grill rack over drip pan. Cover and grill for 25 to 35 minutes or until meat juices run clear (160°F), turning and brushing once with remaining sauce halfway through grilling. (For a gas grill, preheat grill. Reduce heat to medium. Adjust for indirect cooking. Grill as above.) Discard remainder of sauce used for brushing chops. Serve the pork chops with reserved sauce.

NUTRITION FACTS PER SERVING: 356 cal., 19 g total fat (6 g sat. fat), 107 mg chol., 379 mg sodium, 4 g carbo., 0 g fiber, 37 g pro.

Zesty Chops

In Midwestern states, thick-cut pork top loin chops are sometimes called Iowa chops. Elsewhere, the boneless version may be called America's cut. No matter what they're called, these slow-cooked beauties will impress your family and friends.

PREP: 5 MINUTES **GRILL:** 18 MINUTES **MAKES:** 4 SERVINGS

4   12- to 14-ounce pork top loin chops, cut 1¼ to 1½ inches thick

Bottled Italian salad dressing

1   recipe Rice Pilaf (optional)

1 For a charcoal grill, grill chops on the rack of an uncovered grill directly over medium coals for 18 to 22 minutes or until meat juices run clear (160°F), turning once and brushing frequently with Italian dressing during the last 5 minutes of grilling. (For a gas grill, preheat grill. Reduce heat to medium. Place chops on grill rack over heat. Cover and grill as above.)

2 Pass additional Italian dressing with the chops. If desired, serve with Rice Pilaf.

NUTRITION FACTS PER SERVING: 510 cal., 27 g total fat (7 g sat. fat), 148 mg chol., 342 mg sodium, 3 g carbo., 0 g fiber, 60 g pro.

Rice Pilaf: In a medium saucepan melt 1 tablespoon butter or margarine over medium heat. Add ½ cup chopped onion, ½ cup sliced fresh mushrooms, ¼ cup chopped celery, and ½ teaspoon bottled minced garlic (1 clove); cook until tender. Carefully stir in 1½ cups water, ¾ cup uncooked long grain rice, 1½ teaspoons instant chicken bouillon granules, and ¼ teaspoon ground black pepper. Bring to boiling; reduce heat. Cover and simmer about 15 minutes or until rice is tender and liquid is absorbed. Makes 4 servings.

Glazed Pork Chops and Pineapple Relish

Put this glaze from the Orient on an express to your table.
A pineapple relish transports these pork chops far from the ordinary.

PREP: 30 MINUTES   GRILL: 17 MINUTES   MAKES: 4 SERVINGS

¼   cup pineapple preserves

4   teaspoons soy sauce

1½   teaspoons grated fresh ginger

1   teaspoon toasted sesame oil

½   teaspoon bottled minced garlic (1 clove)

4   boneless pork top loin chops, cut 1¼ inches thick

1   tablespoon sesame seeds, toasted (optional)

1   recipe Pineapple Relish

1 For glaze, in a small saucepan combine pineapple preserves, soy sauce, ginger, toasted sesame oil, and garlic. Cook and stir over low heat just until preserves are melted; set aside. Trim fat from chops.

2 For a charcoal grill, grill chops on rack of an uncovered grill directly over medium coals for 17 to 21 minutes or until meat juices run clear (160°F), turning and brushing once with glaze halfway through grilling. (For a gas grill, preheat grill. Reduce heat to medium. Place chops on the grill rack over heat. Cover and grill as above.) Discard any remaining glaze.

3 If desired, sprinkle chops with sesame seeds. Serve with Pineapple Relish.

Pineapple Relish: In a small bowl stir together 1 cup chopped fresh pineapple; ½ cup chopped red sweet pepper; ¼ cup chopped green onions; 3 tablespoons snipped fresh cilantro; and ½ to 1 fresh jalapeño chile pepper, seeded and finely chopped.* Cover and chill until ready to serve or up to 4 hours. Before serving, bring to room temperature.

NUTRITION FACTS PER SERVING: 364 cal., 16 g total fat (5 g sat. fat), 102 mg chol., 425 mg sodium, 21 g carbo., 1 g fiber, 33 g pro.

*NOTE: Because chile peppers contain volatile oils that can burn your skin and eyes, avoid direct contact with them as much as possible. When working with chile peppers, wear plastic or rubber gloves. If your bare hands do touch the chile peppers, wash your hands and nails well with soap and warm water.

Jamaican Pork Chops with Melon Salsa

You'll find jerk seasoning in the seasoning aisle of the supermarket or in food specialty shops. Another time, sprinkle it on skinless, boneless chicken breast halves before grilling.

PREP: 15 MINUTES GRILL: 12 MINUTES MAKES: 4 SERVINGS

1 cup chopped honeydew melon

1 cup chopped cantaloupe

1 tablespoon snipped fresh mint

1 tablespoon honey

4 teaspoons Jamaican jerk seasoning

4 boneless pork top loin chops, cut ¾ to 1 inch thick

Star anise (optional)

Fresh mint sprigs (optional)

1 For salsa, in a medium bowl combine honeydew, cantaloupe, the snipped mint, and the honey. Cover and refrigerate until ready to serve or up to 8 hours.

2 Sprinkle Jamaican jerk seasoning evenly over both sides of each chop; rub in with your fingers. For charcoal grill, grill chops on the rack of an uncovered grill directly over medium coals for 12 to 15 minutes or until meat juices run clear (160°F), turning once halfway through grilling. (For a gas grill, preheat grill. Reduce heat to medium. Place chops on grill rack over heat. Cover and grill as above.) Serve salsa with chops. If desired, garnish with star anise and/or mint sprigs.

NUTRITION FACTS PER SERVING: 189 cal., 8 g total fat (3 g sat. fat), 51 mg chol., 231 mg sodium, 13 g carbo., 1 g fiber, 17 g pro.

Maple-Mustard Pork Chops

For this hearty dish, acorn squash halves grill alongside the chops.

PREP: 30 MINUTES GRILL: 55 MINUTES MAKES: 4 SERVINGS

¼ cup pure maple syrup

2 tablespoons country Dijon-style mustard

1 to 2 teaspoons cider vinegar

¼ teaspoon ground black pepper

1 medium acorn squash (about 1 pound)

1 teaspoon olive oil

   Salt (optional)

4 pork rib or loin chops, cut 1½ inches thick
   (2½ to 3 pounds total)

1 For glaze, in a small saucepan combine maple syrup, mustard, vinegar, and pepper. Cook over low heat until slightly thickened, stirring occasionally.

2 Meanwhile, cut squash in half lengthwise; remove seeds. Lightly brush cut surfaces of squash with olive oil. If desired, sprinkle with salt.

3 For a charcoal grill, arrange medium-hot coals around a drip pan. Test for medium heat above the pan. Place squash, cut sides down, on grill rack over drip pan. Cover and grill for 15 minutes. Add pork chops to grill rack over drip pan. Cover and grill for 25 minutes, turning after 18 minutes. Turn squash cut side up; brush chops and squash with glaze. Cover and grill about 15 minutes more or until squash is tender and meat juices run clear (160°F). (For a gas grill, preheat grill. Reduce heat to medium. Adjust for indirect cooking. Grill squash and chops as above.)

4 To serve, cut each squash half into 2 wedges. Reheat any remaining glaze until bubbly; spoon over chops and squash.

NUTRITION FACTS PER SERVING: 599 cal., 20 g total fat (6 g sat. fat), 168 mg chol., 347 mg sodium, 23 g carbo., 2 g fiber; 56 g pro.

Sage-Marinated Chops with Sweet Potatoes

A blend of cider vinegar, balsamic vinegar, and sage gives
the chops, sweet potatoes, and onion superb flavor.

PREP: 25 MINUTES MARINATE: 8 TO 24 HOURS GRILL: 25 MINUTES MAKES: 4 SERVINGS

- **4** pork rib or loin chops, cut 1¼ inches thick
- **⅔** cup cider vinegar
- **⅓** cup balsamic vinegar
- **2** tablespoons olive oil
- **2** teaspoons dried sage, crushed
- **½** teaspoon salt
- **¼** teaspoon ground black pepper
- **2** sweet potatoes, quartered lengthwise (about 1 pound)
- **1** medium sweet onion (such as Vidalia), cut into ¾-inch-thick slices

1 Trim fat from chops. Place chops in a resealable plastic bag set in a shallow dish. For marinade, in a small saucepan combine cider vinegar and balsamic vinegar. Bring to boiling; reduce heat. Boil gently, uncovered, about 8 minutes or until reduced to about ⅔ cup. Cool slightly. Stir in oil, sage, salt, and pepper. Set aside ¼ cup of the marinade to brush on sweet potatoes and onion. Pour remaining marinade over chops. Seal bag; turn to coat chops. Marinate in the refrigerator for at least 8 hours or up to 24 hours, turning bag occasionally.

2 Drain chops, discarding marinade. Brush sweet potatoes and onion with the reserved marinade. For a charcoal grill, arrange medium coals in bottom of a grill with a cover. Place chops, sweet potatoes, and onion on grill rack directly over coals. Cover and grill for 25 to 30 minutes or until meat juices run clear (160°F) and vegetables are tender, turning chops once and vegetables occasionally. (For a gas grill, preheat grill. Reduce heat to medium. Place chops, sweet potatoes, and onion on grill rack over heat. Grill as above.)

NUTRITION FACTS PER SERVING: 354 cal., 16 g total fat (4 g sat. fat), 77 mg chol., 249 mg sodium, 28 g carbo., 4 g fiber, 26 g pro.

Rosemary Pork Chops

If you have fresh rosemary on hand, snip it for this luscious entrée. Other times, use dried rosemary.

PREP: 10 MINUTES **MARINATE:** 2 TO 4 HOURS **GRILL:** 22 MINUTES **MAKES:** 4 SERVINGS

4 pork loin or rib chops, cut ¾ inch thick (about 1¾ pounds total)

2 tablespoons Dijon-style mustard

2 tablespoons balsamic vinegar

2 tablespoons lemon juice

2 tablespoons olive oil

4 teaspoons snipped fresh rosemary or 1 teaspoon dried rosemary, crushed

1½ teaspoons bottled minced garlic (3 cloves)

½ teaspoon salt

½ teaspoon ground black pepper

1 Place meat in a resealable plastic bag set in a shallow dish. For marinade, in a small bowl whisk together mustard, balsamic vinegar, lemon juice, olive oil, rosemary, garlic, salt, and pepper. Pour marinade over meat. Seal bag; turn to coat meat. Marinate in refrigerator for at least 2 hours or up to 4 hours, turning bag occasionally.

2 Drain meat, discarding marinade. For a charcoal grill, arrange medium-hot coals around a drip pan. Test for medium heat above drip pan. Place chops on the grill rack over drip pan. Cover and grill for 22 to 25 minutes or until meat juices run clear (160°F). (For a gas grill, preheat grill. Reduce heat to medium. Adjust for indirect cooking. Grill as above.)

NUTRITION FACTS PER SERVING: 300 cal., 14 g total fat (4 g sat. fat), 105 mg chol., 244 mg sodium, 2 g carbo., 0 g fiber, 39 g pro.

Savory Pork Steaks

What an unlikely combination! Italian salad dressing, beer, maple syrup, and barbecue sauce create a marinade for these pork shoulder steaks. The result is a savory-sweet entrée that's sure to please.

PREP: 10 MINUTES   **MARINATE:** 6 TO 24 HOURS   **GRILL:** 15 MINUTES   **MAKES:** 5 TO 7 SERVINGS

1	8-ounce bottle zesty Italian salad dressing
¾	cup lemon juice
¾	cup beer
⅔	cup maple syrup
½	cup bottled barbecue sauce
⅓	cup dried minced onion
1½	teaspoons bottled minced garlic (3 cloves)
5	to 7 pork shoulder steaks, cut ¾ inch thick (4½ to 5 pounds total)

1 For the marinade, in a medium bowl stir together salad dressing, lemon juice, beer, maple syrup, barbecue sauce, dried minced onion, and garlic.

2 Place the pork steaks in a resealable plastic bag set in a very large bowl. Pour marinade over steaks. Seal bag; turn to coat steaks. Marinate in refrigerator for at least 6 hours or up to 24 hours, turning bag occasionally.

3 Drain, discarding marinade. For a charcoal grill, grill steaks on the rack of an uncovered grill directly over medium coals for 15 to 20 minutes or until juices run clear (160°F), turning steaks once halfway through grilling. (For a gas grill, preheat grill. Reduce heat to medium. Place pork steaks on grill rack over heat. Cover and grill as above.)

NUTRITION FACTS PER SERVING: 438 cal., 20 g total fat (6 g sat. fat), 147 mg chol., 358 mg sodium, 15 g carbo., 0 g fiber, 46 g pro.

Fennel and Pork Sausage with Grape Relish

Aromatic fennel seeds lend the pork patties their essence, and alongside the patties, crisp fresh fennel cooks with balsamic vinegar and red grapes to make an elegant relish.

PREP: 15 MINUTES **GRILL:** 14 MINUTES **MAKES:** 4 SERVINGS

1	slightly beaten egg
1	tablespoon bourbon (optional)
½	cup quick-cooking rolled oats
1	tablespoon fennel seeds, crushed
1	teaspoon finely shredded lemon peel
1	teaspoon paprika
½	teaspoon salt
½	teaspoon bottled minced garlic (1 clove)
½	teaspoon ground black pepper
1	pound lean ground pork
1½	cups red seedless grapes, halved
1	small fennel bulb, coarsely chopped (1 cup)
1	tablespoon butter or margarine
2	tablespoons balsamic vinegar
	Salt
	Ground black pepper
¼	cup snipped fresh parsley

① In a large bowl combine the egg and, if desired, bourbon. Stir in rolled oats, fennel seeds, lemon peel, paprika, the ½ teaspoon salt, the garlic, and the ½ teaspoon pepper. Add ground pork. Mix well. Shape the pork mixture into four ¾-inch-thick patties. Set aside.

② Fold a 36×18-inch piece of heavy foil in half to make a double thickness of foil that measures 18×18 inches. Place the grapes, chopped fennel, butter, and vinegar in the center of the foil. Sprinkle with additional salt and additional pepper. Bring up 2 opposite edges of foil and seal with a double fold. Fold remaining edges to completely enclose the grape mixture, leaving space for steam to build.

③ For a charcoal grill, grill the pork patties and the foil packet on the rack of an uncovered grill directly over medium coals for 14 to 18 minutes or until patties are done (160°F),* turning once halfway through grilling. (For a gas grill, preheat grill. Reduce heat to medium. Place the pork patties and the foil packet on grill rack over heat. Cover and grill as above.)

④ To serve, spoon grape mixture over the grilled patties. Sprinkle with the fresh parsley.

NUTRITION FACTS PER SERVING: 284 cal., 14 g total fat (6 g sat. fat), 114 mg chol., 409 mg sodium, 23 g carbo., 7 g fiber, 18 g pro.

***NOTE:** The internal color of a meat patty is not a reliable doneness indicator. A pork patty cooked to 160°F is safe, regardless of color. To measure the doneness of a patty, insert an instant-read thermometer through the side of the patty to a depth of 2 to 3 inches.

Grilled Italian Sausage with Sweet and Sour Peppers

If you like, serve the sausages and vegetables with purchased polenta that you slice and heat on the grill.

PREP: 20 MINUTES GRILL: 20 MINUTES MAKES: 6 SERVINGS

- **3** tablespoons slivered almonds
- **¼** cup raisins
- **3** tablespoons red wine vinegar
- **2** tablespoons sugar
- **¼** teaspoon salt
- **⅛** teaspoon ground black pepper
- **1** tablespoon olive oil
- **2** green sweet peppers, cut into 1-inch-wide strips
- **2** red sweet peppers, cut into 1-inch-wide strips
- **1** medium red onion, thickly sliced
- **6** uncooked sweet (mild) Italian sausage links

1 In a small nonstick skillet cook and stir almonds for 1 to 2 minutes or until golden brown. Stir in raisins. Remove skillet from heat. Let stand for 1 minute. Carefully stir in vinegar, sugar, salt, and black pepper. Cook and stir just until the sugar dissolves. Set aside.

2 Drizzle oil over sweet pepper strips and onion slices. Prick sausages several times with a fork. For charcoal grill, arrange medium-hot coals around a drip pan. Test for medium heat above the pan. Place sausages on grill rack over pan. Cover and grill for 10 minutes. Turn sausages. Place vegetables on rack alongside sausages. Cover and grill for 10 to 20 minutes more or until sausages are cooked through (160°F)* and vegetables are tender, turning vegetables once halfway through grilling. Remove vegetables when done. (For a gas grill, preheat grill. Reduce heat to medium. Adjust for indirect cooking. Grill sausages and vegetables as above.)

3 In a large bowl toss the vegetables with the almond mixture; spoon onto a serving platter. Top with sausages.

NUTRITION FACTS PER SERVING: 276 cal., 19 g total fat (6 g sat. fat), 59 mg chol., 604 mg sodium, 15 g carbo., 1 g fiber, 13 g pro.

*NOTE: The internal color of a sausage link is not a reliable doneness indicator. A pork sausage link cooked to 160°F is safe, regardless of color. To measure the doneness of a sausage link, insert an instant-read thermometer through the end of the link into the center of the link.

Homemade Pork Sausage

Why make your own sausage? Because it is lower in fat than store-bought and you can tailor the seasonings to your liking. Slip these grilled and skewered sausages onto a plate or nestle them in hot dog buns.

PREP: 15 MINUTES   GRILL: 14 MINUTES   MAKES: 4 SERVINGS

3	**tablespoons finely snipped fresh basil**
1	**teaspoon sugar**
1	**teaspoon fennel seeds**
1	**teaspoon crushed red pepper**
1	**teaspoon bottled minced garlic (2 cloves)**
¾	**teaspoon salt**
½	**teaspoon ground black pepper**
1½	**pounds lean ground pork**

1 In a large bowl combine basil, sugar, fennel seeds, crushed red pepper, garlic, salt, and black pepper. Add ground pork; mix well. Divide the meat mixture into 4 equal portions. Shape each portion around a flat-sided metal skewer into a 6-inch-long log.

2 For a charcoal grill, grill meat on skewers on rack of an uncovered grill directly over medium coals for 14 to 18 minutes or until meat juices run clear (160°F),* turning once halfway through grilling. (For a gas grill, preheat grill. Reduce heat to medium. Place meat on skewers on grill rack over heat. Cover and grill as above.)

3 To serve, use the tines of a fork to remove the meat from skewers.

NUTRITION FACTS PER SERVING: 210 cal., 12 g total fat (5 g sat. fat), 79 mg chol., 469 mg sodium, 2 g carbo., 0 g fiber, 21 g pro.

*NOTE: The internal color of a sausage log is not a reliable doneness indicator. A sausage log cooked to 160°F is safe, regardless of color. To measure the doneness of a sausage log, insert an instant-read thermometer from an end into the center of the log, making sure the tip of the thermometer does not touch the skewer.

Polish Sausage Foil Dinner

Try this recipe with slices of smoked turkey kielbasa, smoked Italian sausage with fennel, or your favorite smoked sausage. If you want to serve more than one person, increase the ingredients and make a packet for each serving.

PREP: 5 MINUTES **GRILL:** 15 MINUTES **STAND:** 5 MINUTES **MAKES:** 1 SERVING

1 cup frozen loose-pack diced hash brown potatoes with onion and peppers, thawed

3 ounces smoked sausage, sliced (½ cup)

1 tablespoon bottled Italian salad dressing

2 tablespoons shredded cheddar cheese

1 Fold a 24×12-inch piece of heavy foil in half to make a 12-inch square. Place potatoes and sausage in center of the foil square. Drizzle Italian salad dressing over potatoes and sausage. Bring up 2 opposite edges of foil; seal with a double fold. Fold remaining edges to completely enclose the mixture, leaving space for steam to build.

2 For a charcoal grill, grill packet on the rack of an uncovered grill directly over medium coals about 15 minutes or until potatoes are tender, turning once. (For a gas grill, preheat grill. Reduce heat to medium. Place packet on grill rack over heat. Cover and grill as above.)

3 Remove from grill; carefully open packet. Sprinkle mixture with cheese. Reseal packet; let stand about 5 minutes or until cheese is melted.

NUTRITION FACTS PER SERVING: 577 cal., 40 g total fat (14 g sat. fat), 73 mg chol., 1,499 mg sodium, 29 g carbo., 0 g fiber, 25 g pro.

Double Sausage Kabobs

Rolling the vegetables in an herb mixture is an easy way to add scrumptious flavor.

PREP: 30 MINUTES   GRILL: 15 MINUTES   MAKES: 6 SERVINGS

12	ounces tiny new potatoes, halved, or small potatoes, quartered
1/3	cup finely snipped fresh parsley
2	tablespoons finely snipped fresh oregano or 2 teaspoons dried oregano, crushed
1	teaspoon bottled minced garlic (2 cloves)
2	medium yellow sweet peppers, cut into 2×1-inch strips
2	tablespoons olive oil
8	ounces cooked Polish sausage links, bias-cut into 1½-inch slices
4	ounces cooked Italian sausage links, bias-cut into 1½-inch slices
	Honey mustard (optional)
	Fresh oregano sprigs (optional)

1 In a covered medium saucepan cook potatoes in a moderate amount of boiling salted water for 10 to 12 minutes or just until tender. Drain; set aside to cool slightly. In a shallow dish stir together the parsley, snipped or dried oregano, and garlic; set aside.

2 Place potatoes and sweet peppers in a large bowl; drizzle with olive oil and toss to coat. Roll vegetables in the herb mixture, patting herb mixture onto vegetables to lightly coat.

3 On long metal skewers, alternately thread sausage slices, sweet peppers, and potatoes, leaving ¼-inch space between pieces.

4 For a charcoal grill, arrange medium-hot coals around a drip pan. Test for medium heat above the pan. Place kabobs on grill rack over pan. Cover and grill about 15 minutes or until sausage is heated through and peppers are just tender, turning once halfway through grilling. (For a gas grill, preheat grill. Reduce heat to medium. Adjust for indirect cooking. Grill as above.) If desired, serve with honey mustard. If desired, garnish with oregano sprigs.

NUTRITION FACTS PER SERVING: 293 cal., 22 g total fat (6 g sat. fat), 40 mg chol., 527 mg sodium, 16 g carbo., 1 g fiber; 9 g pro.

Sausage and Fennel Kabobs

Italian sausage and fennel unite for a wonderful taste combination made all the better by the cider-and-fennel glaze.

PREP: 20 MINUTES **GRILL:** 7 MINUTES **MAKES:** 4 SERVINGS

1 pound uncooked sweet or hot Italian sausage links

3 small fennel bulbs with tops

1⅓ cups apple juice or apple cider

2 tablespoons brown sugar

1 teaspoon snipped fresh oregano

1 teaspoon fennel seeds, crushed

1 teaspoon olive oil

¼ teaspoon ground cumin

1 Use the tines of a fork to prick each sausage link several times. Trim tops from fennel. If desired, reserve tops. Quarter fennel bulbs lengthwise. In a large saucepan combine the sausage links, fennel bulbs, and 1 cup of the apple juice. Bring to boiling; reduce heat. Cover and simmer about 15 minutes or until sausage is done and fennel is almost tender. Drain; cool slightly.

2 For glaze, in a small bowl combine the remaining ⅓ cup apple juice, the brown sugar, oregano, fennel seeds, oil, and cumin. Bias-slice each sausage link into 3 pieces. On four 10-inch metal skewers, alternately thread sausage pieces and fennel quarters, leaving ¼-inch space between pieces. Brush with some of the glaze.

3 For a charcoal grill, grill kabobs on the rack of an uncovered grill directly over medium coals for 7 to 8 minutes or until sausage and fennel are browned and heated through, turning once and brushing occasionally with glaze. (For a gas grill, preheat grill. Reduce heat to medium. Place kabobs on grill rack over heat. Cover and grill as above.) To serve, if desired, arrange kabobs on a bed of the reserved fennel tops.

NUTRITION FACTS PER SERVING: 382 cal., 23 g total fat (8 g sat. fat), 65 mg chol., 835 mg sodium, 28 g carbo., 33 g fiber, 18 g pro.

Barbecued Baby Back Ribs

A rub featuring paprika, garlic salt, onion powder, sage, celery seeds, and cayenne pepper spices up these pork loin back ribs.

PREP: 15 MINUTES   GRILL: 1½ HOURS   MAKES: 8 SERVINGS

3½ to 4 pounds pork loin back ribs

1 tablespoon paprika

1½ teaspoons garlic salt

1 teaspoon onion powder

1 teaspoon dried sage, crushed

½ teaspoon celery seeds

¼ teaspoon cayenne pepper

½ cup apple juice or apple cider

1 Trim fat from ribs. For rub, in a small bowl combine paprika, garlic salt, onion powder, sage, celery seeds, and cayenne pepper. Sprinkle evenly over both sides of ribs; rub in with your fingers.

2 For a charcoal grill, arrange medium-hot coals around drip pan. Test for medium heat above the pan. Place ribs, bone sides down, on grill rack over pan. (Or place ribs in a rib rack; place on grill rack.) Cover and grill for 1½ to 1¾ hours or until tender, brushing occasionally with apple juice after the first hour of grilling. Add coals as necessary to maintain heat. (For a gas grill, preheat grill. Reduce heat to medium. Adjust for indirect cooking. Place ribs in a roasting pan, place on grill rack, and grill as above.)

NUTRITION FACTS PER SERVING: 324 cal., 14 g total fat (5 g sat. fat), 94 mg chol., 253 mg sodium, 3 g carbo., 0 g fiber, 43 g pro.

Gingery Apricot-Glazed Pork Ribs

You're gonna love these baby back ribs. Maybe it's the apricot flavor or the ginger that you can't resist. Don't dwell on it—the combination of flavors is perfect.

PREP: 20 MINUTES **MARINATE:** 6 TO 24 HOURS **GRILL:** 1½ HOURS **MAKES:** 4 SERVINGS

4 pounds pork loin back ribs

1 cup finely chopped onion

⅓ cup dry sherry

¼ cup finely grated fresh ginger

¼ cup rice vinegar

¼ cup soy sauce

2 tablespoons bottled minced garlic (12 cloves)

½ teaspoon ground black pepper

⅔ cup apricot preserves

3 tablespoons spicy brown mustard

1 tablespoon toasted sesame oil

¼ teaspoon cayenne pepper

1 Trim fat from ribs. Place ribs in a large resealable plastic bag set in a shallow dish. For marinade, in a medium bowl combine onion, sherry, ginger, rice vinegar, soy sauce, garlic, and black pepper. Pour marinade over ribs. Seal bag; turn to coat ribs. Marinate in the refrigerator for at least 6 hours or up to 24 hours, turning bag occasionally.

2 Drain, reserving ¼ cup of the marinade. For sauce, in a small saucepan combine apricot preserves, mustard, toasted sesame oil, and cayenne pepper. Stir in the reserved marinade. Bring to boiling; reduce heat. Simmer, uncovered, about 3 minutes or until slightly thickened.

3 For charcoal grill, arrange medium-hot coals around a drip pan. Test for medium heat above the pan. Place ribs, bone sides down, on grill rack over drip pan. (Or place ribs in a rib rack; place on grill rack.) Cover and grill for 1½ to 1¾ hours or until ribs are tender, brushing occasionally with sauce during the last 15 minutes of grilling. Add coals as necessary to maintain heat. (For a gas grill, preheat grill. Reduce heat to medium. Adjust for indirect cooking. Place ribs on a rack in a roasting pan, place on grill rack, and grill as above.)

NUTRITION FACTS PER SERVING: 740 cal., 42 g total fat (14 g sat. fat), 176 mg chol., 637 mg sodium, 42 g carbo., 1 g fiber, 45 g pro.

Molasses-Rum Baby Back Ribs

It will take about 1 pound of pork loin back ribs to feed each person at your dinner table.

PREP: 30 MINUTES   **CHILL:** 2 TO 24 HOURS   **GRILL:** 1½ HOURS   **MAKES:** 4 SERVINGS

2 tablespoons brown sugar

1 to 2 tablespoons paprika

1 tablespoon garlic powder

3 to 4 teaspoons coarsely ground black pepper

1½ teaspoons salt

½ teaspoon ground cumin

3¾ to 4 pounds pork loin back ribs

½ cup chopped onion

½ teaspoon bottled minced garlic (1 clove)

1 tablespoon cooking oil

1 8-ounce can tomato sauce

⅓ cup pineapple rum, light rum, or unsweetened pineapple juice

⅓ cup honey and/or light-flavored molasses

2 tablespoons Worcestershire sauce

2 tablespoons vinegar

2 teaspoons dry mustard

2 teaspoons chili powder

1 For rub, in a small bowl combine brown sugar, paprika, garlic powder, pepper, salt, and cumin. Sprinkle rub evenly over ribs; rub in with your fingers. Cover and chill in the refrigerator for at least 2 hours or up to 24 hours.

2 For a charcoal grill, arrange medium-hot coals around a drip pan. Test for medium heat above pan. Place ribs, bone sides down, on grill rack over pan. (Or place ribs in a rib rack; place on grill rack.) Cover and grill for 1½ to 1¾ hours or until ribs are tender. Add coals as necessary to maintain heat. (For a gas grill, preheat grill. Reduce heat to medium. Adjust for indirect cooking. Grill as above.)

3 Meanwhile, for sauce, in a medium saucepan cook onion and garlic in hot oil until tender. Remove from heat. Stir in tomato sauce, rum or juice, honey and/or molasses, Worcestershire sauce, vinegar, dry mustard, and chili powder. Bring to boiling; reduce heat. Simmer, uncovered, about 20 minutes or until thickened and reduced to 1½ cups; stir occasionally.

4 To serve, cut ribs into serving-size pieces. Spoon some of the sauce over ribs; pass remaining sauce.

NUTRITION FACTS PER SERVING: 701 cal., 31 g total fat (10 g sat. fat), 126 mg chol., 1,356 mg sodium, 38 g carbo., 2 g fiber, 54 g pro.

Thai-Coconut Ribs

You'll think you're in Thailand when you enjoy these ginger- and coconut-accented ribs.

PREP: 15 MINUTES   **MARINATE:** 8 TO 24 HOURS   **GRILL:** 1½ HOURS   **MAKES:** 6 SERVINGS

4	pounds pork loin back ribs
1	cup purchased unsweetened coconut milk
3	tablespoons brown sugar
3	tablespoons soy sauce
1	tablespoon grated fresh ginger
1	teaspoon finely shredded lime peel
1	tablespoon lime juice
2	teaspoons bottled minced garlic (4 cloves)
1	teaspoon crushed red pepper

1 Trim fat from ribs. Cut into serving-size pieces. Place ribs in a resealable plastic bag set in a shallow dish. For marinade, in a small bowl combine coconut milk, brown sugar, soy sauce, ginger, lime peel, lime juice, garlic, and red pepper. Pour over ribs. Seal bag; turn to coat ribs. Marinate in the refrigerator for at least 8 hours or up to 24 hours, turning bag occasionally.

2 Drain ribs, reserving marinade. For a charcoal grill, arrange medium-hot coals around a drip pan. Test for medium heat above the pan. Place the ribs, bone sides down, on grill rack over pan. (Or place ribs in a rib rack; place on grill rack.) Cover and grill for 1½ to 1¾ hours or until ribs are tender, brushing frequently with reserved marinade during the first hour of grilling. Add coals as necessary to maintain heat. (For a gas grill, preheat grill. Reduce heat to medium. Adjust for indirect cooking. Grill as above.) Discard any remaining marinade.

NUTRITION FACTS PER SERVING: 431 cal., 32 g total fat (16 g sat. fat), 99 mg chol., 607 mg sodium, 9 g carbo., 0 g fiber, 25 g pro.

Marinated Barbecued Spareribs

Seven seasonings give meaty pork ribs plenty of zip.
Serve them with slices of grilled buttered French bread and your favorite coleslaw.

PREP: 15 MINUTES   MARINATE: 6 TO 24 HOURS   GRILL: 1½ HOURS   MAKES: 6 SERVINGS

1   cup bottled chili sauce

¼   cup ketchup

¼   cup soy sauce

2   tablespoons coarse German mustard

1   tablespoon balsamic vinegar

1   tablespoon lemon juice or lime juice

2   teaspoons grated fresh ginger

1   3½- to 4-pound slab meaty pork spareribs

1 For marinade, in small bowl stir together chili sauce, ketchup, soy sauce, mustard, balsamic vinegar, lemon juice, and ginger. Line a roasting pan with plastic wrap; coat ribs with marinade and place on plastic wrap (if necessary, cut ribs to fit in pan). Cover and marinate in refrigerator for at least 6 hours or up to 24 hours.

2 Remove ribs, reserving marinade. For a charcoal grill, arrange medium-hot coals around a drip pan. Test for medium heat above the pan. Place the ribs, bone side down, on the grill rack over the drip pan. (Or place ribs in a rib rack; place on grill rack.) Cover and grill 1½ to 1¾ hours or until the ribs are tender, brushing with reserved marinade occasionally during the first hour of grilling. Add coals as necessary to maintain heat. (For a gas grill, preheat grill. Reduce heat to medium. Adjust for indirect cooking. Grill as above.) Discard any remaining marinade.

NUTRITION FACTS PER SERVING: 458 cal., 34 g total fat (14 g sat. fat), 124 mg chol., 443 mg sodium, 4 g carbo., 0 g fiber, 29 g pro.

Maple-Glazed Country Ribs

If you have a grill rack, use it to hold the ribs for grilling.

PREP: 15 MINUTES **GRILL:** 1½ HOURS **MAKES:** 4 SERVINGS

½ cup apple jelly

½ cup pure maple syrup or maple-flavored syrup

1 tablespoon cider vinegar

1 tablespoon coarse-grain brown mustard

½ teaspoon bottled minced garlic (1 clove)

2½ to 3 pounds pork country-style ribs

1 For sauce, in a small saucepan combine apple jelly, maple syrup, vinegar, mustard, and garlic. Bring to boiling; reduce heat. Simmer, uncovered, about 10 minutes or until desired consistency, stirring frequently. Remove from heat. Trim fat from ribs.

2 For a charcoal grill, arrange medium-hot coals around a drip pan. Test for medium heat above the pan. Place ribs, bone sides down, on grill rack over drip pan. (Or place ribs in a rib rack; place on grill rack.) Cover and grill for 1½ to 2 hours or until ribs are tender, brushing occasionally with sauce during the last 10 minutes of grilling. Add coals as necessary to maintain heat. (For a gas grill, preheat grill. Reduce heat to medium. Adjust for indirect cooking. Place ribs in a roasting pan, place on grill rack, and grill as above.) Pass remaining sauce with ribs.

NUTRITION FACTS PER SERVING: 572 cal., 21 g total fat (7 g sat. fat), 98 mg chol., 155 mg sodium, 53 g carbo., 0 g fiber, 41 g pro.

Indonesian Pork and Noodles

Use your food processor to grind the Brazil nuts or hazelnuts with the seasonings into an almost-smooth mixture.

PREP: 20 MINUTES   **MARINATE:** 30 MINUTES TO 1 HOUR   **GRILL:** 12 MINUTES

MAKES: 4 SERVINGS

1	1-pound pork tenderloin
¼	cup Brazil nuts or hazelnuts (filberts)
¼	cup light soy sauce
3	tablespoons lemon juice
1	tablespoon olive oil
1	tablespoon ground coriander
1	tablespoon brown sugar
¾	teaspoon ground black pepper
½	teaspoon bottled minced garlic (1 clove)
8	ounces dried thin egg noodles
1	tablespoon butter or margarine, softened
2	tablespoons sesame seeds, toasted

1 Trim fat from meat. Cut meat into 1-inch cubes. Place meat in a resealable plastic bag set in a shallow dish. For marinade, in a food processor bowl combine nuts, soy sauce, lemon juice, oil, coriander, brown sugar, ½ teaspoon of the pepper, and the garlic. Cover; process until combined. Pour marinade over meat. Seal bag; turn to coat meat cubes. Marinate in refrigerator for at least 30 minutes or up to 1 hour, turning bag occasionally.

2 Drain meat, discarding marinade. Thread meat cubes onto 4 long metal skewers, leaving ¼-inch space between cubes.

3 For a charcoal grill, grill skewers on the rack of an uncovered grill directly over medium coals for 12 to 14 minutes or until meat juices run clear, turning once halfway through grilling. (For a gas grill, preheat grill. Reduce heat to medium. Place skewers on the grill rack. Cover and grill as above.)

4 Meanwhile, cook noodles according to package directions. Drain and return noodles to hot pan. Toss with butter, sesame seeds, and the remaining ¼ teaspoon pepper. Serve noodles with pork.

NUTRITION FACTS PER SERVING: 490 cal., 20 g total fat (5 g sat. fat), 138 mg chol., 458 mg sodium, 43 g carbo., 3 g fiber, 36 g pro.

Jamaican Pork Kabobs

Mango chutney and Pickapeppa sauce—a Jamaican seasoning sauce—
lend an air of the island to the pork and vegetables.

PREP: 25 MINUTES **GRILL:** 10 MINUTES **MAKES:** 4 SERVINGS

2 fresh ears of corn, husked and cleaned

1 12- to 14-ounce pork tenderloin, cut into 1-inch-thick slices

1 small red onion, cut into ½-inch-thick wedges

16 baby pattypan squash (about 1 inch in diameter) or 4 fresh tomatillos, husked and quartered

¼ cup mango chutney, finely chopped

3 tablespoons Pickapeppa sauce*

1 tablespoon cooking oil

1 tablespoon water

1 Cut corn crosswise into 1-inch pieces. In a covered medium saucepan cook corn pieces in a small amount of boiling water for 3 minutes; drain and rinse with cold water. On long metal skewers, alternately thread tenderloin slices, onion wedges, squash or tomatillos, and corn pieces, leaving ¼-inch space between pieces. In a small bowl combine chutney, Pickapeppa sauce, oil, and the water; set aside.

2 For charcoal grill, grill kabobs on rack of an uncovered grill directly over medium coals for 10 to 14 minutes or until meat juices run clear and vegetables are tender, turning once halfway through grilling and brushing with the chutney mixture during the last 3 minutes of grilling. (For a gas grill, preheat grill. Reduce heat to medium. Place kabobs on grill rack over heat. Cover and grill as above.) Discard any remaining chutney mixture.

NUTRITION FACTS PER SERVING: 252 cal., 7 g total fat (2 g sat. fat), 60 mg chol., 127 mg sodium, 27 g carbo., 3 g fiber, 21 g pro.

***NOTE:** If Pickapeppa sauce is difficult to find, substitute 3 tablespoons Worcestershire sauce plus a dash bottled hot pepper sauce.

Pork Satay with Tahini-Coconut Sauce

Sail with the South Sea winds. Here's a sweet and lively dish that will find a port on any shore. Tahini, coconut, curry powder, and curry paste—it just keeps getting better.

PREP: 40 MINUTES   **MARINATE:** 2 TO 3 HOURS   **GRILL:** 10 MINUTES   **MAKES:** 6 SERVINGS

1½	pounds pork tenderloin
¼	cup purchased unsweetened coconut milk
2	tablespoons lime juice
1	tablespoon brown sugar
1	tablespoon mild curry powder
1½	teaspoons cooking oil
1	tablespoon prepared red curry paste
⅛	teaspoon crushed red pepper
¾	cup purchased unsweetened coconut milk
¼	cup tahini (sesame seed paste)
4	teaspoons orange juice
2	teaspoons brown sugar
1½	teaspoons bottled fish sauce

1 Trim fat from meat. Cut meat into ¾-inch cubes. Place meat cubes in a resealable plastic bag. For marinade, in a medium bowl stir together the ¼ cup coconut milk, the lime juice, the 1 tablespoon brown sugar, and the curry powder. Pour marinade over meat cubes. Seal bag; turn to coat meat cubes. Marinate in the refrigerator for at least 2 hours or up to 3 hours, turning bag occasionally.

2 For dipping sauce, in a small saucepan heat oil over medium heat. Add the curry paste and crushed red pepper; reduce heat to low. Cook and stir about 1 minute or until fragrant. Stir in the ¾ cup coconut milk, the tahini, orange juice, the 2 teaspoons brown sugar, and the fish sauce. Bring just to simmering. Simmer gently, uncovered, about 5 minutes or until combined and thickened, stirring frequently. Cover and keep warm.

3 Drain meat, discarding marinade. Thread the meat cubes onto long metal skewers, leaving ¼-inch space between cubes.

4 For a charcoal grill, grill skewers on the rack of an uncovered grill directly over medium coals for 10 to 12 minutes or until meat juices run clear, turning occasionally to brown evenly. (For a gas grill, preheat grill. Reduce heat to medium. Place skewers on grill rack over heat. Cover and grill as above.) Serve with dipping sauce.

NUTRITION FACTS PER SERVING: 283 cal., 15 g total fat (7 g sat. fat), 81 mg chol., 223 mg sodium, 9 g carbo., 1 g fiber, 28 g pro.

Smoky Pork and Mushroom Kabobs

These kabobs boast the flavors of fall: maple syrup, cider vinegar, hickory smoke, and sweet-tart apples. Choose a good cooking apple, such as Rome Beauty, York Imperial, Newtown Pippin, or Granny Smith.

PREP: 15 MINUTES **MARINATE:** 10 MINUTES **GRILL:** 14 MINUTES **MAKES:** 4 SERVINGS

1   pound lean boneless pork

8   ounces fresh mushroom caps

2   medium apples, cored and quartered

1   medium onion, cut into wedges

¼   cup maple-flavored syrup

¼   cup tomato paste

2   tablespoons cider vinegar

¼   to ½ teaspoon hickory smoke flavoring

⅛   teaspoon ground black pepper

1 Trim fat from pork. Cut pork into 1½-inch cubes. Place the pork, mushrooms, apples, and onion in a resealable plastic bag set in a shallow dish. For marinade, in a small bowl combine the syrup, tomato paste, vinegar, smoke flavoring, and pepper. Set aside ¼ cup of the marinade for dipping sauce. Pour remaining marinade over the pork mixture. Seal bag; turn to coat pork cubes. Marinate in refrigerator for at least 10 minutes or up to 4 hours, turning bag once.

2 Drain pork mixture, reserving marinade. On four 12-inch metal skewers, alternately thread pork cubes, mushrooms, apples, and onion, leaving ¼-inch space between pieces.

3 For a charcoal grill, grill kabobs on the greased rack of an uncovered grill directly over medium coals for 14 to 16 minutes or until meat juices run clear, turning and brushing once with reserved marinade halfway through grilling. (For a gas grill, preheat grill. Reduce heat to medium. Place kabobs on grill rack over heat. Cover and grill as above.) Serve with dipping sauce.

NUTRITION FACTS PER SERVING: 261 cal., 8 g total fat (3 g sat. fat), 51 mg chol., 54 mg sodium, 32 g carbo., 3 g fiber, 18 g pro.

Apple-Glazed Pork Kabobs

There's a hint of cinnamon and cloves in the sweet jelly-based glaze used on the kabobs.

PREP: 20 MINUTES   GRILL: 12 MINUTES   MAKES: 4 SERVINGS

8	12-inch wooden skewers
1	cup apple jelly
2	tablespoons honey
2	tablespoons lemon juice
2	tablespoons butter or margarine
1	teaspoon ground cinnamon
¼	teaspoon ground cloves
1	pound boneless pork loin, cut into 1-inch cubes
1	teaspoon garlic powder
½	teaspoon celery salt
½	to 1 teaspoon ground black pepper
1	large onion, cut into 1-inch pieces
2	large green sweet peppers, cut into 1-inch pieces
1	tablespoon olive oil

1 In a shallow dish soak wooden skewers in enough warm water to cover for 30 minutes. In a small saucepan combine apple jelly, honey, lemon juice, butter, cinnamon, and cloves. Bring to boiling; reduce heat. Simmer, uncovered, 4 to 5 minutes or until of glaze consistency, stirring frequently.

2 Sprinkle pork with garlic powder, celery salt, and black pepper. Thread pork, onion, and sweet peppers alternately onto soaked skewers, leaving ¼-inch space between pieces. Drizzle with oil.

3 For a charcoal grill, place kabobs on grill rack directly over medium coals for 12 to 15 minutes or until meat juices run clear and vegetables are tender, turning frequently and brushing with glaze after 6 minutes of grilling. (For a gas grill, preheat grill. Reduce heat to medium. Place kabobs on grill rack over heat. Cover and grill as above.)

NUTRITION FACTS PER SERVING: 521 cal., 15 g total fat (6 g sat. fat), 83 mg chol., 266 mg sodium, 73 g carbo., 3 g fiber, 26 g pro.

Apricot-Dijon Pork Salad

A mixture of apricot preserves, vinegar, Dijon-style mustard, and ginger serves as both a basting sauce and dressing for the fruit-studded salad.

PREP: 20 MINUTES   GRILL: 12 MINUTES   MAKES: 4 SERVINGS

- **1** cup apricot preserves
- **¼** cup white wine vinegar
- **2** tablespoons Dijon-style mustard
- **½** teaspoon ground ginger
- **1** pound pork tenderloin
- **1** 10-ounce package torn mixed salad greens
- **1** 15¼-ounce can apricot halves, drained and sliced
- **½** cup dried tart cherries
- **8** green onions, cut into ½-inch-long pieces
- **¼** cup pecan pieces, toasted
- **2** ounces provolone cheese, shredded (¼ cup)

1 Snip any large pieces of preserves. In a medium bowl combine preserves, vinegar, mustard, and ginger. Reserve ⅓ cup of the preserves mixture for brushing on pork. Set aside remaining preserves mixture for dressing.

2 Split tenderloin lengthwise, cutting to but not through the opposite side. Spread meat open. For charcoal grill, grill tenderloin on the rack of an uncovered grill directly over medium-hot coals about 12 minutes or until meat juices run clear (160°F), turning once halfway through grilling and brushing frequently with the ⅓ cup preserves mixture during the last 5 minutes of grilling. (For a gas grill, preheat grill. Reduce heat to medium-hot. Place tenderloin on grill rack over heat. Cover and grill as above.) Discard remainder of preserves mixture used as brush-on.

3 Meanwhile, in a large bowl combine greens, apricots, cherries, green onions, and pecans. Divide among 4 dinner plates. Slice grilled pork ½ inch thick. Arrange pork slices on top of greens mixture; drizzle with reserved preserves mixture. Sprinkle with provolone cheese.

NUTRITION FACTS PER SERVING: 604 cal., 12 g total fat (4 g sat. fat), 76 mg chol., 259 mg sodium, 94 g carbo., 6 g fiber, 35 g pro.

Moroccan Pork with Wilted Greens

*The cumin-and-coriander combination gives this flame-kissed pork roll
the wonderful exotic flavors of traditional Moroccan fare.*

PREP: 40 MINUTES   **GRILL:** 40 MINUTES   **MAKES:** 4 SERVINGS

1	12-ounce pork tenderloin
⅓	cup snipped dried apricots
2	tablespoons snipped fresh cilantro
1	tablespoon raisins
2	teaspoons lemon juice
1	teaspoon ground cumin
1	teaspoon ground coriander
1	teaspoon paprika
⅛	teaspoon salt
1	to 1½ pounds mixed greens (such as Swiss chard, beet greens, mustard greens, and/or fresh spinach)
2	tablespoons olive oil
1	teaspoon bottled minced garlic (2 cloves)
	Lemon wedges

1 Trim fat from pork. Cut tenderloin in half lengthwise almost to opposite side; open and lay flat. Place knife in the "V" of the first cut. Cut away from the first cut and parallel to the cut surface to within ½ inch of the other side of the meat. Repeat on opposite side of "V." Spread these sections open. Sprinkle apricots, cilantro, and raisins over pork. Sprinkle with lemon juice. Starting from a long side, roll up into a spiral. Tie with 100%-cotton kitchen string at 1-inch intervals.

2 For rub, in a small bowl combine cumin, coriander, paprika, and salt. Sprinkle rub evenly over pork; rub in with your fingers.

3 For a charcoal grill, arrange hot coals around a drip pan. Test for medium-hot heat above pan. Place pork on grill rack over drip pan. Cover and grill for 40 to 50 minutes or until meat juices run clear (160°F). (For a gas grill, preheat grill. Reduce heat to medium-hot. Adjust for indirect cooking. Grill as above.)

4 Meanwhile, wash greens. Pat greens dry with paper towels. If desired, remove stems. Cut greens lengthwise into 2-inch-wide strips; set aside. In a heavy, large skillet heat oil over medium-hot heat. Cook and stir garlic in hot oil for 30 to 60 seconds or just until brown. Add the greens. Cook and stir for 2 to 3 minutes or just until greens are limp.

5 To serve, slice meat across the grain; serve with greens. Squeeze the juice from lemon wedges over meat and greens.

NUTRITION FACTS PER SERVING: 234 cal., 11 g total fat (2 g sat. fat), 60 mg chol., 317 mg sodium, 15 g carbo., 3 g fiber, 22 g pro.

Peppered Pork and Pasta Salad

Pork and pasta are peppered with colors.
These flavors are just as bright to the tongue as this vinaigrette-tossed salad is to the eye.

PREP: 10 MINUTES **GRILL:** 10 MINUTES + 20 MINUTES **MAKES:** 6 SERVINGS

2   12-ounce pork tenderloins
1   recipe Italian Balsamic Vinaigrette
2   red sweet peppers, halved lengthwise
1   yellow sweet pepper, halved lengthwise
1   green sweet pepper, halved lengthwise
8   ounces dried bow tie pasta
⅓   cup thinly sliced fresh basil

1 Trim fat from meat. Measure 2 tablespoons of the Italian Balsamic Vinaigrette. Set remaining Italian Balsamic Vinaigrette aside for dressing. Lightly brush meat and insides of sweet peppers with the 2 tablespoons Italian Balsamic Vinaigrette; discard remainder of the Italian Balsamic Vinaigrette used as brush-on.

2 For a charcoal grill, grill peppers, cut sides up, on the rack of an uncovered grill directly over medium coals for 10 to 12 minutes or until tender. Wrap peppers in foil; let stand for 20 minutes. While peppers are standing, add meat to grill. Grill about 20 minutes or until meat juices run clear (160°F), turning occasionally to brown evenly. (For a gas grill, preheat grill. Reduce heat to medium. Place peppers, cut sides up, on grill rack over heat. Cover and grill peppers, then meat as above.) Using a paring knife, gently pull the skin off peppers. Cut peppers into 1-inch pieces; set aside.

3 Meanwhile, cook pasta according to package directions; drain. Set aside.

4 To serve, slice each tenderloin in half lengthwise; cut into ¼-inch-thick slices. In a large bowl combine pork, pasta, peppers, and basil. Add the remaining Italian Balsamic Vinaigrette; toss gently to coat. Serve immediately. (Or cover and chill for up to 8 hours.)

Italian Balsamic Vinaigrette: In a screw-top jar combine 3 tablespoons balsamic vinegar, 3 tablespoons olive oil, ½ teaspoon bottled minced garlic (1 clove), ½ teaspoon salt, and ¼ teaspoon ground black pepper. Cover and shake well. Shake before serving.

NUTRITION FACTS PER SERVING: 359 cal., 13 g total fat (3 g sat. fat), 113 mg chol., 245 mg sodium, 30 g carbo., 2 g fiber, 30 g pro.

Blackberry-Glazed Smoked Ham

At your next family reunion or for a neighborhood block party,
serve this smoky ham dressed up with a blackberry-and-mustard brush-on.

PREP: 10 MINUTES **GRILL:** 2¼ HOURS **STAND:** 15 MINUTES **MAKES:** 20 TO 28 SERVINGS

1	6- to 8-pound cooked ham shank
1½	cups seedless blackberry jam or other seedless berry jam
¼	cup coarse-grain brown mustard
2	tablespoons balsamic vinegar

1 Score ham on both sides in a diamond pattern by cutting diagonally at 1-inch intervals.

2 For a charcoal grill, arrange medium coals around edge of grill, leaving center of grill without coals. Test for medium-low heat above center of grill (not over coals). Place ham on a rack in a roasting pan. Place pan on grill rack over center of grill (not over coals). Cover and grill for 2 to 2½ hours or until heated through (135°F). Add coals as necessary to maintain heat. (For a gas grill, preheat grill. Reduce heat to medium-low. Adjust for indirect cooking. Place ham on rack in a roasting pan; place on grill rack. Cover and grill as above.)

3 Meanwhile, for berry sauce, in a medium saucepan stir together jam, mustard, and vinegar. Bring just to boiling; reduce heat. Simmer, uncovered, for 5 minutes.

4 Brush ham with some of the sauce. Cover and grill for 15 minutes more, brushing once or twice with sauce. Remove ham from grill. Cover with foil; let stand for 15 minutes before carving. The meat's temperature after standing should be 140°F.

5 To serve, slice ham. Reheat any remaining sauce until bubbly and pass with ham.

NUTRITION FACTS PER SERVING: 210 cal., 6 g total fat (2 g sat. fat), 51 mg chol., 1,202 mg sodium, 19 g carbo., 0 g fiber, 20 g pro.

Lemon-Pepper Lamb

Leftovers of this savory roast make great sandwiches.

PREP: 10 MINUTES **GRILL:** 1½ HOURS **STAND:** 15 MINUTES **MAKES:** 8 SERVINGS

1 2- to 3-pound boneless rolled lamb shoulder roast

1 teaspoon lemon-pepper seasoning

1 teaspoon dried marjoram, crushed

1 teaspoon bottled minced garlic (2 cloves)

1 Trim fat from meat. For rub, in a small bowl combine lemon-pepper seasoning, marjoram, and garlic. Sprinkle rub evenly over meat; rub in with your fingers.

2 For a charcoal grill, arrange medium coals around a drip pan. Test for medium-low heat above the pan. Place meat on grill rack over drip pan. Cover and grill for 1½ to 2 hours or until done (155°F). Add coals as necessary to maintain heat. (For a gas grill, preheat grill. Reduce heat to medium-low. Adjust for indirect cooking. Place meat on a rack in a roasting pan, place on grill rack, and grill as above.)

3 Remove the meat from the grill; cover with foil and let stand for 15 minutes before slicing. The meat's temperature after standing should be 160°F.

NUTRITION FACTS PER SERVING: 148 cal., 6 g total fat (2 g sat. fat), 72 mg chol., 195 mg sodium, 0 g carbo., 0 g fiber, 23 g pro.

Dijon-Crusted Lamb Rib Roast

Sour cream, Dijon mustard, garlic, and thyme grill up into a wonderful crust that has a twofold purpose—to provide flavor, of course, and to seal in the juices of the succulent lamb rib roast.

PREP: 10 MINUTES   GRILL: 50 MINUTES   STAND: 15 MINUTES   MAKES: 4 SERVINGS

1	2½-pound lamb rib roast (8 ribs)
3	tablespoons Dijon-style mustard
1	tablespoon olive oil
1	teaspoon bottled minced garlic (2 cloves)
1	teaspoon snipped fresh thyme or ½ teaspoon dried thyme, crushed
¼	teaspoon salt
¼	teaspoon ground black pepper
¼	cup dairy sour cream

1 Trim fat from meat. In a small bowl stir together mustard, oil, garlic, thyme, salt, and pepper. Set aside 2 tablespoons of the mustard mixture; cover and chill. Brush meat with remaining mustard mixture.

2 For a charcoal grill, arrange medium-hot coals around a drip pan. Test for medium heat above pan. Place meat, bone side down, on grill rack over drip pan. Cover and grill until desired doneness. Allow 50 to 60 minutes for medium-rare doneness (140°F) or 1 to 1¼ hours for medium doneness (155°F). Add coals as necessary to maintain heat. (For a gas grill, preheat grill. Reduce heat to medium. Adjust for indirect cooking. Place meat on a rack in a roasting pan, place on grill rack, and grill as above.)

3 Remove meat from grill. Cover with foil; let stand for 15 minutes before carving. The meat's temperature after standing should be 145°F for medium-rare or 160°F for medium.

4 Meanwhile, for sauce, in a small bowl stir together sour cream and reserved mustard mixture. To serve, cut meat into four 2-rib portions. Pass sauce with meat.

NUTRITION FACTS PER SERVING: 404 cal., 26 g total fat (9 g sat. fat), 129 mg chol., 539 mg sodium, 2 g carbo., 0 g fiber, 38 g pro.

104

Greek Lamb Chops

*Grilled tomatoes, sliced and tossed with a kalamata olive
and feta cheese mixture, add an authentic Greek touch to the lamb.*

PREP: 20 MINUTES   **MARINATE:** 8 TO 24 HOURS   **GRILL:** 14 MINUTES   **MAKES:** 6 SERVINGS

6   lamb sirloin chops, cut ¾ to 1 inch thick
1   tablespoon finely shredded lemon peel
⅔   cup lemon juice
6   tablespoons olive oil
⅓   cup snipped fresh oregano
½   teaspoon salt
⅛   teaspoon ground black pepper
½   cup snipped fresh parsley
½   cup crumbled feta cheese (2 ounces)
¼   cup pitted sliced kalamata olives
¼   teaspoon ground cinnamon
¼   teaspoon ground black pepper
2   pounds plum tomatoes

1 Place lamb chops in a resealable plastic bag set in a shallow dish. For marinade, in a medium bowl stir together the lemon peel, half of the lemon juice, 4 tablespoons of the oil, the oregano, salt, and the ⅛ teaspoon pepper. Pour marinade over lamb. Seal bag; turn to coat meat. Marinate in the refrigerator for at least 8 hours or up to 24 hours, turning bag occasionally.

2 In a large bowl combine remaining ⅓ cup lemon juice, 1 tablespoon of the remaining oil, the parsley, feta cheese, olives, cinnamon, and the ¼ teaspoon pepper; set aside.

3 Drain lamb chops, discarding marinade. Brush tomatoes with the remaining 1 tablespoon oil. For charcoal grill, grill lamb chops on the rack of an uncovered grill directly over medium coals for 14 to 17 minutes or until lamb is medium doneness (160°F), turning once halfway through grilling. Grill tomatoes alongside lamb chops for last 8 to 10 minutes of grilling or until tomatoes are slightly charred, turning once. (For a gas grill, preheat grill. Reduce heat to medium. Place lamb, then tomatoes on the grill rack over heat. Cover and grill as above.)

4 Transfer tomatoes to cutting board; cool slightly and slice. Toss sliced tomatoes with the feta cheese mixture; serve with the lamb.

NUTRITION FACTS PER SERVING: 263 cal., 15 g total fat (4 g sat. fat), 72 mg chol., 292 mg sodium, 10 g carbo., 2 g fiber, 23 g pro.

Lamb and Vegetable Salad

Oven-roasted vegetables and medallions of Parmesan-stuffed grilled lamb star in this company-special entrée.

PREP: 45 MINUTES **GRILL:** 45 MINUTES **STAND:** 15 MINUTES
ROAST: 30 MINUTES **MAKES:** 8 TO 10 SERVINGS

3 pounds boneless leg of lamb, butterflied

3 tablespoons grated Parmesan cheese

2 tablespoons snipped fresh parsley

1 tablespoon bottled minced garlic (6 cloves)

2 teaspoons finely shredded lemon peel

Salt

Freshly ground black pepper

2 fresh ears of corn, kernels removed (about 2 cups) or 2 cups loose-pack frozen corn, thawed

1 pound tiny new potatoes, scrubbed and quartered

1 small red onion, cut into ½-inch wedges

2 tablespoons olive oil

1 pound fresh asparagus, ends removed and spears cut into 2-inch pieces; and/or small green beans, trimmed

½ cup bottled lemon-dill sauce

¼ cup snipped fresh dill

8 cups torn mixed salad greens

1 cup crumbled feta cheese (4 ounces)

¼ cup pine nuts, toasted

¼ cup Greek ripe olives, pitted and halved

1 Unroll lamb; trim off fat. In a small bowl combine Parmesan cheese, parsley, garlic, and lemon peel. Sprinkle lamb with salt and freshly ground pepper. Top with Parmesan-garlic mixture. Roll up lamb; tie securely with 100%-cotton kitchen string.

2 For a charcoal grill, arrange medium coals around a drip pan. Test for medium-low heat above the pan. Place meat on grill rack, fat side up, over drip pan. Cover and grill until desired doneness. Allow 45 minutes to 1 hour for medium-rare doneness (140°F) or 1 to 1¼ hours for medium doneness (155°F). (For a gas grill, preheat grill. Reduce heat to medium-low. Adjust for indirect cooking. Place lamb on rack in a roasting pan, place on grill rack, and grill as above.)

3 Remove lamb roast from grill. Cover the roast with foil; let stand for 15 minutes. The meat's temperature after standing should be 145°F for medium-rare or 160°F for medium. Slice the meat into medallions.

4 Meanwhile, in a roasting pan, toss together the corn, potatoes, and red onion. Drizzle with olive oil; season with additional salt and pepper. Roast vegetables in a 425°F oven for 15 minutes.

5 Remove from oven; add asparagus and/or green beans. Toss together. Return to oven; roast for 15 minutes more or until potatoes are tender. (You can serve vegetables warm or at room temperature.)

6 Just before serving, toss the vegetables with the lemon-dill sauce. Season vegetables with additional salt and pepper and snipped dill. Place greens on large platter; top with roasted vegetables. Arrange lamb medallions alongside the vegetables with some greens showing. Top with feta cheese, pine nuts, and olives.

NUTRITION FACTS PER SERVING: 473 cal., 22 g total fat (6 g sat. fat), 122 mg chol., 468 mg sodium, 25 g carbo., 4 g fiber, 43 g pro.

Apple-Glazed Lamb Chops

Having friends over for dinner? Serve these curry-spiked chops with couscous as a side dish and sorbet for dessert.

PREP: 15 MINUTES   GRILL: 12 MINUTES   MAKES: 4 SERVINGS

3   tablespoons apple jelly

1   green onion, thinly sliced

1   tablespoon soy sauce

2   teaspoons lemon juice

⅛   teaspoon curry powder

Dash ground cinnamon

Dash cayenne pepper

2   small red and/or green apples, cored and cut crosswise into ¼-inch-thick slices

Lemon juice

8   lamb loin chops, cut 1 inch thick (about 2 pounds total)

Hot cooked couscous (optional)

1   tablespoon snipped fresh mint

1 For glaze, in a small saucepan heat and stir apple jelly, green onion, soy sauce, lemon juice, curry powder, cinnamon, and cayenne pepper over medium heat until bubbly. Remove from heat. Brush apple slices with lemon juice. Set aside.

2 For charcoal grill, grill chops on the rack of an uncovered grill directly over medium coals until desired doneness, turning and brushing once with glaze halfway through grilling. Allow 12 to 14 minutes for medium-rare doneness (145°F) or 15 to 17 minutes for medium doneness (160°F). Place apples on grill rack next to chops during the last 5 minutes of grilling, turning and brushing once with glaze. (For a gas grill, preheat grill. Reduce heat to medium. Place chops, then apple slices on grill rack over heat. Cover and grill as above.) If desired, serve with couscous. Sprinkle chops with mint.

NUTRITION FACTS PER SERVING: 385 cal., 14 g total fat (5 g sat. fat), 133 mg chol., 378 mg sodium, 20 g carbo., 1 g fiber, 43 g pro.

Lamb Chops with Mint Marinade

Lamb and mint are longtime partners. Fresh mint in this marinade is a refreshing change from the traditional mint jelly.

PREP: 10 MINUTES **MARINATE:** 30 MINUTES TO 24 HOURS **GRILL:** 12 MINUTES

MAKES: 4 SERVINGS

8	lamb loin chops, cut 1 inch thick (about 2 pounds total)
2	tablespoons lemon juice
2	tablespoons olive oil
¼	cup snipped fresh mint
1½	teaspoons bottled minced garlic (3 cloves)
¼	teaspoon ground black pepper
¼	teaspoon salt

1 Trim fat from chops. Place chops in a resealable plastic bag set in a shallow dish. For marinade, combine lemon juice, oil, 3 tablespoons of the mint, the garlic, and pepper. Pour marinade over the chops. Seal bag; turn to coat chops. Marinate in the refrigerator for at least 30 minutes or up to 24 hours.

2 Drain chops, discarding marinade. Sprinkle chops with the salt. For charcoal grill, grill chops on rack of an uncovered grill directly over medium coals until desired doneness, turning once halfway through grilling. Allow 12 to 14 minutes for medium-rare doneness (145°F) or 15 to 17 minutes for medium doneness (160°F). (For a gas grill, preheat grill. Reduce heat to medium. Place chops on grill rack over heat. Cover and grill as above.) Sprinkle with remaining 1 tablespoon mint.

NUTRITION FACTS PER SERVING: 310 cal., 18 g total fat (5 g sat. fat), 107 mg chol., 229 mg sodium, 2 g carbo., 0 g fiber, 34 g pro.

Tandoori-Style Lamb Chops

Yellow summer squash, pita bread, and a cooling
yogurt-mint mixture complement these chutney-topped chops.

PREP: 20 MINUTES   GRILL: 12 MINUTES   MAKES: 4 SERVINGS

2 tablespoons cooking oil

1 tablespoon bottled minced garlic (6 cloves)

2 teaspoons grated fresh ginger

1 tablespoon garam masala*

½ teaspoon salt

8 lamb loin chops, cut 1 inch thick (about 2 pounds total)

2 medium yellow summer squash and/or zucchini, halved lengthwise

4 pita bread rounds

½ cup plain low-fat yogurt

1 tablespoon snipped fresh mint

¼ cup chutney or hot chutney

1 In a small bowl combine oil, garlic, ginger, garam masala, and salt. Brush oil mixture onto all sides of lamb chops and squash.

2 For a charcoal grill, grill chops and squash on the rack of an uncovered grill directly over medium coals until chops are desired doneness and squash is tender, turning once halfway through grilling. Allow 12 to 14 minutes for medium-rare doneness (145°F) or 15 to 17 minutes for medium doneness (160°F). For the last 2 minutes of grilling, place pita rounds on grill rack to heat. (For a gas grill, preheat grill. Reduce heat to medium. Place chops and squash, then pita rounds on grill rack over heat. Cover and grill as above.)

3 Meanwhile, in a small bowl combine yogurt and mint. Transfer squash to a cutting board; cool slightly and slice diagonally into ½-inch-thick pieces. Serve yogurt mixture, squash, pita bread, and chutney with chops.

NUTRITION FACTS PER SERVING: 471 cal., 15 g total fat (4 g sat. fat), 82 mg chol., 750 mg sodium, 49 g carbo., 3 g fiber, 34 g pro.

*NOTE: Look for garam masala at Indian food markets or in the specialty foods section of larger supermarkets. If it's not available locally, make your own blend by combining 1 teaspoon ground cumin, 1 teaspoon ground coriander, ½ teaspoon ground black pepper, ½ teaspoon ground cardamom, ¼ teaspoon ground cinnamon, and ¼ teaspoon ground cloves. Store the mixture in a cool, dry place.

Apricot-Stuffed Lamb Chops

*There's sweetness in the center of these chops, which are stuffed
with dried apricots, raisins, onion, and orange peel.*

PREP: 15 MINUTES   **GRILL:** 12 MINUTES   **MAKES:** 4 SERVINGS

⅓   cup snipped dried apricots

3   tablespoons raisins

1   tablespoon finely chopped onion

1   teaspoon finely shredded orange peel

8   lamb rib chops, cut 1 inch thick
(about 2 pounds total)

2   teaspoons ground coriander

½   teaspoon salt

¼   teaspoon ground black pepper

1 For stuffing, in a small bowl combine the apricots, raisins, onion, and orange peel.

2 Trim fat from chops. Make a pocket in each chop by cutting horizontally from the fat side almost to the bone. Divide stuffing among pockets in chops. If necessary, secure openings with wooden toothpicks.

3 For rub, in a small bowl combine coriander, salt, and pepper. Sprinkle rub evenly over chops; rub in with your fingers.

4 For charcoal grill, grill chops on the rack of an uncovered grill directly over medium coals until desired doneness, turning once halfway through grilling. Allow 12 to 14 minutes for medium-rare doneness (145°F) or 15 to 17 minutes for medium doneness (160°F). (For a gas grill, preheat grill. Reduce heat to medium. Place chops on grill rack over heat. Cover and grill as above.) If using toothpicks, remove before serving.

NUTRITION FACTS PER SERVING: 210 cal., 9 g total fat (3 g sat. fat), 64 mg chol., 353 mg sodium, 13 g carbo., 2 g fiber, 20 g pro.

Fragrant Minted Lamb Chops

Celebrate the arrival of the grilling season with the traditional springtime treat of lamb, given classic-with-a-twist treatment here in an aromatic mint-infused marinade.

PREP: 15 MINUTES   **MARINATE:** 4 TO 24 HOURS   **GRILL:** 12 MINUTES   **MAKES:** 4 SERVINGS

8	lamb rib chops, cut 1 inch thick (about 2 pounds total)
¼	cup snipped fresh mint
¼	cup lemon juice
2	tablespoons cooking oil
2	tablespoons water
1	tablespoon grated fresh ginger
1½	teaspoons paprika
1	teaspoon ground cumin
½	teaspoon salt
½	teaspoon bottled minced garlic (1 clove)
⅛	teaspoon cayenne pepper
1	to 2 tablespoons finely shredded fresh mint
	Hot cooked rice pilaf (optional)
	Fresh mint sprigs (optional)

1 Trim fat from chops. Place chops in a resealable plastic bag set in a shallow dish. For marinade, in a small bowl combine the snipped mint, lemon juice, oil, the water, ginger, paprika, cumin, salt, garlic, and cayenne pepper. Pour marinade over chops. Seal bag; turn to coat chops. Marinate in the refrigerator for at least 4 hours or up to 24 hours, turning bag occasionally.

2 Drain chops, discarding marinade. For a charcoal grill, grill chops on the rack of an uncovered grill directly over medium coals until desired doneness, turning once halfway through grilling. Allow 12 to 14 minutes for medium-rare doneness (145°F) or 15 to 17 minutes for medium doneness (160°F). (For gas grill, preheat grill. Reduce heat to medium. Place chops on the grill rack directly over heat. Cover and grill as above.)

3 Transfer lamb chops to a serving platter; sprinkle with the shredded mint. If desired, serve with rice pilaf and garnish with mint sprigs.

NUTRITION FACTS PER SERVING: 232 cal., 15 g total fat (4 g sat. fat), 64 mg chol., 354 mg sodium, 3 g carbo., 1 g fiber, 20 g pro.

L A M B

Mustard-Rosemary Lamb Chops

*A touch of honey mellows the mustard, wine, and vinegar in
the rosemary-accented mixture that coats the chops.*

PREP: 20 MINUTES **CHILL:** 2 TO 3 HOURS **GRILL:** 12 MINUTES **MAKES:** 4 SERVINGS

8   lamb rib or loin chops, cut 1 inch thick
    (about 2 pounds total)

¼   cup stone ground mustard

2   green onions, thinly sliced

2   tablespoons dry white wine

1   tablespoon balsamic vinegar or rice vinegar

1½ teaspoons bottled minced garlic (3 cloves)

1   teaspoon snipped fresh rosemary

1   teaspoon honey

½   teaspoon salt

½   teaspoon freshly ground black pepper

1 Trim fat from chops; set chops aside. In a small bowl stir together mustard, green onions, wine, vinegar, garlic, rosemary, honey, salt, and pepper. Spread mixture evenly over both sides of each chop. Place chops on a large plate; cover loosely with plastic wrap. Chill in the refrigerator for at least 2 hours or up to 3 hours.

2 For a charcoal grill, grill chops on the rack of an uncovered grill directly over medium coals until desired doneness, turning once halfway through grilling. Allow 12 to 14 minutes for medium-rare doneness (145°F) or 15 to 17 minutes for medium doneness (160°F). (For a gas grill, preheat grill. Reduce heat to medium. Place chops on grill rack over heat. Cover and grill as above.)

NUTRITION FACTS PER SERVING: 194 cal., 9 g total fat (3 g sat. fat), 64 mg chol., 557 mg sodium, 4 g carbo., 0 g fiber, 21 g pro.

112

Lamb with Dill-Mustard Marinade

A profusion of flavored mustards is available in most supermarkets. Choose a dill mustard for this zesty marinade.

PREP: 25 MINUTES   **MARINATE:** 6 TO 24 HOURS   **GRILL:** 12 MINUTES   **MAKES:** 4 SERVINGS

3 tablespoons dill mustard

3 tablespoons balsamic vinegar

1 tablespoon molasses

½ teaspoon onion powder

½ teaspoon salt

1 sprig fresh rosemary

1 pound lean boneless lamb, cut into 1-inch cubes

Very sturdy fresh rosemary twigs or metal skewers

❶ In a resealable plastic bag set in a deep bowl combine mustard, vinegar, molasses, onion powder, salt, and the 1 sprig rosemary. Add lamb cubes to bag. Seal bag; turn to coat lamb. Marinate in the refrigerator for at least 6 hours or up to 24 hours, turning bag occasionally.

❷ Drain lamb, discarding marinade. Thread lamb cubes onto sturdy rosemary twigs or metal skewers, leaving ¼ inch space between cubes.

❸ For charcoal grill, grill kabobs on rack of an uncovered grill directly over medium coals for 12 to 15 minutes or until done, turning once halfway through grilling. (For gas grill, preheat grill. Reduce heat to medium. Place kabobs on grill rack over heat. Cover and grill as above.)

NUTRITION FACTS PER SERVING: 321 cal., 24 g total fat (10 g sat. fat), 80 mg chol., 269 mg sodium, 4 g carbo., 0 g fiber, 20 g pro.

Venison Tenderloin and Onions

Onions, green onions, and their relatives, shallots and leeks, cook in foil for a full-flavored side dish that's equally delicious with pork or lamb.

PREP: 25 MINUTES **MARINATE:** 2 TO 3 HOURS **GRILL:** 25 MINUTES **MAKES:** 4 SERVINGS

2 8- to 10-ounce venison tenderloins

3 tablespoons olive oil

2 tablespoons balsamic vinegar

2 teaspoons coarsely cracked mixed peppercorns

1 teaspoon Dijon-style mustard

1 large onion, sliced

4 green onions, cut into 1-inch-long pieces

4 shallots, sliced

2 leeks (white parts only), cut in half lengthwise and sliced

3 cloves garlic, sliced

2 tablespoons balsamic vinegar

1 teaspoon brown sugar

1 Place meat in resealable plastic bag set in shallow dish. For marinade, in a small bowl combine oil, 2 tablespoons balsamic vinegar, the peppercorns, and mustard. Pour marinade over meat. Seal bag; turn to coat meat. Marinate in the refrigerator for at least 2 hours or up to 3 hours, turning bag occasionally.

2 Drain meat, discarding marinade. Fold a 36×18-inch piece of heavy foil in half to make an 18-inch square. Place onion slices, green onions, shallots, leeks, and garlic in the center of foil. In a small bowl stir together 2 tablespoons balsamic vinegar and the brown sugar. Drizzle over vegetables. Bring up opposite edges of foil and seal with a double fold. Fold remaining edges together to completely enclose vegetables, leaving space for steam to build.

3 For a charcoal grill, arrange medium-hot coals around a drip pan. Test for medium heat above the drip pan. Place the meat on the grill rack over the drip pan. Place vegetable packet on grill rack directly over the coals. Cover and grill for 25 to 35 minutes or until done (155°F), turning the vegetable packet once halfway through grilling. (For a gas grill, preheat the grill. Reduce heat to medium. Adjust for indirect cooking. Place meat on a rack in a roasting pan, place on grill rack. Place vegetable packet over heat. Grill as above.)

4 To serve, slice meat. Transfer vegetables to a large serving platter. Arrange meat slices on top.

NUTRITION FACTS PER SERVING: 211 cal., 5 g total fat (1 g sat. fat), 93 mg chol., 80 mg sodium, 14 g carbo., 3 g fiber, 26 g pro.

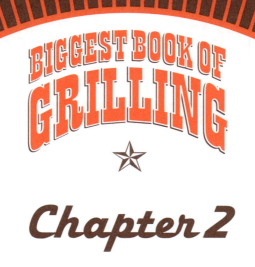

Chapter 2

POULTRY

Aloha Chicken

Marinate chicken with the island seasonings of soy and ginger, then grill.

PREP: 15 MINUTES **MARINATE:** 4 TO 24 HOURS **GRILL:** 50 MINUTES **MAKES:** 6 SERVINGS

3   whole large chicken breasts (about 4 pounds total), halved lengthwise

⅓   cup soy sauce

¼   cup packed brown sugar

¼   cup sliced green onions

2   tablespoons grated fresh ginger

2   teaspoons bottled minced garlic (4 cloves)

1 Skin chicken, if desired. Place chicken in a resealable plastic bag set in a shallow dish. For marinade, in a small bowl combine soy sauce, brown sugar, green onions, ginger, and garlic. Pour marinade over chicken. Seal bag; turn to coat chicken. Marinate in refrigerator for at least 4 hours or up to 24 hours, turning bag occasionally.

2 Drain chicken, discarding marinade.

3 For a charcoal grill, arrange medium-hot coals around drip pan. Test for medium heat above the pan. Place chicken, bone sides down, on grill rack over the drip pan. Cover and grill for 50 to 60 minutes or until chicken is no longer pink (170°F). Watch chicken closely because the sweet marinade may cause overbrowning. (For a gas grill, preheat grill. Reduce heat to medium. Adjust for indirect cooking. Grill as above.)

NUTRITION FACTS: 310 cal., 17 g total fat (5 g sat. fat), 113 mg chol., 299 mg sodium, 2 g carbo., 0 g fiber, 35 g pro.

116

Apricot-and-Mustard-Glazed Chicken

*Apricot spreadable fruit is the foundation for this glaze,
while rosemary and mustard add interesting flavor.*

PREP: 15 MINUTES GRILL: 50 MINUTES MAKES: 6 SERVINGS

½ **cup apricot spreadable fruit**

1 **tablespoon white vinegar**

1 **tablespoon Dijon-style mustard**

1 **tablespoon snipped fresh rosemary
or 1 teaspoon dried rosemary, crushed**

1 **teaspoon bottled minced garlic (2 cloves)**

¼ **teaspoon ground black pepper**

3 **whole medium chicken breasts
(about 3 pounds total), halved lengthwise**

1 For glaze, in a small saucepan combine spreadable fruit, vinegar, mustard, rosemary, garlic, and pepper. Cook and stir over low heat until heated through. Remove from heat.

2 For a charcoal grill, arrange medium-hot coals around a drip pan. Test for medium heat above the pan. Place chicken, skin sides down, on grill rack over drip pan. Cover and grill for 50 to 60 minutes or until chicken is no longer pink (170°F), brushing with some of the glaze during the last 15 minutes of grilling. (For a gas grill, preheat grill. Reduce heat to medium. Adjust for indirect cooking. Grill as above.)

NUTRITION FACTS PER SERVING: 255 cal., 8 g total fat (2 g sat. fat), 83 mg chol., 132 mg sodium, 17 g carbo., 0 g fiber, 29 g pro.

Chicken Caribbean

Experience the islands without venturing from your patio. Fresh basil (try cinnamon basil if you can find it) infuses aroma and peppery-clove flavor into the slightly sweet coconut-orange sauce—perfect with the spicy jerk-seasoned chicken.

PREP: 10 MINUTES **GRILL:** 12 MINUTES **MAKES:** 4 SERVINGS

4   skinless, boneless chicken breast halves (about 1¼ pounds total)

½   teaspoon Jamaican jerk seasoning

½   cup purchased unsweetened coconut milk*

¼   cup orange juice

2   tablespoons snipped fresh basil

1   teaspoon finely shredded orange peel (optional)

2   cups hot cooked rice

1 Rub both sides of chicken with jerk seasoning. For a charcoal grill, grill chicken on the rack of an uncovered grill directly over medium coals for 12 to 15 minutes or until chicken is no longer pink (170°F), turning once halfway through grilling. (For a gas grill, preheat grill. Reduce heat to medium. Place chicken on grill rack over heat. Cover and grill as above.)

2 Meanwhile, for sauce, in a small saucepan combine coconut milk, orange juice, and 1 tablespoon of the basil. Bring to boiling; reduce heat. Simmer, uncovered, about 5 minutes or until reduced to ½ cup.

3 If desired, stir the orange peel into cooked rice. Serve chicken and sauce over rice. Sprinkle with the remaining 1 tablespoon basil.

NUTRITION FACTS PER SERVING: 319 cal., 9 g total fat (6 g sat. fat), 75 mg chol., 100 mg sodium, 25 g carbo., 0 g fiber, 31 g pro.

*NOTE: Look for canned coconut milk in the Asian food section of your supermarket or at an Asian specialty store.

Spicy Moroccan-Glazed Chicken

Yogurt combined with hot pepper sauce, turmeric, and other seasonings gives chicken a deliciously exotic flair.

PREP: 10 MINUTES **MARINATE:** 4 TO 8 HOURS **GRILL:** 12 MINUTES **MAKES:** 4 SERVINGS

4   skinless, boneless chicken breast halves (about 1¼ pounds total)

½   cup plain yogurt

⅓   cup lime juice

2   tablespoons olive oil

2   tablespoons honey

1   teaspoon bottled minced garlic (2 cloves)

1   teaspoon bottled hot pepper sauce

½   teaspoon ground turmeric

½   teaspoon ground cardamom

½   teaspoon ground allspice

½   teaspoon ground cumin

¼   teaspoon salt

¼   teaspoon ground white pepper

1 Place chicken in a resealable plastic bag set in a shallow dish. For marinade, in a small bowl combine yogurt, lime juice, oil, honey, garlic, hot pepper sauce, turmeric, cardamom, allspice, cumin, salt, and white pepper. Pour marinade over chicken. Seal bag; turn to coat chicken. Marinate in the refrigerator for at least 4 hours or up to 8 hours.

2 Drain chicken, reserving marinade. For a charcoal grill, grill chicken on the rack of an uncovered grill directly over medium coals for 12 to 15 minutes or until chicken is no longer pink (170°F), turning once halfway through grilling and brushing often with reserved marinade during the first 5 minutes of grilling. (For a gas grill, preheat grill. Reduce heat to medium. Place chicken on grill rack over heat. Cover and grill as above.) Discard any remaining marinade.

NUTRITION FACTS PER SERVING: 223 cal., 6 g total fat (1 g sat. fat), 83 mg chol., 165 mg sodium, 7 g carbo., 0 g fiber, 34 g pro.

Chicken with Corn Salsa

During the summer, use fresh corn for the salsa.
Just cut enough corn off the cobs to measure 2 cups of kernels.

PREP: 30 MINUTES   MARINATE: 2 TO 4 HOURS   GRILL: 12 MINUTES   MAKES: 6 SERVINGS

6   skinless, boneless chicken breast halves (about 2 pounds total)

½   cup light beer

1   tablespoon reduced-sodium soy sauce

1   tablespoon snipped fresh cilantro

2   teaspoons lime juice

2   teaspoons finely chopped seeded fresh jalapeño chile pepper*

1   10-ounce package frozen whole kernel corn, thawed (2 cups)

¼   cup chopped red onion

¼   cup chopped red sweet pepper

¼   cup snipped fresh cilantro

2   tablespoons lime juice

2   tablespoons finely chopped seeded fresh jalapeño chile pepper*

½   teaspoon salt

1 Place chicken in a resealable plastic bag set in a shallow dish. For marinade, in a small bowl combine the beer, soy sauce, the 1 tablespoon cilantro, the 2 teaspoons lime juice, and the 2 teaspoons jalapeño pepper. Pour marinade over the chicken. Seal bag; turn to coat chicken. Marinate in the refrigerator for at least 2 hours or up to 4 hours, turning bag occasionally.

2 Meanwhile, for corn salsa, in a small bowl combine corn, red onion, sweet pepper, the ¼ cup cilantro, the 2 tablespoons lime juice, the 2 tablespoons jalapeño pepper, and the salt. Cover; refrigerate for at least 2 hours or up to 4 hours. Remove salsa from refrigerator about 30 minutes before serving.

3 Drain chicken, discarding marinade. For a charcoal grill, grill chicken on the rack of an uncovered grill directly over medium coals for 12 to 15 minutes or until chicken is no longer pink (170°F), turning once halfway through grilling. (For a gas grill, preheat grill. Reduce heat to medium. Place chicken on grill rack over heat. Cover and grill as above.) Serve with corn salsa.

NUTRITION FACTS PER SERVING: 215 cal., 5 g total fat (1 g sat. fat), 81 mg chol., 277 mg sodium, 12 g carbo., 1 g fiber, 32 g pro.

*NOTE: Because chile peppers contain volatile oils that can burn your skin and eyes, avoid direct contact with them as much as possible. When working with chile peppers, wear plastic or rubber gloves. If your bare hands do touch the chile peppers, wash your hands and nails well with soap and warm water.

Honey-Rosemary Chicken

Opt for bone-in or boneless chicken breasts.
The honey, mustard, and herb marinade is great with either choice.

PREP: 20 MINUTES **MARINATE:** 4 TO 24 HOURS **GRILL:** 50 MINUTES **MAKES:** 8 SERVINGS

⅓ cup honey

¼ cup olive oil

2 tablespoons coarse-grain mustard

1½ teaspoons bottled minced garlic (3 cloves)

1 tablespoon snipped fresh rosemary

2 teaspoons lemon juice

½ teaspoon salt

¼ teaspoon ground black pepper

4 whole medium chicken breasts (about 4 pounds total), halved lengthwise, or 8 skinless, boneless chicken breast halves

1 For marinade, in a small bowl combine honey, olive oil, mustard, garlic, rosemary, lemon juice, salt, and pepper.

2 If desired, skin bone-in chicken. Place chicken in a resealable plastic bag set in a shallow dish. Pour marinade over chicken. Seal bag; turn to coat chicken. Marinate in the refrigerator for at least 4 hours or up to 24 hours, turning bag occasionally.

3 Drain chicken, reserving marinade. For a charcoal grill, arrange medium-hot coals around a drip pan. Test for medium heat above the pan. Place chicken on grill rack over drip pan. Cover and grill for 50 to 60 minutes for bone-in chicken breasts or 15 to 18 minutes for boneless chicken breasts or until chicken is no longer pink (170°F), brushing once with reserved marinade halfway through grilling. (For a gas grill, preheat grill. Reduce heat to medium. Adjust for indirect cooking. Grill as above.) Discard any remaining marinade.

NUTRITION FACTS PER SERVING: 354 cal., 17 g total fat (4 g sat. fat), 105 mg chol., 286 mg sodium, 12 g carbo., 0 g fiber, 38 g pro.

Italian-Seasoned Chicken

A marinade made with wine, olive oil, Italian seasoning, and garlic—now that's Italian!

PREP: 10 MINUTES **MARINATE:** 8 TO 24 HOURS **GRILL:** 50 MINUTES **MAKES:** 4 TO 6 SERVINGS

2 to 3 whole medium chicken breasts (2 to 3 pounds total), halved lengthwise

1½ cups dry white wine

½ cup olive oil

1 tablespoon dried Italian seasoning, crushed

2 teaspoons bottled minced garlic (4 cloves)

Fresh herb sprigs (optional)

1 If desired, skin chicken. Place chicken in a resealable plastic bag set in a shallow dish.

2 For marinade, in a small bowl combine wine, olive oil, Italian seasoning, and garlic. Pour marinade over chicken. Seal bag; turn to coat chicken. Marinate in the refrigerator for at least 8 hours or up to 24 hours, turning bag occasionally.

3 Drain chicken, reserving marinade. For a charcoal grill, arrange medium-hot coals around a drip pan. Test for medium heat above the pan. Place chicken, bone sides down, on grill rack over drip pan. Cover and grill for 50 to 60 minutes or until chicken is no longer pink (170°F), brushing with some of the reserved marinade during the first 40 minutes of grilling. (For a gas grill, preheat grill. Reduce heat to medium. Adjust for indirect cooking. Grill as above.) Discard any remaining marinade. If desired, garnish with fresh herbs.

NUTRITION FACTS PER SERVING: 276 cal., 11 g total fat (2 g sat. fat), 90 mg chol., 87 mg sodium, 1 g carbo., 0 g fiber, 36 g pro.

Jalapeño and Basil-Glazed Chicken

Basil and jalapeño? Sure!
They marry perfectly when brushed on this red pepper-rubbed chicken.

PREP: 15 MINUTES GRILL: 50 MINUTES MAKES: 4 SERVINGS

2 whole medium chicken breasts (about 2 pounds total), halved lengthwise

1 tablespoon olive oil

½ teaspoon bottled minced garlic (1 clove)

¼ teaspoon salt

¼ teaspoon cayenne pepper

½ cup jalapeño chile pepper jelly

2 tablespoons snipped fresh basil

1 tablespoon lime juice

1 If desired, skin chicken. For rub, in a small bowl combine oil, garlic, salt, and cayenne pepper. Spoon rub evenly over chicken; rub in with your fingers.

2 For sauce, in a small saucepan combine jalapeño jelly, basil, and lime juice. Cook and stir over low heat until jelly is melted. Remove from heat.

3 For a charcoal grill, arrange medium-hot coals around a drip pan. Test for medium heat above the pan. Place chicken, bone sides down, on grill rack over drip pan. Cover and grill for 50 to 60 minutes or until chicken is no longer pink (170°F), brushing with some of the sauce during the last 15 minutes of grilling. (For a gas grill, preheat grill. Reduce heat to medium. Adjust for indirect cooking. Grill as above.)

4 To serve, reheat remaining sauce until bubbly; pass with chicken.

NUTRITION FACTS PER SERVING: 377 cal., 13 g total fat (3 g sat. fat), 104 mg chol., 226 mg sodium, 27 g carbo., 0 g fiber, 37 g pro.

Middle-Eastern Grilled Chicken

The cucumber sauce served alongside this grilled chicken has nuances of tsatsiki, the yogurt, cucumber, and garlic sauce served at tavernas on the Greek isles. Cucumbers are added to half of the spiced yogurt; the remaining half doubles as a brush-on.

PREP: 15 MINUTES GRILL: 15 MINUTES MAKES: 4 SERVINGS

1	**8-ounce carton plain fat-free yogurt**
1	**small onion, finely chopped**
1	**tablespoon snipped fresh oregano or savory or 1 teaspoon dried oregano or savory, crushed**
1½	**teaspoons bottled minced garlic (3 cloves)**
1	**teaspoon sesame seeds, toasted**
½	**teaspoon ground cumin**
¼	**teaspoon ground turmeric (optional)**
⅛	**teaspoon salt**
1	**small cucumber, seeded and chopped (about ⅔ cup)**
4	**skinless, boneless chicken breast halves (about 1¼ pounds total)**
	Hot cooked couscous (optional)

1 In a medium bowl combine yogurt, onion, oregano or savory, garlic, sesame seeds, cumin, turmeric (if desired), and salt. Transfer half of the yogurt mixture to a small bowl and stir in cucumber; cover and refrigerate until ready to serve. Set the remaining yogurt mixture aside.

2 For a charcoal grill, arrange medium-hot coals around a drip pan. Test for medium heat above the pan. Place chicken on grill rack over drip pan. Spoon the remaining yogurt mixture over chicken. Cover and grill for 15 to 18 minutes or until chicken is no longer pink (170°F). (For a gas grill, preheat grill. Reduce heat to medium. Adjust for indirect cooking. Grill as above.)

3 Serve chicken with the cucumber mixture and, if desired, couscous.

NUTRITION FACTS PER SERVING: 201 cal., 4 g total fat (1 g sat. fat), 76 mg chol., 257 mg sodium, 7 g carbo., 0 g fiber, 33 g pro.

Fusion Chicken

For an easy, tasty side dish, serve wild rice pilaf made from a mix.

PREP: 15 MINUTES **MARINATE:** 1 TO 2 HOURS **GRILL:** 50 MINUTES **MAKES:** 4 SERVINGS

2 whole medium chicken breasts (about 2 pounds total), halved lengthwise

1 cup dry red wine

¼ cup bottled hoisin sauce

¼ cup chopped onion

1 tablespoon soy sauce

1 teaspoon bottled minced garlic (2 cloves)

½ teaspoon grated fresh ginger

½ teaspoon five-spice powder

¼ teaspoon crushed red pepper

Wild rice pilaf (optional)

1 Place chicken in a resealable plastic bag set in a shallow dish. For marinade, in a medium bowl combine wine, hoisin sauce, onion, soy sauce, garlic, ginger, five-spice powder, and crushed red pepper. Pour marinade over chicken. Seal bag; turn to coat chicken. Marinate in refrigerator for at least 1 hour or up to 2 hours.

2 Drain chicken, reserving marinade. For a charcoal grill, arrange medium-hot coals around a drip pan. Test for medium heat above the pan. Place chicken, bone sides down, on grill rack over drip pan. Cover and grill for 50 to 60 minutes or until chicken is no longer pink (170°F). (For a gas grill, preheat grill. Reduce heat to medium. Adjust for indirect cooking. Grill as above.)

3 Meanwhile, place reserved marinade in a small saucepan. Bring to boiling; reduce heat. Simmer, uncovered, for 10 minutes. If desired, strain marinade. If desired, serve chicken with rice pilaf. Drizzle hot marinade over chicken.

NUTRITION FACTS PER SERVING: 333 cal., 12 g total fat (4 g sat. fat), 90 mg chol., 620 mg sodium, 12 g carbo., 0 g fiber, 30 g pro.

Pineapple-Lemon Chicken

Be warned—this saucy chicken is messy, but oh so good.

PREP: 30 MINUTES **MARINATE:** 2 TO 24 HOURS **GRILL:** 50 MINUTES **MAKES:** 4 SERVINGS

2   **whole medium chicken breasts (about 2 pounds total), halved lengthwise**

1   **20-ounce can crushed pineapple (juice pack)**

1   **small lemon, very thinly sliced**

⅓   **cup ketchup**

⅓   **cup honey**

1   **tablespoon Worcestershire sauce**

1   **teaspoon bottled minced garlic (2 cloves)**

1   **teaspoon salt**

¼   **teaspoon dried rosemary, crushed**

1   **teaspoon cornstarch**

     Hot cooked rice

1 Place chicken in a resealable plastic bag set in a shallow dish. Drain pineapple, reserving ¼ cup juice. For marinade, in a medium bowl combine pineapple, reserved pineapple juice, lemon slices, ketchup, honey, Worcestershire sauce, garlic, salt, and rosemary. Pour marinade over chicken. Seal bag; turn to coat chicken. Marinate in refrigerator for at least 2 hours or up to 24 hours.

2 Drain chicken, reserving marinade. For a charcoal grill, arrange medium-hot coals around a drip pan. Test for medium heat above the pan. Place chicken, bone sides down, on grill rack over drip pan. Brush with some of the reserved marinade. Cover and grill for 50 to 60 minutes or until chicken is no longer pink (170°F), brushing once with reserved marinade halfway through grilling. (For a gas grill, preheat grill. Reduce heat to medium. Adjust for indirect cooking. Grill as above.)

3 In a medium saucepan combine remaining reserved marinade and the cornstarch. Cook and stir over medium heat until thickened and bubbly. Cook for 2 minutes more. To serve, spoon sauce over chicken and rice.

NUTRITION FACTS PER SERVING: 426 cal., 2 g total fat (0 g sat. fat), 66 mg chol., 949 mg sodium, 74 g carbo., 2 g fiber, 29 g pro.

Raspberry Chicken with Plantains

Cousins of bananas, plantains must be cooked before eating.
Here a brown sugar glaze adds a touch of sweetness to the plantain slices.

PREP: 20 MINUTES GRILL: 12 MINUTES MAKES: 4 SERVINGS

1 cup fresh raspberries or one 10-ounce package frozen lightly sweetened raspberries

2 tablespoons granulated sugar

1 teaspoon butter or margarine

2 ripe plantains or firm bananas, sliced

2 tablespoons brown sugar

2 tablespoons white wine vinegar

2 green onions, thinly sliced

1 small fresh jalapeño chile pepper, seeded and finely chopped*

1 pound skinless, boneless chicken breast halves

Salt

Ground black pepper

1 For sauce, in a small saucepan combine raspberries and granulated sugar. Heat over low heat about 3 minutes or until the berries are softened. Press berries through a fine-mesh sieve; discard seeds.

2 In a large nonstick skillet melt butter over medium heat. Add the plantains (if using); cook and stir about 2 minutes or until plantains are lightly browned and slightly softened. Stir in brown sugar and vinegar; heat through. Remove from heat; stir in green onions and jalapeño pepper. (Or if using bananas, melt butter. Stir in bananas, brown sugar, and vinegar; heat through. Remove from heat; stir in green onions and jalapeño pepper.)

3 Sprinkle chicken with salt and black pepper. For a charcoal grill, grill chicken on the rack of an uncovered grill directly over medium coals for 12 to 15 minutes or until chicken is no longer pink (170°F), turning once halfway through grilling. (For a gas grill, preheat grill. Reduce heat to medium. Place chicken on grill rack over heat. Cover and grill as above.)

4 If desired, place each chicken breast on a ti leaf. Spoon sauce over chicken. Serve with plantain or banana mixture.

NUTRITION FACTS PER SERVING: 300 cal., 5 g total fat (1 g sat. fat), 62 mg chol., 103 mg sodium, 45 g carbo., 4 g fiber, 23 g pro.

*NOTE: Because chile peppers contain volatile oils that can burn your skin and eyes, avoid direct contact with them as much as possible. When working with chile peppers, wear plastic or rubber gloves. If your bare hands do touch the chile peppers, wash your hands and nails well with soap and warm water.

Sesame-Ginger Barbecued Chicken

Oriental chile sauce makes this robust barbecue sauce downright awesome.

PREP: 10 MINUTES GRILL: 12 MINUTES MAKES: 6 SERVINGS

⅓ cup bottled plum sauce or sweet-sour sauce

¼ cup water

3 tablespoons bottled hoisin sauce

1½ teaspoons sesame seeds (toasted, if desired)

1 teaspoon grated fresh ginger
or ¼ teaspoon ground ginger

½ teaspoon bottled minced garlic (1 clove)

¼ to ½ teaspoon Oriental chile sauce or several
dashes bottled hot pepper sauce

6 skinless, boneless chicken breast halves
and/or thighs (about 2 pounds total)

1 For sauce, in a small saucepan combine plum sauce or sweet-sour sauce, the water, hoisin sauce, sesame seeds, ginger, garlic, and chile sauce or bottled hot pepper sauce. Bring to boiling over medium heat, stirring frequently; reduce heat. Cover and simmer for 3 minutes. Set aside.

2 For a charcoal grill, grill chicken on the rack of an uncovered grill directly over medium coals for 12 to 15 minutes or until chicken is no longer pink (170°F), turning once halfway through grilling and brushing with some of the sauce during the last 5 minutes of grilling. (For a gas grill, preheat grill. Reduce heat to medium. Place chicken on grill rack over heat. Cover and grill as above.)

3 To serve, reheat the remaining sauce until bubbly; pass with chicken.

NUTRITION FACTS PER SERVING: 209 cal., 5 g total fat (1 g sat. fat), 81 mg chol., 237 mg sodium, 9 g carbo., 0 g fiber, 31 g pro.

128

Tarragon Chicken with Rice

The airy sweetness of tarragon lifts this dish of rice, grilled vegetables, and chicken completely out of the ordinary.

PREP: 30 MINUTES GRILL: 12 MINUTES MAKES: 4 SERVINGS

12	ounces fresh asparagus spears, trimmed
4	medium carrots, halved lengthwise
¼	cup dry white wine
2	tablespoons olive oil or cooking oil
1	tablespoon snipped fresh tarragon or 1 teaspoon dried tarragon, crushed
½	teaspoon bottled minced garlic (1 clove)
¼	teaspoon ground black pepper
4	skinless, boneless chicken breast halves (about 1¼ pounds total)
1⅓	cups chicken broth
⅔	cup basmati or regular rice
1	teaspoon snipped fresh tarragon or ¼ teaspoon dried tarragon, crushed
1	green onion, thinly sliced
	Fresh tarragon sprigs (optional)

1 In a covered large skillet cook asparagus and carrots in a small amount of boiling water for 3 minutes; drain. In a small bowl combine white wine, oil, the 1 tablespoon fresh or 1 teaspoon dried tarragon, the garlic, and pepper. Brush some of the wine mixture over chicken and vegetables.

2 Meanwhile, in a medium saucepan bring chicken broth to boiling. Add rice and the ¼ teaspoon dried tarragon (if using). Return to boiling; reduce heat. Cover and simmer about 20 minutes or until rice is tender (do not lift cover). Stir in the 1 teaspoon snipped fresh tarragon (if using). Cover; keep warm.

3 Place asparagus and carrots in a grill basket. For a charcoal grill, grill chicken and vegetables in basket on the rack of an uncovered grill directly over medium coals until chicken and vegetables are tender and chicken is no longer pink (170°), turning and brushing chicken with the remaining wine mixture during the first 5 minutes of grilling. Allow about 5 minutes for vegetables and 12 to 15 minutes for chicken. (For a gas grill, preheat grill. Reduce heat to medium. Place chicken and vegetables in basket on grill rack over heat. Cover and grill as above.) Discard any remaining wine mixture.

4 Coarsely chop vegetables. Toss chopped vegetables and green onion with hot cooked rice. Serve chicken with rice mixture. If desired, garnish with fresh tarragon sprigs.

NUTRITION FACTS PER SERVING: 396 cal., 11 g total fat (2 g sat. fat), 76 mg chol., 378 mg sodium, 35 g carbo., 4 g fiber, 35 g pro.

West Indies Chicken with Grilled Fruit

Who says exotic has to be hard? This innovative, island-inspired, sweet-and-savory dish of grilled tropical fruit and chicken glossed with a spicy, herb-infused marmalade glaze is as easy as can be.

PREP: 15 MINUTES GRILL: 12 MINUTES MAKES: 4 SERVINGS

3	tablespoons orange marmalade
2	teaspoons finely shredded grapefruit peel or orange peel
2	teaspoons olive oil
1	tablespoon snipped fresh thyme
2½	teaspoons ground coriander
½	teaspoon hot Hungarian paprika or ⅛ teaspoon cayenne pepper
¼	teaspoon salt
1	small ruby red grapefruit
2	ripe, yet firm, kiwifruit
2	medium ripe, yet firm, nectarines
2	ripe, yet firm, star fruit (carambola)
4	skinless, boneless chicken breast halves (about 1¼ pounds total)

1 In a small bowl combine orange marmalade, grapefruit or orange peel, oil, thyme, coriander, paprika or cayenne pepper, and salt; set aside.

2 Peel and quarter grapefruit and kiwifruit. Pit and quarter nectarines. Cut star fruit into ½-inch-thick slices. Thread fruits on 4 metal skewers.

3 For a charcoal grill, grill chicken on the rack of an uncovered grill directly over medium coals for 12 to 15 minutes or until chicken is no longer pink (170°F), turning once halfway through grilling. Halfway through grilling, add fruit skewers. Brush chicken and fruit with marmalade mixture during the last 5 minutes of grilling. Turn fruit once. (For a gas grill, preheat grill. Reduce heat to medium. Place chicken, then fruit skewers on grill rack over heat. Cover and grill as above.)

NUTRITION FACTS PER SERVING: 320 cal., 7 g total fat (1 g sat. fat), 75 mg chol., 207 mg sodium, 36 g carbo., 3 g fiber, 31 g pro.

Chicken and Prosciutto Roll-Ups

For an attractive presentation, nestle the sliced chicken spirals on a bed of hot cooked spinach fettuccine.

PREP: 25 MINUTES GRILL: 15 MINUTES MAKES: 4 SERVINGS

¼ **cup dry white wine**

2 **teaspoons snipped fresh thyme or ½ teaspoon dried thyme, crushed**

4 **skinless, boneless chicken breast halves (about 1¼ pounds total)**

4 **thin slices prosciutto (about 1 ounce total), trimmed of fat**

2 **ounces fontina cheese, thinly sliced**

½ **of a 7-ounce jar roasted red sweet peppers, cut into thin strips (about ½ cup)**

Hot cooked spinach fettuccine (optional)

Fresh thyme sprigs (optional)

1 For sauce, in a small bowl combine wine and the snipped fresh or dried thyme. Set aside.

2 Place each chicken piece between 2 pieces of plastic wrap. Using the flat side of a meat mallet, lightly pound chicken into a rectangle about ⅛ inch thick. Remove plastic wrap.

3 Place a slice of prosciutto and one-quarter of the cheese on each chicken piece. Arrange one-quarter of the roasted peppers on cheese near bottom edge of each chicken piece. Starting from bottom edge, roll into a spiral; secure with wooden toothpicks.

4 For a charcoal grill, grill chicken on the rack of an uncovered grill directly over medium coals for 15 to 18 minutes or until chicken is no longer pink (170°F), turning once halfway through grilling and brushing with some of the sauce during the last 5 minutes of grilling. (For a gas grill, preheat grill. Reduce heat to medium. Place chicken on grill rack over heat. Cover and grill as above.) If desired, serve over spinach fettuccine. If desired, garnish with thyme sprigs.

NUTRITION FACTS PER SERVING: 246 cal., 9 g total fat (4 g sat. fat), 92 mg chol., 309 mg sodium, 2 g carbo., 0 g fiber, 34 g pro.

Chicken Rolls with Apple Filling

Great any time of year—but a perfect way to celebrate a beautiful fall day—these pretty chicken bundles are full of autumnal flavors.

PREP: 25 MINUTES GRILL: 15 MINUTES MAKES: 4 SERVINGS

4	**skinless, boneless chicken breast halves (about 1¼ pounds total)**
4	**ounces bulk pork sausage**
¼	**cup coarsely shredded apple**
1	**tablespoon snipped fresh parsley**
⅓	**cup apple jelly**
¼	**teaspoon dried sage, crushed**
2	**medium red and/or green cooking apples, cut crosswise into ½-inch-thick slices**

1 Place each chicken breast half between 2 pieces of plastic wrap. Using the flat side of a meat mallet, lightly pound the chicken into a rectangle about ⅛ inch thick. Remove plastic wrap.

2 For filling, in a small bowl combine the sausage, shredded apple, and parsley. Divide filling among chicken pieces, spreading almost to the edges. Starting from a narrow end, roll each chicken piece into a spiral; secure with wooden toothpicks.* For glaze, stir apple jelly until smooth; stir in sage.

3 For a charcoal grill, grill chicken on the rack of an uncovered grill directly over medium coals for 15 to 18 minutes or until chicken is no longer pink (170°F), turning once halfway through grilling and brushing with glaze during the last 5 minutes of grilling. (For a gas grill, preheat grill. Reduce heat to medium. Place chicken on grill rack over heat. Cover and grill as above.)

4 While the chicken is grilling, add apple slices to grill. Cover and grill about 5 minutes or until apples are tender and slightly charred, turning and brushing once with some of the glaze halfway through grilling. Serve the chicken with apples.

NUTRITION FACTS PER SERVING: 336 cal., 7 g total fat (2 g sat. fat), 103 mg chol., 220 mg sodium, 30 g carbo., 2 g fiber, 37 g pro.

*NOTE: If you like, wrap the chicken rolls and refrigerate for up to 4 hours before grilling. You may need to add a few minutes to the grilling time.

Fiery Chicken and Potato Fingers

Hot and sweet describe the flavors of this dynamic duo.
Grilled zucchini would make a fine side dish.

PREP: 20 MINUTES **MARINATE:** 30 MINUTES TO 24 HOURS
GRILL: 24 MINUTES **MAKES:** 4 SERVINGS

4 skinless, boneless chicken breast halves (about 1¼ pounds total)

3 tablespoons olive oil

3 tablespoons bottled hot pepper sauce

2 tablespoons snipped fresh parsley (optional)

1 tablespoon honey or brown sugar

1½ teaspoons bottled minced garlic (3 cloves)

½ teaspoon salt

½ teaspoon cayenne pepper

½ teaspoon cracked black pepper

2 large baking potatoes (about 1 pound total)

① Cut each chicken breast half lengthwise into 3 strips. Place chicken in a resealable plastic bag set in a shallow dish. For sauce, in a small bowl stir together oil, hot pepper sauce, parsley (if desired), honey or brown sugar, garlic, salt, cayenne pepper, and black pepper. Pour 2 tablespoons of the sauce over chicken. Seal bag; turn to coat chicken. Marinate in the refrigerator for at least 30 minutes or up to 24 hours, turning bag occasionally. Cover and chill the remaining sauce to use as a brush-on.

② Drain chicken, discarding marinade. Just before grilling, cut each potato lengthwise into 8 wedges. Lightly brush potato wedges with some of the remaining chilled sauce.

③ For a charcoal grill, grill potato wedges on the rack of an uncovered grill directly over medium coals for 15 minutes. Turn potato wedges. Add chicken to grill. Grill for 9 to 12 minutes more or until chicken and potato wedges are tender and chicken is no longer pink (170°), turning chicken and brushing once with remaining sauce during the last 5 minutes of grilling. (For a gas grill, preheat grill. Reduce heat to medium. Place potatoes, then chicken on grill rack over heat. Cover and grill as above.) Discard any remaining sauce.

NUTRITION FACTS PER SERVING: 367 cal., 12 g total fat (2 g sat. fat), 75 mg chol., 355 mg sodium, 32 g carbo., 1 g fiber, 32 g pro.

Szechwan Chicken Strips

Szechwan in the title indicates spicy.
Here the spiciness comes from Szechwan chile sauce or crushed red pepper.

PREP: 15 MINUTES MARINATE: 15 MINUTES TO 2 HOURS GRILL: 10 MINUTES MAKES: 4 SERVINGS

1 pound skinless, boneless chicken breast halves, cut into bite-size strips

⅓ cup rice vinegar

¼ cup bottled hoisin sauce

1 to 2 teaspoons Szechwan chile sauce or ½ teaspoon crushed red pepper

½ teaspoon bottled minced garlic (1 clove)

12 cherry tomatoes

2 cups packaged shredded broccoli (broccoli slaw mix)

1 tablespoon chopped dry-roasted peanuts

1 Place chicken in a resealable plastic bag set in a shallow dish. For marinade, in a small bowl combine vinegar, hoisin sauce, Szechwan chile sauce or crushed red pepper, and garlic. Set aside half of the vinegar mixture to use for the dressing. Pour remaining marinade over chicken. Seal bag; turn to coat chicken. Marinate in the refrigerator for at least 15 minutes or up to 2 hours, turning bag occasionally.

2 Drain chicken, reserving marinade. On metal skewers, thread chicken (accordion style). For a charcoal grill, grill kabobs on the rack of an uncovered grill directly over medium coals for 10 to 12 minutes or until chicken is no longer pink, turning once and brushing once with reserved marinade halfway through grilling. Add tomatoes to ends of skewers for the last 2 to 3 minutes of grilling. (For a gas grill, preheat grill. Reduce heat to medium. Place kabobs on grill rack over heat. Cover and grill as above.) Discard any remaining marinade.

3 Serve chicken over shredded broccoli. Drizzle with the reserved vinegar mixture; sprinkle with peanuts.

NUTRITION FACTS PER SERVING: 205 cal., 4 g total fat (1 g sat. fat), 59 mg chol., 401 mg sodium, 16 g carbo., 2 g fiber, 23 g pro.

Barbara Bush's Barbecued Chicken

This former First Lady's lemon-marinated chicken is brushed with a homemade barbecue sauce and grilled to perfection.

PREP: 30 MINUTES **MARINATE:** 4 TO 24 HOURS **COOK:** 20 MINUTES + 50 MINUTES
GRILL: 50 MINUTES **MAKES:** 4 SERVINGS

1	2½- to 3-pound broiler-fryer chicken, quartered
3	tablespoons lemon juice
1	tablespoon cooking oil
1	teaspoon salt
½	teaspoon freshly ground black pepper
½	teaspoon bottled minced garlic (1 clove)
2½	cups water
1	cup coarsely chopped onion
½	to ¾ cup sugar
½	cup butter or margarine
⅓	cup prepared mustard
¼	cup cider vinegar
½	teaspoon freshly ground black pepper
2½	cups ketchup
½	cup Worcestershire sauce
6	to 8 tablespoons lemon juice
½	teaspoon cayenne pepper

1 Place chicken in a resealable plastic bag set in a shallow dish. For marinade, stir together the 3 tablespoons lemon juice, the cooking oil, salt, ½ teaspoon black pepper, and garlic. Pour over chicken. Seal bag; turn to coat chicken. Marinate in the refrigerator for at least 4 hours or up to 24 hours, turning bag occasionally.

2 For sauce, in a large saucepan combine the water, onion, sugar, butter, mustard, vinegar, and ½ teaspoon black pepper. Bring to boiling; reduce heat. Simmer, uncovered, for 20 minutes. Stir in ketchup, Worcestershire sauce, the 6 to 8 tablespoons lemon juice, and the cayenne pepper. Return to boiling; reduce heat. Simmer, uncovered, for 50 to 60 minutes or until reduced to about 4 cups.

3 Meanwhile, drain chicken, discarding marinade. For a charcoal grill, arrange medium-hot coals around a drip pan. Test for medium heat above the pan. Place chicken, bone sides down, on grill rack over drip pan. Cover and grill for 50 to 60 minutes or until chicken is no longer pink (170°F for breast portions; 180°F for drumstick portions), brushing with some of the sauce during the last 15 minutes of grilling. (For a gas grill, preheat grill. Reduce heat to medium. Adjust for indirect cooking. Grill as above.)

4 To serve, pass the remaining sauce* with the chicken.

NUTRITION FACTS PER SERVING: 433 cal., 25 g total fat (9 g sat. fat), 115 mg chol., 1,307 mg sodium, 21 g carbo., 1 g fiber, 32 g pro.

*NOTE: Cover and chill any leftover sauce in the refrigerator for up to 1 week.

Honey-Dijon Barbecued Chicken

The mild mustard marinade enhances the flavor of grilled chicken quarters.

PREP: 15 MINUTES MARINATE: 2 TO 4 HOURS GRILL: 50 MINUTES MAKES: 4 SERVINGS

1 3-pound broiler-fryer chicken, quartered

¼ cup olive oil

¼ cup white Zinfandel wine

2 tablespoons honey

2 tablespoons Dijon-style mustard

½ teaspoon ground black pepper

½ teaspoon bottled minced garlic (1 clove)

¼ teaspoon salt

1 Place chicken in a resealable plastic bag set in a shallow dish. For marinade, in a small bowl combine oil, wine, honey, mustard, pepper, garlic, and salt. Pour marinade over chicken. Seal bag; turn to coat chicken. Marinate in the refrigerator for at least 2 hours or up to 4 hours, turning bag occasionally.

2 Drain chicken, reserving marinade. For a charcoal grill, arrange medium-hot coals around a drip pan. Test for medium heat above the pan. Place chicken, bone sides down, on grill rack over drip pan. Cover and grill for 50 to 60 minutes or until chicken is no longer pink (170°F for breast portions; 180°F for drumstick portions), brushing with some of the reserved marinade during the first 40 minutes of grilling. (For a gas grill, preheat grill. Reduce heat to medium. Adjust for indirect cooking. Grill as above.) Discard any remaining marinade.

NUTRITION FACTS PER SERVING: 380 cal., 23 g total fat (6 g sat. fat), 118 mg chol., 171 mg sodium, 3 g carbo., 0 g fiber, 37 g pro.

136

Sweet-and-Smoky Chicken

A mixture of vinegar, brown sugar, Worcestershire sauce, and liquid smoke makes an easy basting sauce that's luscious on chicken and pork.

PREP: 15 MINUTES **GRILL:** 50 MINUTES **MAKES:** 4 SERVINGS

2½ to 3 pounds chicken breast halves and thighs
½ cup vinegar
⅓ cup packed brown sugar
2 tablespoons Worcestershire sauce
¾ teaspoon liquid smoke
½ teaspoon salt
¼ teaspoon ground black pepper

1 Skin chicken. For basting sauce, in a small saucepan stir together vinegar, brown sugar, Worcestershire sauce, liquid smoke, salt, and pepper. Bring to boiling; reduce heat. Simmer, uncovered, for 5 to 8 minutes or until sauce is reduced to ⅔ cup.

2 For a charcoal grill, arrange medium-hot coals around a drip pan. Test for medium heat above the pan. Place chicken, bone sides down, on grill rack over drip pan. Cover and grill for 50 to 60 minutes or until chicken is no longer pink (170°F for breast halves; 180°F for thighs), brushing with the basting sauce during the last 15 minutes of grilling. (For a gas grill, preheat grill. Reduce heat to medium. Adjust for indirect cooking. Grill as above.) Discard any remaining basting sauce.

NUTRITION FACTS PER SERVING: 500 cal., 27 g total fat (8 g sat. fat), 161 mg chol., 518 mg sodium, 22 g carbo., 0 g fiber, 40 g pro.

Sticky-Sloppy Barbecue Chicken

Country meets city in this finger-lickin' barbecue recipe.
Dry sherry supplies the uptown flavor.

PREP: 15 MINUTES **MARINATE:** 2 TO 4 HOURS **COOK:** 30 MINUTES **GRILL:** 50 MINUTES
MAKES: 6 SERVINGS

3 to 4 pounds meaty chicken pieces
(breast halves, thighs, and drumsticks)

1½ cups dry sherry

1 cup finely chopped onion

¼ cup lemon juice

1 tablespoon bottled minced garlic (6 cloves)

2 bay leaves

1 15-ounce can tomato puree

¼ cup honey

3 tablespoons molasses

1 teaspoon salt

½ teaspoon dried thyme, crushed

¼ to ½ teaspoon cayenne pepper

¼ teaspoon ground black pepper

2 tablespoons white vinegar

1 Place chicken in a resealable plastic bag set in a shallow dish. For marinade, in a medium bowl stir together sherry, onion, lemon juice, garlic, and bay leaves. Pour marinade over chicken. Seal bag; turn to coat chicken. Marinate in the refrigerator for at least 2 hours or up to 4 hours, turning bag occasionally.

2 Drain chicken, reserving marinade. Cover and chill chicken until ready to grill. For sauce, in a large saucepan combine the reserved marinade, the tomato puree, honey, molasses, salt, thyme, cayenne pepper, and black pepper. Bring to boiling; reduce heat. Simmer, uncovered, about 30 minutes or until reduced to 2 cups. Remove from heat. Discard bay leaves. Stir in white vinegar.

3 For a charcoal grill, arrange medium-hot coals around a drip pan. Test for medium heat above the pan. Place chicken pieces, bone sides down, on grill rack over drip pan. Cover and grill for 50 to 60 minutes or until tender and no longer pink (170°F for breast halves; 180°F for thighs and drumsticks), brushing with some of the sauce during the last 15 minutes of grilling. (For a gas grill, preheat grill. Reduce heat to medium. Adjust for indirect cooking. Grill as above.)

4 To serve, reheat remaining sauce until bubbly; pass with chicken.

NUTRITION FACTS PER SERVING: 446 cal., 13 g total fat (4 g sat. fat), 104 mg chol., 735 mg sodium, 33 g carbo., 2 g fiber, 35 g pro.

138

Chicken Drumsticks Extraordinaire

Drumsticks become company fare when brushed with a pestolike mixture made with aromatic fresh basil and pecans.

PREP: 15 MINUTES GRILL: 35 MINUTES MAKES: 4 SERVINGS

1 cup lightly packed fresh basil leaves
½ cup broken pecans
¼ cup olive oil
1 teaspoon bottled minced garlic (2 cloves)
¼ teaspoon salt
¼ teaspoon ground black pepper
8 meaty chicken drumsticks

1 In a blender container or small food processor bowl combine basil leaves, broken pecans, olive oil, garlic, salt, and pepper. Cover and blend or process until pureed, scraping down side as needed. Divide mixture in half; chill half of the mixture.

2 Skin chicken, if desired. Before grilling, brush chicken with the unchilled basil mixture; discard remainder of the basil mixture used as a brush-on. For a charcoal grill, grill chicken on the rack of an uncovered grill directly over medium coals for 35 to 45 minutes or until chicken is no longer pink (180°F), turning once halfway through grilling and brushing with the chilled basil mixture during the last 5 minutes of grilling. (For a gas grill, preheat grill. Reduce heat to medium. Place chicken on grill rack over heat. Cover and grill as above.) (Watch carefully for flare-ups after turning chicken. Move chicken to a different area of the grill until the flare-up ends.)

NUTRITION FACTS PER SERVING: 451 cal., 36 g total fat (6 g sat. fat), 118 mg chol., 243 mg sodium, 3 g carbo., 2 g fiber, 30 g pro.

Chicken with Peach Salsa

Fruit salsas, such as this peach of a salsa, are marvelous with almost any grilled poultry.

PREP: 30 MINUTES MARINATE: 1 TO 4 HOURS GRILL: 35 MINUTES MAKES: 4 SERVINGS

4   whole chicken legs (drumstick and thigh) (about 3 pounds total)

½   cup dry white wine

1½ teaspoons finely shredded orange peel

⅓   cup orange juice

2   tablespoons olive oil or cooking oil

1½ teaspoons snipped fresh rosemary or ½ teaspoon dried rosemary, crushed

2   medium peaches or nectarines or 1⅓ cups frozen unsweetened peach slices, thawed

1   ripe avocado, halved, seeded, peeled, and finely chopped

½   cup chopped red or green sweet pepper

2   green onions, finely chopped

2   tablespoons lime juice

1   tablespoon snipped fresh cilantro

1 Skin chicken, if desired. Place chicken in a resealable plastic bag set in a shallow dish. For marinade, in a small bowl combine wine, orange peel, orange juice, oil, and rosemary. Pour marinade over chicken. Seal bag; turn to coat chicken. Marinate in refrigerator for at least 1 hour or up to 4 hours, turning bag occasionally.

2 Meanwhile, for salsa, peel and pit the fresh peaches or pit the nectarines. Finely chop peaches or nectarines. In a medium bowl combine peaches or nectarines, avocado, sweet pepper, green onions, lime juice, and cilantro. Cover and chill until serving time.

3 Drain chicken, reserving marinade. For a charcoal grill, grill chicken on the rack of an uncovered grill directly over medium coals for 35 to 45 minutes or until chicken is tender and no longer pink (180°F), turning once halfway through grilling and brushing with reserved marinade during the first 30 minutes of grilling. (For a gas grill, preheat grill. Reduce heat to medium. Place chicken on grill rack over heat. Cover and grill as above.) Discard any remaining marinade. Serve chicken with salsa.

NUTRITION FACTS PER SERVING: 650 cal., 43 g total fat (10 g sat. fat), 205 mg chol., 166 mg sodium, 13 g carbo., 4 g fiber, 47 g pro.

Cranberry-Chipotle Drumsticks

Finger food at its finest! Baste the chicken legs with zesty sauce during grilling, then pass more sauce for dipping.

PREP: 10 MINUTES GRILL: 35 MINUTES MAKES: 6 SERVINGS

1   16-ounce can whole cranberry sauce

½   cup bottled barbecue sauce

1   canned chipotle pepper in adobo sauce, finely chopped

12   chicken drumsticks or 6 skinless, boneless chicken breast halves

1 For sauce, in a medium saucepan stir together the cranberry sauce, barbecue sauce, and chipotle pepper. For dipping sauce, pour 1 cup of the cranberry sauce mixture into an airtight container; cover and chill. For basting sauce, transfer the remaining cranberry sauce mixture to a blender container or food processor bowl; cover and blend or process until smooth.

2 For a charcoal grill, grill chicken on the rack of an uncovered grill directly over medium coals, turning once halfway through grilling and brushing frequently with the basting sauce during the last 5 minutes of grilling. Allow 35 to 45 minutes for drumsticks (180°F) or 12 to 15 minutes for chicken breast halves (170°F). (For a gas grill, preheat grill. Reduce heat to medium. Place chicken on grill rack over heat. Cover and grill as above.) Serve with the dipping sauce.

NUTRITION FACTS PER SERVING: 371 cal., 12 g total fat (3 g sat. fat), 95 mg chol., 415 mg sodium, 36 g carbo., 1 g fiber, 28 g pro.

Greek Chicken Thighs

Chicken thighs are an often-overlooked cut.
They're a good dark-meat alternative to breasts and usually less expensive too.

PREP: 20 MINUTES **MARINATE:** 4 TO 24 HOURS **GRILL:** 35 MINUTES **STAND:** 2 MINUTES

MAKES: 4 TO 6 SERVINGS

8	chicken thighs (about 2½ pounds)
¼	cup dry red wine
2	tablespoons olive oil
2	tablespoons finely chopped red onion
1	teaspoon finely shredded lemon peel
1	teaspoon snipped fresh rosemary
1	teaspoon snipped fresh oregano
½	teaspoon bottled minced garlic (1 clove)
¼	teaspoon salt
¼	teaspoon ground black pepper
½	cup crumbled basil-and tomato-flavored feta cheese or plain feta cheese

1 Skin chicken thighs. Place chicken in a resealable plastic bag set in a shallow dish. For marinade, in a small bowl combine red wine, olive oil, onion, lemon peel, rosemary, oregano, garlic, salt, and pepper. Pour marinade over chicken. Seal bag; turn to coat chicken. Marinate in the refrigerator for at least 4 hours or up to 24 hours, turning bag occasionally.

2 Drain chicken, reserving marinade. For a charcoal grill, grill chicken on the rack of an uncovered grill directly over medium coals for 35 to 40 minutes or until chicken is no longer pink (180°F), turning once halfway through grilling and brushing with reserved marinade frequently during the first 20 minutes of grilling. (For a gas grill, preheat grill. Reduce heat to medium. Place chicken on grill rack over heat. Cover and grill as above.) Discard any remaining marinade.

3 Sprinkle chicken with feta cheese. Cover loosely with foil; let stand for 2 minutes before serving.

NUTRITION FACTS PER SERVING: 389 cal., 19 g total fat (6 g sat. fat), 205 mg chol., 512 mg sodium, 2 g carbo., 0 g fiber, 47 g pro.

Citrus Chicken Thighs and Onions

The blend of orange, lime, cilantro, and seasonings complements juicy chicken thighs.

PREP: 20 MINUTES **MARINATE:** 2 TO 24 HOURS **GRILL:** 50 MINUTES **MAKES:** 4 SERVINGS

8 chicken thighs (2½ to 2¾ pounds total)
¾ cup orange juice
1 teaspoon finely shredded lime peel
⅓ cup lime juice
2 tablespoons snipped fresh cilantro
2 teaspoons bottled minced garlic (4 cloves)
½ teaspoon salt
½ teaspoon dried oregano, crushed
½ teaspoon ground cumin
¼ teaspoon ground black pepper
1 large red onion, cut into ¾-inch-thick slices
2 teaspoons olive oil
Snipped fresh cilantro

1 Place chicken thighs in a resealable plastic bag set in a shallow dish. For marinade, in a medium bowl stir together orange juice, lime peel, lime juice, the 2 tablespoons cilantro, the garlic, salt, oregano, cumin, and pepper. Pour marinade over chicken. Seal bag; turn to coat chicken. Marinate in the refrigerator for at least 2 hours or up to 24 hours, turning bag occasionally.

2 Drain chicken, reserving marinade. For a charcoal grill, arrange medium-hot coals around a drip pan. Test for medium heat above the pan. Place chicken on grill rack over drip pan. Cover and grill for 50 to 60 minutes or until chicken is no longer pink (180°F), brushing frequently with reserved marinade during the first 40 minutes of grilling. (For a gas grill, preheat grill. Reduce heat to medium. Adjust for indirect cooking. Grill as above.) Brush onion slices with the olive oil. Add onion slices to the outside edge of the grill rack above the coals for the last 15 to 20 minutes of grilling or until tender, turning and brushing once with reserved marinade halfway through grilling. Discard any remaining marinade.

3 To serve, separate onion into rings and serve with chicken. Sprinkle with additional cilantro.

NUTRITION FACTS PER SERVING: 466 cal., 31 g total fat (8 g sat. fat), 165 mg chol., 272 mg sodium, 10 g carbo., 2 g fiber, 36 g pro.

Buffalo Chicken Wings

*Although these zesty wings make a great appetizer,
you also can serve them as a main dish for four.*

PREP: 15 MINUTES GRILL: 18 MINUTES MAKES: 32 APPETIZER SERVINGS

16 chicken wings (about 3 pounds total)

2 tablespoons butter or margarine

1 2-ounce bottle hot pepper sauce (¼ cup)

1 recipe Blue Cheese Dip

Celery sticks

1 Cut off and discard wing tips. Bend the 2 larger sections of each wing back and forth, breaking the cartilage connecting them. Use a knife or cleaver to cut through the cartilage and skin, cutting each wing into 2 sections.

2 In a small saucepan melt butter. Stir in hot pepper sauce. Brush the butter mixture generously over wing pieces.

3 For a charcoal grill, grill wing pieces on the rack of an uncovered grill directly over medium coals for 18 to 20 minutes or until chicken is no longer pink (170°F), turning once and brushing with the remaining butter mixture during the first 5 minutes of grilling. (For a gas grill, preheat grill. Reduce heat to medium. Place wing pieces on grill rack over heat. Cover and grill as above.) Discard any remaining butter mixture. Serve wing pieces with Blue Cheese Dip and celery sticks.

Blue Cheese Dip: In a blender container or food processor bowl combine ½ cup dairy sour cream; ½ cup crumbled blue cheese; ¼ cup mayonnaise or salad dressing; 1 teaspoon bottled minced garlic (2 cloves); 2 tablespoons lemon juice; 2 tablespoons thinly sliced green onion; and 1 tablespoon milk. Cover and blend or process just until combined. Transfer to a small bowl; cover and chill in refrigerator until serving time or up to 1 hour.

NUTRITION FACTS PER SERVING WITH 2 TEASPOONS DIP: 71 cal., 6 g total fat (2 g sat. fat), 19 mg chol., 55 mg sodium, 0 g carbo., 0 g fiber, 4 g pro.

144

Polynesian Chicken Wings

Honey and pineapple juice partner in a delicious marinade that doubles as a gorgeous glaze.

PREP: 25 MINUTES **COOL: 30 MINUTES** **MARINATE: 6 TO 24 HOURS**
GRILL: 20 MINUTES **MAKES: 12 SERVINGS**

½ cup unsweetened pineapple juice

¼ cup honey

¼ cup Worcestershire sauce

1 tablespoon grated fresh ginger
or 1 teaspoon ground ginger

2 teaspoons bottled minced garlic (4 cloves)

1 teaspoon salt

12 chicken wings (about 2½ pounds total)

1 fresh pineapple, cored, halved lengthwise,
and cut into ½-inch-thick slices

1 For marinade, in a small saucepan stir together pineapple juice, honey, Worcestershire sauce, ginger, garlic, and salt. Bring to boiling; reduce heat. Simmer, uncovered, about 12 minutes or until the marinade is reduced to ½ cup, stirring occasionally. Let mixture cool to room temperature.

2 Bend the sections of each wing back and forth at the large joint, breaking the cartilage connecting them. Use a knife or cleaver to cut through the cartilage and skin, cutting each wing into 2 sections. Place chicken pieces in a resealable plastic bag set in a shallow dish. Pour marinade over chicken pieces. Seal bag; turn to coat chicken. Marinate in the refrigerator for at least 6 hours or up to 24 hours, turning bag occasionally.

3 Drain chicken pieces, reserving marinade. For a charcoal grill, arrange medium-hot coals around a drip pan. Test for medium heat above the pan. Place chicken, bone sides down, on grill rack over drip pan. Cover and grill for 20 to 25 minutes or until chicken is no longer pink, brushing with reserved marinade during the first 15 minutes of grilling. (For a gas grill, preheat grill. Reduce heat to medium. Adjust for indirect cooking. Grill as above.) Discard any remaining marinade.

4 Halve pineapple slices. Place on grill rack directly over the heat for the last 5 minutes of grilling; turn once.

NUTRITION FACTS PER SERVING: 167 cal., 8 g total fat (2 g sat. fat), 39 mg chol., 291 mg sodium, 14 g carbo., 1 g fiber, 10 g pro.

Garlic-Grilled Chicken

A mixture of garlic and basil inserted under the skin and a combination of lemon, sweet pepper, and additional garlic in the cavity flavor every bite of this grilled chicken.

PREP: 20 MINUTES GRILL: 1 HOUR STAND: 15 MINUTES MAKES: 5 SERVINGS

- **1** 2½- to 3-pound whole broiler-fryer chicken
- **3** cloves garlic, peeled
- **½** of a lemon, sliced
- **½** of a red sweet pepper, sliced
- **1** tablespoon snipped fresh basil or 1 teaspoon dried basil, crushed
- **⅛** teaspoon salt
- **1** tablespoon olive oil or cooking oil
- **1** tablespoon lemon juice

  Steamed new potatoes (optional)

  Fresh oregano (optional)

1 Soak several wooden toothpicks in enough water to cover for 15 minutes; drain before using. Remove the neck and giblets from chicken. Twist wing tips under the back. Cut one of the garlic cloves lengthwise in half. Rub skin of chicken with cut edge of garlic. Place garlic halves, lemon slices, and sweet pepper slices in cavity of chicken.

2 Mince remaining 2 cloves garlic. In a small bowl combine minced garlic, basil, and salt; set aside. Starting at the neck on one side of the breast, slip your fingers between skin and meat, loosening the skin as you work toward the tail end. Once your entire hand is under the skin, free the skin around the thigh and leg area up to, but not around, the tip of the drumstick. Repeat on the other side of the breast. Rub garlic mixture over entire surface under skin. Securely fasten opening with water-soaked toothpicks.

3 Stir together oil and lemon juice; brush over chicken. Reserve remaining lemon juice mixture. Insert an oven-going meat thermometer into the center of an inside thigh muscle, making sure bulb does not touch bone.

4 For a charcoal grill, arrange medium-hot coals around a drip pan. Test for medium heat above the pan. Place chicken, breast side up, on grill rack over drip pan. Cover and grill for 1 to 1¼ hours or until thermometer registers 180°F, brushing occasionally with oil-lemon mixture during first 30 minutes of grilling. Add coals as necessary to maintain heat. (For a gas grill, preheat grill. Reduce heat to medium. Adjust for indirect cooking. Grill as above.) Discard any remaining oil-lemon mixture.

5 Remove chicken from grill and cover with foil. Let stand for 15 minutes before carving. If desired, serve on a platter with steamed new potatoes and garnish with fresh oregano.

NUTRITION FACTS PER SERVING: 253 cal., 15 g total fat (4 g sat. fat), 82 mg chol., 193 mg sodium, 2 g carbo., 0 g fiber, 26 g pro.

Garlicky Grilled Chicken

The unusual duo of garlic and coffee works together beautifully in this recipe.

PREP: 15 MINUTES GRILL: 1 HOUR STAND: 15 MINUTES MAKES: 4 SERVINGS

1 tablespoon cooking oil

1 teaspoon bottled minced garlic (2 cloves)

1 2½- to 3-pound whole broiler-fryer chicken

1 teaspoon dark roast ground coffee

Salt

Freshly ground black pepper

1 In a small bowl combine oil and garlic. Remove the neck and giblets from chicken. Brush chicken with garlic mixture. Sprinkle with coffee, salt, and pepper. Skewer neck skin to back. Tie legs to tail. Twist wing tips under back. Insert an oven-going meat thermometer into the center of an inside thigh muscle, making sure bulb does not touch bone.

2 For a charcoal grill, arrange medium-hot coals around a drip pan. Test for medium heat above the pan. Place chicken, breast side up, on grill rack over drip pan. Cover and grill for 1 to 1¼ hours or until thermometer registers 180°F. Add coals as necessary to maintain heat. (For a gas grill, preheat grill. Reduce heat to medium. Adjust for indirect cooking. Grill as above.)

3 Remove chicken from grill and cover with foil. Let stand for 15 minutes before carving.

NUTRITION FACTS PER SERVING: 200 cal., 12 g total fat (3 g sat. fat), 66 mg chol., 110 mg sodium, 0 g carbo., 0 g fiber, 20 g pro.

Herbed Chicken

During grilling, the flavorful juices get locked in to make the meat tender and moist.

PREP: 15 MINUTES GRILL: 1 HOUR STAND: 15 MINUTES MAKES: 4 TO 6 SERVINGS

1   2½- to 3-pound whole broiler-fryer chicken
2   tablespoons butter or margarine
3   tablespoons lemon juice
1½ teaspoons bottled minced garlic (3 cloves)
1   teaspoon dried thyme, savory, or sage, crushed
¼   teaspoon salt
¼   teaspoon ground black pepper
    Fresh thyme sprigs (optional)

1 Remove the neck and giblets from chicken. Skewer neck skin to back. Tie legs to tail. Twist wing tips under back. Insert an oven-going meat thermometer into the center of an inside thigh muscle, making sure bulb does not touch bone. In a small saucepan melt butter; stir in lemon juice, garlic, dried herb, salt, and black pepper. Brush chicken with some of the butter mixture.

2 For a charcoal grill, arrange medium-hot coals around a drip pan. Test for medium heat above the pan. Place chicken, breast side up, on grill rack over drip pan. Cover and grill for 1 to 1¼ hours or until thermometer registers 180°F, brushing with the remaining butter mixture during the first 45 minutes of grilling. Add coals as necessary to maintain heat. (For a gas grill, preheat grill. Reduce heat to medium. Adjust for indirect cooking. Grill as above.) Discard any remaining butter mixture.

3 Remove chicken from grill and cover with foil. Let stand for 15 minutes before carving. If desired, garnish with fresh thyme.

NUTRITION FACTS PER SERVING: 237 cal., 16 g total fat (6 g sat. fat), 81 mg chol., 262 mg sodium, 2 g carbo., 0 g fiber, 21 g pro.

Spice-Grilled Chicken

Jasmine rice and broiled apricots are flavorful partners for the spicy chicken.

PREP: 20 MINUTES **GRILL:** 1 HOUR **STAND:** 15 MINUTES **MAKES:** 4 TO 6 SERVINGS

2 teaspoons brown sugar

1½ teaspoons ground cinnamon

1 teaspoon smoked paprika or regular paprika

½ teaspoon salt

½ teaspoon ground black pepper

½ teaspoon ground allspice

1 3-pound whole broiler-fryer chicken or 12 chicken drumsticks

4 teaspoons cooking oil

2 cups chicken broth

1 cup jasmine or long grain rice

¼ cup snipped dried apricots

¼ cup golden raisins

4 lemon wedges (optional)

Swiss chard (optional)

Halved fresh apricots, broiled (optional)*

2 tablespoons chopped peanuts

1 In a small bowl combine brown sugar, cinnamon, paprika, salt, pepper, and allspice. Set aside 1½ teaspoons of the cinnamon mixture. Remove neck and giblets from whole chicken. Skewer neck skin to back. Twist wing tips under back. Brush whole chicken or drumsticks with oil; gently rub remaining cinnamon mixture onto chicken. Tie legs to tail. Insert an oven-going meat thermometer in the center of an inside thigh muscle, making sure bulb does not touch bone.

2 For a charcoal grill, arrange medium-hot coals around a drip pan. Test for medium heat above the pan. Place chicken, breast side up, on grill rack over drip pan. Cover and grill for 1 to 1¼ hours or until thermometer registers 180°F. Add coals as necessary to maintain heat. (For a gas grill, preheat grill. Reduce heat to medium. Adjust for indirect cooking. Grill as above.)

3 Meanwhile, in a medium saucepan combine the reserved 1½ teaspoons cinnamon mixture, the broth, and the uncooked rice. Bring to boiling; reduce heat. Cover and simmer for 15 minutes. Remove from heat. Stir in dried apricots and raisins. Cover and let stand for 5 minutes before serving.

4 Remove chicken from grill and cover with foil. Let stand for 15 minutes before carving. Spoon rice onto platter; top with chicken. If desired, serve with lemon wedges, Swiss chard, and broiled apricots. Pass chopped peanuts.

NUTRITION FACTS PER SERVING: 646 cal., 23 g total fat (6 g sat. fat), 207 mg chol., 1,012 mg sodium, 54 g carbo., 2 g fiber, 58 g pro.

***NOTE:** For broiled apricots, halve and pit fresh apricots. Brush cut sides lightly with melted butter. Place, cut sides up, on the unheated rack of a broiler pan. Broil 3 inches from the heat for 3 to 6 minutes or until lightly browned.

Guava-Glazed Chicken

*The technique of removing the backbone and flattening
the chicken—called spatchcocking—shortens its cooking time.*

PREP: 20 MINUTES COOK: 15 MINUTES GRILL: 45 MINUTES MAKES: 6 SERVINGS

1	3- to 4-pound whole broiler-fryer chicken
½	teaspoon salt
¼	teaspoon ground black pepper
1	cup guava, peach, or apricot nectar
¼	cup bottled hoisin sauce
1	teaspoon bottled minced garlic (2 cloves)
	Several dashes bottled hot pepper sauce (optional)
	Sliced fresh guava (optional)
	Sliced green onions (optional)

1 Remove the neck and giblets from chicken. Place the chicken, breast side down, on a cutting board. Use kitchen shears to make a lengthwise cut down 1 side of the backbone, starting from the neck end. Repeat the lengthwise cut on the opposite side of the backbone. Remove and discard the backbone. Turn chicken cut side down. Flatten the chicken with your hands. (Try to make it as flat as possible.) Use kitchen shears to remove the wing tips. Sprinkle chicken with the salt and pepper.

2 For sauce, in a small saucepan combine nectar, hoisin sauce, garlic, and, if desired, hot pepper sauce. Bring to boiling; reduce heat. Boil gently, uncovered, about 15 minutes or until thickened and sauce is reduced to about ¾ cup. Set aside.

3 For a charcoal grill, grill chicken, bone side down, on the rack of an uncovered grill directly over medium coals for 45 to 50 minutes or until chicken is no longer pink (170°F for breast; 180°F for thigh and drumsticks), turning once halfway through grilling and brushing with some of the sauce during the last 5 minutes of grilling. (For a gas grill, preheat grill. Reduce heat to medium. Place chicken on grill rack over heat. Cover and grill as above.)

4 Bring remaining sauce to boiling; pass with chicken. If desired, serve chicken with sliced fresh guava and green onions.

NUTRITION FACTS PER SERVING: 272 cal., 12 g total fat (3 g sat. fat), 79 mg chol., 478 mg sodium, 13 g carbo., 0 g fiber, 25 g pro.

Chicken and Sausage Kabobs

The sour cream-based dipping sauce is a refreshing serve-along for these double-meat kabobs.

PREP: 25 MINUTES MARINATE: 2 TO 8 HOURS GRILL: 12 MINUTES MAKES: 6 SERVINGS

1 pound skinless, boneless chicken breast halves

2 tablespoons olive oil

2 tablespoons finely chopped green onion

1 tablespoon lime juice

1 tablespoon snipped fresh flat-leaf parsley

1 tablespoon snipped fresh oregano

½ teaspoon bottled minced garlic (1 clove)

8 ounces apple-flavored smoked chicken sausage or smoked sausage, halved lengthwise and cut into ¾-inch-thick pieces

1 recipe Herbed Dipping Sauce

Grilled lime wedges

1 Cut chicken into long strips, about ½ inch thick. Place in a medium bowl. For marinade, in a small bowl combine oil, green onion, lime juice, parsley, oregano, and garlic. Pour marinade over chicken; stir to coat. Cover and marinate in the refrigerator for at least 2 hours or up to 8 hours.

2 Drain chicken, discarding marinade. On 6 long metal skewers, thread chicken strips (accordion-style) and sausage pieces, leaving ¼-inch space between pieces.

3 For a charcoal grill, grill kabobs on the rack of an uncovered grill directly over medium coals for 12 to 15 minutes or until chicken is no longer pink, turning once halfway through grilling. (For a gas grill, preheat grill. Reduce heat to medium. Place kabobs on grill rack over heat. Cover and grill as above.) Remove kabobs from grill. Serve with Herbed Dipping Sauce and grilled lime wedges.

Herbed Dipping Sauce: In a small bowl combine ¼ cup dairy sour cream, ¼ cup mayonnaise or salad dressing, 2 tablespoons finely chopped green onion and/or chives, 1 tablespoon lime juice, 1 tablespoon snipped fresh flat-leaf parsley, 1 tablespoon snipped fresh oregano, and ½ teaspoon bottled minced garlic (1 clove).

NUTRITION FACTS PER SERVING: 262 cal., 18 g total fat (4 g sat. fat), 61 mg chol., 347 mg sodium, 1 g carbo., 0 g fiber, 23 g pro.

Mixed Grill Kabobs

With chicken, two other meats, and assorted vegetables, these skewers are like a mixed grill—on a grill.

PREP: 25 MINUTES **MARINATE:** 6 TO 24 HOURS **GRILL:** 18 MINUTES **MAKES:** 6 SERVINGS

6 pieces chicken-wing drumettes (about 6 ounces total)

6 ounces lean boneless lamb, cut into 1-inch cubes

6 ounces boneless beef sirloin steak, cut into 1-inch cubes

12 ounces assorted fresh vegetables (such as whole baby squash; sweet peppers cut into 1-inch pieces; and mushrooms, whole or quartered) (about 2½ cups total)

1 small sweet onion (sauce as Vidalia or Walla Walla), finely chopped

⅓ cup Worcestershire sauce

1 tablespoon finely shredded lime peel

¼ cup lime juice

2 tablespoons snipped fresh rosemary

1 tablespoon olive oil

1 Place chicken, lamb, beef, and vegetables in a resealable plastic bag set in a shallow dish. For marinade, in a small bowl combine onion, Worcestershire sauce, lime peel, lime juice, rosemary, and oil. Pour marinade over meat and vegetables. Seal bag; turn to coat meat and vegetables. Marinate in the refrigerator for at least 6 hours or up to 24 hours, turning bag occasionally.

2 Drain meat and vegetables, reserving marinade. On separate 8-inch metal skewers, thread chicken, lamb, beef, and vegetables, leaving ¼-inch space between pieces.

3 For a charcoal grill, grill kabobs on the rack of an uncovered grill directly over medium coals until done, turning several times and brushing frequently with reserved marinade during the first 5 minutes of grilling. Allow 18 to 20 minutes for chicken; 8 to 12 minutes for beef and lamb; and 6 to 8 minutes for vegetables. Remove individual kabobs when done. (For a gas grill, preheat grill. Reduce heat to medium. Place kabobs on grill rack over heat. Cover and grill as above.) Discard any remaining marinade.

NUTRITION FACTS PER SERVING: 191 cal., 11 g total fat (3 g sat. fat), 62 mg chol., 182 mg sodium, 7 g carbo., 1 g fiber, 17 g pro.

Pakistani Chicken Kabobs

Fresh fruit is the perfect partner for the curried chicken.
In a pinch, you can use canned pineapple cubes rather than fresh fruit.

PREP: 30 MINUTES **MARINATE:** 30 MINUTES TO 2 HOURS **GRILL:** 12 MINUTES **MAKES:** 4 SERVINGS

1 pound skinless, boneless chicken breast halves, cut into 1-inch pieces

⅓ cup plain yogurt

2 teaspoons curry powder

2 teaspoons brown sugar

1 teaspoon grated fresh ginger

⅛ teaspoon salt

2 limes

4 cups peeled and cubed mango, papaya, and/or pineapple

1 Place chicken in resealable plastic bag set in a shallow dish. For marinade, in a small bowl combine yogurt, curry powder, brown sugar, ginger, and salt. Squeeze the juice from half of 1 lime; stir into yogurt mixture. Pour marinade over chicken. Seal bag; turn to coat chicken. Marinate in the refrigerator for at least 30 minutes or for up to 2 hours. Cut the remaining 1½ limes into wedges; set aside.

2 Drain chicken, discarding marinade. Thread chicken onto 8 long metal skewers, leaving ¼-inch space between pieces.

3 For a charcoal grill, grill kabobs on the rack of an uncovered grill directly over medium coals for 12 to 15 minutes or until chicken is no longer pink, turning once halfway through grilling. (For a gas grill, preheat grill. Reduce heat to medium. Place chicken on grill rack over heat. Cover and grill as above.) Remove from grill.

4 To serve, place fruit on the ends of kabobs. Serve with lime wedges.

NUTRITION FACTS PER SERVING: 227 cal., 4 g total fat (1 g sat. fat), 61 mg chol., 138 mg sodium, 25 g carbo., 3 g fiber, 24 g pro.

Potato and Chicken Kabobs

To assure that the chicken and potatoes cook evenly, be sure to leave a ¼-inch space between pieces. Use the same general guideline for other kabobs.

PREP: 20 MINUTES GRILL: 12 MINUTES MAKES: 4 SERVINGS

12	whole tiny new potatoes (about 1 pound total)
12	ounces skinless, boneless chicken breast halves, cut into 1½-inch pieces
1	lemon, cut into 4 wedges
3	tablespoons olive oil
1	tablespoon snipped fresh oregano or 1 teaspoon dried oregano, crushed
½	teaspoon bottled minced garlic (1 clove)

1 In a small saucepan bring a small amount of water to boiling; add potatoes. Cover and simmer about 10 minutes or until almost tender. Drain well; halve potatoes lengthwise.

2 On 4 long metal skewers, alternately thread chicken and potatoes, leaving ¼-inch space between pieces. Add a lemon wedge to the end of each skewer. In a small bowl combine olive oil, oregano, and garlic; brush kabobs with oil mixture.

3 For a charcoal grill, grill kabobs on the rack of an uncovered grill directly over medium coals for 12 to 15 minutes or until chicken is no longer pink, turning kabobs once and brushing once with remaining oil mixture halfway through grilling. (For a gas grill, preheat grill. Reduce heat to medium. Place kabobs on grill rack over heat. Cover and grill as above.) Discard any remaining oil mixture.

4 To serve, remove chicken and potatoes from skewers; squeeze lemon over chicken and potatoes.

NUTRITION FACTS PER SERVING: 293 cal., 13 g total fat (2 g sat. fat), 45 mg chol., 49 mg sodium, 26 g carbo., 1 g fiber, 19 g pro.

Zesty Curried-Lime Chicken Kabobs

To easily snip cilantro or other fresh herbs,
place the herb in a small bowl and use kitchen shears to snip it.

PREP: 20 MINUTES **MARINATE:** 4 TO 24 HOURS **GRILL:** 15 MINUTES **MAKES:** 4 SERVINGS

1 pound skinless, boneless chicken breast halves, cut into 1½-inch pieces

½ cup plain yogurt

¼ cup snipped fresh cilantro

1 teaspoon finely shredded lime peel

2 tablespoons lime juice

2 tablespoons olive oil or cooking oil

1 tablespoon honey

1 tablespoon Dijon-style mustard

1 teaspoon bottled minced garlic (2 cloves)

½ teaspoon curry powder

¼ teaspoon salt

¼ teaspoon ground black pepper

2 medium green and/or red sweet peppers, cut into 1-inch pieces

1 medium zucchini, cut into ½-inch-thick slices

8 cherry tomatoes

1 Place chicken in a resealable plastic bag set in a shallow dish. For marinade, in a small bowl stir together yogurt, cilantro, lime peel, lime juice, oil, honey, Dijon-style mustard, garlic, curry powder, salt, and black pepper. Pour marinade over chicken. Seal bag; turn to coat chicken. Marinate in the refrigerator for at least 4 hours or up to 24 hours, turning bag occasionally.

2 Drain chicken, reserving marinade. On 8 long metal skewers, alternately thread chicken pieces, sweet pepper pieces, and zucchini slices, leaving ¼-inch space between pieces. Brush vegetables with reserved marinade. Discard any remaining marinade.

3 For a charcoal grill, arrange medium-hot coals around a drip pan. Test for medium heat above the pan. Place kabobs on grill rack over drip pan. Cover and grill for 15 to 18 minutes or until chicken is no longer pink. Place a cherry tomato on the end of each skewer for the last 1 minute of grilling. (For a gas grill, preheat grill. Reduce heat to medium. Adjust for indirect cooking. Grill as above.)

NUTRITION FACTS PER SERVING: 261 cal., 9 g total fat (2 g sat. fat), 68 mg chol., 256 mg sodium, 15 g carbo., 2 g fiber, 30 g pro.

Margarita Fajitas with Sub-Lime Salsa

To boost the heat in the salsa, stir in some of the adobo sauce from the chipotles or add more jalapeños.

PREP: 20 MINUTES **MARINATE: 1 HOUR** **GRILL: 12 MINUTES** **MAKES: 4 SERVINGS**

- **1** 15-ounce can black beans, rinsed and drained
- **1** 8-ounce can pineapple tidbits (juice pack), drained
- **¼** cup finely chopped red onion
- **2** fresh jalapeño chile peppers, seeded and finely chopped*
- **2** tablespoons snipped fresh cilantro
- **1** canned chipotle chile pepper in adobo sauce, drained and finely chopped*
- **4** teaspoons lime juice
- **¼** teaspoon salt
- **1¼** pounds skinless, boneless chicken breast halves
- **¼** cup tequila
- **¼** cup lime juice
- **1** tablespoon cooking oil
- **¼** teaspoon salt
- **¼** teaspoon ground black pepper
- **8** 6- to 7-inch flour tortillas

1 For salsa, in a medium bowl stir together beans, pineapple, onion, jalapeño peppers, cilantro, chipotle pepper, the 4 teaspoons lime juice, and ¼ teaspoon salt. Cover and chill in the refrigerator while chicken marinates.

2 Place the chicken in a resealable plastic bag set in a shallow dish. For marinade, in a small bowl stir together tequila, the ¼ cup lime juice, the oil, ¼ teaspoon salt, and the ground black pepper. Pour marinade over chicken. Seal bag; turn to coat chicken. Marinate in the refrigerator for 1 hour; turning bag occasionally. Meanwhile, wrap tortillas in heavy foil; set aside.

3 Drain chicken, discarding marinade. For a charcoal grill, grill chicken on the rack of an uncovered grill directly over medium coals for 12 to 15 minutes or until chicken is no longer pink (170°F), turning once halfway through grilling. During the last 5 minutes of grilling, place foil-wrapped tortillas alongside chicken on the grill rack; heat through, turning once. (For a gas grill, preheat grill. Reduce heat to medium. Place chicken, then tortillas on grill rack over heat. Cover and grill as above.) Remove chicken to a cutting board.

4 Cut chicken into ½-inch-thick slices. Divide chicken among tortillas and top with salsa. Roll up.

NUTRITION FACTS PER SERVING: 489 cal., 7 g total fat (2 g sat. fat), 82 mg chol., 835 mg sodium, 61 g carbo., 8 g fiber, 46 g pro.

*NOTE: Because chile peppers contain volatile oils that can burn your skin and eyes, avoid direct contact with them as much as possible. When working with chile peppers, wear plastic or rubber gloves. If your bare hands do touch the chile peppers, wash your hands and nails well with soap and warm water.

Chicken and Citrus Salad

This Florida-style chicken salad is freshened up with the citrus that made the Sunshine State famous. Serve it with warm corn bread and iced fruit tea.

PREP: 15 MINUTES GRILL: 15 MINUTES MAKES: 4 SERVINGS

- 2/3 cup bottled fat-free honey Dijon salad dressing
- 1½ teaspoons finely shredded lime peel
- 1 tablespoon lime juice
- 1 pound skinless, boneless chicken breast halves
- Salt
- Ground black pepper
- Nonstick cooking spray
- 1 medium grapefruit, peeled and cut into ½-inch-thick slices
- 2 medium oranges, peeled and cut into ½-inch-thick slices
- 6 cups torn romaine or mixed salad greens

1. For dressing, in a small bowl combine Dijon salad dressing, lime peel, and lime juice. Set aside 2 tablespoons of the dressing to brush on chicken. Cover and refrigerate the remaining dressing until ready to serve.

2. Sprinkle chicken lightly with salt and pepper. Brush both sides of chicken with the reserved 2 tablespoons dressing. Discard remainder of the dressing used as a brush-on.

3. For a charcoal grill, arrange medium-hot coals around a drip pan. Test for medium heat above the pan. Place chicken on grill rack over drip pan. Cover and grill for 15 to 18 minutes or until chicken is no longer pink (170°F). (For a gas grill, preheat grill. Reduce heat to medium. Adjust for indirect cooking. Grill as above.)

4. While the chicken is grilling, lightly coat a grill tray with cooking spray. Place grapefruit and oranges on grill tray; add to grill. Cover and grill about 4 minutes or until grapefruit and oranges are heated through, turning once halfway through grilling.

5. Transfer chicken and fruit to cutting board. Cut chicken diagonally into thin slices. Coarsely chop grapefruit and quarter orange slices. Divide romaine or salad greens among 4 dinner plates. Arrange warm chicken and fruit on top of romaine. Drizzle with remaining dressing.

NUTRITION FACTS PER SERVING: 229 cal., 2 g total fat (0 g sat. fat), 66 mg chol., 519 mg sodium, 24 g carbo., 4 g fiber, 29 g pro.

Chutney Chicken Salad

The warm curried chicken on cool, crisp greens provides a delicious contrast of flavors, texture, and temperature.

PREP: 30 MINUTES CHILL: 30 MINUTES GRILL: 12 MINUTES MAKES: 4 SERVINGS

1	**small onion**
4	**teaspoons lime juice or lemon juice**
2	**teaspoons curry powder**
¼	**teaspoon garlic salt**
1¼	**pounds skinless, boneless chicken breast halves**
6	**cups torn mixed salad greens**
1	**medium cucumber, seeded and chopped**
1	**medium carrot, cut into thin bite-size strips**
1	**medium tomato, cut into thin wedges**
½	**of a medium red sweet pepper, chopped**
½	**cup chopped, peeled jicama***
1	**recipe Chutney Dressing**

1 In a blender container combine onion, lime juice, curry powder, and garlic salt. Cover and blend until the consistency of paste.

2 Rub onion mixture on both sides of chicken. Cover; chill for 30 minutes.

3 For salad, in a large bowl toss together greens, cucumber, carrot, tomato, sweet pepper, and jicama. Divide among 4 serving plates.

4 For a charcoal grill, grill chicken on the greased rack of an uncovered grill directly over medium coals for 12 to 15 minutes or until chicken is no longer pink (170°F), turning once halfway through grilling. (For a gas grill, preheat grill. Reduce heat to medium. Place chicken on grill rack over heat. Cover and grill as above.)

5 To serve, slice chicken breasts and arrange sliced chicken on top of greens. Drizzle Chutney Dressing over chicken-and-greens mixture.

Chutney Dressing: In a food processor bowl or blender container combine ¼ cup rice vinegar or white wine vinegar; 3 tablespoons chutney; 1 tablespoon Dijon-style mustard; 2 teaspoons sugar; 1 teaspoon finely shredded lime peel or lemon peel; 1 clove garlic, quartered; and ⅛ teaspoon ground black pepper. Cover and process or blend until nearly smooth. Gradually add 2 tablespoons olive oil to mixture in food processor or blender, processing or blending until combined.

NUTRITION FACTS PER SERVING: 336 cal., 10 g total fat (2 g sat. fat), 82 mg chol., 255 mg sodium, 25 g carbo., 4 g fiber, 36 g pro.

***NOTE:** If you can't find jicama, use more carrot and sweet pepper.

Grilled Chicken Salad

Steak seasoning adds just the right touch of spiciness to the chicken.

PREP: 20 MINUTES STAND: 1 HOUR GRILL: 12 MINUTES MAKES: 4 SERVINGS

¼ **cup olive oil**

3 **tablespoons balsamic vinegar**

1 **tablespoon dried dillweed**

½ **teaspoon bottled minced garlic (1 clove)**

¼ **teaspoon freshly ground black pepper**

¼ **teaspoon dried oregano, crushed**

1 **pound skinless, boneless chicken breast halves**

Montreal steak seasoning or Kansas City steak seasoning

8 **cups mesclun or spring salad greens or fresh spinach**

¾ **cup seedless red grapes, halved**

⅓ **cup crumbled goat cheese**

¼ **cup pine nuts, toasted**

1 For dressing, in a screw-top jar combine oil, balsamic vinegar, dillweed, garlic, pepper, and oregano. Cover and shake well; let stand for 1 hour.

2 Meanwhile, sprinkle chicken breast halves lightly with steak seasoning. For a charcoal grill, grill chicken on the rack of an uncovered grill directly over medium coals for 12 to 15 minutes or until chicken is no longer pink (170°F), turning once halfway through grilling. (For a gas grill, preheat grill. Reduce heat to medium. Place chicken on grill rack over heat. Cover and grill as above.) Cool slightly.

3 Divide mesclun or salad greens among 4 dinner plates; top with grapes, goat cheese, and pine nuts. Slice chicken breast halves and arrange sliced chicken on top of salads. Shake dressing and drizzle over the salads.

NUTRITION FACTS PER SERVING: 400 cal., 23 g total fat (4 g sat. fat), 86 mg chol., 167 mg sodium, 12 g carbo., 2 g fiber, 38 g pro.

Southwest Chicken Salad

Grilling lends sweet oranges a pleasing smoky flavor
in this refreshingly different chicken salad.

PREP: 15 MINUTES GRILL: 12 MINUTES MAKES: 4 SERVINGS

½ cup bottled poppy seed salad dressing

1 small fresh jalapeño chile pepper, seeded and finely chopped*

½ teaspoon finely shredded orange peel

1 pound skinless, boneless chicken breast halves

2 oranges, peeled and cut into ½-inch-thick slices

1 red sweet pepper, seeded and quartered

8 cups torn mixed salad greens

1 small jicama, peeled and sliced into thin bite-size strips

Ground black pepper

1 In a small bowl combine salad dressing, jalapeño pepper, and orange peel. Remove 1 tablespoon of the dressing mixture to use as a brush-on. Set aside remaining mixture to use as dressing. Brush the chicken, orange slices, and sweet pepper with the 1 tablespoon dressing mixture.

2 For a charcoal grill, grill chicken, orange slices, and sweet pepper on the rack of an uncovered grill directly over medium coals for 12 to 15 minutes or until chicken is no longer pink (170°F), turning once halfway through grilling. (For a gas grill, preheat grill. Reduce heat to medium. Place chicken, orange slices, and sweet pepper on grill rack over heat. Cover and grill as above.) Transfer the chicken, orange slices, and sweet pepper to a cutting board; cool slightly. Cut chicken and sweet pepper into bite-size strips; quarter the orange slices.

3 Meanwhile, in a large salad bowl toss together the greens and jicama. Add the chicken, oranges, and sweet pepper to the salad bowl; drizzle with the reserved dressing mixture. Season to taste with black pepper.

NUTRITION FACTS PER SERVING: 339 cal., 18 g total fat (3 g sat. fat), 59 mg chol., 194 mg sodium, 22 g carbo., 3 g fiber, 24 g pro.

*NOTE: Because chile peppers contain volatile oils that can burn your skin and eyes, avoid direct contact with them as much as possible. When working with chile peppers, wear plastic or rubber gloves. If your bare hands do touch the chile peppers, wash your hands and nails well with soap and warm water.

Chicken and Pasta Salad

*Green grapes, dried cranberries, and mandarin oranges
perk up this hearty main-dish salad.*

PREP: 20 MINUTES **GRILL:** 12 MINUTES **CHILL:** 4 TO 24 HOURS **MAKES:** 6 SERVINGS

12	ounces skinless, boneless chicken breast halves
8	ounces dried pasta
4	cups torn fresh spinach
1	14-ounce can artichoke hearts, drained and quartered
½	cup seedless green grapes, halved
½	cup dried cranberries
¼	cup sliced green onions
½	cup mayonnaise or salad dressing
3	tablespoons seasoned rice vinegar
¼	teaspoon salt
¼	teaspoon ground black pepper
1	11-ounce can mandarin oranges, drained

1 For a charcoal grill, grill chicken on the rack of an uncovered grill directly over medium coals for 12 to 15 minutes or until chicken is no longer pink (170°F). (For a gas grill, preheat grill. Reduce heat to medium. Place chicken on grill rack over heat. Cover and grill as above.) Cool chicken slightly; coarsely chop. Set aside.

2 Meanwhile, cook pasta according to package directions. Drain pasta. Rinse with cold water; drain again.

3 In a large bowl, combine chicken, pasta, spinach, artichoke hearts, grapes, cranberries, and green onions. In a small bowl combine mayonnaise, rice vinegar, salt, and pepper. Pour over pasta mixture; toss. Cover; chill at least 4 hours or up to 24 hours.

4 To serve, stir in mandarin oranges.

NUTRITION FACTS PER SERVING: 434 cal., 17 g total fat (3 g sat. fat), 40 mg chol., 303 mg sodium, 54 g carbo., 6 g fiber, 19 g pro.

Chicken and Kiwi Tacos

Use purchased taco shells or make your own. To make taco shells, heat ½ inch of cooking oil in a large, heavy skillet. Cook six 5-inch tortillas, one at a time, in hot oil just until golden. Fold over a paper towel-lined rolling pin; cool.

PREP: 25 MINUTES GRILL: 12 MINUTES MAKES: 6 TACOS

½ teaspoon ground cumin

¼ teaspoon salt

⅛ to ¼ teaspoon crushed red pepper

8 ounces skinless, boneless chicken breast halves

1 teaspoon cooking oil

6 taco shells

1 cup shredded romaine

½ cup shredded Monterey Jack cheese or Monterey Jack cheese with jalapeño peppers (2 ounces)

3 kiwifruit, peeled and chopped

1 small tomato, chopped

1 tablespoon lime juice or lemon juice

1 For rub, in a small bowl combine cumin, salt, and crushed red pepper. Brush chicken breasts with oil. Sprinkle rub evenly over brushed chicken breasts; rub in with your fingers. Place each breast half between 2 pieces of plastic wrap. Using the flat side of a meat mallet, lightly pound chicken into a rectangle about ½ inch thick.

2 For a charcoal grill, grill chicken on the rack of an uncovered grill directly over medium coals for 12 to 15 minutes or until chicken is no longer pink (170°F), turning once halfway through grilling. (For a gas grill, preheat grill. Reduce heat to medium. Place chicken on grill rack over heat. Cover and grill as above.) Remove chicken; set aside until cool enough to handle. Meanwhile, if using purchased taco shells, heat shells according to the package directions.

3 Cut chicken into thin strips and arrange in taco shells. Top with romaine and cheese. In a small bowl toss together chopped kiwifruit, tomato, and lime juice. Sprinkle over tacos.

NUTRITION FACTS PER SERVING: 170 cal., 7 g total fat (3 g sat. fat), 30 mg chol., 219 mg sodium, 13 g carbo., 2 g fiber, 13 g pro.

Chicken Mole Sandwich

A little chocolate is traditional to round out the flavor in mole, a delicious Mexican sauce.

PREP: 30 MINUTES **GRILL:** 12 MINUTES **CHILL:** 30 MINUTES TO 24 HOURS **MAKES:** 4 SERVINGS

3	dried New Mexico peppers or dried pasilla peppers
¼	cup chopped onion
1½	teaspoons bottled minced garlic (3 cloves)
1	tablespoon cooking oil
½	cup water
1½	ounces Mexican-style sweet chocolate or semisweet chocolate, chopped (about 3 tablespoons)
1	pound skinless, boneless chicken breast halves
	Salt (optional)
1	small avocado, pitted, peeled, and mashed
2	tablespoons light mayonnaise dressing or salad dressing
¼	teaspoon cayenne pepper (optional)
⅛	teaspoon salt
2	bolitos, bollilos, or other Mexican rolls or hard rolls (approximately 6 inches in diameter), split
	Baby romaine or other green lettuce leaves
	Tomato slices
½	of a medium papaya, peeled, seeded, and sliced

1 For mole, remove stems and seeds from dried peppers; coarsely chop peppers and set aside.* In a large skillet cook onion and garlic in hot oil over medium-high heat for 4 to 5 minutes or just until onion is browned. Add the dried peppers and the water; reduce heat. Stir in chocolate. Cook and stir over medium heat for 3 to 5 minutes or until thickened and bubbly. Cool slightly. Transfer mixture to a food processor bowl or blender container; cover and process or blend until a smooth paste forms. Set mixture aside to cool. Transfer 1 to 2 tablespoons of the mole to a small bowl.

2 If desired, sprinkle chicken with salt. Using a sharp knife, carefully butterfly-cut each breast by cutting a slit horizontally two-thirds of the way through; spread open. Spread inside face of each breast with mole from food processor bowl or blender container. Fold closed.

3 Rub the outside of each chicken breast with the reserved 1 to 2 tablespoons mole. For a charcoal grill, grill chicken on the rack of an uncovered grill directly over medium coals for 12 to 15 minutes or until chicken is no longer pink (170°F), turning once halfway through grilling. (For a gas grill, preheat grill. Reduce heat to medium. Place chicken on grill rack over heat. Cover and grill as above.) Remove chicken from grill. Cover and chill in the refrigerator for at least 30 minutes or up to 24 hours.

4 In a small bowl stir together avocado, light mayonnaise dressing, the cayenne pepper (if desired), and the ⅛ teaspoon salt. Cut chicken into ¼- to ½-inch-thick slices. Spread avocado mixture on split rolls. Layer each roll half with chicken slices, romaine leaves, and tomato slices. Top with sliced papaya.

NUTRITION FACTS PER SERVING: 524 cal., 24 g total fat (6 g sat. fat), 59 mg chol., 448 mg sodium, 52 g carbo., 7 g fiber, 28 g pro.

*NOTE: Because chile peppers contain volatile oils that can burn your skin and eyes, avoid direct contact with them as much as possible. When working with chile peppers, wear plastic or rubber gloves. If your bare hands do touch the chile peppers, wash your hands and nails well with soap and warm water.

Pesto Chicken Fettuccine

*Toss the grilled chicken with Homemade Pesto
and serve it over fettuccine with a creamy sauce. It's wonderful!*

PREP: 20 MINUTES GRILL: 12 MINUTES MAKES: 6 SERVINGS

12 ounces dried fettuccine

1 pound skinless, boneless chicken breast halves

1 cup whipping cream

⅓ cup butter

¾ cup grated Parmesan cheese

¼ cup Homemade Pesto or purchased pesto

Dash ground black pepper

1 Cook fettuccine according to package directions. Drain the pasta. Return to hot pan and keep warm.

2 For a charcoal grill, grill chicken on the rack of an uncovered grill directly over medium coals for 12 to 15 minutes or until chicken is no longer pink (170°F), turning once halfway through grilling. (For a gas grill, preheat grill. Reduce heat to medium. Place chicken on grill rack over heat. Cover and grill as above.)

3 Meanwhile, in a small saucepan heat whipping cream and butter until the butter melts. Gradually stir in Parmesan cheese and stir until combined. Cover and keep warm over low heat.

4 Cut chicken into bite-size pieces. In a medium bowl toss chicken with 1 tablespoon of Homemade Pesto.

5 Add the remaining 3 tablespoons Homemade Pesto and the warm Parmesan sauce to the hot, cooked fettuccine. Toss to coat. Arrange the fettuccine on a platter; season with pepper. Top with grilled chicken.

NUTRITION FACTS PER SERVING: 619 cal., 35 g total fat (20 g sat. fat), 140 mg chol., 410 mg sodium, 44 g carbo., 2 g fiber, 31 g pro.

Homemade Pesto: Spread ¼ cup pine nuts in a shallow baking pan. Toast in a 350°F oven for 5 to 10 minutes or until nuts are light golden brown. In a food processor bowl or blender container combine toasted pine nuts, 1 teaspoon bottled minced garlic (2 cloves), 1 cup lightly packed fresh spinach, 1 cup lightly packed fresh basil, ½ cup lightly packed fresh parsley, and dash salt. Cover; process or blend until finely chopped.

Add ¾ cup grated Parmesan cheese, ¼ cup olive oil, and 3 tablespoons softened butter. Process or blend until a paste forms. Divide into ¼-cup portions. Use the pesto immediately or place each portion in a small, airtight container or plastic freezer bag and refrigerate for 1 to 2 days or freeze for up to 3 months. Makes about 1¼ cups.

NUTRITION FACTS PER 1 TABLESPOON: 66 cal., 6 g total fat (2 g sat. fat), 7 mg chol., 84 mg sodium, 1 g carbo., 0 g fiber, 2 g pro.

Provençal Grilled Chicken and Herbed Penne

Fresh herbs, olive oil, and grilled fresh vegetables make this pasta recipe seem like it's straight from the South of France.

PREP: 25 MINUTES **GRILL:** 12 MINUTES **MAKES:** 4 SERVINGS

8 ounces dried tomato or garlic-and-herb-flavored penne pasta or plain penne pasta

1 pound skinless, boneless chicken breast halves

1 medium zucchini, halved lengthwise

8 thick fresh asparagus spears (8 to 10 ounces total), trimmed

3 tablespoons olive oil

½ teaspoon salt

1 tablespoon snipped fresh thyme

1 tablespoon snipped fresh chives

½ cup finely shredded Asiago cheese (2 ounces) (optional)

Ground black pepper (optional)

1 Cook pasta according to package directions; drain. Return pasta to hot pan and keep warm.

2 Meanwhile, brush chicken, zucchini, and asparagus with 1 tablespoon of the oil. Sprinkle all sides of chicken and vegetables with salt.

3 For a charcoal grill, place asparagus on a small piece of foil; place on grill rack of an uncovered grill directly over medium coals. Add chicken and zucchini to grill rack; grill for 12 to 15 minutes or until chicken is no longer pink (170°F) and vegetables are tender, turning once halfway through grilling. (For a gas grill, preheat grill. Reduce heat to medium. Place chicken, zucchini, and asparagus [on foil] on grill rack over heat. Cover and grill as above.)

4 Transfer chicken and vegetables to cutting board; cool slightly. Cut chicken and zucchini into 1-inch cubes; slice asparagus into 1-inch pieces. Add chicken, vegetables, the remaining 2 tablespoons oil, the thyme, and chives to pasta; toss to coat.

5 To serve, divide among 4 dinner plates. If desired, top with cheese and sprinkle with pepper.

NUTRITION FACTS PER SERVING: 441 cal., 13 g total fat (2 g sat. fat), 66 mg chol., 360 mg sodium, 44 g carbo., 3 g dietary fiber, 35 g pro.

Asian Chicken with Noodles

Cold udon noodles flavored with sesame-ginger dressing and tossed with crisp cabbage, warm chicken, and eggplant allow you to keep your cool with this quick-to-fix dish.

PREP: 20 MINUTES GRILL: 12 MINUTES COOL: 5 MINUTES MAKES: 4 SERVINGS

8	ounces dried udon or Chinese curly noodles
¼	cup light soy sauce
2	tablespoons toasted sesame oil
2	tablespoons rice vinegar
2	teaspoons bottled minced garlic (4 cloves)
1½	teaspoons grated fresh ginger
¼	teaspoon crushed red pepper
1	pound skinless, boneless chicken breast halves
1	small eggplant, sliced
4	cups packaged shredded cabbage with carrot (coleslaw mix)
¼	cup chopped cashews (optional)
2	to 3 tablespoons snipped fresh cilantro

1 Cook noodles according to package directions. Meanwhile, combine soy sauce, sesame oil, vinegar, garlic, ginger, and crushed red pepper. Set aside 2 tablespoons of the soy sauce mixture. Drain noodles. In a large bowl toss noodles with the remaining soy sauce mixture. Place noodle mixture in freezer to quick chill.

2 For a charcoal grill, grill chicken on the rack of an uncovered grill directly over medium coals for 12 to 15 minutes or until chicken is no longer pink (170°F), turning once halfway through grilling and brushing with some of the reserved soy sauce mixture during the last 2 minutes of grilling. (For a gas grill, preheat grill. Reduce heat to medium. Place chicken on grill rack over heat. Cover and grill as above.) For the last 8 minutes of grilling, place eggplant slices on the rack alongside the chicken; turn once and brush occasionally with reserved soy sauce mixture. Transfer chicken and eggplant to cutting board; cool for 5 minutes and cut into cubes.

3 Toss chicken, eggplant, and cabbage with noodles. Sprinkle with cashews (if desired) and cilantro.

NUTRITION FACTS PER SERVING: 442 cal., 12 g total fat (2 g sat. fat), 108 mg chol., 646 mg sodium, 51 g carbo., 6 g fiber, 32 g pro.

Curried Chicken and Potato Packets

*You'll curry favor from your family with the Indian flavors
of chicken and vegetables cooked in a velvety sour cream sauce.
Individual serving packets give this dish flair and precooked chicken strips make it fast.*

PREP: 10 MINUTES **GRILL:** 25 MINUTES **MAKES:** 4 SERVINGS

1 9-ounce package frozen cooked chicken breast strips

4 medium potatoes, cut into ¾-inch cubes

1½ cups packaged peeled baby carrots

1 small onion, thinly sliced

½ cup dairy sour cream or plain low-fat yogurt

1 teaspoon curry powder

1 teaspoon Dijon-style mustard

½ teaspoon salt

½ teaspoon paprika

⅛ teaspoon crushed red pepper

1 Tear off four 24×18-inch pieces of heavy foil. Fold each piece in half to make a double thickness of foil that measures 12×18 inches; set aside.

2 In a large bowl combine frozen chicken, potatoes, carrots, and onion; set aside. In a small bowl combine sour cream, curry powder, mustard, salt, paprika, and crushed red pepper. Pour over chicken mixture; toss gently.

3 Divide mixture among the foil pieces. Bring up opposite long edges of foil and seal with a double fold. Fold ends to completely enclose chicken mixture, leaving space for steam to build.

4 For a charcoal grill, grill chicken mixture on the rack of an uncovered grill directly over medium coals about 25 minutes or until vegetables are tender, turning once halfway through grilling. (For a gas grill, preheat grill. Reduce heat to medium. Place chicken mixture on grill rack over heat. Cover and grill as above.)

NUTRITION FACTS PER SERVING: 371 cal., 11 g total fat (5 g sat. fat), 70 mg chol., 414 mg sodium, 44 g carbo., 3 g fiber, 24 g pro.

Grilled Turkey Piccata

A dish done piccata-style always includes lemon, parsley, and capers in it. Another time, try making this Italian specialty with boneless chicken breasts in place of the turkey tenderloin pieces.

PREP: 15 MINUTES GRILL: 15 MINUTES MAKES: 4 SERVINGS

1¼ to 1½ pounds turkey breast tenderloins

2 lemons

4 teaspoons olive oil

2 teaspoons snipped fresh rosemary
or ½ teaspoon dried rosemary, crushed

¼ teaspoon salt

¼ teaspoon freshly ground black pepper

1 tablespoon drained capers

1 tablespoon snipped fresh flat-leaf parsley

① Split each turkey breast tenderloin in half horizontally. Finely shred enough peel from 1 of the lemons to make 1 teaspoon; set aside. Halve and squeeze the juice from that lemon (should have about 3 tablespoons); set aside. Cut the other lemon into very thin slices; set aside.

② For rub, in a small bowl combine the shredded lemon peel, 2 teaspoons of the olive oil, the rosemary, salt, and pepper. Sprinkle the mixture evenly over both sides of each turkey piece; rub in with your fingers.

③ For a charcoal grill, arrange medium-hot coals around a drip pan. Test for medium heat above the pan. Place turkey on grill rack over drip pan. Cover and grill for 8 minutes. Turn turkey. Arrange lemon slices on top of turkey, overlapping if necessary. Cover and grill for 7 to 10 minutes more or until turkey is no longer pink (170°F). (For a gas grill, preheat grill. Reduce heat to medium. Adjust for indirect cooking. Grill as above.)

④ Meanwhile, in a small saucepan combine the remaining 2 teaspoons olive oil, the lemon juice, and the capers. Heat through.

⑤ Remove turkey to a serving platter. Drizzle with the warm caper mixture. Sprinkle with parsley.

NUTRITION FACTS PER SERVING: 159 cal., 5 g total fat (1 g sat. fat), 71 mg chol., 269 mg sodium, 1 g carbo., 0 g fiber, 26 g pro.

Stuffed Turkey Tenderloins

Turkey tenderloins stuffed with spinach and goat cheese make a delicious headliner for a party.

PREP: 15 MINUTES GRILL: 16 MINUTES MAKES: 4 SERVINGS

- **2** 8-ounce turkey breast tenderloins
- **2** cups chopped fresh spinach leaves
- **3** ounces semisoft goat cheese (chèvre) or feta cheese, crumbled (about ¾ cup)
- **½** teaspoon ground black pepper
- **1** tablespoon olive oil
- **1** teaspoon paprika
- **½** teaspoon salt
- **⅛** to ¼ teaspoon cayenne pepper

1 Make a pocket in each turkey breast tenderloin by cutting horizontally from one side almost to, but not through, the opposite side; set aside. In a medium bowl combine spinach, goat cheese, and black pepper. Spoon spinach mixture into pockets. Tie 100%-cotton kitchen string around each tenderloin in 3 or 4 places to hold in stuffing. In a small bowl combine oil, paprika, salt, and cayenne pepper; brush evenly over tenderloins.

2 For a charcoal grill, grill turkey on the rack of an uncovered grill directly over medium coals for 16 to 20 minutes or until turkey is no longer pink (170°F), turning once halfway through grilling. (For a gas grill, preheat grill. Reduce heat to medium. Place turkey on grill rack over heat. Cover and grill as above.) Remove and discard strings; slice tenderloins crosswise.

NUTRITION FACTS PER SERVING: 220 cal., 12 g total fat (4 g sat. fat), 68 mg chol., 458 mg sodium, 1 g carbo., 1 g fiber, 26 g pro.

Thai Curried Turkey with Scallion Slaw

The spicy curry and tangy scallions are tempered by the cool and sweet coconut. Purchase the green curry paste and coconut milk from an Asian specialty store.

PREP: 15 MINUTES GRILL: 12 MINUTES MAKES: 4 SERVINGS

6	scallions or green onions
2	cups finely shredded savoy cabbage, napa cabbage, bok choy, or gai choy
3	tablespoons dry-roasted cashew halves
¼	cup rice vinegar
½	teaspoon sugar
1	pound turkey breast tenderloins
2	to 3 tablespoons Thai green curry paste
¼	cup dry white wine
½	cup purchased unsweetened coconut milk

1 Using a sharp knife, cut scallions or green onions lengthwise into thin slivers. In a medium bowl toss together scallion or green onion slivers; cabbage, bok choy, or gai choy; and cashews. In a small bowl stir together vinegar and sugar until sugar dissolves. Set aside.

2 Cut turkey breast tenderloins crosswise into 1-inch-thick slices; place each slice between 2 sheets of plastic wrap. Using the flat side of a meat mallet, lightly pound turkey to ½-inch thickness. Spread turkey lightly with half of the green curry paste.

3 For a charcoal grill, grill turkey on the rack of an uncovered grill directly over medium coals for 12 to 15 minutes or until turkey is no longer pink (170°F), turning once halfway through grilling. (For a gas grill, preheat grill. Reduce heat to medium. Place turkey on grill rack over heat. Cover and grill as above.) Set aside; keep warm.

4 For sauce, in a small skillet stir together the remaining green curry paste and the wine. Cook, uncovered, over medium-high heat for 1 to 2 minutes or until liquid is almost evaporated, stirring often. Carefully add coconut milk. Bring to boiling; reduce heat. Cook, uncovered, for 1 to 2 minutes or until thickened to a sauce.

5 To serve, toss scallion mixture with vinegar mixture; divide among 4 dinner plates. Arrange warm turkey on plates and drizzle with sauce.

NUTRITION FACTS PER SERVING: 297 cal., 14 g total fat (6 g sat. fat), 68 mg chol., 637 mg sodium, 10 g carbo., 2 g fiber, 29 g pro.

Peppered Turkey Steaks

These spicy turkey steaks have a kick reminiscent of Buffalo wings.

PREP: 15 MINUTES **MARINATE:** 4 TO 6 HOURS **GRILL:** 15 MINUTES **MAKES:** 5 TO 7 SERVINGS

1½ pounds turkey breast tenderloins
1 cup bottled Italian salad dressing
½ cup finely chopped onion
⅓ cup lemon juice
2 teaspoons bottled minced garlic (4 cloves)
1½ to 2 teaspoons cayenne pepper
1 teaspoon taco seasoning
1 teaspoon Cajun seasoning
⅛ to ¼ teaspoon ground black pepper

❶ Split each turkey breast tenderloin in half horizontally. Place turkey pieces in a resealable plastic bag set in a shallow dish. For marinade, in a medium bowl combine Italian salad dressing, onion, lemon juice, garlic, cayenne pepper, taco seasoning, Cajun seasoning, and black pepper. Pour marinade over turkey. Seal bag; turn to coat turkey. Marinate in refrigerator for at least 4 hours or up to 6 hours, turning bag occasionally.

❷ Drain turkey, discarding marinade. For a charcoal grill, arrange medium-hot coals around a drip pan. Test for medium heat above the pan. Place turkey on grill rack over drip pan. Cover and grill for 15 to 18 minutes or until turkey is no longer pink (170°F). (For a gas grill, preheat grill. Reduce heat to medium. Adjust for indirect cooking. Grill as above.)

NUTRITION FACTS PER SERVING: 234 cal., 10 g total fat (2 g sat. fat), 81 mg chol., 209 mg sodium, 3 g carbo., 0 g fiber, 32 g pro.

Turkey Steaks and Vegetables

Vegetable juice—with a few added ingredients—doubles as a basting sauce for turkey steaks. Serve these savory grilled turkey steaks and grilled vegetables with chewy Italian bread and a glass of Chianti.

PREP: 10 MINUTES GRILL: 12 MINUTES MAKES: 4 SERVINGS

1 pound turkey breast tenderloins

¼ cup vegetable juice

3 tablespoons mayonnaise or salad dressing

1 tablespoon snipped fresh chives or green onion tops

2 teaspoons snipped fresh thyme or ½ teaspoon dried thyme, crushed

½ teaspoon bottled minced garlic (1 clove)

Salt

Ground black pepper

2 small zucchini, halved lengthwise

2 large plum tomatoes, halved lengthwise

1 Split each turkey breast tenderloin in half horizontally. For sauce, in a small bowl gradually stir vegetable juice into mayonnaise; stir in chives or green onion tops, thyme, and garlic. Set aside.

2 Sprinkle turkey with salt and pepper. For a charcoal grill, grill turkey and halved zucchini and tomatoes, cut sides down, on the rack of an uncovered grill directly over medium coals for 12 to 15 minutes or until turkey is no longer pink (170°F), zucchini is tender, and tomatoes are heated through,* turning once halfway through grilling and brushing with some of the sauce during the last 3 minutes of grilling. (For a gas grill, preheat grill. Reduce heat to medium. Place turkey, zucchini, and tomatoes on grill rack over heat. Cover and grill as above.)

3 Serve with any remaining sauce.

NUTRITION FACTS PER SERVING: 209 cal., 11 g total fat (2 g sat. fat), 56 mg chol., 200 mg sodium, 6 g carbo., 1 g fiber, 22 g pro.

*NOTE: If the zucchini and tomatoes are done before the turkey, remove them from the grill and keep warm.

Chili-Mustard Turkey Breast

Spreading a mustard mixture under the skin gives turkey another flavor dimension.

PREP: 20 MINUTES **GRILL:** 1¼ HOURS **STAND:** 15 MINUTES **MAKES:** 6 TO 8 SERVINGS

3 tablespoons honey mustard

1 tablespoon packed brown sugar

½ teaspoon chili powder

⅛ teaspoon ground cumin

⅛ teaspoon ground black pepper

1 2- to 2½-pound bone-in turkey breast half

1 In a small bowl stir together the mustard, brown sugar, chili powder, cumin, and black pepper.

2 Starting at the edge of the turkey breast, slip your fingers between the skin and meat, loosening the skin to make a pocket. Using your fingers or a spoon, spread mustard mixture evenly over the meat under the skin. Secure with wooden skewers or toothpicks, if necessary. Insert an oven-going meat thermometer into the thickest portion of the turkey breast, making sure bulb does not touch bone.

3 For a charcoal grill, arrange medium-hot coals around a drip pan. Test for medium heat above the pan. Place turkey, bone side down, on grill rack over drip pan. Cover and grill for 1¼ to 2 hours or until meat thermometer registers 170°F. Add coals as necessary to maintain heat. (For a gas grill, preheat grill. Reduce heat to medium. Adjust for indirect cooking. Place turkey on rack in a roasting pan, place on grill rack, and grill as above.)

4 Remove turkey from grill; cover with foil. Let stand for 15 minutes before carving.

NUTRITION FACTS PER SERVING: 217 cal., 9 g total fat (2 g sat. fat), 83 mg chol., 120 mg sodium, 4 g carbo., 0 g fiber, 28 g pro.

Hazelnut-Pesto Turkey Breast

Spread the savory mixture of nuts, spinach, basil, garlic, and Parmesan cheese between the skin and meat of the turkey breast half.

PREP: 25 MINUTES **GRILL:** 1¼ HOURS **STAND:** 15 MINUTES **MAKES:** 6 TO 8 SERVINGS

¼ cup chopped hazelnuts or almonds, toasted

1 egg yolk

1 cup loosely packed fresh spinach leaves

1 cup loosely packed fresh basil leaves

2 tablespoons cooking oil

½ teaspoon bottled minced garlic (1 clove)

¼ cup grated Parmesan or Romano cheese (1 ounce)

1 2½- to 3-pound bone-in turkey breast half

Cooking oil

❶ For pesto, blend nuts in a covered blender container until very finely chopped. Add egg yolk, spinach, basil, the 2 tablespoons oil, and garlic to blender. Cover and blend until nearly smooth. Stir in Parmesan cheese.

❷ Remove bone from turkey. Starting at the edge of the turkey breast, slip your fingers between skin and meat, loosening the skin to make a pocket. Using your fingers or a spoon, spread pesto evenly over the meat under the skin. Secure with wooden skewers or toothpicks. Tuck thinner portion of breast half under thicker portion. Tie with 100%-cotton kitchen string. Insert an oven-going meat thermometer into the thickest portion of the turkey breast.

❸ For a charcoal grill, arrange medium-hot coals around a drip pan. Test for medium heat above the pan. Place turkey, skin side up, on grill rack over drip pan. Brush skin with cooking oil. Cover and grill for 1¼ to 2 hours or until meat thermometer registers 170°F. Add coals as necessary to maintain heat. (For a gas grill, preheat grill. Reduce heat to medium. Adjust for indirect cooking. Place turkey on rack in a roasting pan, place on grill rack, and grill as above.)

❹ Remove turkey from grill; cover with foil. Let stand for 15 minutes before carving.

NUTRITION FACTS PER SERVING: 324 cal., 18 g total fat (4 g sat. fat), 154 mg chol., 127 mg sodium, 2 g carbo., 1 g fiber, 38 g pro.

Mayan Turkey with Peanut Mole

You'll enjoy every bite when you dine on this dark and fiery turkey breast.
The peanut mole sauce seals in the juiciness as a glaze
and adds a wonderful kick as the serving sauce.

PREP: 40 MINUTES **GRILL:** 1½ HOURS **STAND:** 15 MINUTES **MAKES:** 12 SERVINGS

1	cup chopped onion
2	tablespoons olive oil
1	cup chopped seeded tomato
2	tablespoons chili powder
2	teaspoons bottled minced garlic (4 cloves)
½	teaspoon ground cinnamon
1	14-ounce can chicken broth
2	6-inch corn tortillas, torn into small pieces
1	to 3 canned chipotle chile peppers in adobo sauce plus 1 tablespoon of the sauce
½	cup creamy peanut butter
3	tablespoons honey or brown sugar
1	3- to 4-pound boneless whole turkey breast
2	tablespoons olive oil
1½	teaspoons chili powder
1	teaspoon ground cumin
1	teaspoon bottled minced garlic (2 cloves)
½	teaspoon salt

1 For mole, in a large skillet cook the onion in 2 tablespoons hot oil over medium-high heat for 2 minutes. Stir in tomato, the 2 tablespoons chili powder, the 2 teaspoons garlic, and the cinnamon. Cook and stir for 4 minutes more. Add ½ cup of the chicken broth, the tortillas, and the chipotle peppers and adobo sauce. Bring to boiling; reduce heat. Simmer, uncovered, for 4 minutes. Cool mole slightly.

2 Transfer mixture to a blender container or food processor bowl. Cover and blend or process until smooth. Return mixture to skillet; stir in the remaining broth, the peanut butter, and 1 tablespoon of the honey or brown sugar. Simmer, uncovered, about 10 minutes more or until desired consistency. (Mole may be made up to 2 days ahead; store, covered, in the refrigerator.) For basting sauce, transfer ⅓ cup of the mole to a small bowl; stir in the remaining 2 tablespoons honey or brown sugar. Place remaining mole in a small bowl and reserve to pass with turkey. Cover and refrigerate basting sauce and mole.

3 Spread open turkey. For rub, in a small bowl combine 2 tablespoons oil, the 1½ teaspoons chili powder, the cumin, the 1 teaspoon garlic, and the salt. Spoon rub evenly over turkey; rub in with your fingers. Insert an oven-going meat thermometer into thickest part of turkey breast.

4 For a charcoal grill, arrange medium-hot coals around a drip pan. Test for medium heat above the pan. Place turkey breast, skin side up, on grill rack over drip pan. Cover and grill for 1½ to 2 hours or until turkey is no longer pink (170°F), brushing with the basting sauce during the last 10 minutes of grilling. Add coals as necessary to maintain heat. (For a gas grill, preheat grill. Reduce heat to medium. Adjust for indirect cooking. Place turkey on a rack in a roasting pan, place on grill rack, and grill as above.) Discard remainder of the basting sauce.

5 Remove turkey from grill; cover with foil. Let stand for 15 minutes. To serve, slice turkey. Reheat reserved mole until bubbly; pass with turkey.

NUTRITION FACTS PER SERVING: 264 cal., 13 g total fat (2 g sat. fat), 50 mg chol., 333 mg sodium, 12 g carbo., 2 g fiber, 26 g pro.

Cranberry Margarita Turkey Legs

Look for chipotle chile peppers in adobo sauce in the
Mexican food section of your supermarket or at a Mexican market.

PREP: 20 MINUTES **MARINATE:** 2 TO 24 HOURS **GRILL:** 45 MINUTES **MAKES:** 6 SERVINGS

6	turkey drumsticks (about 3 pounds total)
¼	cup cranberry juice
¼	cup tequila
1	tablespoon finely shredded lime peel
¼	cup lime juice
1	teaspoon bottled minced garlic (2 cloves)
1	teaspoon salt
¼	teaspoon cayenne pepper (optional)
1	16-ounce can whole cranberry sauce
2	or 3 canned chipotle chile peppers in adobo sauce, mashed

1 Place turkey in a resealable plastic bag set in a shallow dish. For marinade, in a small bowl stir together cranberry juice, 2 tablespoons of the tequila, 1½ teaspoons of the lime peel, 2 tablespoons of the lime juice, the garlic, salt, and, if desired, cayenne pepper. Pour marinade over turkey. Seal bag; turn to coat turkey. Marinate in the refrigerator for at least 2 hours or up to 24 hours, turning bag occasionally.

2 For sauce, in a small saucepan combine remaining 2 tablespoons tequila, remaining 1½ teaspoons lime peel, remaining 2 tablespoons lime juice, the cranberry sauce, and chipotle peppers. Bring to boiling; reduce heat. Simmer, uncovered, for 5 minutes. Transfer 1¼ cups of the sauce to a small bowl; chill in refrigerator. Reserve remaining sauce for brush-on.

3 Drain turkey, discarding marinade. For a charcoal grill, arrange medium-hot coals around a drip pan. Test for medium heat above the pan. Place turkey on grill rack over drip pan. Cover and grill for 45 minutes to 1¼ hours or until turkey is no longer pink (180°F), brushing with remaining sauce during the last 10 minutes of grilling. (For a gas grill, preheat grill. Reduce heat to medium. Adjust for indirect cooking. Grill as above.) Discard remainder of sauce used as a brush-on.

4 To serve, reheat the chilled sauce; pass with turkey.

NUTRITION FACTS PER SERVING: 372 cal., 9 g total fat (3 g sat. fat), 105 mg chol., 290 mg sodium, 32 g carbo., 1 g fiber, 36 g pro.

Behemoth Drumsticks

For a medieval twist, eat the huge turkey drumsticks out-of-hand. If you prefer smaller servings, grill 1 or 2 chicken drumsticks for each person.

PREP: 5 MINUTES **GRILL:** 45 MINUTES **MAKES:** 4 SERVINGS

4 turkey drumsticks (2 to 4 pounds total)

1 tablespoon cooking oil

Salt

Ground black pepper

1 Brush drumsticks with cooking oil. Sprinkle with salt and pepper.

2 For a charcoal grill, arrange medium-hot coals around a drip pan. Test for medium heat above the pan. Place turkey drumsticks on grill rack over drip pan. Cover and grill for 45 minutes to 1¼ hours or until turkey is tender and no longer pink (180°F). Add coals as necessary to maintain heat. (For a gas grill, preheat grill. Reduce heat to medium. Adjust for indirect cooking. Grill as above.)

NUTRITION FACTS PER SERVING: 283 cal., 16 g total fat (4 g sat. fat), 119 mg chol., 235 mg sodium, 0 g carbo., 0 g fiber, 32 g pro.

Behemoth-Style Chicken Drumsticks: Prepare as directed, except use 8 chicken drumsticks. Cover and grill for 50 to 60 minutes or until chicken is tender and no longer pink (180°F). Makes 4 to 8 servings.

NUTRITION FACTS PER SERVING: 262 cal., 16 g total fat (4 g sat. fat), 118 mg chol., 242 mg sodium, 0 g carbo., 0 g fiber, 28 g pro.

Best-Ever Turkey on the Grill

Rubbing the seasoning under the turkey or chicken skin before cooking results in a moist, juicy bird that's sure to get rave reviews.

PREP: 20 MINUTES GRILL: 2½ HOURS MAKES: 8 TO 10 SERVINGS

1 8- to 12-pound fresh or frozen whole turkey

2 teaspoons dried Italian seasoning, basil, or oregano, crushed

1 teaspoon poultry seasoning

½ teaspoon salt

½ teaspoon ground black pepper

1 Thaw turkey, if frozen. Remove the neck and giblets. Rinse turkey; pat dry with paper towels. In a small bowl combine Italian seasoning, poultry seasoning, salt, and pepper.

2 Starting at the neck on one side of the breast, slip your fingers between skin and meat, loosening the skin as you work toward the tail end. Once your entire hand is under the skin, free the skin around the top of the thigh and leg area up to, but not around, the tip of the drumstick. Repeat on the other side of the breast. Rub seasonings under the skin of turkey breast and legs. Skewer the neck skin to the back. Tie legs to tail. Twist wing tips under the back. Insert an oven-going meat thermometer into the center of an inside thigh muscle, making sure bulb does not touch bone.

3 For a charcoal grill, arrange medium-hot coals around a drip pan. Test for medium heat above the pan. Place turkey, breast side up, on grill rack over drip pan. Cover and grill for 2½ to 3½ hours or until meat thermometer registers 180°F. Add coals as necessary to maintain the heat. (For a gas grill, preheat grill. Reduce heat to medium. Adjust for indirect cooking. Place the turkey on a rack in a roasting pan, place on grill rack, and grill as above.)

4 Remove from grill; cover with foil. Let stand for 15 minutes before carving.

NUTRITION FACTS PER SERVING: 449 cal., 14 g total fat (4 g sat. fat), 275 mg chol., 221 mg sodium, 0 g carbo., 0 g fiber, 76 g pro.

Cajun Barbecue Turkey

Look for Cajun seasoning in the spice section of the supermarket.

PREP: 30 MINUTES **STAND:** 1 HOUR + 15 MINUTES **GRILL:** 2½ HOURS **MAKES:** 8 TO 10 SERVINGS

1   8- to 10-pound fresh or frozen whole turkey

3   cups water

3   tablespoons Cajun seasoning

1   tablespoon poultry seasoning

½   teaspoon instant chicken bouillon granules

½   teaspoon garlic powder

¼   to ½ teaspoon cayenne pepper

2   tablespoons butter or margarine

1 Thaw turkey, if frozen. Rinse turkey; pat dry with paper towels. Skewer the neck skin to the back. Tie legs to tail. Twist wing tips under the back.

2 In a large saucepan combine the water, Cajun seasoning, poultry seasoning, bouillon granules, garlic powder, and cayenne pepper. Bring to boiling. Remove from heat. Stir in butter until melted. Cover; let stand for 1 hour. Strain through a fine-mesh sieve; discard spices.

3 Using a flavor-injector syringe, inject the water-spice mixture deep into the meat of the turkey. (This may take up to 20 injections, so try to evenly distribute the seasoned broth in the turkey. If the syringe gets clogged with a bit of seasoning, flush it out with water and a toothpick.) Insert an oven-going meat thermometer into the center of an inside thigh muscle, making sure bulb does not touch bone.

4 For charcoal grill, arrange medium-hot coals around a drip pan. Test for medium heat above pan. Place turkey, breast side up, on grill rack over drip pan. Cover and grill for 2½ to 3 hours or until meat thermometer registers 180°F. Add coals as necessary to maintain heat. (For gas grill, preheat grill. Reduce heat to medium. Adjust for indirect cooking. Place turkey on a rack in a roasting pan, place on grill rack, and grill as above.)

5 Remove turkey from grill; cover with foil. Let stand for 15 minutes before carving.

NUTRITION FACTS PER SERVING: 487 cal., 17 g total fat (6 g sat. fat), 283 mg chol., 458 mg sodium, 3 g carbo., 1 g fiber, 77 g pro.

Turkey Tenderloins with Sweet Pepper Salsa

*The roasted red sweet pepper and orange salsa
is equally delicious with grilled or broiled chicken.*

PREP: 15 MINUTES MARINATE: 2 TO 4 HOURS GRILL: 12 MINUTES MAKES: 6 SERVINGS

1½ pounds turkey breast tenderloins
⅓ cup olive oil
¼ cup lemon juice
1 teaspoon finely shredded orange peel
¼ cup orange juice
2 teaspoons bottled minced garlic (4 cloves)
¼ teaspoon salt
¼ teaspoon ground black pepper
1 recipe Sweet Pepper–Citrus Salsa

1 Split each turkey breast tenderloin in half horizontally. Place turkey in a resealable plastic bag set in a shallow dish. For marinade, in a small bowl combine oil, lemon juice, orange peel, orange juice, garlic, salt, and pepper. Pour marinade over turkey. Seal bag; turn to coat turkey. Marinate in the refrigerator for at least 2 hours or up to 4 hours, turning bag occasionally.

2 Drain turkey, reserving marinade. For a charcoal grill, grill turkey on the rack of an uncovered grill directly over medium coals for 12 to 15 minutes or until turkey is no longer pink (170°F), turning once and brushing once with reserved marinade halfway through grilling. (For a gas grill, preheat grill. Reduce heat to medium. Place turkey on grill rack over heat. Cover and grill as above.) Discard any remaining marinade. Serve with Sweet Pepper–Citrus Salsa.

Sweet Pepper–Citrus Salsa: In a small bowl combine one 7-ounce jar roasted red sweet peppers, drained and chopped; 1 orange, peeled, seeded, and cut up; 2 green onions, sliced; 2 tablespoons balsamic vinegar; and 1 tablespoon snipped fresh basil or 1 teaspoon dried basil, crushed. Cover and refrigerate until serving time.

NUTRITION FACTS PER SERVING: 206 cal., 10 g total fat (2 g sat. fat), 50 mg chol., 107 mg sodium, 6 g carbo., 1 g fiber, 22 g pro.

Turkey Tenderloins with Cilantro Pesto

Substituting cilantro for basil in pesto gives it a Southwestern flair. Another time, savor the pesto with chicken, fish, or shrimp.

PREP: 15 MINUTES **GRILL:** 12 MINUTES **MAKES:** 8 SERVINGS

2 pounds turkey breast tenderloins

Salt

Ground black pepper

1½ cups lightly packed fresh cilantro sprigs and/or fresh basil leaves

⅓ cup walnuts

3 tablespoons olive oil

2 tablespoons lime juice

1 teaspoon bottled minced garlic (2 cloves)

¼ teaspoon salt

Lime wedges or lemon wedges (optional)

1 Split each turkey breast tenderloin in half horizontally. Sprinkle turkey with salt and pepper; set aside.

2 For cilantro pesto, in a blender container or food processor bowl combine cilantro and/or basil, walnuts, oil, lime juice, garlic, and the ¼ teaspoon salt. Cover and blend or process until nearly smooth. Divide pesto in half. Chill half of the pesto to serve with turkey.

3 For a charcoal grill, grill turkey on the rack of an uncovered grill directly over medium coals for 7 minutes; turn. Brush lightly with the unchilled half of the cilantro pesto. Grill for 5 to 8 minutes more or until turkey is tender and no longer pink (170°F). (For gas grill, preheat grill. Reduce heat to medium. Place turkey on grill rack over heat. Cover and grill as above.) Discard remainder of cilantro pesto used as a brush-on.

4 Serve turkey with remaining chilled pesto. If desired, serve with lime wedges to squeeze over turkey.

NUTRITION FACTS PER SERVING: 213 cal., 10 g total fat (2 g sat. fat), 68 mg chol., 134 mg sodium, 2 g carbo., 1 g fiber, 28 g pro.

Garlic Turkey Sausage with Garlic Cranberry Sauce

This recipe uses a lot of garlic; but the garlic enhances—
without overpowering—the sausage and the sauce.
Consider making the sauce again to serve with your Thanksgiving turkey.

PREP: 20 MINUTES **GRILL:** 15 MINUTES **MAKES:** 6 SERVINGS

1 16-ounce can whole berry cranberry sauce

1 tablespoon finely shredded orange peel

¼ cup orange juice

2 teaspoons bottled minced garlic (4 cloves)

1¼ pounds uncooked ground turkey

4 ounces bulk pork sausage

5 teaspoons bottled minced garlic (10 cloves)

1 tablespoon snipped fresh marjoram
or 1 teaspoon dried marjoram, crushed

1 tablespoon snipped fresh oregano
or 1 teaspoon dried oregano, crushed

1 tablespoon snipped fresh parsley

1 teaspoon salt

¼ teaspoon freshly ground black pepper

Dash cayenne pepper

1 For sauce, in a medium bowl combine cranberry sauce, orange peel, orange juice, and the 2 teaspoons garlic. Set aside ¼ cup of the sauce to brush on turkey sausage. Cover and chill the remaining sauce.

2 For sausage, in a large bowl combine turkey, pork sausage, the 5 teaspoons garlic, the marjoram, oregano, parsley, salt, black pepper, and cayenne pepper. Divide mixture into 6 portions. Shape each portion around a metal skewer, forming a log about 5 inches long.

3 For a charcoal grill, grill skewers on the rack of an uncovered grill directly over medium coals for 15 to 18 minutes or until sausage is no longer pink (165°F), turning to brown evenly and brushing with the ¼ cup sauce during the last 3 minutes of grilling. (For a gas grill, preheat grill. Reduce heat to medium. Place skewers on grill rack over heat. Cover and grill as above.) Serve with remaining chilled sauce.

NUTRITION FACTS PER SERVING: 350 cal., 15 g total fat (5 g sat. fat), 87 mg chol., 620 mg sodium, 34 g carbo., 2 g fiber, 19 g pro.

Border Grilled Turkey Salad

Try a fresh new twist on taco salad. Chili-and-lime-flavored strips of grilled turkey are served over crisp greens and drizzled with a hot pepper-spiced, dried tomato vinaigrette. It's all topped off with crunchy crumbled tortilla chips.

PREP: 20 MINUTES **MARINATE:** 30 MINUTES TO 3 HOURS **GRILL:** 12 MINUTES **MAKES:** 4 SERVINGS

1	pound turkey breast tenderloins
¼	cup lime juice
1	teaspoon chili powder
1	teaspoon bottled minced garlic (2 cloves)
¾	cup bottled dried tomato vinaigrette*
1	medium fresh jalapeño chile pepper, seeded and finely chopped**
4	cups torn mixed salad greens
1	cup peeled, seeded, and chopped cucumber or peeled and chopped jicama
1	large tomato, coarsely chopped
8	baked tortilla chips, broken into bite-size pieces

1 Split each turkey breast tenderloin in half horizontally. Place turkey in a resealable plastic bag set in a shallow dish. For marinade, in a small bowl combine lime juice, chili powder, and garlic. Pour marinade over turkey. Seal bag; turn to coat turkey. Marinate in refrigerator for at least 30 minutes or up to 3 hours, turning bag occasionally.

2 Drain turkey, reserving marinade. For a charcoal grill, grill turkey on rack of an uncovered grill directly over medium coals for 12 to 15 minutes or until turkey is no longer pink (170°F), turning once and brushing with the reserved marinade during the first 5 minutes of grilling. (For a gas grill, preheat grill. Reduce heat to medium. Place turkey on grill rack over heat. Cover and grill as above.) Discard any remaining marinade. Cut turkey into bite-size strips.

3 Meanwhile, for dressing, in a small bowl stir together tomato vinaigrette and jalapeño pepper. In a large bowl combine greens, cucumber or jicama, and tomato; toss to mix. Divide greens mixture among 4 dinner plates; arrange turkey on top of greens. Drizzle with dressing and sprinkle with tortilla chips.

NUTRITION FACTS PER SERVING: 363 cal., 19 g total fat (3 g sat. fat), 79 mg chol., 402 mg sodium, 13 g carbo., 2 g fiber, 36 g pro.

*NOTE: If you can't find dried tomato vinaigrette, substitute ⅔ cup bottled red wine vinaigrette and 2 tablespoons snipped, drained oil-packed dried tomatoes.

**NOTE: Because chile peppers contain volatile oils that can burn your skin and eyes, avoid direct contact with them as much as possible. When working with chile peppers, wear plastic or rubber gloves. If your bare hands do touch the chile peppers, wash your hands and nails well with soap and warm water.

Turkey and Couscous Salad

The mint and kalamata olives give this summer salad a Mediterranean touch.

PREP: 15 MINUTES **MARINATE:** 4 TO 24 HOURS **GRILL:** 45 MINUTES **MAKES:** 4 SERVINGS

1 turkey thigh (about 1 pound)

2 cups chicken broth

3 tablespoons lemon juice

2 tablespoons olive oil

½ teaspoon bottled minced garlic (1 clove)

¼ teaspoon salt

¼ teaspoon cayenne pepper

1 cup quick-cooking couscous

1 stalk celery, chopped

½ cup whole pitted kalamata or ripe olives (sliced, if desired)

2 tablespoons thinly sliced green onion

2 tablespoons snipped fresh mint

Shredded lettuce (optional)

1 medium tomato, seeded and chopped

1 Place turkey in a resealable plastic bag set in a shallow dish. In a screw-top jar combine ½ cup of the chicken broth, the lemon juice, oil, garlic, salt, and cayenne pepper. Cover and shake well. Pour ¼ cup of the broth mixture over turkey. Seal bag; turn to coat turkey. Marinate in the refrigerator for at least 4 hours or up to 24 hours, turning bag occasionally. Cover and chill the remaining mixture for dressing.

2 Drain turkey, discarding marinade. For a charcoal grill, arrange medium-hot coals around a drip pan. Test for medium heat above the pan. Place turkey on grill rack over drip pan. Cover and grill for 45 minutes to 1¼ hours or until tender and no longer pink (180°F). (For a gas grill, preheat grill. Reduce heat to medium. Adjust for indirect cooking. Grill as above.)

3 Remove turkey from grill. When turkey is cool enough to handle, remove skin and bone; shred meat or cut into cubes.

4 Meanwhile, in a medium saucepan bring remaining 1½ cups chicken broth to boiling; stir in couscous. Remove from heat. Cover; let stand about 5 minutes or until liquid is absorbed.

5 Transfer couscous to a large bowl. Add turkey, celery, olives, green onion, and mint; toss to combine. Drizzle with the chilled dressing; toss to coat. Serve warm. (Or cover and chill for up to 24 hours.) If desired, serve on shredded lettuce. Sprinkle with chopped tomato.

NUTRITION FACTS PER SERVING: 398 cal., 12 g total fat (3 g sat. fat), 68 mg chol., 688 mg sodium, 40 g carbo., 9 g fiber, 30 g pro.

Turkey-Peach Salad

Fresh fruit and poultry are a pleasing pair with a natural lightness. Here, juicy grilled turkey breast, peaches, and plums are drizzled with a light-as-air lemon-poppy seed dressing made with yogurt.

PREP: 15 MINUTES GRILL: 12 MINUTES MAKES: 4 SERVINGS

1 **pound turkey breast tenderloins**

1 **teaspoon olive oil**

  Salt

  Ground black pepper

2 **peaches, pitted and cut up**

2 **plums, pitted and sliced**

2 **tablespoons lemon juice**

½ **cup lemon low-fat yogurt**

2 **tablespoons thinly sliced green onion**

¼ **teaspoon poppy seeds**

  Lemon juice (optional)

  Mixed salad greens

1 Split each turkey breast tenderloin in half horizontally. Rub all sides of turkey breast tenderloin pieces with oil. Sprinkle with salt and pepper.

2 For a charcoal grill, grill turkey on the rack of an uncovered grill directly over medium coals for 12 to 15 minutes or until turkey is tender and no longer pink (170°F), turning once halfway through grilling. (For a gas grill, preheat grill. Reduce heat to medium. Place turkey on grill rack over heat. Cover and grill as above.) Cut turkey into bite-size strips.

3 Meanwhile, in a medium bowl combine the peaches and plums. Add the 2 tablespoons lemon juice; toss gently to coat. For dressing, in a small bowl combine yogurt, green onion, and poppy seeds. If necessary, stir in 1 to 2 teaspoons additional lemon juice to reach drizzling consistency.

4 Divide greens among 4 dinner plates. Arrange turkey and fruit on top of greens. Drizzle with dressing.

NUTRITION FACTS PER SERVING: 209 cal., 4 g total fat (1 g sat. fat), 51 mg chol., 96 mg sodium, 20 g carbo., 2 g fiber, 24 g pro.

Turkey with Pesto and Pasta

Buttery cashews are a nice change of pace in this pesto,
which does delicious double duty as a rub for the turkey tenderloins
and a savory sauce for the accompanying pasta.

PREP: 25 MINUTES GRILL: 25 MINUTES MAKES: 6 SERVINGS

1	cup firmly packed fresh cilantro leaves
½	cup firmly packed fresh flat-leaf parsley leaves
½	cup grated Parmesan cheese (2 ounces)
½	cup salted cashews
½	teaspoon bottled minced garlic (1 clove)
¼	cup olive oil or cooking oil
2	8-ounce turkey breast tenderloins
12	ounces dried fettuccine or linguine
	Fresh cilantro sprigs (optional)

1 For pesto, in a blender container or food processor bowl combine the 1 cup cilantro, the parsley, Parmesan cheese, ¼ cup of the cashews, and the garlic. Cover and blend or process with several on-off turns until a paste forms, stopping the machine several times and scraping the side. With the machine running, gradually add oil and blend or process until the consistency of soft butter. Remove about 2 tablespoons of the pesto mixture; rub over all sides of turkey breast tenderloins.

2 For a charcoal grill, arrange medium-hot coals around a drip pan. Test for medium heat above the pan. Place turkey on grill rack over drip pan. Cover and grill for 25 to 30 minutes or until turkey is no longer pink (170°F). (For a gas grill, preheat grill. Reduce heat to medium. Adjust for indirect cooking. Grill as above.)

3 Meanwhile, cook pasta according to package directions. Drain pasta; return to saucepan. Add the remaining pesto and the remaining ¼ cup cashews; toss well. Divide the pasta mixture among 6 dinner plates. Thinly slice turkey and arrange on top of pasta mixture. If desired, garnish with cilantro sprigs.

NUTRITION FACTS PER SERVING: 483 cal., 18 g total fat (4 g sat. fat), 53 mg chol., 197 mg sodium, 47 g carbo., 2 g fiber, 31 g pro.

Cornish Game Hens Provençal

Choose Merlot or your favorite dry red wine for the robust, herbed marinade. If you like, have an extra bottle on hand to serve with the meal.

PREP: 15 MINUTES **MARINATE:** 24 HOURS **GRILL:** 40 MINUTES **MAKES:** 4 SERVINGS

- **2** 1¼- to 1½-pound Cornish game hens, halved lengthwise
- **½** cup Merlot or other dry red wine
- **2** tablespoons olive oil
- **1** tablespoon snipped fresh rosemary
- **1** tablespoon snipped fresh thyme
- **2** teaspoons bottled minced garlic (4 cloves)
- **½** teaspoon salt
- **½** teaspoon cracked black pepper

1 Place hen halves in a resealable plastic bag set in a deep bowl. For marinade, in a small bowl combine wine, olive oil, rosemary, thyme, garlic, salt, and pepper. Pour marinade over hens. Seal bag; turn to coat hens. Marinate in refrigerator for 24 hours, turning bag occasionally.

2 Drain hens, reserving marinade. Twist wing tips of hens under backs. For a charcoal grill, arrange medium-hot coals around a drip pan. Test for medium heat above the pan. Place Cornish hens, bone sides down, on grill rack over drip pan. Cover and grill for 40 to 50 minutes or until tender and no longer pink (180°F), brushing often with reserved marinade during the first 30 minutes of grilling. (For a gas grill, preheat grill. Reduce heat to medium. Adjust for indirect cooking. Grill as above.) Discard any remaining marinade.

NUTRITION FACTS PER SERVING: 373 cal., 26 g total fat (5 g sat. fat), 100 mg chol., 361 mg sodium, 2 g carbo., 0 g fiber, 31 g pro.

Mediterranean Game Hens with Herb Sauce

Garlic and Dijon-style mustard with fresh basil, rosemary, and parsley gives these tender hens plenty of zesty flavor. Complete the meal with couscous, broccoli spears, and fresh fruit.

PREP: 20 MINUTES **MARINATE:** 2 TO 6 HOURS **GRILL:** 40 MINUTES **MAKES:** 4 SERVINGS

2	1¼- to 1½-pound Cornish game hens, halved lengthwise
⅓	cup loosely packed fresh basil leaves
⅓	cup loosely packed fresh parsley
¼	cup olive oil
2	tablespoons lemon juice
1	tablespoon Dijon-style mustard
2	teaspoons snipped fresh rosemary
½	teaspoon bottled minced garlic (1 clove)
¼	teaspoon salt
¼	teaspoon ground black pepper
¼	cup dairy sour cream
	Fresh rosemary sprigs (optional)

❶ Place hens in a resealable plastic bag set in a deep bowl. In a blender container or food processor bowl combine basil, parsley, oil, lemon juice, mustard, snipped rosemary, garlic, salt, and pepper. Cover and blend or process until nearly smooth. Pour ¼ cup of the herb mixture over hens. Seal bag; turn to coat hens. Marinate in the refrigerator for at least 2 hours or up to 6 hours, turning bag occasionally. Cover and chill remaining herb mixture for sauce.

❷ Drain hens, discarding marinade. Twist wing tips of hens under back. For a charcoal grill, arrange medium-hot coals around a drip pan. Test for medium heat above the pan. Place hens, bone sides down, on grill rack over drip pan. Cover and grill for 40 to 50 minutes or until tender and no longer pink (180°F). (For a gas grill, preheat grill. Reduce heat to medium. Adjust for indirect cooking. Grill as above.)

❸ For sauce, in a small bowl stir together chilled herb mixture and sour cream. Serve with hens. If desired, garnish with rosemary sprigs.

NUTRITION FACTS PER SERVING: 489 cal., 38 g total fat (9 g sat. fat), 127 mg chol., 300 mg sodium, 2 g carbo., 0 g fiber, 37 g pro.

Game Hens with Grilled Peppers

Cutting the Cornish hens in half accomplishes two things: It allows them to cook faster than they would whole and makes two servings of one bird (which is just enough).

PREP: 25 MINUTES **GRILL:** 40 MINUTES **MAKES:** 4 SERVINGS

2   1½-pound Cornish game hens, halved lengthwise

¼   cup butter or margarine, melted

½   teaspoon salt

½   teaspoon freshly ground black pepper

½   teaspoon ground cumin

3   red, yellow, and/or green sweet peppers, quartered

1   fresh ancho chile pepper, quartered*

1   medium red onion, cut into ½-inch-thick slices

1 Twist wing tips of hens under backs. For cumin butter, in a small bowl combine melted butter, salt, pepper, and cumin. Divide mixture in half. Set one portion aside. Use the other portion to brush over both sides of each hen half. Discard remainder of the butter mixture used as a brush-on.

2 For a charcoal grill, arrange medium-hot coals around a drip pan. Test for medium heat above the pan. Place Cornish hens, bone sides down, on grill rack over drip pan. Cover and grill for 40 to 50 minutes or until tender and no longer pink (180°F). (For a gas grill, preheat grill. Reduce heat to medium. Adjust for indirect cooking. Grill as above.)

3 While the hens are grilling, brush the sweet peppers, ancho pepper, and onion with the reserved butter mixture; place peppers and onion on grill rack directly over medium-hot coals. Cover and grill about 10 minutes or until tender and slightly charred, turning once halfway through grilling. Remove vegetables from grill when done.

4 Remove hens from grill; keep hens warm. Cut peppers into strips; chop onion. Toss together peppers and onion. To serve, divide pepper mixture among 4 dinner plates. Arrange hens on top of pepper mixture.

NUTRITION FACTS PER SERVING: 493 cal., 35 g total fat (13 g sat. fat), 153 mg chol., 509 mg sodium, 9 g carbo., 2 g fiber, 38 g pro.

*NOTE: Because chile peppers contain volatile oils that can burn your skin and eyes, avoid direct contact with them as much as possible. When working with chile peppers, wear plastic or rubber gloves. If your bare hands do touch the chile peppers, wash your hands and nails well with soap and warm water.

Duck Breast with Berry-Balsamic Sauce

Order duck breast from the butcher at your local supermarket or, instead of duck, use skinless, boneless chicken breast halves or turkey tenderloins, halved horizontally.

PREP: 30 MINUTES **GRILL:** 12 MINUTES **MAKES:** 4 SERVINGS

½ cup lingonberry or seedless raspberry jam or preserves

¼ cup sweet red wine (such as ruby port)

3 tablespoons balsamic vinegar

1 teaspoon butter

4 skinless, boneless duck breast halves (1 to 1½ pounds total)

2 teaspoons walnut oil

½ teaspoon salt

½ teaspoon freshly ground black pepper

1 recipe Pickled Carrots and Radishes (optional)

1 For sauce, in a small saucepan combine jam or preserves, wine, and vinegar. Cook over medium heat just until boiling, stirring frequently; reduce heat to medium-low. Simmer, uncovered, about 15 minutes or until sauce is slightly thickened and reduced to ½ cup, stirring occasionally. Remove from heat; stir in butter. Keep sauce warm.

2 Place duck breast halves between 2 sheets of plastic wrap. Using the flat side of a meat mallet, lightly pound duck to an even thickness. Remove plastic wrap. Brush oil over both sides of each breast half; season duck with salt and pepper.

3 For a charcoal grill, grill duck on the rack of an uncovered grill directly over medium coals for 12 to 15 minutes or until duck is no longer pink (180°F), turning once halfway through grilling and brushing with some of the sauce during the last 5 minutes of grilling. (For a gas grill, preheat grill. Reduce heat to medium. Place duck on grill rack over heat. Cover and grill as above.)

4 Reheat remaining sauce until bubbly. Using a sharp knife, cut grilled duck crosswise into ½-inch-thick slices. Arrange duck slices on 4 dinner plates; drizzle with sauce. If desired, serve with Pickled Carrots and Radishes.

NUTRITION FACTS PER SERVING: 299 cal., 5 g total fat (1 g sat. fat), 124 mg chol., 406 mg sodium, 33 g carbo., 1 g fiber, 24 g pro.

Pickled Carrots and Radishes: Using a sharp peeler, cut 1 medium peeled carrot into wide ribbons. In a large container combine carrot ribbons with 6 red radishes, sliced and/or cut up. Toss gently with ¼ cup seasoned rice vinegar and 2 tablespoons walnut oil. Cover and chill until serving time.

Duck Breast with Lime Sauce

When company's coming, serve these elegant grilled duck breast halves
with hot cooked brown rice and buttered, steamed asparagus.

PREP: 20 MINUTES **GRILL:** 12 MINUTES **MAKES:** 4 SERVINGS

½ cup currant jelly

¼ cup sweet or semi-dry white wine (such as Riesling or Sauternes)

1 tablespoon raspberry vinegar

1 teaspoon finely shredded lime peel

1 tablespoon lime juice

¼ teaspoon grated fresh ginger

⅛ teaspoon salt

Dash ground black pepper

1 tablespoon butter or margarine

2 teaspoons olive oil

4 skinless, boneless duck breast halves (about 12 ounces total) or 4 skinless, boneless chicken breast halves (about 1¼ pounds total)

Fresh red raspberries (optional)

1 For sauce, in a small saucepan combine jelly, wine, vinegar, lime peel, lime juice, ginger, salt, and pepper. Bring just to boiling; reduce heat. Simmer, uncovered, about 12 minutes or until sauce is slightly thickened and reduced to ½ cup. Remove from heat; stir in butter. Set aside ¼ cup of the sauce. Keep remaining sauce warm until serving time.

2 Brush oil over both sides of duck or chicken pieces. Lightly grease the rack of an uncovered grill. For a charcoal grill, grill duck or chicken on the rack of an uncovered grill directly over medium coals for 12 to 15 minutes or until tender and no longer pink (180°F for duck; 170°F for chicken), turning once halfway through grilling and brushing with the ¼ cup sauce during the last 5 minutes of grilling. (For a gas grill, preheat grill. Reduce heat to medium. Place duck or chicken on grill rack over heat. Cover and grill as above.) Discard remainder of the ¼ cup sauce used as a brush-on. Serve duck with warm sauce. If desired, garnish with raspberries.

NUTRITION FACTS PER SERVING: 336 cal., 14 g total fat (4 g sat. fat), 124 mg chol., 189 mg sodium, 28 g carbo., 0 g fiber, 21 g pro.

Duck Salad with Orange-Hazelnut Dressing

A double dose of orange—juice concentrate in the marinade and orange sections on the salad—complements the duck.

PREP: 20 MINUTES MARINATE: 4 TO 24 HOURS GRILL: 12 MINUTES MAKES: 4 SERVINGS

- **3** skinless, boneless duck breasts (about 12 ounces total)
- **¼** cup water
- **¼** cup olive oil
- **3** tablespoons frozen orange juice concentrate, thawed
- **2** tablespoons finely chopped shallots
- **2** tablespoons balsamic vinegar
- **1½** teaspoons bottled minced garlic (3 cloves)
- **¼** teaspoon salt
- **¼** teaspoon ground black pepper
- **8** cups mesclun or torn mixed salad greens
- **2** oranges, peeled and sectioned
- **⅓** cup chopped hazelnuts (filberts) or almonds, toasted

1 Place duck breasts in a resealable plastic bag set in a shallow dish. For marinade, in a small bowl combine the water, oil, orange juice concentrate, shallots, vinegar, garlic, salt, and pepper. Transfer ⅓ cup of the mixture to a small bowl for salad dressing; cover and chill until ready to serve (let stand at room temperature for 30 minutes before serving). Pour remaining marinade over duck. Seal bag; turn to coat duck. Marinate in refrigerator for at least 4 hours or up to 24 hours, turning bag occasionally.

2 Drain duck, discarding marinade. For a charcoal grill, grill duck on the rack of an uncovered grill directly over medium coals for 12 to 15 minutes or until tender and no longer pink (180°F), turning once halfway through grilling. (For a gas grill, preheat grill. Reduce heat to medium. Place duck on grill rack over heat. Cover and grill as above.)

3 Meanwhile, for salad, in a large bowl combine mesclun or salad greens, oranges, and nuts; toss gently to mix. Shake dressing. Pour dressing over salad; toss gently to coat. To serve, divide salad among 4 dinner plates. Thinly slice duck breasts. Arrange slices on top of salad.

NUTRITION FACTS PER SERVING: 246 cal., 19 g total fat (3 g sat. fat), 19 mg chol., 126 mg sodium, 13 g carbo., 2 g fiber, 7 g pro.

Classic French-Style Quail

For semiboneless quail, check a large butcher shop. It can provide you with whole quail prepared for cooking European style. This means each bird is split open and the rib cage removed, but the wing and leg bones are left intact.

PREP: 15 MINUTES **MARINATE:** 4 TO 6 HOURS **GRILL:** 7 MINUTES **MAKES:** 4 SERVINGS

8 semiboneless quail

¾ cup dry white wine

2 tablespoons fresh rosemary leaves

1 tablespoon olive oil

2 teaspoons bottled minced garlic (4 cloves)

Salt

Ground black pepper

2 lemons, cut into wedges

1 Using kitchen shears, cut down center of back of each quail and press open on firm surface to lie flat. Twist wing tips under back. Tie legs together with 100%-cotton kitchen string. Place quail in a resealable plastic bag set in a shallow dish.

2 For marinade, in a small bowl combine wine, rosemary, oil, and garlic. Pour marinade over quail. Seal bag; turn to coat quail. Marinate in the refrigerator for at least 4 hours or up to 6 hours, turning bag occasionally.

3 Drain quail, discarding marinade. Sprinkle lightly with salt and pepper. For a charcoal grill, grill quail on the rack of an uncovered grill directly over medium coals for 7 to 10 minutes or until quail is no longer pink (180°F), turning once halfway through grilling. (For a gas grill, preheat grill. Reduce heat to medium. Place quail on grill rack over heat. Cover and grill as above.)

4 Serve lemon wedges with quail; squeeze lemon over quail before eating.

NUTRITION FACTS PER SERVING: 438 cal., 27 g total fat (7 g sat. fat), 0 mg chol., 183 mg sodium, 1 g carbo., 0 g fiber, 43 g pro.

Maple-Glazed Quail

Farm-raised quail have a mild flavor that is less gamey than their wild cousins and slightly sweeter than chicken. The maple glaze in this recipe will also work well on skinless, boneless chicken breast halves.

PREP: 10 MINUTES **MARINATE:** 2 TO 24 HOURS **GRILL:** 15 MINUTES **MAKES:** 8 SERVINGS

2 teaspoons hot chili powder

1 teaspoon dried thyme, crushed

¾ teaspoon salt

8 semiboneless quail

½ cup pure maple syrup

2 tablespoons peanut oil or cooking oil

Fresh pineapple wedges (optional)

Torn mixed salad greens (optional)

1 For rub, in a small bowl combine chili powder, thyme, and salt. Sprinkle mixture evenly over the quail; rub in with your fingers. Place quail in a shallow baking dish. In a small bowl combine ¼ cup of the maple syrup and the oil; spoon over quail, turning to coat. Cover and chill for at least 2 hours or up to 24 hours.

2 For a charcoal grill, arrange medium-hot coals around a drip pan. Test for medium heat above the pan. Place quail, breast sides down, on grill rack over drip pan. Cover and grill for 15 to 20 minutes or until quail is no longer pink (180°F), brushing with the remaining ¼ cup maple syrup frequently during the last 3 minutes of grilling. (For a gas grill, preheat grill. Reduce heat to medium. Adjust for indirect cooking. Grill as above.)

3 If desired, serve with fresh pineapple wedges and salad greens.

NUTRITION FACTS PER SERVING: 299 cal., 17 g total fat (4 g sat. fat), 86 mg chol., 275 mg sodium, 14 g carbo., 0 g fiber, 22 g pro.

BIGGEST BOOK OF GRILLING

Chapter 3

FISH & SEAFOOD

Honey-Bourbon Salmon

Brown sugar, bourbon, soy sauce, and ginger combine to create an extraordinary marinade for salmon steaks.

PREP: 10 MINUTES **MARINATE:** 1 HOUR **GRILL:** 8 MINUTES **MAKES:** 4 SERVINGS

4   6- to 8-ounce fresh or frozen salmon steaks, cut 1 inch thick

¾   cup bourbon whiskey

½   cup packed brown sugar

2   tablespoons honey

2   teaspoons soy sauce

½   teaspoon ground ginger

¼   teaspoon ground black pepper

1 Thaw salmon, if frozen; rinse and pat dry with paper towels. Place in a resealable plastic bag set in a shallow dish.

2 For marinade, in a small bowl stir together the bourbon, brown sugar, honey, soy sauce, ginger, and pepper. Pour over fish in the bag. Seal bag; turn gently to coat fish. Marinate in refrigerator for 1 hour, turning bag occasionally.

3 Drain fish, reserving marinade. For a charcoal grill, grill fish on the greased rack of an uncovered grill directly over medium coals for 8 to 12 minutes or until fish flakes easily when tested with a fork, gently turning once and brushing once with reserved marinade halfway through grilling. (For a gas grill, preheat grill. Reduce heat to medium. Place fish on greased grill rack over heat. Cover and grill as above.) Discard any remaining marinade.

NUTRITION FACTS PER SERVING: 322 cal., 6 g total fat (1 g sat. fat), 88 mg chol., 197 mg sodium, 19 g carbo., 0 g fiber, 34 g pro.

Sizzling Salmon with Minted Lentils

This all-purpose Cucumber Sauce also tastes terrific with all kinds of white fish and chicken.

PREP: 45 MINUTES COOK: 20 MINUTES GRILL: 8 MINUTES CHILL: 2 HOURS MAKES: 4 SERVINGS

4 6- to 8-ounce fresh or frozen salmon steaks, cut 1 inch thick

8 cups lightly salted water

12 ounces fresh green beans or long beans

1 recipe Cucumber Sauce

1 14-ounce can reduced-sodium chicken broth

⅔ cup dry brown lentils, rinsed and drained

Salt

Ground black pepper

Lemon wedges (optional)

Fresh mint sprigs (optional)

1 Thaw fish steaks, if frozen; rinse and pat dry with paper towels.

2 In a large saucepan bring the lightly salted water to boiling. Add beans. Cover and cook about 4 minutes or just until crisp-tender. Drain well. In a medium bowl combine beans with ½ cup of the Cucumber Sauce. Set aside while preparing lentils and salmon.

3 In a medium saucepan combine broth and lentils. Bring to boiling; reduce heat. Cover and simmer for 20 to 25 minutes or until lentils are tender. Drain, discarding cooking liquid. Return lentils to saucepan; stir in half (about 1 cup) of the remaining Cucumber Sauce. Set aside.

4 Sprinkle fish with salt and pepper. For a charcoal grill, grill fish on the greased rack of an uncovered grill directly over medium coals for 8 to 12 minutes or until fish flakes easily when tested with a fork, gently turning once halfway through grilling. (For a gas grill, preheat grill. Reduce heat to medium. Place fish on greased grill rack over heat. Cover and grill as above.)

5 To serve, place lentil mixture in a serving bowl; place bowl on platter. Arrange bean mixture and fish on platter. Serve with remaining Cucumber Sauce. If desired, garnish with lemon wedges and mint sprigs.

Cucumber Sauce: Seed and chop 2 medium cucumbers. In a medium bowl combine chopped cucumbers, ¼ cup snipped fresh parsley, ¼ cup lemon juice, 2 tablespoons cooking oil, 2 tablespoons thinly sliced green onion, 2 tablespoons snipped fresh mint, and ¼ teaspoon salt. Cover and chill in the refrigerator for at least 2 hours or up to 24 hours. Makes about 2½ cups.

NUTRITION FACTS PER SERVING: 397 cal., 14 g total fat (1 g sat. fat), 31 mg chol., 308 mg sodium, 34 g carbo., 6 g fiber, 37 g pro.

Tuna with Peanut Sauce

Asian flavors—ginger, sesame, soy, and garlic—season this fast-cooking meal.
You can make the sauce ahead and simply reheat at serving time.
This sauce is also tasty on chicken.

PREP: 15 MINUTES GRILL: 8 MINUTES MAKES: 4 SERVINGS

4   4-ounce fresh or frozen tuna steaks
     (albacore or yellow fin), cut 1 inch thick

½   cup lightly salted peanuts

¼   cup water

1   green onion, cut into 1-inch pieces

2   tablespoons toasted sesame oil

1   tablespoon soy sauce

1   tablespoon rice vinegar

1   teaspoon sugar

1   teaspoon grated fresh ginger

½   teaspoon bottled minced garlic (1 clove)

2   to 3 tablespoons water

1   tablespoon bottled teriyaki sauce

1   tablespoon water

     Chopped peanuts (optional)

     Sliced green onion (optional)

1 Thaw fish, if frozen; rinse and pat dry with paper towels. For peanut sauce, in a blender container or food processor bowl combine the ½ cup peanuts, the ¼ cup water, the green onion pieces, sesame oil, soy sauce, rice vinegar, sugar, ginger, and garlic. Cover and blend or process until almost smooth; pour into a small saucepan. Stir in enough of the 2 to 3 tablespoons water to thin slightly; set aside.

2 In a small bowl combine teriyaki sauce and the 1 tablespoon water. Brush both sides of each tuna steak with the teriyaki mixture.

3 For charcoal grill, grill tuna on the greased rack of an uncovered grill directly over medium coals for 8 to 12 minutes or until fish flakes easily when tested with a fork, gently turning once halfway through grilling. (For gas grill, preheat grill. Reduce heat to medium. Place fish on greased grill rack over heat. Cover and grill as above.)

4 Slowly warm peanut sauce over medium-low heat. (Sauce will thicken slightly as it is heated. Stir in additional water, if necessary.) Spoon sauce over tuna. If desired, garnish with chopped peanuts and sliced green onion.

NUTRITION FACTS PER SERVING: 301 cal., 17 g total fat (2 g sat. fat), 51 mg chol., 524 mg sodium, 6 g carbo., 2 g fiber, 32 g pro.

Basil Halibut Steaks

*Make the most of fresh basil—from your garden,
the farmer's market, or the supermarket—in this savory dish.*

PREP: 25 MINUTES GRILL: 8 MINUTES MAKES: 4 SERVINGS

2 fresh or frozen halibut steaks, cut 1 inch thick (about 1½ pounds total)

1 medium onion, chopped

½ teaspoon bottled minced garlic (1 clove)

2 tablespoons olive oil

2 to 3 cups chopped, peeled tomatoes

¼ teaspoon salt

¼ teaspoon ground black pepper

¼ cup snipped fresh basil

1 tablespoon butter or margarine, melted

Salt

Ground black pepper

1 Thaw fish, if frozen; rinse and pat dry with paper towels. Set aside.

2 In a medium skillet cook onion and garlic in hot oil until tender. Stir in tomatoes, the ¼ teaspoon salt, and the ¼ teaspoon pepper. Bring to boiling; reduce heat. Simmer, uncovered, for 15 minutes. Stir in 2 tablespoons of the basil.

3 Meanwhile, in a small bowl combine melted butter and the remaining 2 tablespoons basil; brush over one side of each halibut steak.

4 For a charcoal grill, grill fish on the greased rack of an uncovered grill directly over medium coals for 8 to 12 minutes or until fish flakes easily when tested with a fork, gently turning once halfway through grilling. (For a gas grill, preheat grill. Reduce heat to medium. Place fish on greased grill rack over heat. Cover and grill as above.)

5 Season fish to taste with additional salt and pepper. Serve with tomato mixture.

NUTRITION FACTS PER SERVING: 302 cal., 14 g total fat (3 g sat. fat), 62 mg chol., 265 mg sodium, 7 g carbo., 2 g fiber, 37 g pro.

Halibut with Blueberry-Pepper Jam

If halibut isn't available, opt for sea bass or salmon fillets.

PREP: 25 MINUTES GRILL: 12 MINUTES MAKES: 4 SERVINGS

4   5- to 6-ounce fresh or frozen halibut steaks or fillets or sea bass or salmon fillets, about 1 inch thick

1   cup fresh blueberries, rinsed and drained

1   teaspoon snipped fresh sage

½   teaspoon freshly ground black pepper

1   cup purchased garlic croutons, coarsely crushed

¼   cup snipped fresh sage

1   teaspoon finely shredded orange peel

¼   teaspoon freshly ground black pepper

2   tablespoons orange juice

1   tablespoon olive oil

    Olive oil (optional)

    Fresh sage leaves (optional)

1 Thaw fish, if frozen; rinse and pat dry with paper towels. Set aside.

2 For blueberry-pepper jam, in a medium bowl mash ¾ cup of the blueberries with a potato masher or fork. Stir in the remaining ¼ cup blueberries, the 1 teaspoon sage, and the ½ teaspoon pepper. Cover and chill until ready to serve. In a small bowl combine crushed croutons, the ¼ cup sage, the orange peel, and the ¼ teaspoon pepper. Stir in orange juice and the 1 tablespoon olive oil until lightly moistened; set aside.

3 For a charcoal grill, grill fish on the greased rack of an uncovered grill directly over medium coals for 5 minutes. Carefully turn fish; top evenly with crouton topping, pressing onto fish. Grill for 7 to 10 minutes more or until fish flakes easily when tested with a fork. (For a gas grill, preheat grill. Reduce heat to medium. Place fish on greased grill rack over heat. Cover and grill as above.)

4 To serve, place fish on serving platter. Serve with blueberry-pepper jam. If desired, drizzle fish with additional olive oil and garnish with sage leaves.

NUTRITION FACTS PER SERVING: 222 cal., 7 g total fat (1 g sat. fat), 45 mg chol., 101 mg sodium, 8 g carbo., 1 g fiber, 30 g pro.

Lime-Marinated Halibut

The lime juice in this marinade flavors and tenderizes the fish—
but don't let the fish soak any longer than 20 minutes or the acidic juice will
begin to affect its appearance, turning it white or opaque.

PREP: 8 MINUTES **MARINATE:** 20 MINUTES **GRILL:** 8 MINUTES **MAKES:** 4 SERVINGS

4	5-ounce fresh or frozen halibut steaks, cut 1 inch thick
1	lime
2	teaspoons olive oil
¼	teaspoon salt
1¼	cups chicken broth
1	cup quick-cooking couscous
1	cup cherry tomatoes, halved
2	tablespoons snipped fresh cilantro
2	tablespoons snipped fresh mint

1 Thaw fish, if frozen; rinse and pat dry with paper towels. Finely shred enough peel from the lime to make 1 teaspoon; set aside. For marinade, halve and squeeze enough juice from the lime to make 2 tablespoons. In a shallow dish combine the lime juice, olive oil, and salt. Add fish, turning to coat. Cover and marinate at room temperature for 20 minutes, turning fish once.

2 Drain fish, discarding marinade. For a charcoal grill, grill fish on the greased rack of an uncovered grill directly over medium coals for 8 to 12 minutes or until fish flakes easily when tested with a fork, gently turning once halfway through grilling. (For a gas grill, preheat grill. Reduce heat to medium. Place fish on greased grill rack over heat. Cover and grill as above.)

3 Meanwhile, for couscous, in a medium saucepan bring chicken broth to boiling. Stir in couscous. Remove from heat; cover and let stand for 5 minutes. Fluff with a fork. Stir in cherry tomatoes, cilantro, mint, and the reserved lime peel. Cover and let stand for 2 to 3 minutes more or until tomatoes are warm. Serve with grilled fish.

NUTRITION FACTS PER SERVING: 372 cal., 7 g total fat (1 g sat. fat), 45 mg chol., 545 mg sodium, 39 g carbo., 3 g fiber, 37 g pro.

Minty Halibut with Yellow Squash

Flavored with fresh basil and mint and served with smoky, grilled summer squash, this delicious grilled halibut is ready from start to finish in about 20 minutes!

PREP: 15 MINUTES GRILL: 8 MINUTES MAKES: 4 SERVINGS

1¼ to 1½ pounds fresh or frozen halibut or salmon steaks, cut 1 inch thick

¼ cup lemon juice

2 tablespoons olive oil

1½ teaspoons bottled minced garlic (3 cloves)

2 medium yellow summer squash or zucchini, halved lengthwise

Salt

Ground black pepper

2 tablespoons finely snipped fresh basil

1 tablespoon snipped fresh mint

1 Thaw fish, if frozen; rinse and pat dry with paper towels. In a small bowl whisk together the lemon juice, oil, and garlic. Set aside 3 tablespoons of the mixture. Brush remaining lemon juice mixture on fish and the cut sides of the squash. Lightly sprinkle fish and squash with salt and pepper.

2 For a charcoal grill, grill fish on the greased rack of an uncovered grill directly over medium coals for 8 to 12 minutes or until fish flakes easily when tested with a fork, gently turning once halfway through grilling. During the last 5 to 6 minutes of grilling, grill the squash just until tender, turning once. (For a gas grill, preheat grill. Reduce heat to medium. Place fish, then squash on greased grill rack over heat. Cover and grill as above.)

3 Meanwhile, stir basil and mint into the reserved lemon juice mixture.

4 Transfer the squash to a cutting board; cool slightly and slice ⅛ inch to ¼ inch thick. Place squash on a serving platter; drizzle with some of the basil mixture. Top with fish; drizzle with the remaining basil mixture.

NUTRITION FACTS PER SERVING: 233 cal., 10 g total fat (1 g sat. fat), 46 mg chol., 112 mg sodium, 5 g carbo., 1 g fiber, 30 g pro.

Swordfish with Spicy Tomato Sauce

This vibrant and fresh fish entrée combines two popular Sicilian foods, swordfish and a spicy, fresh tomato sauce. Couscous, a North African favorite, makes a great serve-along.

PREP: 15 MINUTES GRILL: 8 MINUTES MAKES: 4 SERVINGS

4	**fresh or frozen swordfish steaks, cut 1 inch thick (about 1¼ pounds total)**
4	**teaspoons cooking oil**
½	**teaspoon salt**
¼	**teaspoon ground black pepper**
¼	**cup chopped onion**
1	**small fresh serrano or jalapeño chile pepper, seeded and finely chopped***
½	**teaspoon bottled minced garlic (1 clove)**
½	**teaspoon ground turmeric**
¼	**teaspoon ground coriander**
1½	**cups chopped plum tomatoes**
1	**tablespoon snipped fresh cilantro**
	Hot cooked couscous (optional)

1 Thaw fish, if frozen; rinse and pat dry with paper towels. Drizzle 2 teaspoons of the oil over swordfish. Sprinkle with ¼ teaspoon of the salt and the pepper.

2 For a charcoal grill, grill fish steaks on the greased rack of an uncovered grill directly over medium coals for 8 to 12 minutes or until fish flakes easily when tested with a fork, gently turning once halfway through grilling. (For a gas grill, preheat grill. Reduce heat to medium. Place fish on greased grill rack over heat. Cover and grill as above.)

3 Meanwhile, for the spicy tomato sauce, in a medium skillet heat the remaining 2 teaspoons oil over medium heat. Add onion, chile pepper, garlic, turmeric, and coriander; cook about 2 minutes or until onions are tender. Stir in tomatoes and the remaining ¼ teaspoon salt; cook for 2 to 3 minutes or just until tomatoes are tender. Remove from heat; stir in cilantro. Serve spicy tomato sauce over fish. If desired, serve with couscous.

NUTRITION FACTS PER SERVING: 237 cal., 11 g total fat (2 g sat. fat), 56 mg chol., 402 mg sodium, 5 g carbo., 1 g fiber, 29 g pro.

*NOTE: Because chile peppers contain volatile oils that can burn your skin and eyes, avoid direct contact with them as much as possible. When working with chile peppers, wear plastic or rubber gloves. If your bare hands do touch the chile peppers, wash your hands and nails well with soap and warm water.

Dilly Salmon Fillets

A quick, dill-infused, Dijon-flavored mayonnaise caps off these Scandinavian-style salmon fillets. For a built-in salad and extra freshness, serve them on a bed of shredded cucumber.

PREP: 15 MINUTES **MARINATE:** 10 MINUTES **GRILL:** 7 TO 9 MINUTES PER ½-INCH THICKNESS
MAKES: 4 SERVINGS

4   6-ounce fresh or frozen skinless salmon fillets,
    ½ to ¾ inch thick

3   tablespoons lemon juice

2   tablespoons snipped fresh dill

2   tablespoons mayonnaise or salad dressing

2   teaspoons Dijon-style mustard

    Dash ground black pepper

1 Thaw fish, if frozen; rinse and pat dry with paper towels. Measure thickness of fish. Place fish in a shallow dish. In a small bowl combine the lemon juice and 1 tablespoon of the dill; pour over fish. Marinate at room temperature for 10 minutes. Meanwhile, in a small bowl stir together the remaining 1 tablespoon dill, the mayonnaise, mustard, and pepper; set aside.

2 For a charcoal grill, arrange medium-hot coals around a drip pan. Test for medium heat above the pan. Place fish on greased grill rack over drip pan. Cover and grill until fish flakes easily when tested with a fork, gently turning once and spreading with the mayonnaise mixture halfway through grilling. Allow 7 to 9 minutes per ½-inch thickness of fish. (For a gas grill, preheat grill. Reduce heat to medium. Adjust for indirect cooking. Grill as above.)

NUTRITION FACTS PER SERVING: 211 cal., 11 g total fat (2 g sat. fat), 35 mg chol., 204 mg sodium, 1 g carbo., 0 g fiber, 25 g pro.

Fish and Vegetable Packets

The whole meal—except for the accompanying rice—is cooked on the grill in a foil packet. Served in its foil pouch, it makes an attractive, great-tasting dinner with few dishes to wash.

PREP: 40 MINUTES GRILL: 12 TO 14 MINUTES PER ½-INCH THICKNESS MAKES: 4 SERVINGS

- **1** pound fresh or frozen skinless salmon, orange roughy, cod, or tilapia fillets, ½ to ¾ inch thick
- Nonstick cooking spray
- **2** cups carrots cut into thin bite-size strips
- **2** cups red sweet pepper cut into bite-size strips
- **12** fresh asparagus spears (about 12 ounces), trimmed
- **4** small yellow summer squash (about 1 pound), cut into ¼-inch-thick slices
- **½** cup dry white wine or chicken broth
- **2** teaspoons snipped fresh rosemary or ½ teaspoon dried rosemary, crushed
- **1** teaspoon bottled minced garlic (2 cloves)
- **¼** teaspoon salt
- **¼** teaspoon ground black pepper
- **2** tablespoons butter or margarine, cut up
- Hot cooked white or brown rice

1 Thaw fish, if frozen; rinse and pat dry with paper towels. Measure thickness of fish. Cut into 4 serving-size pieces. Set aside.

2 Cut eight 18-inch squares heavy foil. Stack 2 squares together; repeat to form 4 stacks total. Coat 1 side of each stack with nonstick cooking spray. Divide carrots, sweet pepper, and asparagus among stacks of foil. Top with the fish and squash.

3 For seasonings, in a small bowl combine wine or broth, rosemary, garlic, salt, and black pepper. Drizzle over fish and vegetables; dot with butter. Bring up 2 opposite edges of each foil stack; seal with a double fold. Fold remaining ends to completely enclose the fish and vegetables, leaving space for steam to build.

4 For a charcoal grill, place foil packets on the grill rack of an uncovered grill directly over medium coals. Grill until fish flakes easily when tested with a fork and vegetables are tender, carefully opening packets to check doneness. Allow 12 to 14 minutes per ½-inch thickness of fish. (For a gas grill, preheat grill. Reduce heat to medium. Place foil packets on grill rack over heat. Cover and grill as above.) Serve with hot cooked rice.

NUTRITION FACTS PER SERVING: 518 cal., 22 g total fat (8 g sat. fat), 91 mg chol., 294 mg sodium, 43 g carbo., 6 g fiber, 32 g pro.

Sesame-Ginger Grilled Salmon

Toasting sesame seeds is easy. Place them in a small, heavy skillet over low heat and cook, stirring frequently, for 5 to 7 minutes or until they're golden brown and fragrant.

PREP: 15 MINUTES **MARINATE:** 30 MINUTES OR 2 HOURS
GRILL: 7 TO 9 MINUTES PER ½-INCH THICKNESS **MAKES:** 4 SERVINGS

4	5-ounce fresh or frozen skinless salmon fillets, ¾ to 1 inch thick
¼	cup light soy sauce
2	tablespoons lime juice
1	tablespoon grated fresh ginger
1	teaspoon brown sugar
½	teaspoon toasted sesame oil
2	tablespoons sesame seeds, toasted

1 Thaw fish, if frozen; rinse and pat dry with paper towels. Measure thickness of fish. For marinade, in a shallow dish combine soy sauce, lime juice, ginger, brown sugar, and sesame oil. Add fish, turning to coat. Cover and marinate at room temperature for 30 minutes or in the refrigerator for 2 hours, turning fish occasionally.

2 Drain fish, discarding marinade. For a charcoal grill, arrange medium-hot coals around a drip pan. Test for medium heat above the pan. Place fish on greased grill rack over drip pan, tucking under any thin edges. Sprinkle fish with sesame seeds. Cover and grill until fish flakes easily when tested with a fork. Allow 7 to 9 minutes per ½-inch thickness of fish. Do not turn fish. (For a gas grill, preheat grill. Reduce heat to medium. Adjust for indirect cooking. Grill as above.)

NUTRITION FACTS PER SERVING: 282 cal., 17 g total fat (4 g sat. fat), 93 mg chol., 130 mg sodium, 2 g carbo., 1 g fiber, 29 g pro.

Red Snapper with Fresh Herb-Pecan Crust

Butter, chopped pecans, fresh herbs, and a touch of lemon and garlic make a toasty crust on this meaty grilled red snapper. Instead of flat-leaf parsley, you can substitute your favorite herb. It's terrific on fresh walleye too!

PREP: 15 MINUTES **GRILL:** 4 TO 6 MINUTES PER ½-INCH THICKNESS **MAKES:** 4 SERVINGS

4   5- or 6-ounce fresh or frozen red snapper fillets with skin, ½ to 1 inch thick

⅓   cup finely chopped pecans

2   tablespoons fine dry bread crumbs

2   tablespoons butter or margarine, softened

1   teaspoon finely shredded lemon peel

1   teaspoon bottled minced garlic (2 cloves)

1   tablespoon snipped fresh flat-leaf parsley

¼   teaspoon salt

⅛   teaspoon ground black pepper

    Dash cayenne pepper

    Snipped fresh flat-leaf parsley (optional)

    Lemon wedges (optional)

1 Thaw fish, if frozen; rinse and pat dry with paper towels. Measure thickness of fish. In a small bowl combine pecans, bread crumbs, butter, lemon peel, garlic, the 1 tablespoon parsley, the salt, black pepper, and cayenne pepper.

2 For a charcoal grill, place fish, skin side down, on the greased rack of an uncovered grill directly over medium coals. Spoon pecan mixture on top of fillets; spread slightly. Grill until fish flakes easily when tested with a fork. Allow 4 to 6 minutes per ½-inch thickness of fish. (For a gas grill, preheat grill. Reduce heat to medium. Place fish on greased grill rack over heat. Spoon pecan mixture on top of fillets; spread slightly. Cover and grill as above.) If desired, sprinkle fish with additional snipped parsley and serve with lemon wedges.

NUTRITION FACTS PER SERVING: 268 cal., 14 g total fat (4 g sat. fat), 67 mg chol., 287 mg sodium, 7 g carbo., 8 g fiber, 30 g pro.

Snapper with Cilantro Pesto

Cilantro, used in a pesto, has a freshness that goes beautifully with fish. Try the pesto in other recipes. For a change of pace, stir it into angel hair pasta to create a side dish for grilled fish.

PREP: 15 MINUTES **GRILL:** 4 TO 6 MINUTES PER ½-INCH THICKNESS **MAKES:** 4 SERVINGS

4	4- to 5-ounce fresh or frozen red snapper or halibut fillets, ½ to ¾ inch thick
1	cup loosely packed fresh parsley leaves
½	cup loosely packed fresh cilantro leaves
3	tablespoons grated Parmesan cheese
2	tablespoons pine nuts or slivered almonds
2	teaspoons lemon juice
1½	teaspoons bottled minced garlic (3 cloves)
⅛	teaspoon salt
2	tablespoons olive oil
1	tablespoon lemon juice
2	teaspoons olive oil
	Salt
	Ground black pepper
1	plum tomato, seeded and chopped

1 Thaw fish, if frozen; rinse and pat dry with paper towels. Measure thickness of fish.

2 For pesto, in a blender container or food processor bowl combine the parsley, cilantro, Parmesan cheese, nuts, the 2 teaspoons lemon juice, the garlic, and the ⅛ teaspoon salt. Cover and blend or process with several on-off turns until nearly smooth, stopping the machine and scraping down side as necessary. With the machine running slowly, gradually add the 2 tablespoons oil; blend or process until the consistency of softened butter, scraping side as necessary. Transfer to a small bowl. Set aside.

3 In a small bowl stir together the 1 tablespoon lemon juice and the 2 teaspoons oil. Brush fish with lemon mixture. Sprinkle fish with salt and pepper.

4 Place fish in a greased grill basket, tucking under any thin edges. For a charcoal grill, grill fish in basket on the rack of an uncovered grill directly over medium coals until fish flakes easily when tested with a fork, turning basket once halfway through grilling. Allow 4 to 6 minutes per ½-inch thickness of fish. (For a gas grill, preheat grill. Reduce heat to medium. Place fish in basket on grill rack over heat. Cover and grill as above.)

5 To serve, spoon pesto over fish and top with tomato.

NUTRITION FACTS PER SERVING: 254 cal., 15 g total fat (3 g sat. fat), 45 mg chol., 281 mg sodium, 4 g carbo., 0 g fiber, 27 g pro.

Bass with Star Fruit Salsa

Sunny star fruit (carambola) brightens up meaty grilled fish fillets.

PREP: 25 MINUTES GRILL: 14 MINUTES MAKES: 4 SERVINGS

1 pound fresh or frozen sea bass or red snapper fillets, about 1 inch thick

½ to 1 teaspoon cumin seeds

3 large star fruit (carambola)

1 small lime

½ of a small fresh poblano chile pepper, seeded and finely chopped*

2 tablespoons snipped fresh cilantro

½ teaspoon salt

¼ teaspoon cayenne pepper

1 Thaw fish, if frozen; rinse and pat dry with paper towels. Cut into 4 serving-size pieces.

2 In a dry, small skillet cook cumin seeds, uncovered, over medium-high heat for 1 to 2 minutes or until toasted, shaking the skillet frequently. Set cumin seeds aside. Slice 1 star fruit; cover and chill. Chop remaining 2 star fruit; set aside. Finely shred lime peel; set aside. Peel, section, and chop lime. For salsa, in a medium bowl combine toasted cumin seeds, chopped star fruit, chopped lime, poblano pepper, cilantro, and ⅛ teaspoon of the salt; cover and chill.

3 Sprinkle fish with remaining salt, the cayenne pepper, and lime peel.

4 For a charcoal grill, arrange medium-hot coals around a drip pan. Test for medium heat above the pan. Place fish fillets on greased grill rack over drip pan. Cover and grill for 14 to 18 minutes or until fish flakes easily when tested with a fork, gently turning once halfway through grilling. (For a gas grill, preheat grill. Reduce heat to medium. Adjust for indirect cooking. Grill as above.) Serve with salsa; garnish with the sliced star fruit.

NUTRITION FACTS PER SERVING: 143 cal., 3 g total fat (1 g sat. fat), 47 mg chol., 280 mg sodium, 8 g carbo., 1 g fiber, 22 g pro.

*NOTE: Because chile peppers contain volatile oils that can burn your skin and eyes, avoid direct contact with them as much as possible. When working with chile peppers, wear plastic or rubber gloves. If your bare hands do touch the chile peppers, wash your hands and nails well with soap and warm water.

Orange and Dill Sea Bass

*When it's time to give the fish-and-lemon combo
a vacation, explore other citrus possibilities. Here, sea bass is perfumed orange by
"baking" it on your grill on a bed of orange slices.*

PREP: 15 MINUTES GRILL: 6 MINUTES MAKES: 4 SERVINGS

4 5- to 6-ounce fresh or frozen sea bass or
   orange roughy fillets, about ¾ inch thick

2 tablespoons snipped fresh dill

2 tablespoons olive oil

¼ teaspoon salt

¼ teaspoon ground white pepper

4 large oranges, cut into ¼-inch-thick slices

1 orange, cut into wedges

   Fresh dill sprigs (optional)

1 Thaw fish, if frozen; rinse and pat dry with paper towels. In a small bowl stir together the snipped dill, oil, salt, and white pepper. Brush both sides of fish with dill mixture.

2 For a charcoal grill, place medium coals in bottom of a grill with a cover. Arrange a bed of orange slices on the greased grill rack directly over coals. Arrange fish on orange slices. Cover; grill for 6 to 9 minutes or until fish flakes easily when tested with a fork. Do not turn fish. (For a gas grill, preheat grill. Reduce heat to medium. Arrange orange slices and fish on greased grill rack over heat. Grill as above.)

3 To serve, use a spatula to transfer fish and grilled orange slices to a serving platter or dinner plates. Squeeze the juice from orange wedges over fish. If desired, garnish with dill sprigs.

NUTRITION FACTS PER SERVING: 207 cal., 10 g total fat (2 g sat. fat), 59 mg chol., 230 mg sodium, 2 g carbo., 0 g fiber, 26 g pro.

Mahi Mahi with Vegetable Slaw

The cabbage, carrot, and jicama slaw gives this flavorful dish a pleasant crunch.

PREP: 15 MINUTES **MARINATE:** 30 MINUTES **GRILL:** 4 TO 6 MINUTES PER ½-INCH THICKNESS
MAKES: 4 SERVINGS

4   5- to 6-ounce fresh or frozen mahi mahi or pike fillets, ½ to ¾ inch thick

1   teaspoon finely shredded lime peel (set aside)

¼   cup lime juice

¼   cup snipped fresh cilantro

3   tablespoons olive oil

1   tablespoon honey

1   fresh jalapeño chile pepper; seeded and finely chopped*

1½   teaspoons bottled minced garlic (3 cloves)

⅛   teaspoon salt

1½   cups packaged shredded cabbage with carrot (coleslaw mix)

1   cup shredded jicama

① Thaw fish, if frozen; rinse and pat dry with paper towels. Measure thickness of fish. Place fish in a shallow dish. For dressing, in a small bowl combine lime juice, cilantro, oil, honey, jalapeño pepper, garlic, and salt; divide in half. Stir lime peel into 1 portion of the dressing. Pour dressing with lime peel over fish; turn fish to coat. Cover; marinate at room temperature for 30 minutes.

② For slaw, in a medium bowl combine cabbage mixture and jicama. Pour remaining dressing over slaw; toss to coat. Cover and chill until ready to serve.

③ Drain fish, discarding marinade. Place fish in a well-greased wire grill basket, tucking under any thin edges. For a charcoal grill, grill fish in basket on the rack of an uncovered grill directly over medium coals until fish flakes easily when tested with a fork, turning basket once halfway through grilling. Allow 4 to 6 minutes per ½-inch thickness. (For a gas grill, preheat grill. Reduce heat to medium. Place fish in basket on grill rack over heat. Cover and grill as above.) Serve fish with slaw.

NUTRITION FACTS PER SERVING: 276 cal., 10 g total fat (1 g sat. fat), 67 mg chol., 130 mg sodium, 12 g carbo., 1 g fiber, 34 g pro.

*NOTE: Because chile peppers contain volatile oils that can burn your skin and eyes, avoid direct contact with them as much as possible. When working with chile peppers, wear plastic or rubber gloves. If your bare hands do touch the chile peppers, wash your hands and nails well with soap and warm water.

Blackened Catfish with Roasted Potatoes

Vegetables roasted in olive oil add color and variety to this version of a Cajun classic.

PREP: 20 MINUTES GRILL: 35 MINUTES MAKES: 4 SERVINGS

4	4- to 5-ounce fresh or frozen catfish or red snapper fillets, about ½ inch thick
1	tablespoon olive oil
¼	teaspoon salt
	Several dashes bottled hot pepper sauce
1½	pounds tiny new potatoes, thinly sliced
4	medium carrots, thinly sliced
1	medium green sweet pepper, cut into thin strips
1	medium onion, sliced
½	teaspoon Cajun seasoning
	Nonstick cooking spray
1	tablespoon snipped fresh chervil or parsley

1 Thaw fish, if frozen; rinse and pat dry with paper towels. Fold a 48×18-inch piece of heavy foil in half to make a 24×18-inch rectangle. In a large bowl combine oil, salt, and hot pepper sauce. Add the potatoes, carrots, sweet pepper, and onion; toss to coat. Place in the center of foil. Bring up 2 opposite edges of foil; seal with a double fold. Fold remaining ends to completely enclose vegetables, leaving space for steam to build.

2 For a charcoal grill, grill vegetable packet on the greased rack of an uncovered grill directly over medium coals for 35 to 40 minutes or until potatoes and carrots are tender.

3 Sprinkle both sides of fish with Cajun seasoning and lightly coat with nonstick cooking spray. Place fish in a well-greased wire grill basket, tucking under any thin edges. Add grill basket to grill beside vegetable packet for the last 4 to 6 minutes of grilling. Grill until fish flakes easily with a fork, gently turning grill basket once halfway through grilling. (For a gas grill, preheat grill. Reduce heat to medium. Place vegetable packet, then fish in grill basket on grill rack over heat. Cover and grill as above.)

4 To serve, sprinkle fish and vegetables with snipped chervil or parsley.

NUTRITION FACTS PER SERVING: 352 cal., 6 g total fat (1 g sat. fat), 42 mg chol., 266 mg sodium, 48 g carbo., 5 g fiber, 28 g pro.

212

Trout with Mushrooms

Whether you pull it from a stream or from the nearest supermarket, fresh trout needs few seasonings to complement its delicate flavor.

PREP: 15 MINUTES GRILL: 6 MINUTES MAKES: 4 SERVINGS

4 8-ounce fresh or frozen dressed whole trout (heads removed, if desired)

1 large lemon, halved

¼ cup olive oil

4 teaspoons snipped fresh thyme or 1 teaspoon dried thyme, crushed

¼ teaspoon salt

¼ teaspoon crushed red pepper

1½ cups sliced jumbo button mushrooms (4 ounces)

1 bunch green onions (8 to 10)

4 sprigs fresh thyme

1 Thaw fish, if frozen; rinse and pat dry with paper towels. Strain juice from 1 lemon half into a small bowl. Set aside. Thinly slice remaining lemon half. Cut the slices in half. Set aside.

2 In a small bowl stir together the lemon juice, olive oil, snipped or dried thyme, salt, and crushed red pepper. Set aside ¼ cup of the lemon juice mixture. Toss the sliced mushrooms with the remaining lemon juice mixture; cover and set aside.

3 Trim the root end and the first inch of the green tops off each green onion. Brush the onion pieces with some of the reserved ¼ cup lemon juice mixture.

4 Place trout in a grill basket. Tuck 2 halved lemon slices and a thyme sprig inside the cavity of each trout. Brush skin and inside flesh of trout with the remainder of the ¼ cup lemon juice mixture.

5 For a charcoal grill, grill fish on a greased rack of an uncovered grill directly over medium coals for 6 to 9 minutes or until fish flakes easily when tested with a fork. Grill green onions alongside fish for 4 to 6 minutes or until tender, turning once. (For a gas grill, preheat grill. Reduce heat to medium. Place fish, then green onions on greased grill rack over heat. Cover and grill as above.)

6 To serve, arrange green onions on 4 dinner plates. Arrange fish on green onions. Spoon the marinated mushroom slices over fish.

NUTRITION FACTS PER SERVING: 454 cal., 26 g total fat (5 g sat. fat), 133 mg chol., 231 mg sodium, 4 g carbo., 1 g fiber, 49 g pro.

Ginger Tuna Kabobs

A touch of honey added to the reserved marinade makes a delicious brush-on for these grilled tuna, pineapple, and vegetable kabobs.

PREP: 30 MINUTES **MARINATE:** 30 MINUTES **GRILL:** 8 MINUTES **MAKES:** 4 SERVINGS

12	ounces fresh or frozen skinless tuna steaks, cut 1 inch thick
3	tablespoons reduced-sodium soy sauce
3	tablespoons water
1	tablespoon snipped green onion tops or snipped fresh chives
2	teaspoons grated fresh ginger
½	of a medium fresh pineapple, cored and cut into 1-inch cubes
1	medium red or green sweet pepper, cut into 1½-inch squares
6	green onions, cut into 2-inch pieces
¼	cup honey

1 Thaw tuna, if frozen; rinse and pat dry with paper towels. Cut tuna into 1-inch cubes. Place in a resealable plastic bag set in a shallow dish. Add soy sauce, the water, snipped green onion tops or chives, and ginger. Seal bag; turn gently to coat tuna. Marinate in the refrigerator for 30 minutes.

2 Drain tuna, reserving marinade. On long metal skewers, alternately thread tuna, pineapple, sweet pepper, and green onion pieces, leaving ¼-inch space between pieces. For a charcoal grill, grill kabobs on the greased rack of an uncovered grill directly over medium coals for 8 to 12 minutes or until tuna flakes easily when tested with a fork, turning kabobs once halfway through grilling. (For a gas grill, preheat grill. Reduce heat to medium. Place kabobs on greased grill rack over heat. Cover and grill as above.)

3 Meanwhile, bring reserved marinade to boiling; strain. Discard any solids. Stir honey into hot marinade. Brush tuna, pineapple, and vegetables generously with honey-soy mixture just before serving.

NUTRITION FACTS PER SERVING: 251 cal., 5 g total fat (1 g sat. fat), 32 mg chol., 446 mg sodium, 32 g carbo., 2 g fiber, 22 g pro.

214

Fragrant Swordfish Brochettes

Loaded with herbs and spices, the marinade for the fish packs tons of flavor.

PREP: 25 MINUTES **MARINATE:** 1 TO 2 HOURS **GRILL:** 8 MINUTES **MAKES:** 4 SERVINGS

1½ pounds fresh or frozen swordfish or salmon steaks, cut 1½ inches thick

⅓ cup lightly packed fresh parsley leaves

⅓ cup lightly packed fresh mint leaves

⅓ cup lightly packed fresh cilantro leaves

3 tablespoons lemon juice

3 tablespoons olive oil

1 tablespoon bottled minced garlic (6 cloves)

2 teaspoons paprika

½ teaspoon ground coriander

½ teaspoon ground cumin

8 bay leaves*

Hot cooked couscous or rice pilaf (optional)

1 Thaw fish, if frozen; rinse and pat dry with paper towels. Cut fish into 1½-inch cubes. Place fish in a shallow dish. For marinade, in a blender container or food processor bowl combine parsley, mint, cilantro, lemon juice, oil, garlic, paprika, coriander, and cumin. Cover and blend or process until combined, scraping down side of blender or food processor as necessary. Pour over fish; turn fish to coat. Cover and marinate in the refrigerator for at least 1 hour or up to 2 hours, turning fish once.

2 Drain fish, discarding marinade. On 4 long metal skewers, alternately thread fish and bay leaves. For a charcoal grill, grill skewers on the greased rack of an uncovered grill directly over medium coals for 8 to 12 minutes or until fish flakes easily when tested with a fork, gently turning once halfway through grilling. (For a gas grill, preheat grill. Reduce heat to medium. Place skewers on greased grill rack over heat. Cover and grill as above.) Discard bay leaves.

3 If desired, serve with couscous or rice pilaf.

NUTRITION FACTS PER SERVING: 319 cal., 17 g total fat (3 g sat. fat), 67 mg chol., 159 mg sodium, 5 g carbo., 0 g fiber, 35 g pro.

*NOTE: Bay leaves flavor the fish during grilling, but are not to be eaten.

Salmon with Cucumber Kabobs

Cooked cucumbers provide a pleasant change of pace on these kabobs.
Though their characteristic crispness disappears with cooking, their delicacy does not.

PREP: 15 MINUTES **MARINATE:** 10 TO 20 MINUTES
GRILL: 4 TO 6 MINUTES PER ½-INCH THICKNESS **MAKES:** 4 SERVINGS

4   6- to 8-ounce fresh or frozen skinless salmon fillets, ½ to 1 inch thick

⅓   cup lemon juice

1   tablespoon olive oil or cooking oil

2   teaspoons snipped fresh tarragon

1   medium cucumber, halved lengthwise and cut into 1-inch-thick slices

1   medium red onion, cut into wedges

8   cherry tomatoes

   Hot cooked rice (optional)

1 Thaw fish, if frozen; rinse and pat dry with paper towels. Measure thickness of fish. Place fish in a resealable plastic bag set in a shallow dish. For marinade, in a small bowl combine lemon juice, oil, and tarragon. For basting sauce, set aside half of the marinade. Pour the remaining marinade over fish. Seal bag; turn to coat fish. Marinate at room temperature for at least 10 minutes or up to 20 minutes. Meanwhile, on four 10-inch skewers, alternately thread cucumber and onion.

2 Drain fish, discarding marinade. Place fish in a well-greased wire grill basket, tucking under any thin edges. For a charcoal grill, grill the fish and vegetable kabobs on the rack of an uncovered grill directly over medium coals until fish flakes easily when tested with a fork and vegetables are tender, gently turning once and brushing once with basting sauce halfway through grilling. Allow 4 to 6 minutes per ½-inch thickness of fish and 8 to 12 minutes for vegetables. (For a gas grill, preheat grill. Reduce heat to medium. Place fish in basket and vegetables on greased grill rack over heat. Cover and grill as above.) Add the tomatoes to the ends of the kabobs for the last 2 minutes of grilling.

3 If desired, serve fish and vegetables with hot cooked rice.

NUTRITION FACTS PER SERVING: 201 cal., 8 g total fat (2 g sat. fat), 31 mg chol., 106 mg sodium, 6 g carbo., 1 g fiber, 25 g pro.

Panzanella with Grilled Tuna

Pane means bread in Italian, and making panzanella (bread salad) is a wonderful way to use bread that's not as fresh as just-baked but still too good to throw away.

PREP: 20 MINUTES **GRILL:** 4 TO 6 MINUTES PER ½-INCH THICKNESS
STAND: 5 MINUTES **MAKES:** 4 SERVINGS

1 pound fresh or frozen tuna steaks, cut ½ to 1 inch thick

½ cup bottled balsamic vinaigrette or red wine vinegar salad dressing

½ teaspoon finely snipped fresh rosemary

2 cups torn mixed salad greens

1½ cups broccoli florets

2 small tomatoes, chopped

¼ cup thinly sliced green onions

4 cups 1-inch cubes day-old Italian bread

Finely shredded Parmesan cheese (optional)

1 Thaw tuna, if frozen; rinse and pat dry with paper towels. Measure thickness of fish. For sauce, in a small bowl combine vinaigrette and rosemary. Set aside 2 tablespoons of the sauce to use as the dressing.

2 For a charcoal grill, grill fish on the greased rack of an uncovered grill directly over medium coals until fish flakes easily when tested with a fork, gently turning and brushing with remaining sauce once halfway through grilling. Allow 4 to 6 minutes per ½ inch thickness. (For a gas grill, preheat grill. Reduce heat to medium. Place fish on greased grill rack over heat. Cover and grill as above.)

3 Meanwhile, in a large salad bowl combine greens, broccoli, tomatoes, and green onions. Flake fish; add to greens mixture. Drizzle with the reserved 2 tablespoons dressing; toss gently to coat. Add bread cubes; toss gently to combine. Let stand for 5 minutes before serving. If desired, sprinkle with Parmesan cheese.

NUTRITION FACTS PER SERVING: 380 cal., 17 g total fat (3 g sat. fat), 47 mg chol., 608 mg sodium, 24 g carbo., 2 g fiber, 33 g pro.

Jambalaya on a Stick

The combination of shrimp, smoked sausage, chicken, and vegetables is reminiscent of the Creole classic jambalaya.

PREP: 35 MINUTES **MARINATE:** 1 TO 2 HOURS **SOAK:** 30 MINUTES
GRILL: 10 MINUTES **MAKES:** 6 SERVINGS

18 fresh or frozen large shrimp in shells (about 12 ounces)

12 ounces cooked smoked sausage links, cut into 12 pieces

8 ounces skinless, boneless chicken breast halves, cut into 1-inch pieces

1 medium green sweet pepper, cut into 1-inch pieces

1 medium onion, cut into 1-inch wedges

⅓ cup white wine vinegar

⅓ cup tomato sauce

2 tablespoons olive oil

2 teaspoons dried thyme, crushed

2 teaspoons bottled hot pepper sauce

¾ teaspoon dried minced garlic

24 8-inch wooden skewers

3 cups hot cooked rice

2 tablespoons snipped fresh parsley

6 cherry tomatoes

1 Thaw shrimp, if frozen. Peel and devein shrimp. Rinse shrimp; pat dry with paper towels. Place shrimp, sausage, chicken, sweet pepper, and onion in a resealable plastic bag set in a shallow dish.

2 In a small bowl combine vinegar, tomato sauce, oil, thyme, bottled hot pepper sauce, and garlic. Pour half of the tomato sauce mixture over meat and vegetables. Seal bag; turn to coat pieces. Marinate in the refrigerator for at least 1 hour or up to 2 hours, turning bag occasionally. Cover and chill remaining tomato sauce mixture.

3 Meanwhile, soak wooden skewers in enough water to cover for 30 minutes; drain.

4 Drain meat and vegetables, discarding marinade. On soaked skewers, alternately thread meat and vegetables (to secure pieces, use 2 skewers for each kabob—1 skewer through head end of shrimp and another skewer parallel to first skewer but through tail end of shrimp), leaving ¼ inch space between pieces.

5 For a charcoal grill, grill skewers on the greased rack of an uncovered grill directly over medium coals for 10 to 12 minutes or until shrimp are opaque and chicken is no longer pink, turning occasionally. (For a gas grill, preheat grill. Reduce heat to medium. Place skewers on greased grill rack over heat. Cover and grill as above.)

6 Meanwhile, in a small saucepan heat chilled tomato sauce mixture. Combine cooked rice and parsley. Serve rice mixture and cherry tomatoes with kabobs. Pass warmed tomato sauce mixture.

NUTRITION FACTS PER SERVING: 451 cal., 23 g total fat (9 g sat. fat), 112 mg chol., 632 mg sodium, 30 g carbo., 2 g fiber, 27 g pro.

Margarita Kabobs

These shrimp kabobs with a brush-on sauce are based on the classic cocktail. The alcohol helps the flavors blend subtly, but you can omit it.

PREP: 30 MINUTES GRILL: 10 MINUTES MAKES: 6 SERVINGS

1¼ pounds fresh or frozen jumbo shrimp in shells or skinless, boneless chicken breast halves or thighs

1 large red or green sweet pepper, cut into bite-size pieces

1 medium red onion, cut into wedges

1 cup orange marmalade

⅓ cup lime juice

¼ cup tequila (optional)

2 tablespoons snipped fresh cilantro

2 tablespoons cooking oil

1 teaspoon bottled minced garlic (2 cloves)

6 ½-inch-thick slices peeled fresh pineapple

1 Thaw shrimp, if frozen. Peel and devein shrimp, leaving tails intact. Rinse shrimp; pat dry with paper towels. If using chicken, cut it into 1-inch chunks. On long metal skewers alternately thread shrimp and/or chicken, sweet pepper, and onion, leaving ¼ inch space between pieces.

2 For sauce, in a small saucepan stir together orange marmalade, lime juice, tequila (if desired), cilantro, oil, and garlic. Cook and stir just until marmalade is melted.

3 For a charcoal grill, grill kabobs on the greased rack of an uncovered grill directly over medium coals for 10 to 12 minutes or until shrimp are opaque and chicken is no longer pink, turning once halfway through grilling. After 5 minutes of grilling, add pineapple to grill rack. Turn pineapple once and brush pineapple and shrimp and/or chicken once with sauce during the last 3 minutes of grilling. (For a gas grill, preheat grill. Reduce heat to medium. Place skewers, then pineapple on greased grill rack over heat. Cover and grill as above.)

4 To serve, reheat sauce until bubbly; pass warm sauce with kabobs and pineapple.

NUTRITION FACTS PER SERVING: 314 cal., 6 g total fat (1 g sat. fat), 108 mg chol., 141 mg sodium, 52 g carbo., 2 g fiber, 16 g pro.

Rosemary-Orange Shrimp Kabobs

With shrimp, turkey bacon, and a special orange-flavored couscous and sweet pepper combo, this dish is definitely company fare.

PREP: 30 MINUTES GRILL: 8 MINUTES MAKES: 4 SERVINGS

16 fresh or frozen jumbo shrimp in shells (about 1 pound total)

8 slices turkey bacon, halved crosswise

2 red and/or yellow sweet peppers, cut into 1-inch pieces

2 teaspoons finely shredded orange or blood orange peel

2 tablespoons orange or blood orange juice

2 teaspoons snipped fresh rosemary

2 cups hot cooked couscous

1 cup cooked or canned black beans, rinsed and drained

1 Thaw shrimp, if frozen. Peel and devein shrimp, leaving tails intact. Rinse shrimp; pat dry with paper towels.

2 Wrap each shrimp in a half slice of the bacon. On long metal skewers, alternately thread bacon-wrapped shrimp and sweet pepper pieces, leaving ¼ inch space between pieces. In a small bowl combine 1 teaspoon of the orange peel, the orange juice, and rosemary. Brush over kabobs.

3 For a charcoal grill, grill kabobs on the greased rack of an uncovered grill directly over medium coals for 8 to 10 minutes or until shrimp are opaque and bacon is crisp, turning once halfway through grilling. (For a gas grill, preheat grill. Reduce heat to medium. Place kabobs on greased grill rack over heat. Cover and grill as above.)

4 Meanwhile, in a medium saucepan stir together the remaining 1 teaspoon orange peel, the couscous, and black beans; heat through. Serve with shrimp and peppers.

NUTRITION FACTS PER SERVING: 310 cal., 7 g total fat (2 g sat. fat), 149 mg chol., 563 mg sodium, 36 g carbo., 2 g fiber, 26 g pro.

Seafood Skewers with Peanut Sauce

While the coconut milk-and-lime marinade is doing its work,
you make a simple peanut sauce. Then, after just minutes on the grill,
the skewers are ready to be dipped and devoured.

PREP: 20 MINUTES MARINATE: 30 MINUTES GRILL: 5 MINUTES MAKES: 4 TO 6 SERVINGS

8 ounces fresh or frozen peeled and deveined medium shrimp

8 ounces fresh or frozen sea scallops

¼ cup purchased unsweetened coconut milk

2 tablespoons lime juice

1 tablespoon soy sauce

⅓ cup purchased unsweetened coconut milk

¼ cup peanut butter

2 tablespoons snipped fresh cilantro

1 tablespoon thinly sliced green onion

1 tablespoon lime juice

½ teaspoon chile paste or ⅛ teaspoon crushed red pepper

1 Thaw shrimp and scallops, if frozen; rinse and pat dry with paper towels. Place in a medium bowl.

2 For marinade, in a small bowl combine the ¼ cup coconut milk, the 2 tablespoons lime juice, and the soy sauce. Pour marinade over shrimp and scallops, stirring to coat. Cover and marinate at room temperature for 30 minutes, stirring once.

3 Meanwhile, for sauce, in a small bowl whisk together the ⅓ cup coconut milk, the peanut butter, cilantro, green onion, the 1 tablespoon lime juice, and the chile paste or crushed red pepper. Cover and let stand at room temperature for 30 minutes to blend flavors.

4 Drain shrimp and scallops, discarding marinade. On long metal skewers, alternately thread shrimp and scallops, leaving ¼ inch space between pieces.

5 For a charcoal grill, grill skewers on the greased rack of an uncovered grill directly over medium coals for 5 to 8 minutes or until shrimp and scallops are opaque, turning once halfway through grilling. (For a gas grill, preheat grill. Reduce heat to medium. Place skewers on greased grill rack over heat. Cover and grill as above.) Serve seafood with sauce.

NUTRITION FACTS PER SERVING: 270 cal., 16 g total fat (6 g sat. fat), 104 mg chol., 542 mg sodium, 7 g carbo., 1 g fiber, 26 g pro.

BBQ Shrimp on Pineapple Planks

Jumbo shrimp are more impressive, but medium shrimp also work well for these skewers. Use 24 medium shrimp and grill them for 5 to 8 minutes or until they turn opaque.

PREP: 40 MINUTES **MARINATE:** 30 MINUTES **SOAK:** 30 MINUTES **GRILL:** 7 MINUTES

MAKES: 8 SERVINGS

16	fresh or frozen jumbo shrimp in shells (about 1 pound)
¼	cup bottled barbecue sauce
1	to 2 tablespoons chopped canned chipotle chile peppers in adobo sauce*
3	tablespoons butter or margarine, melted
1	teaspoon bottled minced garlic (2 cloves)
8	6- to 8-inch wooden skewers
1	fresh medium pineapple, crown removed and peeled
½	cup chopped seeded cucumber
½	cup chopped peeled jicama
1	tablespoon lime juice or lemon juice
¼	teaspoon salt
	Bottled barbecue sauce
¼	cup snipped fresh cilantro

1 Thaw shrimp, if frozen. Peel and devein shrimp, leaving tails intact. Rinse shrimp; pat dry with paper towels.

2 In a medium bowl combine the ¼ cup barbecue sauce, the chipotle peppers, 2 tablespoons of the melted butter, and the garlic. Stir in shrimp. Cover and marinate in the refrigerator for 30 minutes, stirring occasionally.

3 Meanwhile, soak wooden skewers in enough water to cover for 30 minutes; drain. Cut pineapple lengthwise into ½-inch-thick slices. Chop 1 of the slices to measure ½ cup; set aside for relish. Halve each pineapple slice crosswise (you should have 8 planks of pineapple). Using remaining 1 tablespoon melted butter, brush both sides of each pineapple plank; set aside.

4 For relish, in a bowl combine the chopped pineapple, the chopped cucumber, jicama, lime juice, and salt. Cover and set aside until serving time.

5 Remove shrimp from marinade; discard marinade. Thread 2 jumbo shrimp onto each soaked skewer, leaving ¼ inch space between shrimp. For a charcoal grill, grill skewers and pineapple planks on the greased rack of an uncovered grill directly over medium coals until shrimp are opaque and pineapple is heated through, turning once halfway through grilling and brushing with additional bottled barbecue sauce during the last 1 minute of grilling. Allow 7 to 9 minutes for shrimp and 6 to 8 minutes for pineapple planks. (For a gas grill, preheat grill. Reduce heat to medium. Place skewers and pineapple planks on greased grill rack over heat. Cover and grill as above.)

6 To serve, stir snipped cilantro into the relish. Place pineapple planks on a serving platter. Spoon some of the relish over the pineapple planks; top each pineapple plank with a shrimp skewer.

NUTRITION FACTS PER SERVING: 135 cal., 6 g total fat (5 g sat. fat), 110 mg chol., 228 mg sodium, 8 g carbo., 1 g fiber, 12 g pro.

*NOTE: Because chile peppers contain volatile oils that can burn your skin and eyes, avoid direct contact with them as much as possible. When working with chile peppers, wear plastic or rubber gloves. If your bare hands do touch the chile peppers, wash your hands and nails well with soap and warm water.

Garlic and Shrimp Pasta Toss

As any Italian cook knows, garlic, butter, shrimp, and pasta were made for each other. Using roasted garlic can make the best even better.

PREP: 25 MINUTES GRILL: 30 MINUTES + 8 MINUTES MAKES: 4 SERVINGS

1 pound fresh or frozen large shrimp in shells

1 large garlic bulb

1 tablespoon olive oil

2 tablespoons lemon juice

1 red or yellow sweet pepper, quartered lengthwise

1 onion, cut into ½-inch-thick slices

3 cups dried cavatelli (curled shells) or bow tie pasta (farfalle) (about 8 ounces)

2 tablespoons butter, softened

½ teaspoon salt

½ teaspoon ground black pepper

⅓ cup shredded Asiago or Parmesan cheese

1 Thaw shrimp, if frozen. Peel and devein shrimp, leaving tails intact. Rinse shrimp; pat dry with paper towels. Cover and refrigerate until ready to grill.

2 Using a sharp knife, cut off the top ½ inch from garlic bulb to expose the ends of the individual cloves. Leaving garlic bulb whole, remove any loose, papery outer layers.

3 Fold an 18×9-inch piece of heavy foil in half to make a 9-inch square. Place garlic bulb, cut side up, in center of foil. Drizzle bulb with 1½ teaspoons of the oil. Bring up opposite edges of foil and seal with a double fold. Fold remaining edges together to completely enclose garlic, leaving room for steam to build.

4 For a charcoal grill, arrange medium-hot coals around a drip pan. Test for medium heat above the pan. Place garlic on greased grill rack over drip pan. Cover and grill for 30 minutes.

5 Meanwhile, thread shrimp onto long metal skewers, leaving ¼ inch space between pieces. In a small bowl combine the remaining 1½ teaspoons oil and 1 tablespoon of the lemon juice; brush over shrimp, sweet pepper, and onion. Discard any remaining oil-lemon juice mixture.

6 Add skewers to grill rack over drip pan; add sweet pepper and onion to grill rack directly over coals. Cover and grill for 8 to 10 minutes more or until garlic is soft, shrimp are opaque, and vegetables are tender, turning shrimp and vegetables once halfway through grilling. (For a gas grill, preheat grill. Reduce heat to medium. Adjust for indirect cooking. Grill as above.) Remove from grill. Cool garlic and vegetables slightly. Coarsely chop vegetables.

7 While shrimp and vegetables are grilling, cook pasta according to package directions; drain. Return pasta to hot pan.

8 Squeeze garlic pulp into a small bowl. Thoroughly mash garlic pulp. Add butter, salt, and black pepper; mix well. In a large bowl combine pasta and garlic mixture; toss to coat. Add shrimp, vegetables, remaining 1 tablespoon lemon juice, and the cheese; toss gently to mix. Serve immediately.

NUTRITION FACTS PER SERVING: 404 cal., 16 g total fat (7 g sat. fat), 174 mg chol., 567 mg sodium, 44 g carbo., 3 g fiber, 21 g pro.

Pepper Shrimp in Peanut Sauce

Enjoy grilled shrimp at their best in this colorful pasta dish.

PREP: 30 MINUTES GRILL: 5 MINUTES MAKES: 4 SERVINGS

1 pound fresh or frozen medium shrimp in shells

8 ounces dried bow tie pasta or linguine

½ cup water

¼ cup orange marmalade

2 tablespoons peanut butter

2 tablespoons soy sauce

2 teaspoons cornstarch

¼ teaspoon crushed red pepper

2 medium red, yellow, and/or green sweet peppers, cut into 1-inch pieces

Chopped peanuts (optional)

❶ Thaw shrimp, if frozen. Peel and devein shrimp, leaving tails intact. Rinse shrimp; pat dry with paper towels. Set aside. Cook pasta according to package directions; drain. Return pasta to pan; keep warm.

❷ For sauce, in a small saucepan stir together the water, orange marmalade, peanut butter, soy sauce, cornstarch, and crushed red pepper. Bring to boiling; reduce heat. Cook and stir, uncovered, for 2 minutes. Remove from heat and keep warm.

❸ On long metal skewers, alternately thread shrimp and sweet peppers, leaving ¼ inch space between pieces. For a charcoal grill, grill kabobs on the greased rack of an uncovered grill directly over medium coals for 5 to 8 minutes or until shrimp are opaque, turning once halfway through grilling. (For a gas grill, preheat grill. Reduce heat to medium. Place skewers on greased grill rack over heat. Cover and grill as above.)

❹ To serve, add shrimp and peppers to the cooked pasta. Add the sauce; toss gently to coat. If desired, sprinkle individual servings with chopped peanuts.

NUTRITION FACTS PER SERVING: 382 cal., 7 g total fat (1 g sat. fat), 180 mg chol., 718 mg sodium, 57 g carbo., 3 g fiber, 24 g pro.

Pizza-on-the-Beach

For one large pizza, do not divide dough. Instead, roll the entire package of dough into one circle 12 to 15 inches in diameter. Then prepare the pizza as directed.

PREP: 25 MINUTES **GRILL:** 6 MINUTES + 3 MINUTES **STAND:** 5 MINUTES

MAKES: 8 APPETIZER OR 4 MAIN-DISH SERVINGS

4 ounces fresh or frozen medium shrimp

4 ounces fresh or frozen sea scallops

1 large fennel bulb (1 to 1½ pounds)

2 teaspoons olive oil

½ cup water

Nonstick cooking spray

1 10-ounce package refrigerated pizza dough

½ of a 10-ounce container refrigerated light Alfredo sauce (about ½ cup)

½ teaspoon fennel seeds, crushed (optional)

1 cup shredded provolone, scamorze, mozzarella, and/or other cheese (4 ounces)

1 tablespoon snipped fresh fennel leaf (optional)

1 Thaw shrimp and scallops, if frozen; rinse and pat dry with paper towels. Peel and devein shrimp. Cut scallops in half horizontally. Cut off and discard stalks and base of the fennel. (If desired, reserve some of the feathery leaves for garnish.) Wash fennel bulb; remove any brown or wilted outer layers. Halve, core, and cut fennel crosswise into thin slices. Set aside.

2 In a large nonstick skillet heat oil over medium-high heat. Add shrimp and scallops; cook for 2 to 3 minutes or until opaque. Remove shrimp mixture from skillet. Set aside. Add fennel slices and the water to skillet. Bring to boiling; reduce heat. Cover and simmer for 2 to 3 minutes or just until tender. Drain and set aside.

3 Coat a 16-inch grill pizza pan or a 12- to 13-inch pizza pan with nonstick cooking spray; set aside. Unroll pizza dough; divide into 4 pieces. If desired, shape each piece into a ball for round pizzas, or leave as rectangles. On lightly floured surface, roll out each dough piece to ¼-inch thickness. Transfer to pan. (If necessary, grill pizzas in 2 batches.)

4 For a charcoal grill, in a grill with a cover place pizza pan on grill rack directly over medium coals. Cover and grill for 6 to 8 minutes or until bottoms of crusts turn slightly golden, giving pan a half turn after 4 minutes. Remove pan from grill; cool slightly (about 3 minutes). Carefully turn crusts over.

5 Spread Alfredo sauce on pizza crusts to within about ½ inch of edge. Top each crust with shrimp, scallops, and sliced fennel. Sprinkle with fennel seeds, if using. Sprinkle with cheese. Return pizzas to grill. Cover and grill for 3 to 4 minutes more or until cheese is melted and bottoms of crusts are golden. (For a gas grill, preheat grill. Reduce heat to medium. Grill as above.)

6 Remove pizzas from grill. If desired, sprinkle with snipped fennel leaf. Let stand for 5 minutes before serving.

NUTRITION FACTS PER SERVING: 218 cal., 9 g total fat (4 g sat. fat), 38 mg chol., 524 mg sodium, 23 g carbo., 6 g fiber, 12 g pro.

Soy-Lime Scallops with Leeks

*Grilling lime halves caramelizes the sugar in the fruit
for a sharp-sweet finishing touch to this dish.*

PREP: 10 MINUTES MARINATE: 30 MINUTES GRILL: 5 MINUTES MAKES: 4 SERVINGS

1	**pound fresh or frozen sea scallops**
1	**small leek or 4 baby leeks**
8	**medium green or red scallions or green onions**
¼	**cup soy sauce**
¼	**cup rice vinegar**
1	**medium lime, halved**
	Black sesame seeds (optional)
¼	**cup butter, melted**

1 Thaw scallops, if frozen; rinse and pat dry with paper towels. Trim root end and green tops of leek(s). Rinse leek(s) thoroughly to remove any grit. Cut the 1 small leek lengthwise into quarters; insert a wooden pick crosswise through each leek quarter to hold layers together when grilling. (Or trim the baby leeks.)

2 Place leeks, scallops, and scallions or green onions in a resealable plastic bag set in a shallow dish. For marinade, in a small bowl combine soy sauce and rice vinegar. Pour marinade over scallops and vegetables. Seal bag; turn to coat scallops and vegetables. Marinate in refrigerator for 30 minutes.

3 Drain the scallops and vegetables, discarding marinade. For a charcoal grill, place leeks, scallops, scallions or green onions, and lime halves (cut sides down) on the rack of an uncovered grill directly over medium coals. Grill for 5 to 8 minutes or until scallops are opaque, turning scallops and vegetables occasionally. Remove scallions or green onions from grill rack before they overbrown. (For a gas grill, preheat grill. Reduce heat to medium. Place leeks, scallops, and scallions or green onions on the grill rack over heat. Grill as above.)

4 To serve, transfer leeks and scallions or green onions to serving plates. Top with scallops. Using grilling tongs, remove lime halves from grill and squeeze over scallops. If desired, sprinkle with black sesame seeds. Serve with the melted butter.

NUTRITION FACTS PER SERVING: 229 cal., 13 g total fat (8 g sat. fat), 70 mg chol., 467 mg sodium, 8 g carbo., 1 g fiber, 20 g pro.

Lobster Tails with Basil-Walnut Butter

As with many things so easy, this is sinfully delicious. Combine melted butter, garlic, walnuts, and fresh basil and serve it over sweet lobster meat.

PREP: 15 MINUTES **GRILL:** 12 MINUTES **MAKES:** 4 SERVINGS

4 8-ounce frozen lobster tails

2 teaspoons olive oil

⅓ cup butter

2 tablespoons snipped fresh basil

2 tablespoons finely chopped walnuts, toasted*

½ teaspoon bottled minced garlic (1 clove)

1 Thaw lobster. Rinse and pat dry with paper towels. Place lobster tails, shell sides down, on a cutting board. To butterfly, with kitchen scissors, cut each lobster tail in half lengthwise, cutting to but not through the back shell. Bend backward to crack back shell and expose the meat. Brush lobster meat with oil.

2 For a charcoal grill, grill lobster tails, shell sides down, on the greased rack of an uncovered grill directly over medium coals for 12 to 15 minutes or until lobster meat is opaque in the center and shells are bright red, turning once halfway through grilling. Do not overcook. (For a gas grill, preheat grill. Reduce heat to medium. Place lobster tails, shell sides down, on greased grill rack over heat. Cover and grill as above.)

3 While lobster is grilling, in a small saucepan melt butter over low heat without stirring; cool slightly. Pour off and reserve clear top layer; discard milky bottom layer. In a small bowl combine butter, basil, walnuts, and garlic. To serve, spoon butter mixture over lobster meat.

NUTRITION FACTS PER SERVING: 321 cal., 21 g total fat (10 g sat. fat), 145 mg chol., 706 mg sodium, 3 g carbo., 0 g fiber, 30 g pro.

*NOTE: To toast walnuts, spread them in a single layer in a pie plate. Bake in a 350°F oven for 5 to 10 minutes or until light golden brown, watching carefully and stirring once or twice so nuts don't burn.

Zucchini Crab Cakes

You'll need to start with about 1¼ pounds of crab legs to end up with 8 ounces of crabmeat. Be sure to discard any small pieces of shell or cartilage from the crabmeat.

PREP: 20 MINUTES GRILL: 6 MINUTES MAKES: 4 SERVINGS

1   cup coarsely shredded zucchini (about 5 ounces)

¼   cup thinly sliced green onions

6   teaspoons cooking oil

1   beaten egg

½   cup seasoned fine dry bread crumbs

1   tablespoon Dijon-style mustard

½   teaspoon snipped fresh lemon thyme or snipped fresh thyme

⅛   to ¼ teaspoon cayenne pepper (optional)

8   ounces cooked crabmeat, chopped (1½ cups)

2   red and/or yellow tomatoes, cut into ¼-inch-thick slices

    Red and/or yellow cherry tomatoes (optional)

1   large lemon or lime, cut into wedges (optional)

1   recipe Tomato-Sour Cream Dipping Sauce

1 In a large skillet cook and stir the zucchini and green onions in 2 teaspoons of the hot oil about 3 minutes or just until the vegetables are tender and the liquid is evaporated. Cool slightly.

2 In a large bowl combine the egg, bread crumbs, mustard, thyme, and, if desired, cayenne pepper. Add the zucchini mixture and crabmeat; mix well. Using about ¼ cup of the mixture for each crab cake, shape into 8 patties, each about 2½ inches in diameter. Brush both sides of each patty lightly with the remaining 4 teaspoons oil.

3 For a charcoal grill, grill crab cakes on the greased rack of an uncovered grill or on a grilling tray placed on the rack directly over medium-hot coals for 6 to 8 minutes or until golden brown, gently turning once halfway through grilling. (For a gas grill, preheat grill. Reduce heat to medium. Place crab cakes on greased grill rack or on a grilling tray placed on the rack over heat. Cover and grill as above.)

4 For each serving, overlap 2 patties on a dinner plate along with sliced tomatoes. If desired, garnish with cherry tomatoes and lemon wedges. Serve with Tomato-Sour Cream Dipping Sauce.

Tomato-Sour Cream Dipping Sauce: In a small bowl stir together ½ cup dairy sour cream, 3 tablespoons finely chopped yellow and/or red tomatoes, 1 to 2 tablespoons lemon juice or lime juice, and ⅛ teaspoon seasoned salt. Cover and chill in the refrigerator until serving time (up to 2 hours).

NUTRITION FACTS PER SERVING, WITH 2 TABLESPOONS DIPPING SAUCE: 277 cal., 16 g total fat (5 g sat. fat), 123 mg chol., 424 mg sodium, 16 g carbo., 2 g fiber, 17 g pro.

High-and-Dry Clambake

Nori, a Japanese seaweed that's dried in sheets, adds a hint of ocean flavor. Find nori in Asian markets or the supermarket's Asian section. If you can't find it, use parsley.

PREP: 30 MINUTES **SOAK:** 15 MINUTES + 15 MINUTES + 15 MINUTES **GRILL:** 15 MINUTES
MAKES: 4 SERVINGS

2	7- to 8-ounce frozen lobster tails, thawed and halved lengthwise
20	littleneck, Manila, or cherrystone clams in shells
1	cup salt
¾	cup butter, melted
1	teaspoon finely shredded lemon peel
2	tablespoons lemon juice
2	tablespoons snipped fresh basil or 3 tablespoons snipped fresh dill
4	small fresh ears of corn in husks
8	sheets nori or 1 large bunch fresh parsley
8	ounces cooked kielbasa or other smoked sausage, cut into 8 slices
12	to 16 sprigs fresh basil and/or dill
	Salt
	Ground black pepper

❶ Thaw lobster tails; rinse and pat dry with paper towels. Thoroughly wash clams in shells. In a large pot or kettle combine 4 quarts cold water and ⅓ cup of the salt. Place clams in the saltwater mixture; let stand for 15 minutes. Drain and rinse well. Repeat soaking, draining, and rinsing twice, using new water and salt each time.

❷ In a small bowl stir together butter, lemon peel, lemon juice, and the snipped basil or dill; set aside. Remove cornhusks; clean several husks and set aside. Use hands or a stiff brush to remove silk from corn. Brush corn with about 2 tablespoons of the butter mixture. Lay the clean cornhusks back in place around ears of corn.

❸ Tear off four 24×18-inch pieces of heavy foil. Lay 2 sheets of the nori or 3 or 4 large sprigs of the fresh parsley in the center of each piece of foil. Cut four 12-inch squares of 100%-cotton cheesecloth; place 1 square over nori or parsley on each piece of foil.

❹ For each packet, arrange the following on cheesecloth: 5 clams in shells, 1 ear of corn, half of a lobster tail, and 2 slices of kielbasa. Brush about 2 tablespoons of the butter mixture over cut sides of lobsters. Drizzle about 1 tablespoon of the remaining butter mixture over each packet. (Reserve remaining butter mixture until serving time.) Top with a few sprigs of basil or dill. Sprinkle lightly with salt and pepper. Bring ends of cheesecloth together in center. Bring up 2 opposite edges of each foil rectangle; seal with a double fold. Fold remaining ends to completely enclose seafood, corn, and kielbasa, leaving space for steam to build.

❺ For a charcoal grill, in a grill with a cover place foil packets, seam sides down, on grill rack directly over medium coals. Cover and grill for 15 to 20 minutes or until clams are open, lobster is opaque, and corn is tender, carefully opening packets to check doneness. (For a gas grill, preheat grill. Reduce heat to medium. Grill as above.)

❻ To serve, open packets. Discard any clams that have not opened, the nori, if using, and herb sprigs. (If desired, replace with fresh herb sprigs.) Pass reserved butter mixture.

NUTRITION FACTS PER SERVING: 667 cal., 54 g total fat (29 g sat. fat), 203 mg chol., 1,177 mg sodium, 21 g carbo., 3 g fiber, 28 g pro.

Skillet-Grilled Mussels

The mussels cook beautifully in a skillet, and the sauce that develops is perfect for dipping crusty pieces of bread.

PREP: 20 MINUTES **SOAK:** 15 MINUTES + 15 MINUTES + 15 MINUTES **GRILL:** 6 MINUTES

MAKES: 6 TO 8 APPETIZER SERVINGS

24	fresh mussels in shells
1	cup salt
⅓	cup butter, cut into small pieces
2	tablespoons olive oil
1	tablespoon lemon juice
⅛	teaspoon bottled hot pepper sauce
	French bread or sourdough bread (optional)

1 Scrub mussels under cold running water. Using your fingers, pull out the beards that are visible between the shells. In an 8-quart kettle or Dutch oven combine 4 quarts cold water and ⅓ cup of the salt; add mussels. Soak for 15 minutes; drain and rinse. Discard water. Repeat soaking, draining, and rinsing twice, using new water and salt each time.

2 Evenly distribute the butter pieces in a large cast-iron skillet or a 9×9×2-inch baking pan. Drizzle with olive oil, lemon juice, and hot pepper sauce. Place mussels on top of butter mixture.

3 For a charcoal grill, in a grill with a cover place mussels in skillet on grill rack directly over medium coals. Cover and grill for 6 to 10 minutes or until the mussels have opened. Discard any mussels that do not open. (For a gas grill, preheat grill. Reduce heat to medium. Grill as above.)

4 If desired, serve mussels with French or sourdough bread, dipping bread into pan juices.

NUTRITION FACTS PER SERVING: 227 cal., 17 g total fat (7 g sat. fat), 59 mg chol., 312 mg sodium, 4 g carbo., 0 g fiber, 14 g pro.

BIGGEST BOOK OF GRILLING

★

Chapter 4

BURGERS, SANDWICHES & PIZZAS

BBQ Burgers

Zip up the sauce by adding a few dashes of bottled hot pepper sauce.

PREP: 15 MINUTES **GRILL:** 14 MINUTES **MAKES:** 4 SERVINGS

¼ **cup ketchup**

2 **tablespoons bottled steak sauce**

1 **tablespoon water**

1 **teaspoon sugar**

1 **teaspoon vinegar**

½ **teaspoon bottled minced garlic (1 clove)**

Few dashes bottled hot pepper sauce (optional)

1 **pound lean ground beef**

¼ **teaspoon salt**

¼ **teaspoon ground black pepper**

4 **hamburger buns, split and toasted**

Desired accompaniments (such as American cheese slices, lettuce leaves, tomato slices, onion slices, and/or pickle slices) (optional)

1 For sauce, in a small saucepan combine ketchup, steak sauce, the water, sugar, vinegar, garlic, and, if desired, hot pepper sauce. Bring to boiling; reduce heat. Simmer, uncovered, for 3 minutes. Remove from heat; set aside.

2 In a medium bowl combine beef, salt, and pepper. Shape mixture into four ¾-inch-thick patties.

3 For a charcoal grill, grill patties on the rack of an uncovered grill directly over medium coals for 14 to 18 minutes or until meat is done (160°F),* turning once halfway through grilling and brushing once or twice with sauce during the last 5 minutes of grilling. (For a gas grill, preheat grill. Reduce heat to medium. Place patties on grill rack over heat. Cover and grill as above.)

4 Reheat any remaining sauce until bubbly. Serve patties on buns. Spoon reheated sauce over patties. If desired, serve with your choice of accompaniments.

NUTRITION FACTS PER SERVING: 332 cal., 13 g total fat (5 g sat. fat), 71 mg chol., 713 mg sodium, 29 g carbo., 1 g fiber, 24 g pro.

*NOTE: The internal color of a burger is not a reliable doneness indicator. A beef patty cooked to 160°F is safe, regardless of color. To measure the doneness of a patty, insert an instant-read thermometer through the side of the patty to a depth of 2 to 3 inches.

Burgers Borrachos

Marinating in beer gives the burgers a distinctively delicious flavor.

PREP: 15 MINUTES **MARINATE:** 6 TO 24 HOURS **GRILL:** 14 MINUTES **MAKES:** 6 SERVINGS

¼ cup finely chopped onion

2 tablespoons tomato paste

2 teaspoons bottled minced garlic (4 cloves)

½ teaspoon salt

½ teaspoon dried rosemary, crushed

½ teaspoon ground black pepper

¼ teaspoon ground allspice

1½ pounds lean ground beef

1½ cups beer

1 recipe Mustard Sauce

6 hamburger buns, split and toasted

Shredded lettuce (optional)

Onion slices (optional)

❶ In a small bowl combine onion, tomato paste, garlic, salt, rosemary, pepper, and allspice. Add ground beef; mix well. Shape mixture into six ¾-inch-thick patties. Place in a shallow dish. Set aside 1 tablespoon of the beer for Mustard Sauce; pour remaining beer over burgers. Cover; marinate in the refrigerator for at least 6 hours or up to 24 hours, turning burgers once. Prepare Mustard Sauce. Cover and chill until needed.

❷ Drain burgers, discarding beer. For a charcoal grill, grill patties on the rack of an uncovered grill directly over medium coals for 14 to 18 minutes or until meat is done (160°F),* turning once halfway through grilling. (For a gas grill, preheat grill. Reduce heat to medium. Place patties on grill rack over heat. Cover and grill as above.)

❸ Serve burgers on buns with sauce. If desired, add lettuce and onion slices.

Mustard Sauce: In a small bowl combine the reserved 1 tablespoon beer, 3 tablespoons stone-ground mustard, and ¾ teaspoon Worcestershire sauce.

NUTRITION FACTS PER SERVING: 324 cal., 13 g total fat (5 g sat. fat), 71 mg chol., 547 mg sodium, 24 g carbo., 1 g fiber, 24 g pro.

*NOTE: The internal color of a burger is not a reliable doneness indicator. A beef patty cooked to 160°F is safe, regardless of color. To measure the doneness of a patty, insert an instant-read thermometer through the side of the patty to a depth of 2 to 3 inches.

Caesar Salad Beef Burgers on Garlic Crostini

Another time, serve the crostini topped with grilled chicken breasts.

PREP: 15 MINUTES GRILL: 14 MINUTES MAKES: 4 SERVINGS

1½   pounds ground beef

1½   teaspoons bottled minced garlic (3 cloves)

1   teaspoon salt

½   teaspoon ground black pepper

8   slices sourdough bread

Salt

Ground black pepper

Olive oil

2   large cloves garlic, cut lengthwise into quarters

4   romaine leaves

¼   cup shredded Parmesan cheese (1 ounce)

1 In a large bowl combine beef, minced garlic, the 1 teaspoon salt, and ½ teaspoon pepper. Shape into four ¾-inch-thick patties, shaping to fit the bread.

2 For a charcoal grill, grill patties on the rack of an uncovered grill directly over medium coals for 14 to 18 minutes or until meat is done (160°F),* turning once halfway through grilling. (For a gas grill, preheat grill. Reduce heat to medium. Place patties on grill rack over heat. Cover and grill as above.) Season with additional salt and pepper.

3 Meanwhile, brush both sides of each bread slice with oil. Place bread around outer edge of grill. Grill a few minutes until lightly toasted, turning once; remove from grill. Rub both sides of each slice with a garlic quarter.

4 Place romaine leaves and burgers on half of the bread slices; sprinkle with Parmesan cheese. Cover with remaining bread slices.

NUTRITION FACTS PER SERVING: 481 cal., 23 g total fat (7 g sat. fat), 112 mg chol., 984 mg sodium, 28 g carbo., 1 g fiber, 38 g pro.

*NOTE: The internal color of a burger is not a reliable doneness indicator. A beef patty cooked to 160°F is safe, regardless of color. To measure the doneness of a patty, insert an instant-read thermometer through the side of the patty to a depth of 2 to 3 inches.

234

Spicy Beer Burgers

Add a side of seasoned grilled potato wedges and a
frosty beer for a brew pub–style meal.

PREP: 20 MINUTES GRILL: 14 MINUTES MAKES: 6 SERVINGS

1	slightly beaten egg
½	cup finely chopped onion
¼	cup fine dry bread crumbs
¼	cup beer
1	tablespoon Worcestershire sauce
½	teaspoon dried thyme, crushed
¼	teaspoon dry mustard
¼	teaspoon cayenne pepper
1	pound lean ground beef
6	hamburger buns, split and toasted
	Romaine leaves (optional)
	Tomato slices (optional)

1 In a large bowl combine the egg, onion, bread crumbs, beer, Worcestershire sauce, thyme, mustard, and cayenne pepper. Add ground beef; mix well. Shape meat mixture into six ¾-inch-thick patties.

2 For a charcoal grill, grill patties on the rack of an uncovered grill directly over medium coals for 14 to 18 minutes or until meat is done (160°F),* turning once halfway through grilling. (For a gas grill, preheat grill. Reduce heat to medium. Place patties on grill rack over heat. Cover and grill as above.)

3 Serve burgers on toasted buns. If desired, top burgers with romaine and tomato slices.

NUTRITION FACTS PER SERVING: 284 cal., 10 g total fat (4 g sat. fat), 83 mg chol., 400 mg sodium, 26 g carbo., 2 g fiber, 19 g pro.

*NOTE: The internal color of a burger is not a reliable doneness indicator. A beef patty cooked to 160°F is safe, regardless of color. To measure the doneness of a patty, insert an instant-read thermometer through the side of the patty to a depth of 2 to 3 inches.

Colossal Stuffed Burger

What fun! This giant burger is packed with mushrooms and mozzarella, grilled, then cut into wedges to serve.

PREP: 20 MINUTES **GRILL:** 35 MINUTES **MAKES:** 6 SERVINGS

2	pounds lean ground beef or lamb
¼	cup grated Parmesan cheese (1 ounce)
2	teaspoons dried oregano, crushed
1	teaspoon lemon juice
1	teaspoon bottled teriyaki sauce
½	teaspoon garlic salt
¼	cup tomato paste
1	4-ounce can chopped mushrooms, drained
¼	cup shredded mozzarella cheese (1 ounce)

1 In a large bowl combine ground meat, Parmesan cheese, oregano, lemon juice, teriyaki sauce, and garlic salt. Divide meat mixture in half. Shape each half into a ball; pat each ball onto waxed paper to form a flat patty 8 inches in diameter. Spread tomato paste in the center of 1 circle of the meat. Top tomato paste with mushrooms and mozzarella cheese. Top with the second circle of the meat. Press to seal edge.

2 For a charcoal grill, arrange medium-hot coals around a drip pan. Test for medium heat above the pan. Place the burger on the grill rack over drip pan. Cover and grill about 35 minutes or until meat is done (160°F).* Cut into wedges to serve.

NUTRITION FACTS PER SERVING: 290 cal., 16 g total fat (7 g sat. fat), 102 mg chol., 334 mg sodium, 4 g carbo., 1 g fiber, 30 g pro.

***NOTE:** The internal color of a burger is not a reliable doneness indicator. A beef patty cooked to 160°F is safe, regardless of color. To measure the doneness of a patty, insert an instant-read thermometer through the side of the patty into the meaty section to a depth of 2 to 3 inches.

Creole Carnival Burgers

Add extra kick to these stuffed burgers by substituting Monterey Jack cheese with jalapeño peppers for the plain Monterey Jack cheese.

PREP: 25 MINUTES **GRILL:** 14 MINUTES **MAKES:** 6 SERVINGS

2   pounds ground beef

2   teaspoons Cajun seasoning

½   teaspoon salt

1   medium onion, chopped

1   small green sweet pepper, chopped

½   cup shredded Monterey Jack cheese (2 ounces)

6   hamburger buns, split

Desired accompaniments (such as lettuce, sliced tomatoes, sliced cucumber, pickles, carrot sticks, and/or celery sticks) (optional)

1 In a large bowl combine beef, Cajun seasoning, and salt. Shape into twelve ¼-inch-thick patties.

2 In a medium bowl combine onion, sweet pepper, and cheese. Spoon ¼ cup of cheese mixture into center of each of 6 of the patties. Top with remaining 6 patties; press edges to seal. Reshape patties as necessary.

3 For a charcoal grill, grill patties on the rack of an uncovered grill directly over medium coals for 14 to 18 minutes or until meat is done (160°F),* turning once halfway through grilling. (For a gas grill, preheat grill. Reduce heat to medium. Place patties on grill rack over heat. Cover and grill as above.)

4 Serve on buns. If desired, serve with your choice of accompaniments.

NUTRITION FACTS PER SERVING: 461 cal., 24 g total fat (10 g sat. fat), 103 mg chol., 626 mg sodium, 25 g carbo., 2 g fiber, 35 g pro.

*****NOTE:** The internal color of a burger is not a reliable doneness indicator. A beef patty cooked to 160°F is safe, regardless of color. To measure the doneness of a patty, insert an instant-read thermometer through the side of the patty into the meaty section to a depth of 2 to 3 inches.

Gorgonzola-and-Garlic Stuffed Burger

The burger goes uptown! Tangy, blue cheese makes a creamy, melty center in these far-from-middling hamburgers. Serve 'em with gourmet potato chips and crisp raw vegetables.

PREP: 20 MINUTES GRILL: 14 MINUTES MAKES: 4 SERVINGS

½ cup crumbled Gorgonzola cheese or other blue cheese (2 ounces)

¼ cup snipped fresh basil

½ teaspoon bottled minced garlic (1 clove)

1¼ pounds lean ground beef

Salt

Ground black pepper

4 kaiser rolls, split and toasted

1½ cups arugula or fresh spinach leaves

1 large tomato, sliced

1 For burgers, in a small bowl combine Gorgonzola cheese, basil, and garlic; press into 4 slightly flattened mounds. Shape ground beef into eight ¼-inch-thick patties. Place a cheese mound in center of each of 4 of the patties. Top with remaining 4 patties; press edges to seal. Reshape patties as necessary. Sprinkle with salt and pepper.

2 For a charcoal grill, grill patties on the rack of an uncovered grill directly over medium coals for 14 to 18 minutes or until meat is done (160°F),* turning once halfway through grilling. (For a gas grill, preheat grill. Reduce heat to medium. Place patties on grill rack over heat. Cover and grill as above.)

3 Serve burgers on kaiser rolls with arugula or spinach and tomato.

NUTRITION FACTS PER SERVING: 467 cal., 21 g total fat (9 g sat. fat), 102 mg chol., 675 mg sodium, 33 g carbo., 2 g fiber, 35 g pro.

***NOTE:** The internal color of a burger is not a reliable doneness indicator. A beef patty cooked to 160°F is safe, regardless of color. To measure the doneness of a patty, insert an instant-read thermometer through the side of the patty to a depth of 2 to 3 inches.

Poblano Chile Burgers

Flecks of shredded carrot add a bit of crunch.

PREP: 45 MINUTES **GRILL:** 14 MINUTES + 2 MINUTES **MAKES:** 4 SERVINGS

2 medium fresh poblano chile peppers

1 beaten egg

¾ cup soft bread crumbs (1 slice)

½ cup shredded carrot

2 tablespoons water

1 teaspoon dried oregano, crushed

1 teaspoon bottled minced garlic (2 cloves)

½ teaspoon salt

¼ teaspoon ground black pepper

1 pound lean ground beef

¼ cup purchased guacamole

½ of a medium tomato, sliced

4 kaiser rolls, split and toasted

1 To roast peppers, halve peppers and remove stems, membranes, and seeds.* Place peppers, cut sides down, on a foil-lined baking sheet. Roast in a 425°F oven for 20 to 25 minutes or until skins are bubbly and browned. Wrap the peppers in foil and let stand for 20 to 30 minutes or until cool enough to handle. Using a paring knife, gently and slowly pull the skin off peppers. Chop the peppers.

2 In a large bowl combine chopped peppers, egg, bread crumbs, carrot, the water, oregano, garlic, salt, and black pepper. Add ground beef; mix well. Shape mixture into four ¾-inch-thick patties.

3 For a charcoal grill, grill patties on the rack of an uncovered grill directly over medium coals for 14 to 18 minutes or until meat is done (160°F),** turning once halfway through grilling. (For a gas grill, preheat grill. Reduce heat to medium. Place patties on grill rack over heat. Cover and grill as above.) Top each patty with 1 tablespoon of the guacamole and a tomato slice. Grill for 2 minutes more. Serve on toasted rolls.

NUTRITION FACTS PER SERVING: 482 cal., 21 g total fat (7 g sat. fat), 123 mg chol., 755 mg sodium, 43 g carbo., 3 g fiber, 30 g pro.

***NOTE:** Because chile peppers contain volatile oils that can burn your skin and eyes, avoid direct contact with them as much as possible. When working with chile peppers, wear plastic or rubber gloves. If your bare hands do touch the chile peppers, wash your hands and nails well with soap and warm water.

****NOTE:** The internal color of a burger is not a reliable doneness indicator. A beef patty cooked to 160°F is safe, regardless of color. To measure the doneness of a patty, insert an instant-read thermometer through the side of the patty to a depth of 2 to 3 inches.

Italian–American Cheeseburgers

Complement the savory burgers with a refreshing melon salad.
Toss cubed cantaloupe and honeydew with a splash of white balsamic vinegar.
Cover and chill thoroughly before serving.

PREP: 15 MINUTES **GRILL:** 14 MINUTES **MAKES:** 6 SERVINGS

⅓	cup snipped dried oil-packed tomatoes
1½	pounds lean ground beef
1	cup crumbled Gorgonzola cheese (4 ounces)
1	tablespoon snipped fresh thyme
2	teaspoons bottled minced garlic (4 cloves)
½	teaspoon salt
½	teaspoon coarsely ground black pepper
6	sourdough rolls, split and toasted
	Sliced red onions
	Sliced tomatoes

1 Set aside 1 tablespoon of the snipped dried tomatoes. In a large bowl combine the remaining snipped dried tomatoes, the beef, ¾ cup of the Gorgonzola cheese, the thyme, garlic, salt, and pepper. Shape mixture into six ¾-inch-thick patties.

2 For a charcoal grill, grill patties on the rack of an uncovered grill directly over medium coals for 14 to 18 minutes or until meat is done (160°F),* turning once halfway through grilling. (For a gas grill, preheat grill. Reduce heat to medium. Place patties on grill rack over heat. Cover and grill as above.)

3 Remove burgers from grill. Top with remaining ¼ cup Gorgonzola cheese and reserved 1 tablespoon snipped dried tomatoes. Serve burgers on toasted rolls with red onions and tomatoes.

NUTRITION FACTS PER SERVING: 385 cal., 17 g total fat (8 g sat. fat), 85 mg chol., 723 mg sodium, 27 g carbo., 0 g fiber, 29 g pro.

*NOTE: The internal color of a burger is not a reliable doneness indicator. A beef patty cooked to 160°F is safe, regardless of color. To measure the doneness of a patty, insert an instant-read thermometer through the side of the patty to a depth of 2 to 3 inches.

Latino Barbecue Burgers

You can prepare the Latino Barbecue Ketchup up to 3 days in advance, then cover and chill it until mealtime.

PREP: 35 MINUTES GRILL: 20 MINUTES MAKES: 4 SERVINGS

2 tablespoons olive oil

1 tablespoon butter

8 ounces fresh mushrooms, sliced

¼ teaspoon kosher salt or coarse salt

¼ teaspoon coarsely ground black pepper

1 tablespoon sherry wine vinegar or red wine vinegar

2 pounds extra-lean ground beef

1 recipe Latino Barbecue Ketchup (see recipe, page 284)

4 large hamburger buns, split and toasted

1 In a large skillet heat oil and butter over medium-high heat. Add mushrooms, salt, and pepper. Cook about 3 minutes or just until mushrooms are tender. Add vinegar. Cook and stir about 2 minutes more or until most of the liquid has evaporated. Set aside.

2 Shape ground beef into 8 thin patties, each 3½ to 4 inches in diameter. Divide mushroom mixture among 4 of the patties, placing mushroom mixture in center of each patty. Top with remaining 4 patties; press edges to seal. Reshape burgers as necessary. Measure ¼ cup of the Latino Barbecue Ketchup to use as a brush-on; set aside remaining ketchup.

3 For a charcoal grill, arrange medium-hot coals around a drip pan. Test for medium heat above the pan. Place patties on grill rack over drip pan. Cover and grill for 10 minutes; turn. Brush patties with the ¼ cup Latino Barbecue Ketchup. Grill for 10 to 14 minutes more or until done (160°F).* (For a gas grill, preheat grill. Reduce heat to medium. Adjust for indirect cooking. Grill as above.) Discard remainder of the Latino Barbecue Ketchup used as a brush-on.

4 To serve, place the burgers on the toasted buns. Pass the reserved Latino Barbecue Ketchup.

NUTRITION FACTS PER SERVING: 726 cal., 47 g total fat (16 g sat. fat), 159 mg chol., 666 mg sodium, 27 g carbo., 2 g fiber, 47 g pro.

*NOTE: The internal color of a burger is not a reliable doneness indicator. A beef patty cooked to 160°F is safe, regardless of color. To measure the doneness of a patty, insert an instant-read thermometer through the side of the patty into the meaty section to a depth of 2 to 3 inches.

Southwest Burger with Chili Salsa

*Can't decide whether you're in the mood for Mexican or American, tacos or burgers?
Here's a little bit of both: an herbed beefburger
topped with Monterey Jack cheese and homemade salsa.*

PREP: 30 MINUTES GRILL: 14 MINUTES MAKES: 4 SERVINGS

- **2** medium tomatoes, seeded and chopped
- **½** of a 4-ounce can diced green chile peppers, drained
- **¼** cup finely chopped onion
- **¼** cup snipped fresh cilantro
- **¼** teaspoon salt
- **1** slightly beaten egg
- **¼** cup fine dry bread crumbs
- **2** tablespoons water
- **1** tablespoon snipped fresh oregano or 1 teaspoon dried oregano, crushed
- **1** teaspoon snipped fresh thyme or ¼ teaspoon dried thyme, crushed
- **½** teaspoon salt
- **½** teaspoon ground cumin
- **½** teaspoon chili powder
- **1** pound lean ground beef
- **4** slices Monterey Jack cheese or Monterey Jack cheese with jalapeño peppers
- **4** kaiser rolls or hamburger buns, split and toasted

1 For salsa, in a medium bowl combine tomatoes, chile peppers, onion, cilantro, and the ¼ teaspoon salt. Set aside.

2 For burgers, in a medium bowl combine egg, bread crumbs, the water, oregano, thyme, the ½ teaspoon salt, the cumin, and chili powder. Add ground beef; mix well. Shape into four ¾-inch-thick patties.

3 For a charcoal grill, grill patties on the rack of an uncovered grill directly over medium coals for 14 to 18 minutes or until meat is done (160°F),* turning once halfway through grilling and adding cheese slices for the last 1 minute of grilling. (For a gas grill, preheat grill. Reduce heat to medium. Place patties on grill rack over heat. Cover and grill as above.) Serve burgers on kaiser rolls or hamburger buns with salsa.

NUTRITION FACTS PER SERVING: 489 cal., 22 g total fat (9 g sat. fat), 143 mg chol., 1,097 mg sodium, 38 g carbo., 3 g fiber, 34 g pro.

*NOTE: The internal color of a burger is not a reliable doneness indicator. A beef patty cooked to 160°F is safe, regardless of color. To measure the doneness of a patty, insert an instant-read thermometer through the side of the patty to a depth of 2 to 3 inches.

Sun-Dried Tomato Burgers

Burgers on the grill take on a whole new meaning when they're infused with fresh lemon, studded with dried tomatoes, and slathered with a mayonnaise dressing dressed up with basil and jalapeño pepper.

PREP: 15 MINUTES GRILL: 10 MINUTES MAKES: 4 SERVINGS

1   pound lean ground beef

1   tablespoon finely chopped, drained, oil-packed sun-dried tomatoes

1   teaspoon finely shredded lemon peel or lime peel

½   teaspoon salt

¼   teaspoon ground black pepper

¼   cup light mayonnaise dressing or salad dressing

2   tablespoons snipped fresh basil

1   fresh jalapeño chile pepper, seeded and finely chopped*

4   onion hamburger buns, split

1   cup lightly packed arugula or fresh spinach leaves

1 In a medium bowl combine beef, tomatoes, lemon peel, salt, and black pepper; mix lightly but thoroughly. Shape into four ½-inch-thick patties. For a charcoal grill, grill patties on the rack of an uncovered grill directly over medium coals for 10 to 13 minutes or until meat is done (160°F),** turning once halfway through grilling. (For a gas grill, preheat grill. Reduce heat to medium. Place patties on grill rack over heat. Cover and grill as above.)

2 Meanwhile, in a small bowl combine mayonnaise dressing, basil, and jalapeño pepper; mix well. For the last 1 to 2 minutes of grilling, place buns, cut sides down, on grill rack to toast. Top bottom halves of buns with burgers. Top with mayonnaise dressing mixture and arugula or spinach. Add bun tops.

NUTRITION FACTS PER SERVING: 450 cal., 20 g total fat (6 g sat. fat), 71 mg chol., 784 mg sodium, 40 g carbo., 2 g fiber, 26 g pro.

*NOTE: Because chile peppers contain volatile oils that can burn your skin and eyes, avoid direct contact with them as much as possible. When working with chile peppers, wear plastic or rubber gloves. If your bare hands do touch the chile peppers, wash your hands and nails well with soap and warm water.

**NOTE: The internal color of a burger is not a reliable doneness indicator. A beef patty cooked to 160°F is safe, regardless of color. To measure the doneness of a patty, insert an instant-read thermometer through the side of the patty to a depth of 2 to 3 inches.

Pesto Veal Burgers on Focaccia

*Look for pesto in bottles in the produce section
or in containers in the refrigerated section of your supermarket.*

PREP: 15 MINUTES GRILL: 14 MINUTES MAKES: 4 SERVINGS

1	slightly beaten egg white
½	cup soft bread crumbs
½	teaspoon salt
⅛	teaspoon ground black pepper
1	pound ground veal
¼	cup light mayonnaise dressing or salad dressing
1	tablespoon purchased pesto
8	3-inch squares focaccia bread or 8 slices sourdough bread, toasted
4	lettuce leaves
4	tomato slices

1 In a medium bowl combine egg white, bread crumbs, salt, and pepper. Add ground veal; mix well. Shape mixture into four ¾-inch-thick patties.

2 For a charcoal grill, grill patties on the rack of an uncovered grill directly over medium coals for 14 to 18 minutes or until meat is done (160°F),* turning once halfway through grilling. (For a gas grill, preheat grill. Reduce heat to medium. Place burgers on grill rack over heat. Cover and grill as above.)

3 Meanwhile, for sauce, in a small bowl combine mayonnaise dressing and pesto. Serve burgers on toasted focaccia bread with sauce, lettuce, and tomato slices.

NUTRITION FACTS PER SERVING: 309 cal., 13 g total fat (3 g sat. fat), 95 mg chol., 623 mg sodium, 18 g carbo., 1 g fiber, 29 g pro.

*NOTE: The internal color of a burger is not a reliable doneness indicator. A veal patty cooked to 160°F is safe, regardless of color. To measure the doneness of a patty, insert an instant-read thermometer through the side of the patty to a depth of 2 to 3 inches.

Down Island Burgers

Grilled onions and a mango-mayonnaise sauce top the subtly spiced pork burgers.

PREP: 25 MINUTES GRILL: 14 MINUTES MAKES: 6 SERVINGS

1½ pounds ground pork

2 tablespoons dry white wine or water

1 to 2 tablespoons bottled hot pepper sauce

2 tablespoons fine dry bread crumbs

3 to 4 teaspoons grated fresh ginger

3 to 4 teaspoons curry powder

2 teaspoons bottled minced garlic (4 cloves)

½ teaspoon salt

½ teaspoon ground allspice

6 ¼-inch-thick slices sweet onion (such as Vidalia or Maui)

6 hamburger buns, split

Lettuce leaves or 1 bunch stemmed watercress

1 recipe Mango Mayonnaise

1 In a large bowl combine pork, wine or water, hot pepper sauce, bread crumbs, ginger, curry powder, garlic, salt, and allspice; mix well. Shape into six ¾-inch-thick patties.

2 For a charcoal grill, grill patties and onion slices on the rack of an uncovered grill directly over medium coals for 14 to 18 minutes or until meat is done (160°F)* and onions are crisp-tender, turning once halfway through grilling. (For a gas grill, preheat grill. Reduce heat to medium. Place patties and onions on grill rack over heat. Cover and grill as above.)

3 For the last 2 minutes of grilling, place buns, cut sides down, on grill to toast.

4 To serve, place lettuce leaves on bottom halves of buns. Top with burgers, onion slices, and Mango Mayonnaise. Add bun tops.

Mango Mayonnaise: In a small bowl stir together ¼ cup mayonnaise, salad dressing, or fat-free mayonnaise dressing; ½ cup finely chopped mango or sliced peaches; and 2 tablespoons lime juice. Cover and refrigerate until serving time.

NUTRITION FACTS PER SERVING: 360 cal., 18 g total fat (5 g sat. fat), 56 mg chol., 590 mg sodium, 29 g carbo., 2 g fiber, 19 g pro.

*NOTE: The internal color of a burger is not a reliable doneness indicator. A pork patty cooked to 160°F is safe, regardless of color. To measure the doneness of a patty, insert an instant-read thermometer through the side of the patty to a depth of 2 to 3 inches.

Lebanese Burgers

Don't wait. Try these subtly seasoned lamb or beef burgers with Mediterranean accents for dinner tonight. Serve them with the tomato-yogurt-cucumber sauce.

PREP: 25 MINUTES GRILL: 10 MINUTES MAKES: 6 SERVINGS

¾ cup finely chopped seeded tomato

½ cup plain yogurt

½ cup finely chopped cucumber

2 teaspoons snipped fresh mint
or ¾ teaspoon dried mint, crushed

½ teaspoon bottled minced garlic (1 clove)

⅛ teaspoon salt

½ cup snipped fresh parsley

¼ cup finely chopped onion

2 tablespoons water

1 teaspoon salt

1 teaspoon ground cinnamon

1 teaspoon ground cumin

1 teaspoon paprika

½ teaspoon cayenne pepper

1½ pounds lean ground lamb or ground beef

3 large pita bread rounds, halved crosswise

1 For sauce, in a small bowl stir together tomato, yogurt, cucumber, mint, garlic, and the ⅛ teaspoon salt. Cover and refrigerate until serving time.

2 For burgers, in a large bowl stir together parsley, onion, the water, the 1 teaspoon salt, the cinnamon, cumin, paprika, and cayenne pepper. Add lamb and mix well. Shape into six ½-inch-thick oval patties.

3 For a charcoal grill, grill patties on the rack of an uncovered grill directly over medium coals for 10 to 13 minutes or until done (160°F),* turning once halfway through grilling. (For a gas grill, preheat grill. Reduce heat to medium. Place patties on grill rack over heat. Cover and grill as above.)

4 Serve patties in pita bread halves with the sauce.

NUTRITION FACTS PER SERVING: 332 cal., 16 g total fat (7 g sat. fat), 77 mg chol., 681 mg sodium, 21 g carbo., 2 g fiber, 24 g pro.

*NOTE: The internal color of a burger is not a reliable doneness indicator. A lamb or beef patty cooked to 160°F is safe, regardless of color. To measure the doneness of a patty, insert an instant-read thermometer through the side of the patty to a depth of 2 to 3 inches.

Mediterranean Burgers

Ground lamb burgers are the perfect way to explore some of the magical flavors of the Mediterranean. Feta cheese, tomatoes, and fresh mint are classic regional accents.

PREP: 15 MINUTES GRILL: 14 MINUTES MAKES: 4 SERVINGS

1 pound lean ground lamb or ground beef
2 teaspoons freshly ground black pepper
4 kaiser rolls, split
4 lettuce leaves
½ cup crumbled feta cheese (2 ounces)
4 tomato slices
1 tablespoon snipped fresh mint

1 Shape ground lamb into four ¾-inch-thick patties. Sprinkle pepper evenly over patties; press in with your fingers. For a charcoal grill, grill patties on the rack of an uncovered grill directly over medium coals for 14 to 18 minutes or until meat is done (160°F),* turning once halfway through grilling. (For a gas grill, preheat grill. Reduce heat to medium. Place patties on grill rack over heat. Cover and grill as above.)

2 Serve patties on rolls with lettuce, feta cheese, tomato slices, and mint.

NUTRITION FACTS PER SERVING: 435 cal., 21 g total fat (9 g sat. fat), 88 mg chol., 535 mg sodium, 33 g carbo., 1 g fiber, 28 g pro.

*NOTE: The internal color of a burger is not a reliable doneness indicator. A lamb or beef patty cooked to 160°F is safe, regardless of color. To measure the doneness of a patty, insert an instant-read thermometer through the side of the patty to a depth of 2 to 3 inches.

Chicken Burgers

Complete the meal with garden-fresh accompaniments and corn on the cob.

PREP: 15 MINUTES GRILL: 10 MINUTES MAKES: 4 SERVINGS

1   **pound uncooked ground chicken**

¼   **cup snipped fresh basil**

¼   **cup fine dry bread crumbs**

4   **teaspoons Worcestershire sauce**

⅛   **teaspoon salt**

⅛   **teaspoon ground black pepper**

8   **slices toasted French bread or 4 kaiser rolls or hamburger buns, split and toasted**

     Desired accompaniments (such as lettuce leaves, sliced tomato, and/or sliced onion) (optional)

1 In a medium bowl combine ground chicken, basil, bread crumbs, Worcestershire sauce, salt, and pepper. Shape into four ½-inch-thick patties. (The mixture may be sticky. If necessary, wet hands to shape patties.)

2 For a charcoal grill, grill patties on the greased rack of an uncovered grill directly over medium coals for 10 to 13 minutes or until chicken is no longer pink (165°F),* turning once halfway through grilling. (For a gas grill, preheat grill. Reduce heat to medium. Place patties on grill rack over heat. Cover and grill as above.)

3 Serve patties on toasted French bread, rolls, or buns. If desired, serve with your choice of accompaniments.

NUTRITION FACTS PER SERVING: 243 cal., 5 g total fat (1 g sat. fat), 29 mg chol., 820 mg sodium, 34 g carbo., 2 g fiber, 15 g pro.

***NOTE:** The internal color of a burger is not a reliable doneness indicator. A chicken patty cooked to 165°F is safe, regardless of color. To measure the doneness of a patty, insert an instant-read thermometer through the side of the patty to a depth of 2 to 3 inches.

Tandoori Chicken Burgers

If you can't find the east Indian spice blend garam masala, use curry powder instead.

PREP: 20 MINUTES GRILL: 14 MINUTES MAKES: 4 SERVINGS

¼ cup fine dry bread crumbs

2 teaspoons garam masala or curry powder

¼ teaspoon salt

¼ teaspoon cayenne pepper

1 pound uncooked ground chicken

2 tablespoons plain yogurt

4 seeded hamburger buns or kaiser rolls, split and toasted

1 recipe Minty Cucumbers

Kale or lettuce

1 In a large bowl combine bread crumbs, garam masala or curry powder, salt, and cayenne pepper. Add ground chicken and yogurt; mix well. Shape chicken mixture into four ¾-inch-thick patties.

2 For a charcoal grill, place patties on the rack of an uncovered grill directly over medium coals. Grill for 14 to 18 minutes or until no longer pink (165°F),* turning once halfway through grilling. (For a gas grill, preheat grill. Reduce heat to medium. Place patties on grill rack over heat. Cover and grill as above.) Remove from grill. Serve burgers on toasted buns with Minty Cucumbers and kale or lettuce.

Minty Cucumbers: In a medium bowl combine 1 medium cucumber, thinly sliced; ½ cup thinly sliced red onion; ¼ cup snipped fresh mint; 1 tablespoon bottled balsamic vinaigrette salad dressing; and ¼ teaspoon salt.

NUTRITION FACTS PER SERVING: 269 cal., 7 g total fat (2 g sat. fat), 30 mg chol., 970 mg sodium, 35 g carbo., 3 g fiber; 17 g pro.

*NOTE: The internal color of a burger is not a reliable doneness indicator. A chicken patty cooked to 165°F is safe, regardless of color. To measure the doneness of a patty, insert an instant-read thermometer through the side of the patty to a depth of 2 to 3 inches.

Savory Mushroom Burgers

The produce sections of many supermarkets carry a variety of exotic mushrooms, including chanterelle, porcini, and shiitake.

PREP: 35 MINUTES GRILL: 14 MINUTES MAKES: 4 SERVINGS

7	ounces exotic mushrooms (such as chanterelle, porcini, or shiitake) or button mushrooms
1	teaspoon bottled minced garlic (2 cloves)
¾	cup chicken broth
3	tablespoons bulgur
12	ounces uncooked ground turkey breast
2	tablespoons thinly sliced green onion
2	teaspoons Worcestershire sauce
¼	teaspoon ground black pepper
	Dijon-style mustard (optional)
4	hamburger buns or kaiser rolls, split and toasted

1 Remove stems and finely chop half of the mushrooms (1 cup); slice remaining mushrooms and set aside. In a small saucepan cook the finely chopped mushrooms and garlic in ½ cup of the chicken broth for 4 to 5 minutes or until tender. Stir in bulgur. Return to boiling; reduce heat. Cover and simmer about 10 minutes or until liquid is absorbed and bulgur is tender.

2 Remove from heat; cool slightly. In a large bowl combine turkey breast, green onion, Worcestershire sauce, and pepper. Add bulgur mixture; mix until combined. Shape into four ¾-inch-thick patties.

3 For a charcoal grill, grill patties on the greased rack of an uncovered grill directly over medium coals for 14 to 18 minutes or until meat is done (165°F),* turning once halfway through grilling. (For a gas grill, preheat grill. Reduce heat to medium. Place patties on greased grill rack over heat. Cover and grill as above.)

4 Meanwhile, in a covered small saucepan cook the sliced mushrooms in the remaining ¼ cup broth for 4 to 5 minutes or until tender.

5 If desired, spread mustard on bottom halves of buns or rolls. Serve burgers and sliced mushrooms on buns or rolls.

NUTRITION FACTS PER SERVING: 292 cal., 10 g total fat (2 g sat. fat), 67 mg chol., 520 mg sodium, 30 g carbo., 3 g fiber, 21 g pro.

*NOTE: The internal color of a burger is not a reliable doneness indicator. A turkey patty cooked to 165°F is safe, regardless of color. To measure the doneness of a patty, insert an instant-read thermometer through the side of the patty to a depth of 2 to 3 inches.

Glazed Turkey Burgers

A glaze of mustard and fruit preserves gives these burgers a sweet-sour flavor.

PREP: 20 MINUTES **GRILL:** 14 MINUTES **MAKES:** 4 SERVINGS

1 tablespoon yellow mustard

1 tablespoon cherry, apricot, peach, or pineapple preserves

1 beaten egg

¼ cup quick-cooking rolled oats

¼ cup finely chopped celery

3 tablespoons snipped dried tart cherries or dried apricots (optional)

¼ teaspoon salt

⅛ teaspoon ground black pepper

1 pound uncooked ground turkey or chicken

4 kaiser rolls or hamburger buns, split and toasted

Desired accompaniments (such as mayonnaise or salad dressing, lettuce leaves, and/or tomato slices) (optional)

1 For glaze, in a small bowl stir together mustard and preserves; set aside. In a medium bowl combine egg, rolled oats, celery, dried cherries or apricots (if desired), salt, and pepper. Add ground turkey or chicken; mix well. Shape into four ¾-inch-thick patties.

2 For a charcoal grill, grill patties on the greased rack of an uncovered grill directly over medium coals for 14 to 18 minutes or until no longer pink (165°F),* turning once halfway through grilling and brushing with glaze during the last minute of grilling. (For a gas grill, preheat grill. Reduce heat to medium. Place patties on greased grill rack over heat. Cover and grill as above.) Serve burgers on rolls or buns. Brush any remaining glaze over burgers. If desired, serve with your choice of accompaniments.

NUTRITION FACTS PER SERVING: 397 cal., 14 g total fat (3 g sat. fat), 143 mg chol., 599 mg sodium, 38 g carbo., 2 g fiber, 28 g pro.

***NOTE:** The internal color of a burger is not a reliable doneness indicator. A turkey or chicken patty cooked to 165°F is safe, regardless of color. To measure the doneness of a patty, insert an instant-read thermometer through the side of the patty to a depth of 2 to 3 inches.

Turkey Burgers with Fresh Curry Ketchup

Fresh cilantro and curry powder in the turkey mixture and the tomato topper set these burgers apart.

PREP: 20 MINUTES GRILL: 14 MINUTES MAKES: 4 SERVINGS

- **1** beaten egg
- **¼** cup fine dry bread crumbs
- **2** tablespoons snipped fresh cilantro
- **2** teaspoons grated fresh ginger
- **½** teaspoon bottled minced garlic (1 clove)
- **½** teaspoon salt
- **½** teaspoon curry powder
- **¼** teaspoon freshly ground black pepper
- **1** pound uncooked ground turkey
- **1** recipe Curry Ketchup
- **2** large pita bread rounds (optional)

1 In a large bowl combine egg, bread crumbs, cilantro, ginger, garlic, salt, curry powder, and pepper. Add turkey and mix well. Form turkey mixture into four ¾-inch-thick patties. (If mixture is sticky, moisten hands with water.)

2 For a charcoal grill, grill patties on the greased rack of an uncovered grill directly over medium coals for 14 to 18 minutes or until no longer pink (165°F),* turning once halfway through grilling. (For a gas grill, preheat grill. Reduce heat to medium. Place patties on greased grill rack over heat. Cover and grill as above.)

3 To serve, spoon the Curry Ketchup over the burgers. (Or lightly grill pita rounds for 2 to 4 minutes or until toasted, turning once. Cut rounds in half crosswise; place a burger in each pita half and top with Curry Ketchup.)

Curry Ketchup: Chop 4 medium plum tomatoes. In medium saucepan combine tomatoes, ½ cup ketchup, 3 tablespoons finely chopped onion, 2 tablespoons snipped fresh cilantro, and 2 teaspoons curry powder. Bring to boiling; reduce heat. Cover and simmer for 5 minutes, stirring occasionally. Season to taste with salt and ground black pepper.

NUTRITION FACTS PER SERVING: 407 cal., 11 g total fat (3 g sat. fat), 95 mg chol., 1,113 mg sodium, 52 g carbo., 2 g fiber, 24 g pro.

*NOTE: The internal color of a burger is not a reliable doneness indicator. A turkey patty cooked to 165°F is safe, regardless of color. To measure the doneness of a patty, insert an instant-read thermometer through the side of the patty to a depth of 2 to 3 inches.

252

Slaw-Topped Tuna and Salmon Burgers

Fresh fish and a dill-dressed slaw transform tuna burgers into extraordinary fare.

PREP: 30 MINUTES GRILL: 10 MINUTES MAKES: 6 SERVINGS

1 pound fresh or frozen tuna fillet

8 ounces fresh or frozen salmon fillet

¼ cup snipped fresh cilantro

2 tablespoons lime juice

2 tablespoons olive oil

1 tablespoon purchased pickled ginger, finely chopped

1 tablespoon bottled chili sauce

1 to 2 teaspoons wasabi paste

1 teaspoon bottled minced garlic (2 cloves)

¼ teaspoon sea salt

¼ teaspoon ground black pepper

6 soft flatbreads (such as Afghan bread, naan, or lefsa) or split rolls

1 recipe Napa Cabbage Slaw

Yellow tomato slices (optional)

1 Thaw tuna and salmon, if frozen. Rinse fish; pat dry with paper towels. Finely chop the tuna and salmon. In a large bowl combine tuna, salmon, cilantro, lime juice, 4 teaspoons of the olive oil, the ginger, chili sauce, wasabi paste, garlic, salt, and pepper. Shape into six ¾-inch-thick patties.

2 For a charcoal grill, grill patties on the greased rack of an uncovered grill directly over medium coals for 10 to 12 minutes or until fish is done (160°F),* turning once halfway through grilling. (For a gas grill, preheat grill. Reduce heat to medium. Place patties on greased grill rack over heat. Cover and grill as above.) Brush the flatbread with remaining 2 teaspoons olive oil. Toast on grill rack for 1 to 2 minutes or until golden brown.

3 To serve, place patties on flatbreads; top with Napa Cabbage Slaw. If desired, serve with yellow tomato slices.

Napa Cabbage Slaw: In a food processor bowl or blender container combine ½ cup plain low-fat yogurt, 2 tablespoons snipped fresh parsley, 2 tablespoons snipped fresh dill, 2 tablespoons lime juice, and ½ to 1 teaspoon bottled minced garlic (1 to 2 cloves). Add ⅛ teaspoon sea salt and ⅛ teaspoon freshly ground black pepper. Cover and process or blend until smooth.

In a large bowl toss together yogurt mixture and 3 cups finely shredded napa cabbage. Cover and refrigerate until using or up to 24 hours.

NUTRITION FACTS PER SERVING: 275 cal., 8 g total fat (1 g sat. fat), 55 mg chol., 288 mg sodium, 19 g carbo., 2 g fiber, 30 g pro.

*NOTE: The internal color of a fish patty is not a reliable doneness indicator. A fish patty cooked to 160°F is safe, regardless of color. To measure the doneness of a patty, insert an instant-read thermometer through the side of the patty to a depth of 2 to 3 inches.

Surf and Turf Burgers with Spicy Caramelized Mayo

You can make the mayonnaise topper up to several days ahead of time; refrigerate, covered, until using.

PREP: 30 MINUTES CHILL: 30 MINUTES + 1 HOUR GRILL: 18 MINUTES MAKES: 4 SERVINGS

- **1** tablespoon olive oil
- **1** large onion, finely chopped
- **1** small shallot, finely chopped
- **1** teaspoon purchased red curry paste
- **½** cup mayonnaise or salad dressing or light mayonnaise dressing
- **1½** pounds lean ground beef
- **4** ounces peeled and cooked baby shrimp, chopped
- **2** tablespoons snipped fresh dill
- **½** teaspoon sea salt
- **¼** teaspoon ground black pepper
- **4** large onion or sesame kaiser rolls, split and toasted

  Lettuce (optional)

  Sliced tomatoes (optional)

  Sweet pickle slices (optional)

1 For spicy caramelized mayo, heat oil in a large skillet over medium-high heat. Add onion; cook about 7 minutes or until browned (caramelized), stirring occasionally. Reduce heat to medium. Add shallot and curry paste; cook and stir for 2 minutes more. Transfer mixture to a small bowl; cover and chill for 30 minutes. Stir mayonnaise into chilled onion mixture. Cover and chill about 1 hour or until ready to serve.

2 For burgers, in a large bowl combine ground beef, shrimp, dill, sea salt, and pepper; mix well. Shape mixture into four 1-inch-thick patties.

3 For a charcoal grill, grill patties on the rack of an uncovered grill directly over medium coals for 18 to 23 minutes or until meat is done (160°F),* turning once halfway through grilling. (For a gas grill, preheat grill. Reduce heat to medium. Place patties on grill rack over heat. Cover and grill as above.)

4 Serve burgers on rolls with the spicy caramelized mayo. If desired, serve with lettuce, tomatoes, and sweet pickle slices.

NUTRITION FACTS PER SERVING: 498 cal., 32 g total fat (6 g sat. fat), 93 mg chol., 867 mg sodium, 30 g carbo., 1 g fiber, 21 g pro.

*NOTE: The internal color of a burger is not a reliable doneness indicator. A beef patty cooked to 160°F is safe, regardless of color. To measure the doneness of a patty, insert an instant-read thermometer through the side of the patty to a depth of 2 to 3 inches.

254

Garden Veggie Burgers

Two toppings—sharp red onion and a tangy spinach-feta combination—complement these grilled meatless burgers.

PREP: 10 MINUTES GRILL: 15 MINUTES MAKES: 4 SERVINGS

2 medium red onions

4 refrigerated or frozen meatless burger patties

¼ cup bottled vinaigrette salad dressing (at room temperature)

1 tablespoon olive oil

4 cups fresh spinach leaves

½ teaspoon bottled minced garlic (1 clove)

½ cup crumbled feta cheese (2 ounces)

4 hamburger buns, split

1 For onion topping, cut onions into ½-inch-thick slices. For a charcoal grill, grill onions on the rack of an uncovered grill directly over medium coals for 15 to 20 minutes or until tender, turning once. Add burger patties to the grill for the last 8 to 10 minutes of grilling or until heated through, turning once halfway through grilling. (For a gas grill, preheat grill. Reduce heat to medium. Place onions, then burger patties on grill rack over heat. Cover and grill as above.) Brush grilled onions with the salad dressing.

2 Meanwhile, for spinach topping, in a large skillet heat oil over medium-high heat. Add spinach and garlic; cook and stir about 30 seconds or just until spinach is wilted. Remove from heat. Stir in feta cheese.

3 To serve, place onion slices on bottoms of buns. Top with grilled burger patties, spinach mixture, and bun tops.

NUTRITION FACTS PER SERVING: 350 cal., 14 g total fat (4 g sat. fat), 17 mg chol., 920 mg sodium, 37 g carbo., 7 g fiber, 21 g pro.

Marinated Beef on Sourdough

A sturdy Cabernet, assisted by plenty of garlic, does wonderful things to a round roast.

PREP: 25 MINUTES MARINATE: 4 TO 24 HOURS GRILL: 1¼ HOURS

STAND: 15 MINUTES MAKES: 8 SERVINGS

1	**2-pound beef round tip roast or sirloin tip roast**
8	**cloves garlic, sliced**
⅔	**cup Cabernet Sauvignon or other dry red wine**
½	**cup finely chopped onion**
¼	**cup olive oil**
2	**tablespoons red wine vinegar**
¼	**teaspoon salt**
¼	**teaspoon ground black pepper**
½	**teaspoon bottled minced garlic (1 clove)**
8	**½-inch-thick slices sourdough bread, toasted**

1 Trim fat from meat. With the point of a paring knife, make small slits in meat. Insert garlic slices into slits. Place meat in a resealable plastic bag set in a shallow dish. For marinade, in a small bowl combine the wine, onion, 2 tablespoons of the olive oil, and the vinegar. Pour marinade over meat. Seal bag; turn to coat meat. Marinate in refrigerator for at least 4 hours or up to 24 hours, turning bag occasionally.

2 Drain meat, discarding marinade. Sprinkle meat with salt and pepper. In a small bowl combine the remaining 2 tablespoons olive oil and the minced garlic; brush over one side of each bread slice. Set aside.

3 For a charcoal grill, arrange medium coals around a drip pan. Test for medium-low heat above the pan. Place meat on grill rack over drip pan. Cover and grill until desired doneness. Allow 1¼ to 1½ hours for medium-rare doneness (140°F) or 1½ to 1¾ hours for medium doneness (155°F). Add coals as necessary to maintain heat. A few minutes before meat is done, add bread to grill. (For a gas grill, preheat grill. Reduce heat to medium-low. Adjust for indirect cooking. Place roast on a rack in a roasting pan, place on grill rack, and grill as above.)

4 Remove meat from grill. Cover with foil; let stand for 15 minutes before slicing. The meat's temperature after standing should be 145°F for medium-rare or 160°F for medium doneness. To serve, thinly slice meat. Arrange meat slices on toasted bread.

NUTRITION FACTS PER SERVING: 232 cal., 8 g total fat (2 g sat. fat), 54 mg chol., 265 mg sodium, 14 g carbo., 0 g fiber, 23 g pro.

Italian Steak Sandwiches

Flavors of Italian cuisine dominate this sandwich. The intensely flavorful, garlicky olive oil sauce elevates the steak sandwich from ordinary to outstanding.

PREP: 20 MINUTES **GRILL:** 14 MINUTES + 2 MINUTES **MAKES:** 4 SERVINGS

1 **1-pound boneless beef top sirloin steak, cut 1 inch thick**

1 **cup loosely packed fresh flat-leaf parsley**

3 **tablespoons olive oil**

4 **teaspoons lemon juice**

1 **tablespoon capers, drained**

1 **teaspoon bottled minced garlic (2 cloves)**

Dash salt

Dash bottled hot pepper sauce

4 **1-inch-thick slices sourdough bread**

1 **medium onion, thinly sliced and separated into rings**

1 **cup mesclun**

1 Trim fat from steak. For sauce, in a blender container or food processor bowl combine parsley, olive oil, lemon juice, capers, garlic, salt, and hot pepper sauce. Cover and blend or process until nearly smooth, stopping and scraping side as necessary. Set aside.

2 For a charcoal grill, grill steak on the rack of an uncovered grill directly over medium coals until desired doneness, turning once halfway through grilling. Allow 14 to 18 minutes for medium-rare doneness (145°F) or 18 to 22 minutes for medium doneness (160°F). Remove steak from grill. Add bread slices, cut sides down, to grill. Grill for 2 to 4 minutes or until bread is lightly browned, turning once halfway through grilling. (For a gas grill, preheat grill. Reduce heat to medium. Place steaks, then bread on grill rack over heat. Cover and grill as above.)

3 Thinly slice steak. To serve, arrange onion rings and mesclun on bread slices; top with steak slices. Drizzle with sauce.

NUTRITION FACTS PER SERVING: 211 cal., 13 g total fat (2 g sat. fat), 13 mg chol., 244 mg sodium, 17 g carbo., 1 g fiber, 7 g pro.

Steak Rémoulade Sandwiches

Served in France as an accompaniment to cold meats, fish, and seafood, the classic mayonnaise-based sauce called rémoulade adds a hint of rustic sophistication to this steak sandwich perked up by peppery arugula and grilled sweet pepper.

PREP: 15 MINUTES GRILL: 11 MINUTES MAKES: 4 SERVINGS

¼ cup light mayonnaise dressing or salad dressing

1½ teaspoons finely minced cornichons or gherkins

1 teaspoon drained capers, chopped

¼ teaspoon lemon juice

Freshly ground black pepper

2 8-ounce boneless beef top loin steaks, cut 1 inch thick

2 teaspoons prepared garlic spread or 2 teaspoons bottled minced garlic (4 cloves)

1 large yellow sweet pepper, cut lengthwise into 8 strips

4 kaiser or French-style rolls, split and toasted

1 cup arugula or fresh spinach leaves

1 For rémoulade, in a small bowl combine mayonnaise dressing, cornichons, capers, lemon juice, and several dashes black pepper. Cover and refrigerate until ready to serve.

2 Pat steaks dry with a paper towel. Using your fingers, rub garlic spread over steaks. Sprinkle with additional black pepper.

3 For a charcoal grill, grill steaks and sweet pepper strips on the rack of an uncovered grill directly over medium coals until meat is desired doneness and sweet pepper strips are crisp-tender, turning once halfway through grilling. Allow 11 to 15 minutes for medium-rare doneness (145°F) or 14 to 18 minutes for medium doneness (160°F). (For a gas grill, preheat grill. Reduce heat to medium. Place steak and sweet pepper strips on grill rack over heat. Cover and grill as above.) Transfer cooked steaks and sweet pepper strips to a cutting board; cut steaks into ¼-inch-thick slices.

4 If desired, grill rolls directly over medium heat about 1 minute or until toasted. Spread rémoulade on cut sides of toasted rolls. Fill rolls with arugula or spinach, steak slices, and sweet pepper strips. Add roll tops.

NUTRITION FACTS PER SERVING: 380 cal., 13 g total fat (3 g sat. fat), 65 mg chol., 516 mg sodium, 37 g carbo., 0 g fiber, 29 g pro.

Beef and Swiss Sandwiches

To toast the rolls, grill them, cut sides down, for 1 to 2 minutes or until lightly toasted.

PREP: 15 MINUTES MARINATE: 6 TO 24 HOURS GRILL: 17 MINUTES MAKES: 6 SERVINGS

1	1- to 1¼-pound beef flank steak
1	medium sweet onion (such as Vidalia or Maui), thinly sliced
½	cup bottled clear Italian salad dressing or oil and vinegar salad dressing
2	tablespoons horseradish mustard
1½	cups packaged shredded cabbage with carrot (coleslaw mix)
6	kaiser or French-style rolls, split and toasted
4	ounces thinly sliced Swiss cheese

1. Trim fat from steak. Score both sides of steak in a diamond pattern by making shallow diagonal cuts at 1-inch intervals. Place steak and onion in a resealable plastic bag set in a shallow dish. For marinade, in a bowl combine salad dressing and mustard. Pour over steak and onion. Seal bag; turn to coat meat. Marinate in refrigerator for at least 6 hours or up to 24 hours, turning bag occasionally.

2. Drain steak and onion, reserving marinade. Fold a 24×18-inch piece of heavy foil in half to make an 18×12-inch rectangle. Place onion in center of foil. Drizzle 2 tablespoons of the reserved marinade over onion. Bring up opposite edges of foil; seal with a double fold. Fold remaining edges together to completely enclose onion, leaving space for steam to build.

3. For a charcoal grill, grill steak and onion packet on the rack of an uncovered grill directly over medium coals for 17 to 21 minutes or until steak is medium doneness (160°F) and onion is tender, turning steak and onion packet once and brushing steak once with reserved marinade halfway through grilling. (For a gas grill, preheat grill. Reduce heat to medium. Place steak and onion packet on grill rack over heat. Cover and grill as above.) Discard any remaining marinade.

4. To serve, thinly slice steak diagonally across the grain. Toss together onion and cabbage. Fill the rolls with steak slices and onion mixture. Top with cheese.

NUTRITION FACTS PER SERVING: 394 cal., 22 g total fat (7 g sat. fat), 53 mg chol., 530 mg sodium, 25 g carbo., 1 g fiber, 24 g pro.

Steak and Vegetable Sandwiches

Shaved Parmesan cheese adds a salty tang to these layered sandwiches.

PREP: 25 MINUTES STAND: 30 MINUTES GRILL: 17 MINUTES MAKES: 4 SERVINGS

1	**small eggplant**
½	**teaspoon salt**
1	**tablespoon olive oil**
1	**medium onion, chopped**
2	**teaspoons bottled minced garlic (4 cloves)**
8	**ounces fresh mild red cherry chile peppers or mild banana chile peppers, halved and stems and seeds removed***
2	**tablespoons balsamic vinegar**
¼	**teaspoon salt**
12	**ounces beef flank steak**
	Salt (optional)
	Ground black pepper (optional)
2	**teaspoons dried Italian seasoning, crushed**
4	**6-inch Italian sourdough rolls, split horizontally and toasted**
	Salad greens or romaine leaves
2	**ounces shaved Parmesan cheese**

1 Trim ends from eggplant; discard. Cut eggplant lengthwise into ¼-inch-thick slices, discarding the outside "peel" slices. Spread the eggplant slices in a single layer on a baking sheet. Sprinkle with ½ teaspoon salt; cover and let stand for 30 minutes. Rinse eggplant; pat dry. Rub eggplant slices with half of the olive oil; set aside.

2 For pepper spread, in a large skillet heat remaining oil over medium heat. Add onion and garlic; cook about 5 minutes or until onion turns golden, stirring often. Add chile peppers, balsamic vinegar, and the ¼ teaspoon salt; cook and stir for 2 minutes. Reduce heat; cover. Cook over low heat about 10 minutes or until mixture is soft, stirring occasionally. Remove pepper mixture from heat. Let cool. In a food processor bowl or blender container cover and process or blend pepper mixture until nearly smooth. Set aside.

3 Score both sides of the steak in a diamond pattern by making shallow diagonal cuts at 1-inch intervals. If desired, season steak with additional salt and pepper. Sprinkle Italian seasoning evenly over both sides of steak; rub in with your fingers.

4 For a charcoal grill, grill steak and eggplant on the rack of an uncovered grill directly over medium coals until steak is medium doneness (160°F) and eggplant is tender, turning once. Allow 17 to 21 minutes for steaks and 6 to 8 minutes for eggplant. (For a gas grill, preheat grill. Reduce heat to medium. Place steak and eggplant on grill rack over heat. Cover and grill as above.)

5 To assemble, spread about 1 tablespoon of the pepper spread on bottom half of each Italian roll. Top with greens and eggplant. Slice steak across grain into very thin strips. Arrange sliced steak on eggplant. Top with Parmesan. Lightly spread top halves of Italian rolls with remaining pepper spread. Place roll tops on sandwiches.

NUTRITION FACTS PER SERVING: 616 cal., 18 g total fat (7 g sat. fat), 47 mg chol., 1,300 mg sodium, 75 g carbo., 7 g fiber, 37 g pro.

*NOTE: Because chile peppers contain volatile oils that can burn your skin and eyes, avoid direct contact with them as much as possible. When working with chile peppers, wear plastic or rubber gloves. If your bare hands do touch the chile peppers, wash your hands and nails well with soap and warm water.

Gruyère and Pork Sandwiches

A four-ingredient rub perks up the pork.

PREP: 15 MINUTES GRILL: 1 HOUR STAND: 10 MINUTES MAKES: 8 SERVINGS

1   2-pound boneless pork top loin roast (single loin)

1   tablespoon paprika

1   teaspoon dried oregano, crushed

½   teaspoon salt

½   teaspoon garlic powder

    Coarse-grain brown mustard

1   10- to 12-inch Italian flatbread (focaccia), split horizontally and toasted

3   ounces thinly sliced cooked ham

4   slices Gruyère or Swiss cheese (about 4 ounces)

    Dill pickle slices

1 Trim fat from pork roast. For rub, in a small bowl combine paprika, oregano, salt, and garlic powder. Sprinkle rub evenly over pork roast; rub in with your fingers.

2 For a charcoal grill, arrange medium coals around a drip pan. Test for medium-low heat above the pan. Place roast on grill rack over drip pan. Cover and grill for 1 to 1½ hours or until done (155°F). Add coals as necessary to maintain heat. (For a gas grill, preheat grill. Reduce heat to medium-low. Adjust for indirect cooking. Place roast on rack in roasting pan, place on grill rack, and grill as above.)

3 Remove meat from grill. Cover with foil; let stand for 10 minutes before carving. The meat's temperature after standing should be 160°F.

4 To serve, thinly slice meat. Spread mustard on the bottom half of bread. Layer with grilled pork, ham, cheese, and pickles. Spread mustard on top half of bread; press firmly onto layered sandwich. Cut into wedges.

NUTRITION FACTS PER SERVING: 344 cal., 15 g total fat (6 g sat. fat), 72 mg chol., 425 mg sodium, 25 g carbo., 2 g fiber, 28 g pro.

Honey-Mustard Pork Sandwiches

Stirred together straight from the jars, Dijon-style mustard and honey create a glossy, hot-sweet sauce that clings to pork.

PREP: 10 MINUTES GRILL: 12 MINUTES MAKES: 4 SERVINGS

1 1-pound pork tenderloin
  Ground black pepper

2 tablespoons honey

2 tablespoons Dijon-style mustard

4 kaiser rolls or hamburger buns, split and toasted

¼ cup mayonnaise or salad dressing

4 tomato slices

1 Trim fat from meat. Cut meat into ¾-inch-thick slices. Sprinkle with pepper. For glaze, in a small bowl combine honey and mustard; set aside.

2 For a charcoal grill, grill meat on the rack of an uncovered grill directly over medium coals for 12 to 15 minutes or until meat juices run clear (160°F), turning and brushing once with honey-mustard mixture halfway through grilling. (For a gas grill, preheat grill. Reduce heat to medium. Place meat on grill rack over heat. Cover and grill as above.) Discard any remaining honey-mustard mixture.

3 To serve, spread cut sides of toasted rolls with mayonnaise. Top bottoms of rolls with meat and tomato slices.

NUTRITION FACTS PER SERVING: 459 cal., 18 g total fat (3 g sat. fat), 89 mg chol., 639 mg sodium, 41 g carbo., 0 g fiber, 32 g pro.

262

Barbecued Pork Chop Sandwiches

Two simple ingredients—curry and cumin—transform purchased chili sauce into a perfect brush-on for grilled pork.

PREP: 10 MINUTES GRILL: 17 MINUTES MAKES: 4 SERVINGS

⅓ cup bottled chili sauce

½ to 1 teaspoon curry powder

¼ teaspoon ground cumin

3 boneless pork loin chops, cut 1¼ to 1½ inches thick

  Salt (optional)

  Ground black pepper (optional)

4 kaiser rolls, split and toasted

  Leaf lettuce (optional)

1 For sauce, in a small bowl stir together chili sauce, curry powder, and cumin. Set aside. Trim fat from chops. If desired, sprinkle lightly with salt and pepper.

2 For a charcoal grill, grill chops on the rack of an uncovered grill directly over medium coals for 17 to 21 minutes or until meat juices run clear (160°F), turning once and brushing occasionally with sauce during the last 5 minutes of grilling. (For a gas grill, preheat grill. Reduce heat to medium. Place chops on grill rack over heat. Cover and grill as above.)

3 To serve, thinly slice pork. Top rolls with sliced pork and, if desired, leaf lettuce.

NUTRITION FACTS PER SERVING: 393 cal., 14 g total fat (4 g sat. fat), 77 mg chol., 637 mg sodium, 35 g carbo., 0 g fiber, 30 g pro.

Texas Rib Sandwich with Coleslaw

When you want a barbecue sandwich that's truly a barbecue sandwich, stick to the ribs—country-style boneless ribs, that is. Coleslaw is a must.

PREP: 30 MINUTES GRILL: 1½ HOURS MAKES: 6 TO 8 SERVINGS

2 pounds boneless pork country-style ribs

¾ cup bottled barbecue sauce

6 to 8 crusty dinner rolls or hamburger buns, split and toasted

Bottled hot pepper sauce (optional)

1 recipe Creamy Coleslaw

1 Trim fat from ribs. For a charcoal grill, arrange medium-hot coals around a drip pan. Test for medium heat above the pan. Place ribs on grill rack over drip pan. (Or place ribs in a rib rack; place on grill rack.) Cover and grill for 1½ to 2 hours or until ribs are tender, brushing occasionally with sauce during the last 10 minutes of grilling. Add coals as necessary to maintain heat. (For a gas grill, preheat grill. Reduce heat to medium. Adjust for indirect cooking. Place ribs on a rack in a roasting pan, place on grill rack, and grill as above.) Remove ribs from grill and brush with the remaining sauce. Cut ribs into serving-size pieces.

2 Top the toasted rolls with the ribs, hot pepper sauce (if desired), and Creamy Coleslaw.

Creamy Coleslaw: In a small bowl stir together ¼ cup mayonnaise or salad dressing, 1½ teaspoons vinegar, ½ to 1 teaspoon sugar, ¼ teaspoon celery seeds, and ⅛ teaspoon salt. In a large bowl combine 1½ cups shredded green cabbage; ½ cup shredded red or green cabbage; 1 medium carrot, shredded; and 1 green onion, thinly sliced. Pour mayonnaise mixture over cabbage mixture. Toss lightly to coat. Cover and chill for at least 2 hours or up to 24 hours.

NUTRITION FACTS PER SERVING: 457 cal., 22 g total fat (6 g sat. fat), 99 mg chol., 683 mg sodium, 29 g carbo., 2 g fiber, 34 g pro.

Brats Deluxe

The sauerkraut-onion topping is equally delicious on Polish sausage.

PREP: 15 MINUTES **COOK:** 20 MINUTES **GRILL:** 20 MINUTES **MAKES:** 10 SERVINGS

10   uncooked bratwursts (about 4 ounces each)

2   medium onions, halved and thinly sliced

1   tablespoon cooking oil

1   32-ounce jar sauerkraut, undrained

1   12-ounce can beer

10   hoagie buns, split and toasted (optional)

    Mustard (optional)

1 Pierce bratwursts in several places with tines of fork. For a charcoal grill, arrange medium-hot coals around a drip pan. Test for medium heat above the pan. Place brats on grill rack over drip pan. Cover and grill for 20 to 30 minutes or until meat juices run clear (160°F),* turning occasionally. (For a gas grill, preheat grill. Reduce heat to medium. Adjust for indirect cooking. Grill as above.)

2 Meanwhile, in a Dutch oven cook onions in hot oil until tender. Stir in sauerkraut and beer. Bring to boiling; reduce heat. Simmer, uncovered, for 20 minutes. Add cooked bratwursts; heat through.

3 If desired, serve bratwursts on hoagie buns with mustard. Serve with the sauerkraut mixture.

NUTRITION FACTS PER SERVING: 430 cal., 35 g total fat (17 g sat. fat), 68 mg chol., 1,421 mg sodium, 9 g carbo., 3 g fiber, 15 g pro.

*NOTE: The internal color of a fresh bratwurst is not a reliable doneness indicator. A bratwurst cooked to 160°F is safe, regardless of color. To measure the doneness of a bratwurst, insert an instant-read thermometer from an end into the center of the bratwurst.

Picnic Hot Dog Platter

Setting out a platter loaded with a variety of hot dogs and sausages will please everyone at your gathering.

PREP: 10 MINUTES **GRILL:** 20 MINUTES (FRESH) OR 10 MINUTES (COOKED) **MAKES:** 12 SERVINGS

12 frankfurters, uncooked bratwursts, smoked pork sausages, veal sausages, turkey sausages, vegetarian frankfurters, and/or other favorites

1 dozen frankfurter or bratwurst buns or French-style rolls, split

1 recipe Tart Apple Mustard, 1 recipe Bacon Brown-Sugar Mustard, and/or 1 recipe Tomato Mustard

Desired condiments (such as chopped pickled peppers, sliced tomatoes, pickle relish, and/or crumbled cooked bacon) (optional)

1 Pierce uncooked sausages all over with a fork.

2 For a charcoal grill, arrange medium-hot coals around a drip pan. Test for medium heat above the pan. Place uncooked sausages on grill rack over drip pan. Cover and grill for 20 to 30 minutes or until meat is done (160°F),* turning once halfway through grilling. Add frankfurters and cooked sausage to the grill after the first 10 minutes; grill until heated through, turning once. (For a gas grill, preheat grill. Reduce heat to medium. Adjust for indirect cooking. Grill as above.) Serve with buns and desired mustards and condiments.

NUTRITION FACTS PER FRANKFURTER WITH BUN AND 1 TABLESPOON TART APPLE MUSTARD: 281 cal., 16 g total fat (6 g sat. fat), 24 mg chol., 757 mg sodium, 24 g carbo., 1 g fiber, 9 g pro.

***NOTE:** The internal color of an uncooked sausage is not a reliable doneness indicator. A sausage cooked to 160°F is safe, regardless of color. To measure doneness, insert instant-read thermometer from end into center of sausage.

Tart Apple Mustard: Stir together ½ cup honey mustard; 2 tablespoons shredded, unpeeled tart green apple; and ½ teaspoon ground black pepper. Cover; refrigerate at least 2 hours or up to 24 hours. Makes about ⅔ cup.

NUTRITION FACTS PER TABLESPOON: 23 cal., 0 g total fat (0 g sat. fat), 0 mg chol., 11 mg sodium, 5 g carbo., 0 g fiber, 0 g pro.

Bacon Brown-Sugar Mustard: Stir together ¾ cup yellow mustard; 3 slices bacon, crisp-cooked, drained, and finely crumbled; and 4 teaspoons brown sugar. Cover; refrigerate at least 8 hours or up to 2 days. Makes 1 cup.

NUTRITION FACTS PER TABLESPOON: 22 cal., 1 g total fat (0 g sat. fat), 1 mg chol., 161 mg sodium, 1 g carbo., 0 g fiber, 1 g pro.

Tomato Mustard: Stir together ⅓ cup creamy Dijon-style mustard blend and ½ teaspoon dry mustard. Gently stir in ½ cup peeled, seeded, and chopped tomatoes. Cover; refrigerate for up to 24 hours. Makes about ⅔ cup.

NUTRITION FACTS PER TABLESPOON: 20 cal., 2 g total fat (0 g sat. fat), 0 mg chol., 102 mg sodium, 2 g carbo., 0 g fiber, 0 g pro.

Surf-Side Tuna Sandwiches

All the ingredients you love in the lunch box version of this classic are here with the added smoky charm of barbecued tuna. Soaking the onions briefly in water and lemon juice reduces their harshness without diminishing flavor.

PREP: 20 MINUTES CHILL: 2 HOURS GRILL: 8 MINUTES MAKES: 4 SERVINGS

1 pound fresh or frozen tuna steaks, cut 1 inch thick

2 to 3 tablespoons olive oil or cooking oil

½ teaspoon salt

¼ teaspoon ground black pepper

2 cups water

1 tablespoon lemon juice

1 small red onion, very thinly sliced

⅓ to ½ cup mayonnaise

3 tablespoons dill pickle relish

1 teaspoon finely shredded lemon peel

1 tablespoon lemon juice

1 teaspoon bottled minced garlic (2 cloves)

½ teaspoon prepared mustard

4 6-inch-long Italian-style or French-style rolls, halved lengthwise

Sliced hard-cooked eggs, dill pickle slices, and/or tomato slices (optional)

Fresh dill sprigs (optional)

1 Thaw tuna, if frozen. Brush tuna generously with oil; sprinkle with salt and pepper. Cover and chill for 2 hours.

2 In a medium bowl combine the water and 1 tablespoon lemon juice. Add onion slices; let soak for 15 minutes. Drain.

3 For a charcoal grill, grill tuna on the greased rack of an uncovered grill directly over medium coals for 8 to 12 minutes or until fish flakes easily when tested with a fork, gently turning once halfway through grilling. (For a gas grill, preheat grill. Reduce heat to medium. Place tuna on greased grill rack over heat. Cover and grill as above.) Remove tuna from grill. Using 2 forks, break tuna into chunks.

4 In a medium bowl stir together mayonnaise, pickle relish, lemon peel, 1 tablespoon lemon juice, the garlic, and mustard. Add tuna chunks; stir gently to combine.

5 Spoon mixture onto bottoms of rolls. If desired, top with sliced hard-cooked eggs, dill pickle slices, and/or tomato slices. Top with the onion slices. If desired, add dill. Top with roll tops.

NUTRITION FACTS PER SERVING: 539 cal., 31 g total fat (6 g sat. fat), 155 mg chol., 1,218 mg sodium, 29 g carbo., 2 g fiber, 34 g pro.

Gazpacho Medley Open-Faced Sandwich

Stay as cool as a cucumber with this hearty sandwich featuring the flavors of gazpacho, a cold soup. Cucumbers, tomatoes, garlic, and jalapeños get mixed with black beans, then scooped into grilled French bread bowls and topped with cheese.

PREP: 20 MINUTES **GRILL:** 12 MINUTES + 1 MINUTE + 1 MINUTE **MAKES:** 6 SERVINGS

- **1** medium cucumber, seeded and chopped
- **1** cup cooked or canned black beans, rinsed and drained
- **¼** cup snipped fresh cilantro
- **1** tablespoon olive oil
- **2** tablespoons cider vinegar
- **1** pickled jalapeño pepper, finely chopped*
- **½** to 1 teaspoon chili powder
- **½** teaspoon bottled minced garlic (1 clove)
- **Salt**
- **Ground black pepper**
- **3** large tomatoes, halved
- **1** large sweet onion (such as Vidalia or Maui), cut into ½-inch-thick slices
- **1** loaf French bread
- **1** cup shredded cheddar cheese (4 ounces)

1 In a medium bowl combine the cucumber, beans, cilantro, oil, vinegar, jalapeño pepper, chili powder, garlic, and salt and pepper to taste. Set aside.

2 For a charcoal grill, place tomatoes and onion slices on greased rack of a grill with a cover directly over medium coals; grill, uncovered, for 12 to 15 minutes or until lightly charred, turning onion slices once. (For a gas grill, preheat grill. Reduce heat to medium. Place tomatoes and onion slices on greased grill rack over heat. Cover and grill as above.) Transfer vegetables to a cutting board; cool slightly and coarsely chop. Add chopped vegetables to the cucumber mixture; toss to combine.

3 Meanwhile, halve the French bread lengthwise. Cut each bread half crosswise into 3 pieces. Using a fork, hollow out the bread pieces slightly. Grill the bread pieces, cut sides down, about 1 minute or until toasted. Spoon the vegetable mixture into the bread pieces; sprinkle sandwiches with cheddar cheese. Place the sandwiches on the grill rack, filled sides up. Cover and grill for 1 to 2 minutes or until cheese is melted.

NUTRITION FACTS PER SERVING: 329 cal., 11 g total fat (5 g sat. fat), 20 mg chol., 634 mg sodium, 46 g carbo., 3 g fiber, 14 g pro.

*NOTE: Because chile peppers contain volatile oils that can burn your skin and eyes, avoid direct contact with them as much as possible. When working with chile peppers, wear plastic or rubber gloves. If your bare hands do touch the chile peppers, wash your hands and nails well with soap and warm water.

Foil-Grilled Cheese Sandwiches

Salsa gives these sandwiches a Mexican spin.
They're easy to make and cleanup is a breeze.

PREP: 20 MINUTES GRILL: 6 MINUTES MAKES: 6 SERVINGS

12 slices firm-textured white or whole wheat bread

¼ cup butter or margarine, softened

½ of an 8-ounce tub cream cheese

2 to 4 tablespoons bottled salsa

2 cups shredded cheddar cheese (8 ounces)*

¼ cup finely chopped green sweet pepper

1 Spread 1 side of each bread slice with butter. Spread cream cheese on unbuttered side of 6 of the bread slices. Spoon 1 to 2 teaspoons salsa over cream cheese on each bread slice. Sprinkle with cheddar cheese and sweet pepper. Top with remaining 6 bread slices, buttered sides up. Press sandwiches down to flatten slightly.

2 For a charcoal grill, grill sandwiches on the foil-covered grill rack of an uncovered grill directly over medium coals about 6 minutes or until browned and cheese is melted, turning once halfway through grilling. (For a gas grill, preheat grill. Reduce heat to medium. Place sandwiches on foil-covered grill rack over heat. Cover and grill as above.)

NUTRITION FACTS PER SERVING: 433 cal., 30 g total fat (17 g sat. fat), 80 mg chol., 689 mg sodium, 29 g carbo., 0 g fiber, 15 g pro.

*NOTE: If you prefer, substitute 6 slices of American cheese for the shredded cheddar cheese.

Portobello Flats

Portobello mushrooms add substance to this no-meat sandwich.

PREP: 15 MINUTES **GRILL:** 6 MINUTES + 2 MINUTES **MAKES:** 4 SERVINGS

⅔ cup chopped tomato

2 teaspoons snipped fresh basil, thyme, and/or oregano

⅛ teaspoon salt

2 medium fresh portobello mushrooms (about 4 inches in diameter)

1 teaspoon balsamic vinegar or red wine vinegar

½ teaspoon olive oil

½ of a 12-inch Italian flatbread (focaccia), quartered, or ½ of a 12-inch thin-crust Italian bread shell (Boboli)

Finely shredded Parmesan cheese (optional)

1 In a small bowl stir together tomato, desired herb, and salt; set aside. Cut the mushroom stems even with the caps; discard stems. Rinse mushroom caps; gently pat dry.

2 In a small bowl stir together vinegar and oil. Gently brush mixture over the mushrooms. For a charcoal grill, grill mushrooms on the rack of an uncovered grill directly over medium coals for 6 to 8 minutes or just until mushrooms are tender, turning once halfway through grilling. (For a gas grill, preheat grill. Reduce heat to medium. Place mushrooms on grill rack over heat. Cover and grill as above.) Drain the mushrooms on paper towels; thinly slice the mushrooms.

3 Place bread on grill rack. Grill for 2 to 3 minutes or until heated through.

4 To serve, top bread with sliced mushrooms and tomato mixture. If desired, sprinkle with Parmesan cheese.

NUTRITION FACTS PER SERVING: 157 cal., 3 g total fat (1 g sat. fat), 0 mg chol., 80 mg sodium, 28 g carbo., 4 g fiber, 7 g pro.

Pork Kabobs in Pita Pockets

*Fans of the Greek specialty gyro will love
these yogurt and cucumber-sauced pork sandwiches.*

PREP: 25 MINUTES MARINATE: 6 TO 24 HOURS GRILL: 10 MINUTES MAKES: 8 TO 10 SERVINGS

2 pounds boneless pork, cut into 1-inch pieces

¼ cup cooking oil

¼ cup chopped onion

3 tablespoons lemon juice

1 tablespoon finely snipped fresh parsley

½ teaspoon salt

½ teaspoon dried marjoram, crushed

½ teaspoon bottled minced garlic (1 clove)

⅛ teaspoon ground black pepper

1 8-ounce carton plain yogurt

½ cup finely chopped cucumber

1 tablespoon chopped onion

1 tablespoon finely snipped fresh parsley

1 teaspoon lemon juice

⅛ teaspoon garlic salt

4 or 5 large pita bread rounds, halved crosswise

Chopped tomato (optional)

Shredded lettuce (optional)

1 Place pork in a resealable plastic bag set in a shallow dish. For marinade, in a small bowl combine cooking oil, the ¼ cup onion, the 3 tablespoons lemon juice, the 1 tablespoon parsley, salt, marjoram, garlic, and pepper. Pour marinade over pork. Seal bag; turn to coat meat. Marinate in the refrigerator for at least 6 hours or up to 24 hours, turning bag occasionally.

2 In a medium bowl stir together yogurt, cucumber, the 1 tablespoon onion, the 1 tablespoon parsley, the 1 teaspoon lemon juice, and the garlic salt. Cover and refrigerate until serving time.

3 Drain pork, discarding marinade. On long metal skewers, thread pork pieces, leaving ¼-inch space between pieces. For a charcoal grill, grill kabobs on the rack of an uncovered grill directly over medium coals for 10 to 12 minutes or until meat juices run clear, turning occasionally. (For a gas grill, preheat grill. Reduce heat to medium. Place kabobs on grill rack over heat. Cover and grill as above.) Remove pork from skewers.

4 Serve pork in pita; top with yogurt mixture. If desired, top with tomato and lettuce.

NUTRITION FACTS PER SERVING: 302 cal., 15 g total fat (4 g sat. fat), 53 mg chol., 386 mg sodium, 20 g carbo., 0 g fiber, 20 g pro.

Greek-Inspired Lamb Pockets

Be a dinnertime hero with a meal-in-a-pocket that wins you applause. Meaty lamb leg or shoulder is marinated in balsamic vinegar, pepper, and fresh herbs, quick-grilled to keep it juicy, then tucked into pitas and topped with a creamy yogurt sauce.

PREP: 20 MINUTES **MARINATE:** 10 MINUTES TO 4 HOURS **GRILL:** 10 MINUTES **MAKES:** 4 SERVINGS

1	pound boneless lamb leg or shoulder
¼	cup balsamic vinegar
1	tablespoon snipped fresh savory or 1 teaspoon dried savory, crushed
½	teaspoon ground black pepper
1	8-ounce carton plain low-fat or fat-free yogurt
1	small cucumber, peeled, seeded, and chopped (¾ cup)
2	plum tomatoes, chopped
1	small onion, finely chopped
4	whole wheat pita bread rounds

❶ Trim fat from lamb. Cut lamb into 2×1-inch thin strips. Place lamb in a resealable plastic bag set in a shallow dish. For marinade, in a small bowl combine vinegar, savory, and pepper. Pour marinade over lamb. Seal bag; turn once to coat meat. Marinate in the refrigerator for at least 10 minutes or up to 4 hours, turning bag occasionally.

❷ Meanwhile, for sauce, in a medium bowl combine yogurt, cucumber, tomatoes, and onion. Cover and refrigerate until ready to serve or up to 4 hours. Wrap pita rounds in foil. Set aside.

❸ Drain lamb, reserving marinade. On long metal skewers, thread lamb (accordion-style). For a charcoal grill, grill skewers on the rack of an uncovered grill directly over medium coals for 10 to 12 minutes or until meat is done, turning once halfway through grilling and brushing with reserved marinade for the first 5 minutes of grilling. Place the pita rounds on grill rack next to the skewers for the last 5 minutes of grilling. (For a gas grill, preheat grill. Reduce heat to medium. Place skewers on grill rack over heat. Cover and grill as above.) Discard any remaining marinade.

❹ Cut pita bread rounds in half crosswise. Spoon the sauce into pita halves and fill with lamb strips.

NUTRITION FACTS PER SERVING: 361 cal., 8 g total fat (3 g sat. fat), 61 mg chol., 430 mg sodium, 46 g carbo., 1 g fiber, 28 g pro.

Pork Tenderloin Wrap

Wraps are all the rage and Asian flavors are too.
Here flavorful pork tenderloin is rolled up with crunchy sesame-flavored slaw.
Wrap up dinner with iced green tea garnished with orange slices.

PREP: 15 MINUTES **MARINATE:** 6 TO 24 HOURS **GRILL:** 40 MINUTES **MAKES:** 6 SERVINGS

2   12-ounce pork tenderloins
3   tablespoons soy sauce
2   tablespoons orange juice
1   tablespoon honey
½   teaspoon bottled minced garlic (1 clove)
3   cups packaged shredded cabbage with carrot (coleslaw mix)
¼   cup thinly sliced green onions
2   tablespoons sesame seeds, toasted
1   tablespoon seasoned rice vinegar
1   teaspoon toasted sesame oil
6   12-inch plain or spinach flour tortillas*

1 Trim fat from meat. Place meat in a resealable plastic bag set in a shallow dish. For marinade, in a small bowl combine soy sauce, orange juice, honey, and garlic. Pour marinade over meat. Seal bag; turn to coat meat. Marinate in the refrigerator for at least 6 hours or up to 24 hours, turning bag occasionally.

2 For slaw, in a medium bowl combine cabbage, green onions, sesame seeds, rice vinegar, and sesame oil; toss well. Cover and refrigerate until ready to serve.

3 Drain tenderloins, discarding marinade. For a charcoal grill, arrange hot coals around a drip pan. Test for medium-hot heat above the pan. Place tenderloins on grill rack over drip pan. Cover and grill for 40 to 50 minutes or until meat juices run clear (160°F). (For a gas grill, preheat grill. Reduce heat to medium-hot. Adjust for indirect cooking. Place tenderloins on a rack in a roasting pan, place on grill rack, and grill as above.)

4 Thinly slice tenderloins. Arrange meat slices in a strip down the center of each tortilla. Top with slaw. Fold up bottom edge over filling; fold in sides, overlapping in the center. Serve immediately.

NUTRITION FACTS PER SERVING: 319 cal., 8 g total fat (2 g sat. fat), 66 mg chol., 468 mg sodium, 28 g carbo., 2 g fiber, 32 g pro.

*NOTE: For easier handling, wrap tortillas in heavy foil and heat on the grill about 10 minutes or until warm, turning once halfway through grilling.

Jalapeño Sausages

Homemade Southwestern-style sausages swaddled in warm tortillas make a blazingly satisfying meal.

PREP: 15 MINUTES CHILL: 6 TO 24 HOURS GRILL: 20 MINUTES MAKES: 4 SERVINGS

4   ounces fresh jalapeño chile peppers, seeded and finely chopped, or one 4-ounce can jalapeño chile peppers, drained and chopped*

2   tablespoons snipped fresh cilantro

2   tablespoons beer or water

1   teaspoon cumin seeds, crushed

½   teaspoon salt

½   teaspoon bottled minced garlic (1 clove)

¼   teaspoon ground black pepper

⅛   teaspoon cayenne pepper

1   pound lean ground pork

4   8-inch whole wheat flour or corn tortillas or frankfurter buns

    Leaf lettuce (optional)

1 In a medium bowl combine jalapeño chile peppers, cilantro, beer, cumin seeds, salt, garlic, black pepper, and cayenne pepper. Add ground pork; mix well. Shape meat mixture into four 6-inch-long logs or ¾-inch-thick patties. Cover; chill for at least 6 hours or up to 24 hours or until mixture is firm. Stack tortillas; wrap in foil. Set aside.

2 For a charcoal grill, arrange medium-hot coals around a drip pan. Test for medium heat above the pan. Place meat on grill rack over drip pan. Cover and grill for 15 minutes. Add tortillas to grill directly over coals. Cover and grill for 5 to 10 minutes more or until meat is done (160°F)** and tortillas are heated through, turning once halfway through grilling. (For a gas grill, preheat grill. Reduce heat to medium. Adjust for indirect cooking. Place meat on grill rack over heat. Cover and grill as above.) To serve, place sausages in warm tortillas. If desired, top with lettuce.

NUTRITION FACTS PER SERVING: 240 cal., 11 g total fat (4 g sat. fat), 53 mg chol., 432 mg sodium, 18 g carbo., 1 g fiber, 17 g pro.

*NOTE: Because chile peppers contain volatile oils that can burn your skin and eyes, avoid direct contact with them as much as possible. When working with chile peppers, wear plastic or rubber gloves. If your bare hands do touch the chile peppers, wash your hands and nails well with soap and warm water.

**NOTE: The internal color of a meat log or patty is not a reliable doneness indicator. A pork log or patty cooked to 160°F is safe, regardless of color. To measure doneness of pork logs, insert an instant-read thermometer from an end into the center of log. To measure the doneness of a patty, insert an instant-read thermometer through the side of the patty to a depth of 2 to 3 inches.

Herbed Focaccia with Chicken

Want a meatless entrée? Try the Herbed Focaccia with Eggplant variation.

PREP: 20 MINUTES **RISE:** 20 MINUTES **GRILL:** 15 MINUTES + 15 MINUTES + 5 MINUTES

MAKES: 6 SERVINGS

1	16-ounce package hot roll mix
¼	cup olive oil
1	tablespoon snipped fresh basil
1	teaspoon snipped fresh rosemary
¼	teaspoon freshly ground black pepper
1	pound skinless, boneless chicken breast halves
¼	cup bottled Italian salad dressing
2	or 3 plum tomatoes, cut into ¼-inch-thick slices
¼	cup shredded Parmesan cheese (1 ounce)

1 For focaccia, prepare hot roll mix according to package directions, except substitute 2 tablespoons of the olive oil for the margarine.

2 Lightly oil a 12-inch pizza pan with 1 teaspoon of the olive oil. Press kneaded dough into pan and flatten top. Using your fingertips, press indents into top of dough. Drizzle with the remaining 5 teaspoons olive oil and sprinkle with basil, rosemary, and pepper. Cover and let rise in a warm place for 20 minutes.

3 Meanwhile, brush chicken with Italian dressing. For a charcoal grill, arrange medium-hot coals around a drip pan. Test for medium heat above the pan. Place chicken on grill rack over drip pan. Cover and grill for 15 to 18 minutes or until chicken is no longer pink (170°F), turning once halfway through grilling. (For a gas grill, preheat grill. Reduce heat to medium. Adjust for indirect cooking. Grill as above.) Remove chicken from grill; cool slightly.

4 Place dough on pan on the grill rack. Cover and grill about 15 minutes or until focaccia is puffed and beginning to brown on edges. Meanwhile, thinly slice chicken. Arrange tomato slices on top of focaccia. Top with chicken and sprinkle with Parmesan cheese. Cover and grill for 5 to 10 minutes more or until focaccia is lightly browned on edges and cheese is golden brown. Cut into wedges.

NUTRITION FACTS PER SERVING: 575 cal., 24 g total fat (4 g sat. fat), 90 mg chol., 744 mg sodium, 59 g carbo., 0 g fiber, 31 g pro.

Herbed Focaccia with Eggplant: Prepare as directed, except substitute 1 medium eggplant for the chicken. Cut eggplant into ½-inch-thick slices; lightly coat with olive oil. Place directly over medium coals; cover and grill about 6 minutes or just until tender, turning once. Arrange on partially grilled focaccia with tomatoes. Top with ½ cup shredded fontina cheese in place of Parmesan cheese.

NUTRITION FACTS PER SERVING: 478 cal., 19 g total fat (4 g sat. fat), 46 mg chol., 607 mg sodium, 64 g carbo., 2 g fiber, 15 g pro.

Pizza on the Grill

*Your friends will think you've gone gourmet if you make
either of these grilled pizzas—one with nutty
Asiago and fresh basil, the other with smoked provolone and fresh rosemary.*

PREP: 25 MINUTES GRILL: 3 MINUTES + 2 MINUTES + 5 MINUTES MAKES: 4 SERVINGS

1   16-ounce loaf frozen bread dough, thawed

      Cornmeal

2   medium tomatoes, chopped (1½ cups)

½   cup snipped fresh basil

1   tablespoon olive oil

½   teaspoon bottled minced garlic (1 clove)

1   cup shredded Asiago cheese (4 ounces)

1   cup shredded mozzarella cheese (4 ounces)

1 On a lightly floured surface, roll dough into a ¼-inch-thick circle (about 12 inches in diameter). Lightly dust both sides with cornmeal. Place on a large baking sheet dusted with cornmeal. For a charcoal grill, arrange medium-hot coals around a drip pan. Test for medium heat above the pan. Carefully slide pizza crust from the baking sheet onto the grill rack over drip pan. Cover and grill about 3 minutes or until top is puffed and underside is crisp. Using a large spatula, turn crust. Cover and grill for 2 minutes more. (For a gas grill, preheat grill. Reduce heat to medium. Adjust for indirect cooking. Grill as above.)

2 Meanwhile, in a medium bowl combine tomatoes, basil, olive oil, and garlic. Spread tomato mixture evenly over crust. Top with shredded Asiago cheese and mozzarella cheese.

3 Cover and grill about 5 minutes more or until mozzarella cheese is melted and crust is cooked through.

NUTRITION FACTS PER SERVING: 483 cal., 24 g total fat (11 g sat. fat), 46 mg chol., 808 mg sodium, 46 g carbo., 3 g fiber, 21 g pro.

Smoked Provolone Pizza: Prepare as above, except substitute 2 teaspoons snipped fresh rosemary for the basil and use 1½ cups shredded smoked provolone or Gouda cheese (6 ounces) in place of the Asiago and mozzarella cheeses.

NUTRITION FACTS PER SERVING: 468 cal., 15 g total fat (8 g sat. fat), 29 mg chol., 374 mg sodium, 54 g carbo., 0 g fiber, 20 g pro.

Italian Sausage Pizza

Grill this classic Italian sausage pizza that's set apart by the smoky vigor of outdoor cooking. Suddenly you're a top-notch pizza chef.

PREP: 15 MINUTES **GRILL:** 12 MINUTES + 8 MINUTES + 3 MINUTES + 5 MINUTES

MAKES: 4 SERVINGS

- **1** cup chopped plum tomatoes
- **½** cup snipped fresh basil
- **½** teaspoon bottled minced garlic (1 clove)
- **¼** teaspoon salt
- **12** ounces uncooked sweet or hot Italian sausage links
- **1** medium onion, cut into ½-inch-thick slices
- **1** red or yellow sweet pepper, cut into 1-inch-wide strips
- **4** 7-inch packaged prebaked pizza crusts
- **1** cup shredded mozzarella cheese (4 ounces)
- **¼** cup grated Parmesan cheese (1 ounce)

1 In a small bowl combine the tomatoes, basil, garlic, and salt; set aside.

2 For a charcoal grill, arrange medium-hot coals around a drip pan. Test for medium heat above the pan. Place sausage on grill rack over drip pan. Cover and grill for 12 minutes. Turn sausage. Place onion and sweet pepper on grill tray or in a grill basket; add to grill directly over coals. Cover and grill for 8 to 18 minutes more or until sausage juices run clear (160°F)* and vegetables are tender, turning once halfway through grilling. (For a gas grill, preheat grill. Reduce heat to medium. Adjust for indirect cooking. Place sausage, then onion and sweet pepper on grill rack, and grill as above.) Remove sausage and vegetables from grill. Thinly slice sausage; set aside.

3 Add pizza crusts to grill directly over coals. Cover and grill crusts for 3 minutes. Turn crusts. Divide mozzarella cheese, tomato mixture, sausage, onion, and sweet pepper among the pizza crusts. Sprinkle with Parmesan cheese. Cover and grill about 5 minutes more or until heated through and cheese is melted.

NUTRITION FACTS PER SERVING: 597 cal., 26 g total fat (10 g sat. fat), 70 mg chol., 1,470 mg sodium, 56 g carbo., 1 g fiber, 32 g pro.

*NOTE: The internal color of a sausage link is not a reliable doneness indicator. A sausage cooked to 160°F is safe, regardless of color. To measure the doneness of a sausage link, insert an instant-read thermometer from an end into the center of the sausage link.

Canadian Bacon Pizza

*This fast-grilling appetizer puts all of the sizzle and smoke
you love into one of the world's most popular treats.
Purchased Italian bread shells make the recipe a real snap to prepare.*

PREP: 20 MINUTES GRILL: 5 MINUTES MAKES: 8 SERVINGS

1　6-ounce jar marinated artichoke hearts, quartered

2　6-inch Italian bread shells (Boboli)

1　cup shredded fontina or mozzarella cheese (4 ounces)

6　slices Canadian-style bacon, cut into strips (about 5 ounces)

3　plum tomatoes, sliced

¼　cup crumbled feta cheese (1 ounce)

2　green onions, thinly sliced

1　tablespoon snipped fresh oregano or basil

1 Drain artichoke hearts, reserving marinade. Brush the bread shells with some of the reserved marinade (discard any remaining marinade). Sprinkle ½ cup of the fontina cheese over bread shells. In a large bowl toss together the artichoke hearts, Canadian-style bacon, tomatoes, feta cheese, green onions, and oregano; divide among shells. Sprinkle with remaining ½ cup fontina cheese.

2 Transfer the bread shells to a pizza grill pan or a large piece of double-thickness heavy foil. For a charcoal grill, place the pan or foil on the rack of a grill with a cover directly over medium coals. Cover and grill for 5 to 8 minutes or until cheese is melted and pizza is heated through. (For a gas grill, preheat grill. Reduce heat to medium. Place pan or foil on grill rack over heat. Grill as above.)

NUTRITION FACTS PER SERVING: 186 cal., 9 g total fat (4 g sat. fat), 29 mg chol., 615 mg sodium, 17 g carbo., 0 g fiber, 11 g pro.

278

Middle Eastern-Style Pizza

Lamb, feta cheese, and fresh mint give pizza a whole new dimension.

PREP: 15 MINUTES GRILL: 5 MINUTES + 8 MINUTES MAKES: 4 SERVINGS

12 ounces ground lamb

1 8-ounce can tomato sauce

½ teaspoon bottled minced garlic (1 clove)

¼ teaspoon ground allspice

Nonstick cooking spray

1 10-ounce package refrigerated pizza dough

2 plum tomatoes, thinly sliced

½ cup chopped green sweet pepper

½ cup crumbled feta cheese (2 ounces) (optional)

¼ cup snipped fresh mint

1 tablespoon pine nuts, toasted

Plain low-fat yogurt (optional)

1 For sauce, in a large skillet cook ground lamb over medium heat until meat is brown. Drain off fat. Stir in tomato sauce, garlic, and allspice. Set aside.

2 Lightly coat a 12-inch pizza grill pan with nonstick cooking spray. With your fingers, pat the pizza dough onto the prepared pan.

3 For a charcoal grill, in a grill with a cover place pizza pan on the rack directly over medium coals; grill, uncovered, for 5 minutes. (For a gas grill, preheat grill. Reduce heat to medium. Place pizza pan on grill rack over heat. Cover and grill as above.) Carefully remove pizza crust from grill.

4 Turn crust; spread with the sauce. Top with tomatoes and sweet pepper. Return pizza to grill. Cover and grill for 8 to 10 minutes more or until pizza is heated through, checking occasionally to make sure the crust doesn't overbrown. Remove pizza from grill.

5 Sprinkle with feta cheese (if desired), mint, and pine nuts. If desired, top with yogurt.

NUTRITION FACTS PER SERVING: 388 cal., 16 g total fat (5 g sat. fat), 57 mg chol., 784 mg sodium, 40 g carbo., 2 g fiber, 22 g pro.

Vegetable Pizzas

Grilled garden-fresh vegetables top flour tortilla crusts for these delightful pizzas.

PREP: 25 MINUTES GRILL: 8 MINUTES + 1 MINUTE + 2 MINUTES MAKES: 4 SERVINGS

1 small yellow summer squash, quartered lengthwise

1 small red sweet pepper, quartered lengthwise

1 medium zucchini, quartered lengthwise

2 tablespoons olive oil

1 teaspoon ground black pepper

½ teaspoon salt

1 large tomato, seeded and chopped

¼ cup mayonnaise or salad dressing

2 tablespoons purchased basil pesto

1 tablespoon snipped fresh basil

1 tablespoon snipped fresh oregano

4 6- to 7-inch flour tortillas

1 cup shredded mozzarella or smoked provolone cheese (4 ounces)

1 Brush summer squash, sweet pepper, and zucchini with olive oil; sprinkle with black pepper and salt. For a charcoal grill, place vegetables on the rack of a grill with a cover directly over medium coals; grill, uncovered, until crisp-tender, turning once halfway through grilling. Allow 5 to 6 minutes for summer squash and zucchini and 8 to 10 minutes for sweet pepper. Remove vegetables from grill.

2 Chop grilled vegetables. In a medium bowl combine chopped vegetables, tomato, mayonnaise, pesto, basil, and oregano. Place tortillas on grill rack directly over heat. Cover and grill for 1 to 2 minutes or until lightly toasted on one side. Turn tortillas over and spread the vegetable mixture over the toasted sides of tortillas. Sprinkle with shredded cheese.

3 Cover and grill for 2 to 3 minutes more or just until tortillas are lightly toasted, vegetables are heated, and cheese begins to melt. Carefully remove from grill. (For a gas grill, preheat grill. Reduce heat to medium. Place vegetables, then tortillas over heat. Cover and grill as above.)

NUTRITION FACTS PER SERVING: 426 cal., 31 g total fat (7 g sat. fat), 24 mg chol., 737 mg sodium, 27 g carbo., 3 g fiber, 12 g pro.

280

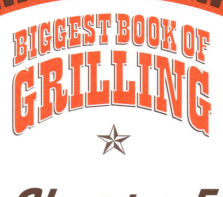

BIGGEST BOOK OF GRILLING

★

Chapter 5

SAUCES, RUBS & MARINADES

Barbecue Sauce

There's enough of this sweet, tangy sauce to slather on during grilling plus pass at the table.

PREP: 10 MINUTES COOK: 30 MINUTES
MAKES: 3 CUPS

1 15-ounce can tomato sauce
½ cup cider vinegar
½ cup packed brown sugar
2 tablespoons finely chopped onion
2 tablespoons liquid smoke
1 tablespoon Worcestershire sauce
1 teaspoon chili powder
½ teaspoon bottled minced garlic (1 clove)
¼ teaspoon celery salt
⅛ to ¼ teaspoon cayenne pepper
⅛ teaspoon ground allspice
3 drops bottled hot pepper sauce

1 In a medium saucepan combine tomato sauce, vinegar, brown sugar, onion, liquid smoke, Worcestershire sauce, chili powder, garlic, celery salt, cayenne pepper, allspice, and hot pepper sauce. Bring to boiling; reduce heat. Simmer, uncovered, about 30 minutes or until desired consistency.

2 Use warm to brush on beef, pork, or poultry during the last 5 to 10 minutes of grilling. Reheat any remaining sauce until bubbly; pass with grilled meat. Cover and store unused sauce in refrigerator for up to 3 days.

NUTRITION FACTS PER 2-TABLESPOON SERVING: 24 cal., 0 g total fat, 0 mg chol., 108 mg sodium, 6 g carbo., 0 g fiber, 0 g pro.

Tangy-Sweet Barbecue Sauce

In your quest to find your signature sauce, be sure to try this honey-sparked one.

START TO FINISH: 15 MINUTES
MAKES: 1¾ CUPS

1 cup ketchup
½ cup packed brown sugar
⅓ cup granulated sugar
3 tablespoons cooking oil
2 tablespoons vinegar
1 tablespoon honey
2 teaspoons Worcestershire sauce

1 In a medium saucepan combine ketchup, brown sugar, granulated sugar, oil, vinegar, honey, and Worcestershire sauce. Cook and stir over medium heat until the sugars dissolve and sauce is heated through.

2 Use warm to brush on beef, pork, or poultry during the last 5 to 10 minutes of grilling. Reheat any remaining sauce until bubbly; pass with grilled meat. Cover and store unused sauce in refrigerator for up to 3 days.

NUTRITION FACTS PER 2-TABLESPOON SERVING: 98 cal., 3 g total fat (0 g sat. fat), 0 mg chol., 216 mg sodium, 19 g carbo., 0 g fiber, 0 g pro.

Basic Moppin' Sauce

Use a pastry or basting brush as a mop for brushing on this coffee-accented sauce.

PREP: 15 MINUTES COOK: 30 MINUTES

MAKES: 2 CUPS

- 1 cup strong coffee
- 1 cup ketchup
- ½ cup Worcestershire sauce
- ¼ cup butter or margarine
- 1 tablespoon sugar
- 1 to 2 teaspoons freshly ground black pepper
- ½ teaspoon salt (optional)

1 In a medium saucepan combine coffee, ketchup, Worcestershire sauce, butter, sugar, pepper, and, if desired, salt. Bring to boiling, stirring occasionally; reduce heat. Simmer, uncovered, for 30 minutes, stirring frequently.

2 Use warm to brush on beef, pork, or poultry during the last 5 to 10 minutes of grilling. Reheat any remaining sauce until bubbly; pass with grilled meat. Cover and store unused sauce in refrigerator for up to 3 days.

NUTRITION FACTS PER 2-TABLESPOON SERVING: 52 cal., 4 g total fat (2 g sat. fat), 7 mg chol., 292 mg sodium, 6 g carbo., 0 g fiber, 0 g pro.

Dried Plum Barbecue Sauce

The California origins of this delectable sauce are easy to find. In fact, ribs brushed with the sauce would be great served with a hearty California Zinfandel.

START TO FINISH: 25 MINUTES

MAKES: ABOUT 4 CUPS

- 2 tablespoons cooking oil
- 1 large onion, finely chopped
- 1 15-ounce can tomato puree
- 1½ cups cut-up pitted dried plums (prunes)
- ⅔ cup water
- ½ cup packed brown sugar
- ⅓ cup Dijon-style mustard
- ¼ cup lemon juice
- ¼ cup Worcestershire sauce
- 4 teaspoons bottled hot pepper sauce
- ½ teaspoon ground allspice
- ½ teaspoon ground ginger
  - Salt
  - Ground black pepper

1 In a medium saucepan heat oil over medium heat. Add onion; cook about 10 minutes or until tender, stirring occasionally. Add tomato puree, dried plums, the water, brown sugar, mustard, lemon juice, Worcestershire, pepper sauce, allspice, and ginger. Bring to boiling; reduce heat. Simmer, uncovered, 5 to 10 minutes or until sauce thickens. Season to taste with salt and pepper.

2 Use warm to brush on pork ribs during the last 5 to 10 minutes of grilling. Reheat any remaining sauce until bubbly; serve with ribs. Cover and store unused sauce in refrigerator for up to 3 days.

NUTRITION FACTS PER 2-TABLESPOON SERVING: 52 cal., 1 g total fat (0 g sat. fat), 0 mg chol., 100 mg sodium, 11 g carbo., 1 g fiber, 0 g pro.

Latino Barbecue Ketchup

Chipotle and jalapeño chile peppers add spark to this burger topper.

START TO FINISH: 15 MINUTES
MAKES: 1²⁄₃ CUPS

1 cup chopped green onions

¼ to ½ cup canned chipotle chile peppers in adobo sauce

1 fresh jalapeño chile pepper, chopped*

1 tablespoon snipped fresh oregano

1 teaspoon bottled minced garlic (2 cloves)

½ teaspoon salt

1 cup ketchup

¼ cup red wine vinegar

2 tablespoons olive oil

1 In a food processor bowl combine green onions, chipotle peppers, jalapeño pepper, oregano, garlic, and salt. Cover; process until combined. Add ketchup, red wine vinegar, and olive oil; process until smooth. Serve with grilled burgers. Cover and store unused ketchup in refrigerator for up to 3 days.

NUTRITION FACTS PER 2-TABLESPOON SERVING: 45 cal., 2 g total fat (0 g sat. fat), 0 mg chol., 332 mg sodium, 6 g carbo., 1 g fiber, 0 g pro.

*NOTE: Because chile peppers contain volatile oils that can burn your skin and eyes, avoid direct contact with them as much as possible. When working with chile peppers, wear plastic or rubber gloves. If your bare hands do touch the chile peppers, wash your hands and nails well with soap and warm water.

Kansas City Barbecue Sauce

Kansas City is a notoriously competitive barbecue town—so much so that some sauce recipes are secrets taken to the grave.

PREP: 10 MINUTES COOK: 30 MINUTES
MAKES: ABOUT 1¹⁄₃ CUPS

½ cup finely chopped onion

1 teaspoon bottled minced garlic (2 cloves)

1 tablespoon olive oil or cooking oil

¾ cup apple juice or apple cider

½ of a 6-ounce can tomato paste (⅓ cup)

¼ cup cider vinegar

2 tablespoons brown sugar

2 tablespoons molasses

1 tablespoon paprika

1 tablespoon prepared horseradish

1 tablespoon Worcestershire sauce

1 teaspoon salt

½ teaspoon ground black pepper

1 In a medium saucepan cook onion and garlic in hot oil until onion is tender. Stir in apple juice, tomato paste, vinegar, brown sugar, molasses, paprika, horseradish, Worcestershire sauce, salt, and pepper. Bring to boiling; reduce heat. Simmer, uncovered, about 30 minutes or until desired consistency, stirring occasionally.

2 Use warm to brush on beef, pork, or poultry during the last 5 to 10 minutes of grilling. Reheat any remaining sauce until bubbly; pass with grilled meat. Cover and store unused sauce in refrigerator for up to 3 days.

NUTRITION FACTS PER 2-TABLESPOON SERVING: 52 cal., 2 g total fat (0 g sat. fat), 0 mg chol., 300 mg sodium, 10 g carbo., 0 g fiber, 0 g pro.

Mango and Pepper BBQ Sauce

What starts out as a chunky, fresh-fruit-and-vegetable salsa you could serve alongside your grilled food winds up being pureed into a terrific barbecue sauce for the top of it.

START TO FINISH: 20 MINUTES
MAKES: ABOUT 2½ CUPS

2	cups chopped red sweet pepper
½	cup chopped onion
2	tablespoons cooking oil
2	medium mangoes, seeded, peeled, and chopped (2 cups)
¼	cup packed brown sugar
2	tablespoons rice vinegar
½	teaspoon crushed red pepper
¼	teaspoon salt
2	tablespoons finely chopped green onion

1 In a large skillet cook the sweet pepper and onion in hot oil just until tender. Stir in the mangoes, brown sugar, vinegar, crushed red pepper, and salt. Bring to boiling; reduce heat. Simmer, uncovered, about 10 minutes or until mangoes are tender. Cool mixture slightly. Transfer mixture to a blender container or food processor bowl. Cover and blend or process until nearly smooth. Stir in green onion.

2 Use warm to brush on pork, chicken, fish, or shrimp during the last 5 to 10 minutes of grilling. Reheat any remaining sauce until bubbly; pass with grilled meat. Cover and store unused sauce in refrigerator for up to 3 days.

NUTRITION FACTS PER 2-TABLESPOON SERVING: 38 cal., 2 g total fat (0 g sat. fat), 0 mg chol., 28 mg sodium, 6 g carbo., 0 g fiber, 0 g pro.

Molasses Barbecue Sauce

Ribs turn out glossy when brushed with this succulent sauce.

START TO FINISH: 10 MINUTES
MAKES: 1½ CUPS

1	cup ketchup
¼	cup full-flavored molasses
¼	cup water
½	teaspoon finely shredded lemon peel
1	tablespoon lemon juice
2	teaspoons Worcestershire sauce
½	teaspoon ground black pepper
⅛	teaspoon salt
2	tablespoons ruby port wine (optional)

1 In a medium bowl combine ketchup, molasses, the water, lemon peel, lemon juice, Worcestershire sauce, pepper, and salt. If desired, stir in wine.

2 Use to brush on beef or pork ribs during the last 5 to 10 minutes of grilling. Heat any remaining sauce until bubbly; pass with grilled ribs. Cover and store unused sauce in refrigerator for up to 3 days.

NUTRITION FACTS PER 2-TABLESPOON SERVING: 40 cal., 0 g total fat, 0 mg chol., 275 mg sodium, 10 g carbo., 0 g fiber, 0 g pro.

Pacific Rim BBQ Sauce

This spunky barbecue brush-on is great for everything from chicken and ribs to steak and burgers.

PREP: 10 MINUTES COOK: 25 MINUTES

MAKES: 1 CUP

1   teaspoon bottled minced garlic (2 cloves)

1   teaspoon grated fresh ginger

2   teaspoons cooking oil

½   cup packed brown sugar

½   cup whiskey

¼   cup bottled hoisin sauce

¼   cup soy sauce

¼   cup frozen pineapple juice concentrate, thawed

¼   cup rice vinegar

1 In a medium saucepan cook and stir garlic and ginger in hot oil for 1 minute. Stir in brown sugar, whiskey, hoisin sauce, soy sauce, pineapple juice concentrate, and rice vinegar. Bring to boiling; reduce heat. Simmer, uncovered, for 25 to 30 minutes or until reduced to 1 cup, stirring occasionally.

2 Use warm to brush on steaks, ribs, poultry, or burgers during the last 5 to 10 minutes of grilling. Reheat any remaining sauce until bubbly; pass with grilled meat. Cover and store unused sauce in refrigerator for up to 3 days.

NUTRITION FACTS PER 2-TABLESPOON SERVING: 140 cal., 2 g total fat (0 g sat. fat), 0 mg chol., 555 mg sodium, 21 g carbo., 0 g fiber, 1 g pro.

Mutha Sauce

This zippy sauce is great on beef or pork.

PREP: 20 MINUTES COOK: 20 MINUTES

MAKES: ABOUT 2 CUPS

⅓   cup finely chopped onion

2   tablespoons finely chopped green onion

1   small fresh jalapeño chile pepper, seeded and finely chopped (see Note, page 284)

1   tablespoon cooking oil

2   teaspoons bottled minced garlic (4 cloves)

1   8-ounce can tomato sauce

½   cup ketchup

¼   cup packed brown sugar

3   tablespoons Worcestershire sauce

2   tablespoons vinegar

1   tablespoon lemon juice

1   tablespoon bottled hot pepper sauce

1   tablespoon spicy brown mustard

1   tablespoon molasses

1   teaspoon chili powder

½   teaspoon coarsely ground black pepper

⅛   teaspoon ground allspice

1   teaspoon liquid smoke

1 In large saucepan cook onion, green onion, and jalapeño pepper in hot oil until onion is tender, stirring occasionally. Add garlic; cook for 1 minute more. Add tomato sauce, ketchup, brown sugar, Worcestershire, vinegar, lemon juice, pepper sauce, mustard, molasses, chili powder, black pepper, and allspice. Stir in ¼ cup water. Bring to boiling; reduce heat. Cover; simmer 20 minutes. Stir in liquid smoke.

2 Use warm to brush on beef or pork during last 5 to 10 minutes of grilling. Reheat any remaining sauce until bubbly; pass with grilled meat. Cover and store unused sauce in refrigerator for up to 3 days.

NUTRITION FACTS PER 2-TABLESPOON SERVING: 44 cal., 1 g total fat (0 g sat. fat), 0 mg chol., 215 mg sodium, 9 g carbo., 0 g fiber, 0 g pro.

Tomato-Molasses Barbecue Sauce

Three forms of pepper give this slightly chunky sauce plenty of zip.

PREP: 15 MINUTES **COOK:** 10 MINUTES

MAKES: ABOUT 4 CUPS

1 12-ounce can tomato paste
1 10-ounce can chopped tomatoes and green chile peppers
½ cup cider vinegar
½ cup mild-flavored molasses
½ cup packed brown sugar
¼ cup finely chopped onion
1 teaspoon bottled minced garlic (2 cloves)
1 tablespoon chili powder
1½ teaspoons ground black pepper
1½ teaspoons paprika
½ teaspoon salt (optional)
½ teaspoon celery seeds
½ teaspoon dry mustard
½ teaspoon bottled hot pepper sauce

1 In a medium saucepan stir together tomato paste, tomatoes and chile peppers, cider vinegar, molasses, brown sugar, onion, garlic, chili powder, black pepper, paprika, salt (if desired), celery seeds, dry mustard, and pepper sauce. Stir in ¼ cup water.

2 Bring the mixture just to boiling over medium heat, stirring frequently; reduce heat. Cover and simmer for 10 to 15 minutes or until the flavors are blended, stirring occasionally.

3 Use warm to brush on steaks, ribs, poultry, or burgers during the last 5 to 10 minutes of grilling. Reheat any remaining sauce until bubbly; pass with grilled meat. Cover and store unused sauce in refrigerator for up to 3 days.

NUTRITION FACTS PER 2-TABLESPOON SERVING: 40 cal., 0 g total fat, 0 mg chol., 48 mg sodium, 10 g carbo., 0 g fiber, 0 g pro.

Tomato-Mustard Sauce

Consider this a melting pot sauce. It has plenty of regional echoes to satisfy purists from all parts of the country.

PREP: 20 MINUTES **COOK:** 10 MINUTES

MAKES: ABOUT 2 CUPS

¼ cup finely chopped onion
1 tablespoon bottled minced garlic (6 cloves)
½ teaspoon paprika
½ teaspoon crushed red pepper
1 tablespoon cooking oil
1 15-ounce can tomato puree
3 tablespoons cider vinegar
3 tablespoons molasses
2 tablespoons brown sugar
2 tablespoons stone-ground mustard
½ teaspoon salt
½ teaspoon dried oregano, crushed
½ teaspoon liquid smoke (optional)

1 In a medium saucepan cook onion, garlic, paprika, and crushed red pepper in hot oil until onion is tender. Stir in the tomato puree, vinegar, molasses, brown sugar, mustard, salt, oregano, and, if desired, liquid smoke. Bring to boiling; reduce heat. Simmer, uncovered, about 10 minutes or until sauce is thickened, stirring frequently.

2 Use warm to brush on beef, pork, or poultry during the last 5 to 10 minutes of grilling. Reheat any remaining sauce until bubbly; pass with grilled meat. Cover and store unused sauce in refrigerator for up to 3 days.

NUTRITION FACTS PER 2-TABLESPOON SERVING: 38 cal., 2 g total fat (0 g sat. fat), 0 mg chol., 200 mg sodium, 8 g carbo., 0 g fiber, 0 g pro.

Apricot Teriyaki Glaze

This sweet and gingery glaze confettied with bits of red and green sweet pepper goes with chicken, beef, lamb, or pork.

PREP: 10 MINUTES COOK: 10 MINUTES

MAKES: 1 CUP

- ¼ cup finely chopped onion
- ½ teaspoon bottled minced garlic (1 clove)
- 1 tablespoon cooking oil
- ⅔ cup apricot preserves
- 2 tablespoons soy sauce
- 2 teaspoons grated fresh ginger or ½ teaspoon ground ginger
- ⅓ cup finely chopped green sweet pepper
- ⅓ cup finely chopped red sweet pepper
- ½ teaspoon toasted sesame oil

1 In a small saucepan cook onion and garlic in hot oil over medium heat for 3 minutes, stirring occasionally. Cut up any large pieces of apricot in preserves.

2 Stir apricot preserves, soy sauce, and ginger into onion mixture. Cook over medium heat until bubbly, stirring occasionally. Reduce heat. Cook, uncovered, about 10 minutes or until slightly thickened. Stir in sweet pepper and sesame oil.

3 Brush glaze on beef, pork, lamb, or poultry during the last 5 to 10 minutes of grilling. Reheat any remaining glaze until bubbly; pass with grilled meat.

NUTRITION FACTS PER 2-TABLESPOON SERVING: 100 cal., 2 g total fat (0 g sat. fat), 0 mg chol., 239 mg sodium, 20 g carbo., 0 g fiber, 1 g pro.

Ginger Sauce

Take your choice of fresh or ground ginger for this full-of-flavor sauce.

PREP: 5 MINUTES CHILL: 6 TO 24 HOURS

MAKES: ⅔ CUP

- ½ cup ketchup
- ¼ cup packed brown sugar
- 3 tablespoons reduced-sodium soy sauce
- 3 tablespoons water
- 1 tablespoon grated fresh ginger or 1 teaspoon ground ginger

1 In a small bowl combine ketchup, brown sugar, soy sauce, the water, and ginger. Cover; refrigerate for at least 6 hours or up to 24 hours.

2 Use to brush on beef, pork, or chicken during the last 5 to 10 minutes of grilling. Discard any remaining sauce.

NUTRITION FACTS PER 2-TABLESPOON SERVING: 76 cal., 0 g total fat, 0 mg chol., 631 mg sodium, 19 g carbo., 0 g fiber, 1 g pro.

Five-Alarm Sauce

If you can't get to Kansas City, Houston, or some other smoke-and-fire-hub, turn your backyard into BBQ central with this multi-spiced sauce.

START TO FINISH: 20 MINUTES
MAKES: 2½ CUPS

- **1** cup ketchup
- **1** large tomato, peeled, seeded, and chopped
- **1** small green sweet pepper, chopped
- **2** tablespoons chopped onion
- **2** tablespoons brown sugar
- **1** to 2 tablespoons bottled steak sauce
- **1** to 2 tablespoons Worcestershire sauce
- **½** teaspoon garlic powder
- **¼** teaspoon ground nutmeg
- **¼** teaspoon ground cinnamon
- **¼** teaspoon ground cloves
- **⅛** teaspoon ground ginger
- **⅛** teaspoon ground black pepper

1 In a small saucepan stir together ketchup, tomato, sweet pepper, onion, brown sugar, steak sauce, Worcestershire sauce, garlic powder, nutmeg, cinnamon, cloves, ginger, and black pepper. Bring to boiling; reduce heat. Cover and simmer about 5 minutes or until sweet pepper is crisp-tender.

2 Use warm to brush on beef or chicken during the last 5 to 10 minutes of grilling. Reheat any remaining sauce until bubbly; pass with grilled meat. Cover and store unused sauce in refrigerator for up to 3 days.

NUTRITION FACTS PER 2-TABLESPOON SERVING: 22 cal., 0 g total fat, 0 mg chol., 165 mg sodium, 6 g carbo., 0 g fiber, 0 g pro.

Honey-Peach Sauce

This sweet sauce is the taste of summer boiled down to the basics: juicy peaches, honey, zingy cracked black pepper, and fresh thyme.

PREP: 10 MINUTES COOK: 15 MINUTES
MAKES: ABOUT 1¾ CUPS

- **4** medium peaches (about 1⅓ pounds total)
- **2** tablespoons lemon juice
- **2** tablespoons honey
- **½** teaspoon cracked black pepper
- **1** to 2 teaspoons snipped fresh thyme

1 Peel and cut up 3 of the peaches. Place cut up peaches in a blender container or food processor bowl. Add lemon juice, honey, and pepper. Cover and blend or process until smooth. Transfer to a medium saucepan.

2 Bring to boiling; reduce heat. Simmer, uncovered, about 15 minutes or until sauce is slightly thickened, stirring occasionally. Remove from heat. Peel and finely chop the remaining peach; stir into the sauce. Stir in thyme.

3 Use warm to brush on beef, lamb, pork, poultry, or fish during the last 5 to 10 minutes of grilling. Reheat any remaining sauce until bubbly; pass with grilled meat. Cover and store unused sauce in refrigerator for up to 24 hours.

NUTRITION FACTS PER 2-TABLESPOON SERVING: 31 cal., 0 g total fat, 0 mg chol., 0 mg sodium, 8 g carbo., 1 g fiber, 0 g pro.

Mushroom-Garlic Sauce

Serve this first-rate sauce with meat, poultry, or fish.

START TO FINISH: 25 MINUTES

MAKES: 2½ CUPS

2 8-ounce packages fresh mushrooms, quartered

¼ cup finely chopped shallots

1 tablespoon bottled minced garlic (6 cloves)

½ teaspoon curry powder

⅛ to ¼ teaspoon crushed red pepper

2 tablespoons olive oil

¾ cup chicken broth

2 teaspoons soy sauce

¼ teaspoon ground nutmeg

¼ cup dry white wine or chicken broth

1 tablespoon cornstarch

1 In large saucepan cook mushrooms, shallots, garlic, curry powder, and crushed red pepper in hot oil until mushrooms are tender. Add the ¾ cup chicken broth, the soy sauce, and nutmeg; bring to boiling. In a small bowl stir together wine or additional chicken broth and cornstarch; add to saucepan. Cook and stir until thickened and bubbly; cook and stir for 2 minutes more. Serve with grilled beef, pork, lamb, poultry, or fish.

NUTRITION FACTS PER ¼-CUP SERVING: 52 cal., 4 g total fat (1 g sat. fat), 0 mg chol., 139 mg sodium, 3 g carbo., 0 g fiber, 2 g pro.

Cucumber-Dill Sauce

Dress up grilled fish steaks or fillets with this fresh-tasting sauce.

START TO FINISH: 10 MINUTES

MAKES: ⅔ CUP

⅓ cup finely chopped seeded cucumber

3 tablespoons plain yogurt

2 tablespoons mayonnaise or salad dressing

2 teaspoons snipped fresh dill

2 teaspoons prepared horseradish

1 In a small bowl combine cucumber, yogurt, mayonnaise, dill, and horseradish. Serve immediately or cover and chill up to 4 hours. Serve with grilled fish.

NUTRITION FACTS PER 2-TABLESPOON SERVING: 59 cal., 6 g total fat (1 g sat. fat), 3 mg chol., 50 mg sodium, 1 g carbo., 0 g fiber, 1 g pro.

Yogurt-Mustard Sauce

Three simple ingredients turn into a magnificent sauce for lamb or chicken.

PREP: 5 MINUTES

CHILL: 1 HOUR

MAKES: ¾ CUP

⅔ cup plain yogurt

2 tablespoons lime juice

4 teaspoons Dijon-style mustard

1 In a small bowl stir together yogurt, lime juice, and mustard. Cover and chill for 1 hour before serving. Serve with grilled lamb or chicken.

NUTRITION FACTS PER 2-TABLESPOON SERVING: 22 cal., 0 g total fat, 2 mg chol., 96 mg sodium, 2 g carbo., 0 g fiber, 1 g pro.

Double-Pepper Barbecue Rub

To get maximum flavor, sprinkle about 2 tablespoons of the spice mixture on each pound of meat or poultry.

START TO FINISH: 15 MINUTES

MAKES: ABOUT ⅔ CUP RUB

(ENOUGH FOR 4 TO 6 POUNDS MEAT OR POULTRY)

¼	cup paprika
1	tablespoon salt
1	tablespoon ground cumin
1	tablespoon brown sugar
1	tablespoon chili powder
1	tablespoon ground black pepper
1½	teaspoons cayenne pepper
¼	teaspoon ground cloves

1 In a small bowl stir together paprika, salt, cumin, brown sugar, chili powder, black pepper, cayenne pepper, and cloves.

2 To use, generously sprinkle spice mixture evenly over beef, pork, or chicken about 10 minutes before grilling; rub in with your fingers. Grill meat or poultry. Cover and store unused spice mixture in a screw-top jar or resealable plastic bag for up to 1 month.

NUTRITION FACTS PER TEASPOON RUB: 7 cal., 0 g total fat, 0 mg chol., 203 mg sodium, 1 g carbo., 0 g fiber, 0 g pro.

Indian Curry Rub

This aromatic rub is essentially a homemade curry. Curries, used extensively in east Indian cooking, are blends of up to 20 spices that range from mild to hot.

START TO FINISH: 10 MINUTES

MAKES: ABOUT ¼ CUP

(ENOUGH FOR 4 TO 5 POUNDS MEAT OR POULTRY)

2	teaspoons ground cinnamon
½	teaspoon sugar
½	teaspoon ground cumin
½	teaspoon ground turmeric
½	teaspoon ground coriander
¼	teaspoon salt
¼	teaspoon ground cardamom
¼	teaspoon ground cloves
¼	teaspoon ground nutmeg
¼	teaspoon cayenne pepper

1 In a small bowl stir together cinnamon, sugar, cumin, turmeric, coriander, salt, cardamom, cloves, nutmeg, and cayenne pepper.

2 To use, rub a little cooking oil evenly onto all sides of beef, pork, lamb, or poultry about 15 minutes before grilling. Sprinkle spice mixture evenly over meat or poultry; rub in with your fingers. Grill meat or poultry. Cover and store unused spice mixture in a screw-top jar or resealable plastic bag for up to 1 month.

NUTRITION FACTS PER TEASPOON RUB: 3 cal., 0 g total fat, 0 mg chol., 49 mg sodium, 1 g carbo., 0 g fiber, 0 g pro.

Best Beef Marinade

Fresh thyme flavors this very simple, very tasty marinade.

PREP: 10 MINUTES

MARINATE: 30 MINUTES OR 3 TO 24 HOURS

MAKES: ABOUT ½ CUP MARINADE

(ENOUGH FOR 1 TO 1½ POUNDS BEEF)

- ¼ cup chopped shallots
- 3 tablespoons soy sauce
- 2 tablespoons olive oil
- 2 tablespoons balsamic vinegar or cider vinegar
- 4 teaspoons snipped fresh thyme
- ½ teaspoon bottled minced garlic (1 clove)
- ½ teaspoon cracked black pepper

1 In a small bowl combine shallots, soy sauce, olive oil, vinegar, thyme, garlic, and cracked pepper.

2 To use, pour marinade over beef in a resealable plastic bag set in a shallow dish. Seal bag; turn to coat meat. Marinate in the refrigerator about 30 minutes for tender cuts (such as tenderloin or sirloin) or at least 3 hours or up to 24 hours for tougher cuts (such as flank steak), turning bag occasionally. Drain, reserving marinade. Grill beef until done, brushing occasionally with reserved marinade up to the last 5 minutes of grilling. Discard any remaining marinade.

NUTRITION FACTS PER TABLESPOON MARINADE: 42 cal., 3 g total fat (0 g sat. fat), 0 mg chol., 387 mg sodium, 3 g carbo., 0 g fiber, 1 g pro.

Pineapple-Ginger Marinade

Five-spice powder is a blend of cinnamon, cloves, fennel seeds, star anise, and Szechwan peppercorns.

PREP: 10 MINUTES

MARINATE: 30 MINUTES OR 2 TO 4 HOURS

MAKES: ABOUT ¾ CUP

(ENOUGH FOR 1½ POUNDS POULTRY, FISH, OR SEAFOOD)

- ½ cup unsweetened pineapple juice
- 2 tablespoons cooking oil
- 2 tablespoons finely chopped green sweet pepper
- 1 tablespoon finely chopped fresh ginger
- 1 teaspoon honey
- ¼ teaspoon five-spice powder

1 In a small bowl combine pineapple juice, oil, sweet pepper, ginger, honey, and five-spice powder. To use, pour marinade over poultry, fish, or seafood in a resealable plastic bag set in a shallow dish. Seal bag; turn to coat poultry, fish, or seafood.

2 Marinate in the refrigerator for at least 2 hours or up to 4 hours for poultry or at room temperature for 30 minutes for fish or seafood, turning bag occasionally. Drain, reserving marinade. Grill poultry, fish, or seafood until done, brushing often with reserved marinade up to the last 5 minutes of grilling. Discard any remaining marinade.

NUTRITION FACTS PER TABLESPOON MARINADE: 28 cal., 3 g total fat (0 g sat. fat), 0 mg chol., 0 mg sodium, 2 g carbo., 0 g fiber, 0 g pro.

Soy-Citrus Marinade

Citrus, salty soy, garlic, and brown sugar zing up this Asian-accented marinade.

PREP: 10 MINUTES

MARINATE: 1 TO 2 HOURS

MAKES: ¾ CUP

(ENOUGH FOR ABOUT 2 POUNDS CHICKEN, FISH, OR SEAFOOD)

- ¼ cup soy sauce
- 1 tablespoon finely shredded orange peel
- ¼ cup orange juice
- 1 tablespoon finely shredded lemon peel
- 3 tablespoons lemon juice
- 1 tablespoon brown sugar
- 1½ teaspoons bottled minced garlic (3 cloves)
- 2 teaspoons toasted sesame oil

1 In a small bowl combine soy sauce, orange peel, orange juice, lemon peel, lemon juice, brown sugar, garlic, and sesame oil. Stir until the brown sugar is dissolved.

2 To use, pour marinade over poultry, fish, or seafood in a resealable plastic bag set in a shallow dish. Seal bag; turn to coat poultry, fish, or seafood. Marinate in the refrigerator for at least 1 hour or up to 2 hours, turning bag occasionally. Drain, discarding marinade. Grill poultry, fish, or seafood until done.

NUTRITION FACTS PER TABLESPOON MARINADE: 21 cal., 1 g total fat (0 g sat. fat), 0 mg chol., 344 mg sodium, 3 g carbo., 0 g fiber, 0 g pro.

Caper Butter

Turn a simple grilled fish steak into a something-special dish by topping it with this simple stir-together butter.

START TO FINISH: 5 MINUTES

MAKES: ABOUT ¼ CUP

¼ cup butter, softened

1 tablespoon capers, drained and finely chopped

½ teaspoon bottled minced garlic (1 clove)

Ground black pepper

1 In small bowl stir together the butter, capers, and garlic. Season to taste with pepper. Serve with grilled salmon or other fish.

NUTRITION FACTS PER 1-TABLESPOON SERVING: 109 cal., 12 g total fat (8 g sat. fat), 33 mg chol., 188 mg sodium, 0 g carbo., 0 g fiber, 0 g pro.

Citrus-Garlic Butter

Sometimes a flourish at the end is all you need to give flair to the most basic grilled food. Look no further than this butter to top off unadorned grilled meat, poultry, fish, or vegetables.

PREP: 10 MINUTES

CHILL: 2 HOURS MAKES: ½ CUP

½ cup butter, softened

2 tablespoons snipped fresh parsley

1 tablespoon finely shredded lemon peel

1 tablespoon finely shredded orange peel

1 teaspoon bottled minced garlic (2 cloves)

1 In a small bowl stir together butter, parsley, lemon peel, orange peel, and garlic. If necessary, chill about 10 minutes or until easy to handle.

2 With your hands, shape the butter mixture into a 4-inch-long log. Wrap in plastic wrap; chill about 2 hours or until firm.

3 To use, unwrap the butter and cut crosswise into 8 slices. Place a slice of butter on top of each serving of grilled chicken, beef, veal, fish, or vegetables.

NUTRITION FACTS PER 1-TABLESPOON SERVING: 103 cal., 11 g total fat (7 g sat. fat), 31 mg chol., 117 mg sodium, 1 g carbo., 0 g fiber, 0 g pro.

Blue Cheese Butter

This full-flavored basil-and-blue cheese topper takes beef steaks to the next level. It's also delicious stirred into steamed vegetables.

START TO FINISH: 10 MINUTES

MAKES: ½ CUP

¼ cup butter or margarine, softened

¼ cup crumbled blue cheese (1 ounce)

1 tablespoon snipped fresh parsley

2 teaspoons snipped fresh basil or ½ teaspoon dried basil, crushed

½ teaspoon bottled minced garlic (1 clove)

1 In a small bowl stir together the butter, blue cheese, parsley, basil, and garlic. Serve with grilled steaks.

NUTRITION FACTS PER 1-TABLESPOON SERVING: 69 cal., 7 g total fat (5 g sat. fat), 20 mg chol., 121 mg sodium, 0 g carbo., 0 g fiber, 1 g pro.

Grilled Papaya Butter

Compliments galore are sure to come your way when you offer guests this unique topper for steaks or burgers. If there is any left over, spread it on your breakfast toast or bagel.

PREP: 10 MINUTES

GRILL: 5 MINUTES

CHILL: 2 HOURS

MAKES: ABOUT 2½ CUPS

½ of a small papaya

Cooking oil

1 pound butter, softened

1 Peel and seed papaya; cut into thick slices. Lightly brush slices with cooking oil. For a charcoal grill, grill papaya slices on the rack of an uncovered grill directly over medium coals for 5 minutes, turning once. Set aside. (For a gas grill, preheat grill. Reduce heat to medium. Cover and grill as above.)

2 Finely chop papaya; stir into butter. Spoon mixture onto a sheet of plastic wrap. Roll into a log. Wrap in the plastic wrap, twisting ends closed. Chill about 2 hours or until firm. Cut into ¼- to ½-inch-thick slices.

3 Serve with grilled steaks or burgers. Wrap and store unused butter in refrigerator for up to 3 days.

NUTRITION FACTS PER 1-TABLESPOON SERVING: 85 cal., 9 g total fat (6 g sat. fat), 25 mg chol., 94 mg sodium, 0 g carbo., 0 g fiber, 0 g pro.

Tomato Aioli

With the addition of dried tomatoes, this flavored mayonnaise makes a perfect finishing touch for grilled lamb chops.

START TO FINISH: 10 MINUTES

MAKES: ⅔ CUP

½ cup mayonnaise or salad dressing

2 tablespoons oil-packed dried tomatoes, drained and finely chopped

1 tablespoon snipped fresh basil

1 teaspoon bottled minced garlic (2 cloves)

1 teaspoon snipped fresh thyme

1 In a small bowl combine mayonnaise, tomatoes, basil, garlic, and thyme. Serve with grilled lamb, pork, or chicken.

NUTRITION FACTS PER 1-TABLESPOON SERVING: 75 cal., 8 g total fat (1 g sat. fat), 6 mg chol., 60 mg sodium, 1 g carbo., 0 g fiber, 0 g pro.

Tangy Avocado Salsa

Leave the salsa on the chunky side so the ingredients retain their individual textures.

PREP: 30 MINUTES **CHILL:** 1 TO 24 HOURS
MAKES: ABOUT 2 CUPS

6	fresh tomatillos, husked and halved
1	cup water
1	avocado, seeded and peeled
½	cup coarsely chopped green onions
½	cup loosely packed fresh cilantro leaves
⅓	cup dairy sour cream
1	fresh jalapeño chile pepper, seeded and coarsely chopped*
½	teaspoon salt

1 In a medium saucepan combine tomatillos and the water. Bring to boiling; reduce heat. Simmer, uncovered, for 5 to 7 minutes or until soft, stirring occasionally. Remove tomatillos with a slotted spoon; cool slightly. Reserve 2 tablespoons of the cooking liquid.

2 In a food processor bowl or blender container combine tomatillos, the reserved 2 tablespoons cooking liquid, the avocado, green onions, cilantro, sour cream, jalapeño pepper, and salt. Cover and process or blend until combined but still slightly chunky. Transfer to a covered container; chill for at least 1 hour or up to 24 hours.

3 Serve with grilled meat, poultry, or seafood or as a dip with fresh vegetables and/or tortilla chips.

NUTRITION FACTS PER 2-TABLESPOON SERVING: 34 cal., 2 g total fat (0 g sat. fat), 2 mg chol., 70 mg sodium, 2 g carbo., 0 g fiber, 0 g pro.

*NOTE: Because chile peppers contain volatile oils that can burn your skin and eyes, avoid direct contact with them as much as possible. When working with chile peppers, wear plastic or rubber gloves. If your bare hands do touch the chile peppers, wash your hands and nails well with soap and warm water.

Mango-Mint Salsa

Though this all-purpose salsa goes with just about anything, it's especially good on grilled fresh tuna or mahi mahi.

PREP: 25 MINUTES
CHILL: 2 TO 24 HOURS **STAND:** 30 MINUTES
MAKES: ABOUT 1½ CUPS

1	mango
½	cup chopped peeled jicama
¼	cup finely chopped red onion
¼	cup snipped fresh mint
1	canned chipotle chile pepper in adobo sauce, chopped*
1	tablespoon honey
1	tablespoon olive oil

1 Peel, seed, and chop mango (you should have about 1 cup). In a medium bowl stir together mango, jicama, onion, mint, and chipotle pepper. Drizzle with honey and oil; stir to combine. Cover and refrigerate for at least 2 hours or up to 24 hours to blend flavors.

2 Before serving, let stand at room temperature for 30 minutes. Serve with grilled meat, poultry, fish, or seafood.

NUTRITION FACTS PER ¼-CUP SERVING: 64 cal., 2 g total fat (0 g sat. fat), 0 mg chol., 27 mg sodium, 11 g carbo., 1 g fiber, 0 g pro.

*NOTE: Because chile peppers contain volatile oils that can burn your skin and eyes, avoid direct contact with them as much as possible. When working with chile peppers, wear plastic or rubber gloves. If your bare hands do touch the chile peppers, wash your hands and nails well with soap and warm water.

Smoky Sicilian Salsa

This flavorful salsa tastes like summer!

PREP: 15 MINUTES

GRILL: 30 MINUTES + 10 MINUTES

MAKES: 2½ CUPS

1	bulb garlic
2	tablespoons olive oil
10	plum tomatoes
2	onion slices (about ¾ inch thick)
1	to 2 fresh jalapeño chile peppers
½	cup fresh basil leaves, cut into thin strips
⅛	teaspoon salt

1 Fold an 18×9-inch piece of heavy foil in half to make a 9-inch square. Place garlic in center of foil. Drizzle with 1 tablespoon of the olive oil. Bring up opposite edges together to completely enclose garlic, leaving space for steam to build.

2 For a charcoal grill, arrange medium coals in the bottom of a grill with a cover, leaving a small area on one side free of coals. Place garlic on grill rack not directly over coals. Cover and grill for 30 minutes, turning once halfway through grilling.

3 Place the tomatoes, onion slices, and jalapeño peppers on the grill rack directly over coals. (Or use a grill basket, grill tray, or heavy foil for vegetables; place on grill rack.) Grill, uncovered, about 10 minutes more or just until the tomato skins brown and onion is crisp-tender, turning once halfway through grilling. (For a gas grill, preheat grill. Reduce heat to medium. Adjust for indirect cooking. Grill as above.)

4 Remove vegetables and garlic from grill; cool until easy to handle. For salsa, if desired, remove and discard the tomato skins and seeds. Coarsely chop tomatoes and onion; place in a medium bowl. Seed and finely chop the jalapeño pepper (see Note, page 295). Stir jalapeño pepper into tomato mixture. Squeeze garlic pulp from each clove; stir into tomato mixture. Stir in remaining 1 tablespoon oil, the basil leaves, and salt. Serve with grilled meat, poultry, or fish.

NUTRITION FACTS PER 2-TABLESPOON SERVING: 22 cal., 2 g total fat (0 g sat. fat), 0 mg chol., 16 mg sodium, 2 g carbo., 0 g fiber, 0 g pro.

Sweet and Spicy Pepper-Pineapple Salsa

This zippy condiment perks up grilled beef and pork particularly well.

PREP: 15 MINUTES

GRILL: 10 MINUTES + 3 MINUTES

MAKES: 6 SERVINGS

12	ounces peeled and cored fresh pineapple, cut into ½-inch-thick slices
2	large red and/or green sweet peppers, seeded and quartered
1	½-inch-thick slice sweet onion (such as Vidalia or Maui)
¼	cup apricot jam
2	tablespoons rice vinegar
¼	teaspoon salt
¼	teaspoon ground cinnamon
¼	teaspoon ground allspice
¼	teaspoon bottled hot pepper sauce

1 For a charcoal grill, grill the pineapple, sweet peppers, and onion on the rack of an uncovered grill directly over medium heat for 10 to 12 minutes or until sweet peppers are slightly charred, turning once. (For a gas grill, preheat grill. Reduce heat to medium. Place pineapple, sweet peppers, and onion on grill rack over heat. Cover and grill as above.) Transfer pineapple and vegetables to a cutting board; cool slightly and coarsely chop.

2 Meanwhile, in a medium saucepan* combine jam, vinegar, salt, cinnamon, allspice, and hot pepper sauce. Place saucepan over coals near edge of grill. Cook and stir for 3 to 5 minutes or until jam is melted. Add the chopped pineapple, sweet peppers, and onion to the saucepan. Serve warm or at room temperature over grilled meat or poultry.

NUTRITION FACTS PER 2-TABLESPOON SERVING: 76 cal., 0 g total fat, 0 mg chol., 93 mg sodium, 20 g carbo., 1 g fiber, 1 g pro.

*NOTE: The heat from the grill will blacken the outside of the saucepan, so use an old one, or use a small cast-iron skillet.

Sweet Pepper Salsa

For less heat, seed the habañero
or jalapeño before using.
Much of a chile pepper's heat is stored
in the seeds and membranes.

PREP: 15 MINUTES CHILL: 1 TO 24 HOURS
MAKES: 1½ CUPS

1 medium red sweet pepper, seeded and finely chopped (¾ cup)

½ cup finely chopped papaya

½ cup snipped fresh cilantro

¼ cup finely chopped jicama

2 tablespoons lime juice

1 small fresh habañero chile pepper or 1 medium fresh jalapeño chile pepper, finely chopped*

1 tablespoon honey (optional)

¼ teaspoon salt

1 In a medium bowl combine sweet pepper, papaya, cilantro, jicama, lime juice, chile pepper, honey (if desired), and salt. Cover and chill for at least 1 hour or up to 24 hours. Serve with grilled beef, pork, or chicken.

NUTRITION FACTS PER 2-TABLESPOON SERVING: 9 cal., 0 g total fat, 0 mg chol., 50 mg sodium, 2 g carbo., 0 g fiber, 0 g pro.

Watermelon and Jicama Salsa

Thanks to sweet and juicy watermelon
combined with crisp jicama, this salsa
stands out in a crowd. The addition of a
jalapeño chile pepper adds heat to sweet.

START TO FINISH: 25 MINUTES
MAKES: ABOUT 5 CUPS

3 cups chopped seeded watermelon

1½ cups thinly sliced, peeled jicama

1 fresh jalapeño chile pepper, seeded and finely chopped*

2 tablespoons chopped green onion

1 tablespoon snipped fresh cilantro or mint

1 tablespoon seasoned rice vinegar

⅛ to ¼ teaspoon cayenne pepper (optional)

1 In a medium bowl stir together the watermelon, jicama, jalapeño pepper, green onion, cilantro or mint, vinegar, and, if desired, cayenne pepper.

2 If desired, cover and chill for up to 2 hours. Serve with grilled pork, chicken, or fish.

NUTRITION FACTS PER ¼-CUP SERVING: 13 cal., 0 g total fat, 0 mg chol., 8 mg sodium, 3 g carbo., 0 g fiber, 0 g pro.

***NOTE:** Because chile peppers contain volatile oils that can burn your skin and eyes, avoid direct contact with them as much as possible. When working with chile peppers, wear plastic or rubber gloves. If your bare hands do touch the chile peppers, wash your hands and nails well with soap and warm water.

Cantaloupe Relish

Allowing the flavors to mingle for as long as 24 hours lets the fruits absorb a whole palette of flavors.

PREP: 20 MINUTES CHILL: 1 TO 24 HOURS

MAKES: ABOUT 3 CUPS

- **1** cup chopped Asian pear or chopped, peeled jicama
- **1** cup chopped cantaloupe
- **1** cup chopped, peeled papaya or mango
- **¼** cup finely chopped green onions
- **3** tablespoons lemon juice
- **1** teaspoon snipped fresh lemon thyme or thyme
- **1** teaspoon olive oil

1 In a medium bowl combine pear or jicama, cantaloupe, papaya or mango, green onions, lemon juice, thyme, and olive oil. Cover and chill for at least 1 hour or up to 24 hours. Serve with grilled chicken or pork.

NUTRITION FACTS PER ¼-CUP SERVING: 24 cal., 0 g total fat, 0 mg chol., 2 mg sodium, 5 g carbo., 1 g fiber, 0 g pro.

Corn and Cucumber Relish

Pair this out-of-the-ordinary relish— with overtones from ginger, sesame oil, and cayenne pepper— with grilled poultry or fish.

PREP: 25 MINUTES STAND: 20 MINUTES

CHILL: 8 HOURS MAKES: 2 CUPS

- **1¾** cups chopped, seeded cucumber
- **2** teaspoons salt
- **1** cup cut fresh corn kernels
- **½** cup sugar
- **½** cup white wine vinegar
- **2** green onions, thinly sliced
- **1** teaspoon grated fresh ginger
- **2** tablespoons diced pimiento
- **½** teaspoon toasted sesame oil
- **⅛** teaspoon cayenne pepper

1 In a medium bowl sprinkle chopped cucumber with the salt. Let stand for 20 minutes. Rinse the cucumber; drain well, pressing out the excess liquid.

2 Meanwhile, in a medium saucepan combine corn, sugar, vinegar, green onions, and ginger. Bring to boiling, stirring occasionally; reduce heat. Simmer, uncovered, for 4 minutes. Remove from heat. Stir in the drained cucumber, pimiento, sesame oil, and cayenne pepper.

3 Transfer relish to a nonmetallic container. Cover and chill in refrigerator for at least 8 hours before serving. Serve with grilled poultry or fish. Cover and store any unused relish in refrigerator for up to 1 week. Drain before serving.

NUTRITION FACTS PER ¼-CUP SERVING: 82 cal., 0 g total fat, 0 mg chol., 634 mg sodium, 18 g carbo., 0 g fiber, 0 g pro.

Grilled Corn Relish

Terrific as an accompaniment for grilled pork or chicken, this colorful corn relish also makes a light meal when stirred with some cooked black beans, rolled up with some shredded Monterey Jack cheese in a flour tortilla, and warmed on the grill.

PREP: 15 MINUTES GRILL: 25 MINUTES

MAKES: 4 SERVINGS

- 3 tablespoons lime juice
- 1 tablespoon cooking oil
- 1 teaspoon bottled minced garlic (2 cloves)
- 2 fresh ears of corn, husked and cleaned
- 1 teaspoon chili powder
- 1 small avocado, seeded, peeled, and cut up
- ½ cup chopped red sweet pepper
- ¼ cup snipped fresh cilantro
- ¼ teaspoon salt

1 In medium bowl combine lime juice, oil, and garlic. Brush corn lightly with juice mixture. Reserve remaining juice mixture. Sprinkle corn with chili powder. For a charcoal grill, grill corn on the rack of an uncovered grill directly over medium coals for 25 to 30 minutes or until tender, turning occasionally. (For a gas grill, preheat grill. Reduce heat to medium. Place corn on grill rack over heat. Cover and grill as above.)

2 Meanwhile, add avocado, sweet pepper, cilantro, and salt to the remaining lime juice mixture; toss well. Cut corn kernels from cobs; stir into avocado mixture. Serve with grilled pork or chicken.

NUTRITION FACTS PER SERVING: 159 cal., 12 g total fat (1 g sat. fat), 0 mg chol., 152 mg sodium, 15 g carbo., 3 g fiber, 3 g pro.

Dried-Fruit Chutney

This chutney keeps in the refrigerator for up to 3 weeks.

PREP: 30 MINUTES STAND: 30 MINUTES

MAKES: ABOUT 2½ CUPS

- ¾ cup coarsely chopped dried apricots
- ¾ cup coarsely chopped dried pineapple
- ¾ cup raisins
- 1 cup boiling water
- ½ cup chopped onion
- ½ cup cider vinegar
- ¼ cup packed brown sugar
- ¼ teaspoon ground ginger
- ⅛ teaspoon ground allspice
- ⅛ teaspoon ground cardamom
- ⅛ teaspoon ground cinnamon
- ⅛ teaspoon cayenne pepper
  - Dash salt
  - Dash ground cloves

1 In a medium bowl combine apricots, pineapple, and raisins. Pour boiling water over mixture. Let stand about 30 minutes or until fruit is softened. Drain, reserving ⅓ cup of the liquid.

2 In a medium saucepan combine the softened fruit, the ⅓ cup reserved liquid, the onion, vinegar, brown sugar, ginger, allspice, cardamom, cinnamon, cayenne pepper, salt, and cloves. Bring to boiling, stirring frequently; reduce heat. Simmer, uncovered, for 8 to 10 minutes or until liquid has evaporated and mixture is thick, stirring frequently; cool.

3 Serve with grilled pork, lamb, or chicken. Cover and store any unused chutney in refrigerator for up to 3 weeks.

NUTRITION FACTS PER ¼-CUP SERVING: 126 cal., 0 g total fat, 0 mg chol., 35 mg sodium, 32 g carbo., 2 g fiber, 1 g pro.

Plum Chutney

Here's an Asian-style chutney special enough to turn a midweek barbecue into a company-special event. Try it on grilled duck.

PREP: 40 MINUTES **COOK:** 25 MINUTES

MAKES: 1¾ CUPS

2½ cups chopped, pitted red or purple plums (about 1 pound total)

⅓ cup packed brown sugar

⅓ cup sliced green onions

¼ cup raspberry vinegar

1 tablespoon soy sauce

1 fresh jalapeño chile pepper, seeded and finely chopped*

1 teaspoon grated fresh ginger

½ teaspoon bottled minced garlic (1 clove)

1 In a medium saucepan combine plums, brown sugar, green onions, vinegar, soy sauce, jalapeño pepper, ginger, and garlic. Bring to boiling; reduce heat. Simmer, uncovered, about 25 minutes or until slightly thickened, stirring occasionally; cool. (Mixture will thicken more as it cools.)

2 Serve with grilled pork or poultry. Cover and store unused chutney in refrigerator for up to 1 week.

NUTRITION FACTS PER ¼-CUP SERVING: 80 cal., 0 g total fat, 0 mg chol., 137 mg sodium, 20 g carbo., 1 g fiber, 1 g pro.

Plantain and Pepper Chutney

Plantains are ripe when they turn dark.

PREP: 35 MINUTES **GRILL:** 8 MINUTES

MAKES: ABOUT 2 CUPS

1 ripe plantain, peeled and cut in half lengthwise

½ of a medium green sweet pepper

½ of a medium red sweet pepper

1 small onion, cut into 1-inch-thick slices

1 fresh Scotch bonnet or jalapeño chile pepper*

1 tablespoon olive oil

2 tablespoons apricot preserves or orange marmalade

1 tablespoon lime juice

¼ teaspoon salt

¼ teaspoon ground allspice

1 Brush plantain, sweet peppers, onion, and chile pepper with oil.

2 For a charcoal grill, grill plantain, sweet peppers, onion, and chile pepper on the rack of an uncovered grill directly over medium coals for 8 to 10 minutes or until tender; turning occasionally. Watch plantain and vegetables closely so they do not char. (For a gas grill, preheat grill. Reduce heat to medium. Place plantain, sweet peppers, onion, and chile pepper on grill rack over heat. Cover and grill as above.)

3 Transfer to a cutting board; cool until easy to handle. Finely chop plantain, sweet peppers, and onion; place in bowl. Seed and finely chop the chile pepper;* stir into plantain mixture. Stir in preserves or marmalade, lime juice, salt, and allspice; toss to coat. If desired, cover and chill for up to 2 hours.

4 Serve at room temperature with grilled chicken or pork.

NUTRITION FACTS PER ¼-CUP SERVING: 64 cal., 2 g total fat (0 g sat. fat), 0 mg chol., 76 mg sodium, 12 g carbo., 1 g fiber, 1 g pro.

*NOTE: Because chile peppers contain volatile oils that can burn your skin and eyes, avoid direct contact with them as much as possible. When working with chile peppers, wear plastic or rubber gloves. If your bare hands do touch the chile peppers, wash your hands and nails well with soap and warm water.

Chapter 6

SIDE DISHES & DESSERTS

Savory Stuffed Breadsticks

After you taste this, you may never again be satisfied with plain breadsticks.
The soft bread, crisp bacon, melted cheeses,
green onions, and fresh thyme make for a satisfying side dish.

PREP: 25 MINUTES GRILL: 8 MINUTES MAKES: 6 BREADSTICKS

4	slices bacon, cut up
½	cup chopped onion
¼	cup finely shredded Parmesan cheese (1 ounce)
¼	cup shredded sharp cheddar cheese (1 ounce)
2	tablespoons sliced green onion
1	tablespoon snipped fresh thyme
6	soft breadsticks or dinner rolls

1 In a medium skillet cook bacon until crisp. Remove bacon; drain on paper towels. Drain off fat, reserving 1 tablespoon drippings in skillet. Add chopped onion to drippings. Cook over medium heat until tender; stirring occasionally. Cool slightly. Stir in bacon, cheeses, green onion, and thyme.

2 Cut each breadstick in half lengthwise, cutting to but not through opposite side. Spread cut surfaces with bacon mixture.

3 Fold six 24×18-inch pieces of heavy foil in half to make 18×12-inch rectangles. Place each breadstick in center of a foil rectangle. Bring up 2 opposite edges of each foil rectangle and seal with a double fold. Fold remaining edges to completely enclose each breadstick, leaving space for steam to build. If desired, chill for up to 8 hours.

4 For a charcoal grill, grill breadstick packets on the rack of an uncovered grill directly over medium coals for 8 to 10 minutes or until cheddar cheese begins to melt, turning packets occasionally. (For a gas grill, preheat grill. Reduce heat to medium. Place breadstick packets on grill rack over heat. Cover and grill as above.)

NUTRITION FACTS PER BREADSTICK: 81 cal., 5 g total fat (2 g sat. fat), 12 mg chol., 165 mg sodium, 4 g carbo., 0 g fiber, 5 g pro.

Asparagus with Parmesan Curls

You don't need new equipment or split-second timing for the cheese curl garnish. A vegetable peeler is all it takes to create a pile of Parmesan shavings. Simply scatter them over grilled asparagus like flower petals to create a stunning dish.

PREP: 15 MINUTES **MARINATE:** 30 MINUTES **GRILL:** 3 MINUTES **MAKES:** 6 SERVINGS

- 1½ **pounds fresh asparagus spears, trimmed**
- 2 **tablespoons olive oil**
- 2 **tablespoons lemon juice**
- ½ **teaspoon salt**
- ¼ **teaspoon ground black pepper**
- 1 **2-ounce block Parmesan cheese**

1 In a large skillet cook the asparagus spears in a small amount of boiling water for 3 minutes. Drain well. Meanwhile, for marinade, in a 2-quart rectangular baking dish stir together olive oil, lemon juice, salt, and pepper. Add drained asparagus, turning to coat. Cover and marinate at room temperature for 30 minutes. Drain asparagus, discarding marinade. Place asparagus on a grilling tray or in a grill basket.

2 For a charcoal grill, grill asparagus on grilling tray or in grill basket on the rack of an uncovered grill directly over medium coals for 3 to 5 minutes or until asparagus is tender and begins to brown, turning once halfway through grilling. (For a gas grill, preheat grill. Reduce heat to medium. Place asparagus on grill rack over heat. Cover and grill as above.)

3 To serve, arrange asparagus on a serving platter. Working over asparagus, use a vegetable peeler or cheese plane to cut thin, wide strips from the side of the block of Parmesan cheese.

NUTRITION FACTS PER SERVING: 95 cal., 7 g total fat (1 g sat. fat), 7 mg chol., 287 mg sodium, 4 g carbo., 1 g fiber, 6 g pro.

Cast-Iron Skillet Cowboy Beans

Cowboy cooking is back. And it's good! Whether you make this over a charcoal grill on a camping trip or on the latest state-of-the-art grill in your backyard, the bubbling satisfaction of a skillet full of beans can't be beat.

PREP: 15 MINUTES GRILL: 15 MINUTES + 15 MINUTES MAKES: 6 SERVINGS

2 15-ounce cans pinto beans, rinsed and drained

½ cup chopped onion

½ cup ketchup

½ cup hot strong coffee

6 slices bacon, crisp-cooked, drained, and crumbled

2 tablespoons Worcestershire sauce

1 tablespoon brown sugar

❶ In a 9-inch cast-iron skillet combine pinto beans, onion, ketchup, coffee, bacon, Worcestershire sauce, and brown sugar.

❷ For a charcoal grill, grill beans in skillet on the rack of an uncovered grill directly over medium coals about 15 minutes or until bubbly. Grill for 15 to 20 minutes more or until beans are desired consistency, stirring occasionally. (For a gas grill, preheat grill. Reduce heat to medium. Place beans in skillet on grill rack over heat. Cover and grill as above.)

NUTRITION FACTS PER SERVING: 184 cal., 4 g total fat (1 g sat. fat), 5 mg chol., 1,003 mg sodium, 30 g carbo., 8 g fiber, 9 g pro.

304

Grilled Corn

Whether you're cooking burgers, steak, or chicken, this recipe for fresh summertime sweet corn makes a mouthwatering side dish grilled alongside the meat.

PREP: 10 MINUTES **SOAK:** 2 TO 4 HOURS **GRILL:** 25 MINUTES **MAKES:** 4 SERVINGS

4   fresh ears of corn

¼   cup butter or margarine, softened

2   tablespoons snipped fresh chives, parsley, cilantro, or tarragon

¼   teaspoon salt

¼   teaspoon ground black pepper

1 Peel back corn husks, but don't remove. Remove the corn silk; discard. Gently rinse the ears of corn. Pull the husks back up around the corn. Using 100%-cotton kitchen string, tie the husks shut. Cover corn with water. Soak for at least 2 hours or up to 4 hours.

2 Drain corn. For a charcoal grill, grill corn on the rack of an uncovered grill directly over medium coals for 25 to 30 minutes or until the kernels are tender, turning once halfway through grilling. (For a gas grill, preheat grill. Reduce heat to medium. Place corn on grill rack over heat. Cover and grill as above.)

3 In a small bowl stir together the butter, fresh herb, salt, and pepper. Remove string from the corn. Serve immediately with butter mixture.

NUTRITION FACTS PER SERVING: 186 cal., 13 g total fat (8 g sat. fat), 33 mg chol., 283 mg sodium, 17 g carbo., 3 g fiber, 3 g pro.

Grilled Eggplant Salad

Few vegetables take to the grill so kindly as eggplant. Its meaty flesh stays firm with grilling and it tastes delicious with the smoky flavor grilling imparts. You can use the smaller, rounder Italian eggplant in place of the Japanese variety.

PREP: 10 MINUTES GRILL: 8 MINUTES MAKES: 4 TO 6 SERVINGS

- **3** tablespoons snipped fresh herbs (basil, oregano, and/or parsley)
- **3** tablespoons balsamic vinegar
- **2** tablespoons olive oil
- **1** teaspoon bottled minced garlic (2 cloves)
-   Salt
-   Ground black pepper
- **3** Japanese eggplants, cut lengthwise into ¼-inch-thick slices (about 12 ounces total)*
- **2** medium red sweet peppers, seeded and cut into 1-inch-wide strips
- **2** medium sweet onions (such as Vidalia or Maui), cut crosswise into ½-inch-thick slices

1 In a small bowl combine the herbs, vinegar, oil, and garlic; stir in salt and pepper to taste.

2 For a charcoal grill, grill vegetables on the rack of an uncovered grill directly over medium coals for 8 to 12 minutes or until vegetables are crisp-tender, turning once and brushing occasionally with some of the herb mixture. (For a gas grill, preheat grill. Reduce heat to medium. Place vegetables on grill rack over heat. Cover and grill as above.) Transfer vegetables to a serving dish; toss with remaining herb mixture.

NUTRITION FACTS PER SERVING: 116 cal., 7 g total fat (1 g sat. fat), 0 mg chol., 39 mg sodium, 13 g carbo., 3 g fiber, 1 g pro.

***NOTE:** If desired, substitute 1 small regular eggplant for the Japanese eggplants. Slice the eggplant and grill as above. Before serving, cut the eggplant slices into quarters.

Garlicky Mushrooms

Ingredients, like people, are sometimes just meant for each other.
That's certainly the case with garlic, butter, and mushrooms.
Portobellos, with their rich, meaty flavor, put butter and garlic to especially good use.

PREP: 15 MINUTES GRILL: 6 MINUTES MAKES: 4 SERVINGS

1   pound fresh portobello mushrooms
¼   cup butter, melted
1½   teaspoons bottled minced garlic (3 cloves)
¼   teaspoon salt
⅛   teaspoon ground black pepper
1   tablespoon snipped fresh chives

1 Cut the mushroom stems even with the caps; discard stems. Rinse mushroom caps; pat dry with paper towels.

2 In a small bowl stir together melted butter, garlic, salt, and pepper; brush over mushrooms.

3 For a charcoal grill, grill mushrooms on the rack of an uncovered grill directly over medium coals for 6 to 8 minutes or just until mushrooms are tender, turning once halfway through grilling. (For a gas grill, preheat grill. Reduce heat to medium. Place mushrooms on grill rack over heat. Cover and grill as above.)

4 To serve, sprinkle mushrooms with chives.

NUTRITION FACTS PER SERVING: 133 cal., 12 g total fat (7 g sat. fat), 31 mg chol., 252 mg sodium, 6 g carbo., 2 g fiber, 3 g pro.

Portobellos and Onions

*These cheese-topped vegetable "medallions" are great with grilled lamb or veal.
Buy similar-size vegetables for aesthetics
and so they all finish grilling about the same time.*

PREP: 15 MINUTES GRILL: 6 MINUTES + 1 MINUTE MAKES: 4 TO 6 SERVINGS

- **4 fresh portobello mushrooms (about 1¼ pounds total)**
- **2 medium sweet onions (such as Vidalia or Maui), cut crosswise into ½-inch-thick slices**
- **2 tablespoons olive oil**
- **4 medium plum tomatoes, halved**
- **1 teaspoon ground black pepper**
- **½ teaspoon salt**
- **2 to 3 tablespoons bottled balsamic vinaigrette salad dressing**
- **2 ounces Gorgonzola cheese or fresh mozzarella cheese, cut up**
- **2 tablespoons snipped fresh oregano**

1 Cut off the mushroom stems even with the caps; discard stems. Rinse mushroom caps; pat dry with paper towels.

2 Brush both sides of each mushroom and onion slice with olive oil. Sprinkle mushrooms, onions, and tomato halves with pepper and salt.

3 For a charcoal grill, place mushroom caps and onion slices on the grill rack of a grill with a cover directly over medium coals. Cover and grill for 6 to 8 minutes or until tender, turning once halfway through grilling. Remove from grill. Add tomatoes to grill. Cover and grill for 1 minute, turning once halfway through grilling. (For a gas grill, preheat grill. Reduce heat to medium. Place mushroom caps and onion slices, then tomatoes on grill rack over heat. Grill as above.)

4 Arrange vegetables on a serving platter. Drizzle with balsamic vinaigrette. Top with Gorgonzola or mozzarella cheese and sprinkle with oregano.

NUTRITION FACTS PER SERVING: 201 cal., 16 g total fat (4 g sat. fat), 11 mg chol., 589 mg sodium, 12 g carbo., 2 g fiber, 9 g pro.

Hearty Grilled Vegetables

Fresh herbs star in this colorful side dish.
For top flavor, use a mixture of two or three herbs.

PREP: 15 MINUTES GRILL: 6 MINUTES MAKES: 4 SERVINGS

¼ cup olive oil

¼ cup snipped fresh thyme, basil, oregano, and/or chives

2 fresh portobello mushrooms (about 4 inches in diameter), halved

8 green onions

2 medium red and/or yellow sweet peppers, seeded and quartered lengthwise

1 medium zucchini, quartered lengthwise

Salt

Ground black pepper

Fresh herbs (optional)

1 In a large bowl stir together olive oil and the ¼ cup fresh herbs. Add mushrooms, green onions, sweet peppers, and zucchini. Toss gently to evenly coat vegetables.

2 If desired, place the vegetables on a grilling tray. For a charcoal grill, grill vegetables on the rack of an uncovered grill directly over medium coals for 6 to 10 minutes or until tender, turning occasionally. (For a gas grill, preheat grill. Reduce heat to medium. Place vegetables on grill rack over heat. Cover and grill as above.)

3 Season with salt and pepper. If desired, garnish with additional fresh herbs.

NUTRITION FACTS PER SERVING: 168 cal., 15 g total fat (2 g sat. fat), 0 mg chol., 45 mg sodium, 9 g carbo., 3 g fiber, 3 g pro.

Grillside Potato Chips

For the best results, use Idaho russet potatoes.
They have a low water content and will make a crisper chip.

PREP: 10 MINUTES **GRILL:** 15 MINUTES **STAND:** 8 MINUTES **MAKES:** 4 SERVINGS

1 pound baking potatoes (such as russet or long white), scrubbed and bias-cut into $\frac{1}{16}$-inch-thick slices

3 tablespoons cooking oil

½ teaspoon dried thyme, crushed

½ teaspoon coarse salt or seasoned salt

1 Place potato slices in a Dutch oven. Add enough water to cover. Bring just to boiling. Cook for 2 to 3 minutes or until crisp-tender. Drain; place in a single layer on paper towels. Carefully brush both sides of each potato slice with cooking oil. Sprinkle with thyme and salt or seasoned salt.

2 For a charcoal grill, grill potato slices on the rack of an uncovered grill directly over medium-hot coals for 15 to 20 minutes or until browned and crisp, turning occasionally. (For a gas grill, preheat grill. Reduce heat. Place potatoes on grill rack over heat. Cover and grill as above.)

3 Meanwhile, line a baking sheet with several layers of paper towels; set aside. Remove potato slices from grill; let stand for 8 to 10 minutes on prepared baking sheet. (Chips will crisp as they stand.)

NUTRITION FACTS PER SERVING: 209 cal., 10 g total fat (1 g sat. fat), 0 mg chol., 276 mg sodium, 27 g carbo., 1 g fiber, 3 g pro.

Hot-Off-the-Grill Potatoes

Dinner is easy when you tuck the vegetable packets alongside meat or poultry on the grill.

PREP: 20 MINUTES **GRILL:** 30 MINUTES **MAKES:** 4 SERVINGS

- **3** tablespoons butter
- **5** medium potatoes, scrubbed and thinly sliced
- **¼** cup chopped green onions
- **2** tablespoons coarsely snipped fresh parsley
- **2** tablespoons snipped fresh dill
- **2** tablespoons snipped fresh chives
- **2** tablespoons grated Parmesan cheese
- **¼** teaspoon salt
- **¼** teaspoon paprika
- **¼** teaspoon ground black pepper
- **3** slices bacon, crisp-cooked, drained, and crumbled

1 Fold a 48×18-inch piece of heavy foil in half to make a 24×18-inch rectangle. Grease the foil with about 1 tablespoon of the butter.

2 Place potatoes in the center of the foil. Sprinkle with green onions, parsley, dill, chives, Parmesan cheese, salt, paprika, and pepper. Top with bacon. (If desired, add the parsley and bacon just before serving instead of adding them to the packet.) Dot with remaining 2 tablespoons butter. Bring up 2 opposite edges of foil and seal with double fold. Fold remaining ends to completely enclose the potatoes, leaving space for steam to build.

3 For a charcoal grill, grill foil packet on the rack of an uncovered grill directly over medium coals for 30 to 40 minutes or until potatoes are tender, turning packet every 10 minutes. (For a gas grill, preheat grill. Reduce heat to medium. Place foil packet on grill rack over heat. Cover and grill as above.)

NUTRITION FACTS PER SERVING: 236 cal., 13 g total fat (7 g sat. fat), 32 mg chol., 393 mg sodium, 24 g carbo., 3 g fiber, 6 g pro.

South-of-the-Border Potato Skins

Grilling gives an old favorite a slightly new twist.

PREP: 15 MINUTES **GRILL:** 20 MINUTES + 5 MINUTES **MAKES:** 12 APPETIZER SERVINGS

6 4- to 6-ounce baking potatoes
(such as russet or long white)

1 tablespoon cooking oil

½ teaspoon bottled minced garlic (1 clove)

⅛ to ¼ teaspoon cayenne pepper

1 cup shredded taco cheese (4 ounces)

1 6-ounce container frozen avocado dip, thawed

¾ cup thick-and-chunky salsa

¾ cup dairy sour cream

1 Scrub potatoes; cut each potato in half lengthwise. In a small bowl combine the oil, garlic, and cayenne pepper. Brush cut surfaces of potato halves with some of the oil mixture.

2 For a charcoal grill, grill potatoes, cut sides down, on the rack of an uncovered grill directly over medium coals for 20 to 25 minutes or until tender, turning once halfway through grilling. (For a gas grill, preheat grill. Reduce heat to medium. Place potatoes, cut sides down, on grill rack over heat. Cover and grill as above.)

3 Carefully scoop out the inside of each potato half, leaving a ½-inch-thick shell. Brush the insides of the potato shells with the remaining oil mixture. Sprinkle potatoes with cheese. Return potatoes to grill, cut sides up. Grill for 5 to 7 minutes more or until cheese is melted. Transfer to a serving platter.

4 To serve, top potato shells with avocado dip, salsa, and sour cream.

NUTRITION FACTS PER SERVING: 148 cal., 10 g total fat (4 g sat. fat), 15 mg chol., 255 mg sodium, 13 g carbo., 0 g fiber, 4 g pro.

Spicy Potato Slices

A spicy blend of thyme, paprika, and garlic salt seasons these grilled sliced potatoes and onions. Sour cream and snipped chives are tasty additions.

PREP: 10 MINUTES **GRILL:** 20 MINUTES **MAKES:** 4 SERVINGS

1	teaspoon dried thyme, crushed
½	teaspoon paprika
½	teaspoon garlic salt
⅛	teaspoon ground black pepper
3	large yellow potatoes or 2 russet potatoes, scrubbed (about 1 pound total)
1	sweet onion (such as Vidalia or Maui), sliced
2	tablespoons olive oil
¼	cup light dairy sour cream (optional)
1	tablespoon snipped fresh chives (optional)

1 For seasoning mixture, in a small bowl combine thyme, paprika, garlic salt, and pepper; set aside. Fold a 36×18-inch piece of heavy foil in half to make an 18-inch square. Cut potatoes crosswise into ¼-inch-thick slices. Place the potato slices and onion slices in the center of the foil. Drizzle with oil. Sprinkle with seasoning mixture. Bring up 2 opposite edges of foil square and seal with a double fold. Fold remaining edges to completely enclose the vegetables, leaving space for steam to build.

2 For a charcoal grill, grill foil packet on the rack of an uncovered grill directly over medium heat for 20 to 25 minutes or until potatoes are tender, turning once halfway through grilling. (For a gas grill, preheat grill. Reduce heat to medium. Place foil packet on grill rack over heat. Cover and grill as above.) If desired, serve with sour cream and chives.

NUTRITION FACTS PER SERVING: 186 cal., 7 g total fat (1 g sat. fat), 0 mg chol., 266 mg sodium, 29 g carbo., 1 g fiber, 3 g pro.

Two-Potato Packet

*Sweet potatoes weren't designed just for marshmallows and Thanksgiving.
You'll find sweet potatoes are great on the grill year-round.*

PREP: 15 MINUTES **GRILL:** 30 MINUTES **STAND:** 1 MINUTE **MAKES:** 4 SERVINGS

2 medium sweet potatoes, peeled and thinly sliced (about 12 ounces total)

4 small red potatoes, thinly sliced (about 8 ounces total)

4 onion slices, separated into rings

2 tablespoons butter or margarine, cut into small pieces

4 small fresh rosemary, basil, or oregano sprigs

⅛ teaspoon salt

⅛ teaspoon ground black pepper

½ cup shredded smoked provolone or Gouda cheese (2 ounces)

1 Fold four 24×18-inch pieces of heavy foil in half to make 18×12-inch rectangles. Divide sweet potatoes and red potatoes among foil rectangles, alternating and overlapping slices. Top with onion, butter, herbs, salt, and pepper. Bring up 2 opposite edges of foil and seal with a double fold. Fold remaining edges together to completely enclose vegetables, leaving space for steam to build.

2 For a charcoal grill, arrange medium-hot coals around edge of a grill with a cover. Test for medium heat above center of grill (not over coals). Place vegetable packets on grill rack over center of grill (not over coals). Cover and grill about 30 minutes or until potatoes are tender. (For a gas grill, preheat grill. Reduce heat to medium. Adjust for indirect cooking. Grill as above.)

3 Remove packets from grill. Carefully open packets; sprinkle vegetables with cheese. Let stand for 1 to 2 minutes or until cheese is melted.

NUTRITION FACTS PER SERVING: 234 cal., 10 g total fat (6 g sat. fat), 25 mg chol., 260 mg sodium, 32 g carbo., 3 g fiber, 6 g pro.

314

Warm Tarragon Potato Salad

A picnic favorite has been lightened and brightened up with a tangy fresh herb and Dijon vinaigrette dressing, crunchy bok choy, and peppery radishes.

PREP: 10 MINUTES GRILL: 25 MINUTES MAKES: 8 SERVINGS

¼ cup salad oil

¼ cup vinegar

1 tablespoon sugar (optional)

1 teaspoon snipped fresh tarragon or dill or ¼ teaspoon dried tarragon, crushed, or dried dillweed

½ teaspoon Dijon-style mustard

1 pound tiny new potatoes and/or small yellow potatoes, cut into bite-size pieces

2 teaspoons salad oil

1 cup chopped bok choy

½ cup chopped red radishes

½ cup thinly sliced green onions

2 thin slices Canadian-style bacon, chopped (1 ounce total)

⅛ teaspoon ground black pepper

4 artichokes, cooked, halved lengthwise, and chokes removed (optional)

1 For dressing, in a small bowl whisk together the ¼ cup oil, the vinegar, sugar (if desired), tarragon or dill, and mustard. Set aside.

2 Lightly grease a 2-quart square disposable foil pan. Combine potatoes and the 2 teaspoons oil in prepared pan; toss to coat.

3 For a charcoal grill, arrange medium-hot coals around the edge of a grill with a cover. Test for medium-hot heat above the center of grill (not over coals). Place potatoes in pan on grill rack over center of grill (not over coals). Cover and grill about 25 minutes or until potatoes are tender. (For a gas grill, preheat grill. Reduce heat to medium. Adjust for indirect cooking. Grill as above.) Cool potatoes slightly.

4 In a large bowl combine potatoes, bok choy, radishes, green onions, Canadian-style bacon, and pepper. Add the dressing; toss gently to coat. If desired, spoon the salad into artichoke halves.

NUTRITION FACTS PER SERVING: 135 cal., 8 g total fat (1 g sat. fat), 2 mg chol., 68 mg sodium, 14 g carbo., 1 g fiber, 2 g pro.

Fire-Roasted Acorn Squash

Falling leaves and chilly evenings set the stage for winter squash. But rather than the usual brown sugar and butter treatment, try basting rings of squash with tarragon butter, then grilling them. They're delicious with grilled pork and a dry white wine.

PREP: 10 MINUTES GRILL: 45 MINUTES MAKES: 4 SERVINGS

1	tablespoon olive oil
½	teaspoon salt
¼	teaspoon ground black pepper
2	small acorn squash, cut crosswise into 1-inch-thick rings and seeded
2	tablespoons butter or margarine, melted
2	teaspoons snipped fresh tarragon or ½ teaspoon dried tarragon, crushed

1 In a small bowl combine oil, salt, and pepper; brush over squash rings. In another small bowl stir together melted butter and tarragon; set aside.

2 For a charcoal grill, arrange medium-hot coals around a drip pan. Test for medium heat above the pan. Place squash rings on grill rack over drip pan. Cover and grill about 45 minutes or until squash is tender, turning squash occasionally and brushing with butter mixture after 30 minutes of grilling. (For a gas grill, preheat grill. Reduce heat to medium. Adjust for indirect cooking. Grill as above.)

NUTRITION FACTS PER SERVING: 156 cal., 9 g total fat (4 g sat. fat), 15 mg chol., 332 mg sodium, 20 g carbo., 4 g fiber, 2 g pro.

Shades of Green Kabobs

Create multicolor skewers with the baby veggies of your choice.

PREP: 20 MINUTES **MARINATE:** 1 TO 24 HOURS **GRILL:** 8 MINUTES **MAKES:** 6 SERVINGS

8 green onions

12 baby green pattypan squash

12 baby zucchini

1 cup sugar snap peas

⅓ cup olive oil

⅓ cup grated Parmesan cheese

3 tablespoons red wine vinegar

3 tablespoons snipped fresh oregano
or 1½ teaspoons dried oregano, crushed

¼ teaspoon salt

¼ teaspoon ground black pepper

❶ Rinse and trim vegetables. Cut a 3-inch portion from the bottom of each of 6 of the green onions. Place pattypan squash, zucchini, sugar snap peas, and the 3-inch green onion portions in a resealable plastic bag set in a shallow dish.

❷ Finely chop remaining 2 green onions. For marinade, in a screw-top jar combine finely chopped green onion, oil, Parmesan cheese, vinegar, oregano, salt, and pepper. Cover and shake well. Pour over vegetables in bag. Seal bag; turn to coat vegetables. Marinate vegetables in the refrigerator for at least 1 hour or up to 24 hours, turning bag occasionally.

❸ Drain vegetables, reserving marinade. On long metal skewers, alternately thread pattypan squash, zucchini, sugar snap peas, and green onion portions. For a charcoal grill, grill kabobs on the rack of an uncovered grill directly over medium coals for 8 to 10 minutes or until vegetables are browned and tender, turning and brushing occasionally with reserved marinade. (For a gas grill, preheat grill. Reduce heat to medium. Place kabobs on grill rack over heat. Cover and grill as above.)

NUTRITION FACTS PER SERVING: 156 cal., 14 g total fat (3 g sat. fat), 4 mg chol., 194 mg sodium, 6 g carbo., 2 g fiber, 4 g pro.

Spaghetti Squash with Grilled Plum Tomatoes

Topped with grilled tomatoes and fresh basil, there's no better way to get acquainted with this variety of squash that, when cooked, separates into spaghetti-like strands.

PREP: 15 MINUTES COOK: 10 MINUTES STAND: 5 MINUTES

GRILL: 10 MINUTES MAKES: 4 TO 6 SERVINGS

1   2½-pound spaghetti squash, halved lengthwise and seeded

2   tablespoons water

4   teaspoons olive oil

1   teaspoon dried Italian seasoning

½   teaspoon salt

¼   teaspoon ground black pepper

½   cup finely shredded Parmesan cheese (2 ounces)

4   medium red and/or yellow plum tomatoes, quartered

2   tablespoons snipped fresh basil

1 Place squash, cut sides down, in a microwave-safe 2-quart rectangular baking dish; add the water. Prick squash skin all over with a fork. Cover with vented plastic wrap. Microwave on 100% power (high) about 10 minutes or until squash is tender. Let squash stand for 5 minutes.

2 In a small bowl combine oil, Italian seasoning, salt, and pepper. Using fork, remove pulp from squash shells, separating it into strands. Transfer to bowl; toss with 2 teaspoons of the oil mixture and the Parmesan cheese. Fold a 36×18-inch piece of heavy foil in half to make an 18-inch square. Place squash mixture in center of foil. Bring up 2 opposite edges of foil and seal with double fold. Fold remaining edges to completely enclose the squash mixture, leaving space for steam to build.

3 For a charcoal grill, grill squash packet on the rack of an uncovered grill directly over medium heat for 10 minutes, turning once. Toss tomatoes with remaining oil mixture. For last 5 minutes of grilling, place tomatoes on grill rack beside packet. Grill tomatoes just until tender; turning once. (For a gas grill, preheat grill. Reduce heat to medium. Place squash packet, then tomatoes on grill rack over heat. Cover and grill as above.) Transfer tomatoes to cutting board; cool slightly and chop. Spoon over squash mixture; sprinkle with basil.

NUTRITION FACTS PER SERVING: 133 cal., 8 g total fat (1 g sat. fat), 10 mg chol., 447 mg sodium, 9 g carbo., 2 g fiber, 6 g pro.

Apples with Caramel Crème Fraîche

When the air cools and the leaves begin to turn, there's nothing sweeter than this elegant take on the caramel apple. Try the sauce on grilled bananas, pineapple, or pound cake.

PREP: 15 MINUTES **GRILL:** 2 MINUTES + 2 MINUTES + 2 MINUTES + 2 MINUTES
MAKES: 6 SERVINGS

4   Granny Smith apples, cored
4   cups water
3   tablespoons lemon juice
½   cup whipping cream
½   cup dairy sour cream
⅓   cup caramel ice cream topping
3   tablespoons butter, melted

1 Cut apples crosswise into ½-inch-thick slices. In a large bowl combine the water and lemon juice. Soak apple slices in water mixture to prevent browning.

2 For caramel crème fraîche, in a food processor bowl or blender container combine whipping cream, sour cream, and caramel ice cream topping. Cover and process or blend for 1 to 2 minutes or until slightly thickened. (Or beat with an electric mixer on high speed about 2 minutes or until slightly thickened.) Set aside.

3 Drain apple slices; pat dry with paper towels. Brush both sides of each apple slice with melted butter. For a charcoal grill, place apple slices on the grill rack of a grill with a cover directly over medium-hot coals. Cover and grill for 2 minutes. Rotate apple slices a half-turn to create a checkerboard grill pattern. Cover and grill for 2 minutes more. Turn apples over and repeat on other side. (For a gas grill, preheat grill. Reduce heat to medium-hot. Place apples on grill rack over heat. Cover and grill as above.)

4 To serve, arrange 3 or 4 apple slices on each dessert plate and top with caramel crème fraîche.

NUTRITION FACTS PER SERVING: 265 cal., 17 g total fat (11 g sat. fat), 51 mg chol., 118 mg sodium, 28 g carbo., 2 g fiber, 2 g pro.

Stuffed Autumn Apples and Pears

Crushed gingersnaps and shredded orange peel enhance the nut filling.

PREP: 20 MINUTES **GRILL:** 20 MINUTES + 5 MINUTES **MAKES:** 4 SERVINGS

2 medium cooking apples (such as Rome Beauty, Granny Smith, or Golden Delicious)

2 medium ripe, yet firm, pears (such as Bosc, Anjou, or Bartlett)

2 tablespoons brown sugar

2 tablespoons butter or margarine, melted

¼ cup coarsely chopped walnuts

¼ cup raisins

4 gingersnaps, finely crushed

1 teaspoon finely shredded orange peel

1 Peel the apples and pears. Cut the apples and pears in half lengthwise. Core the apples and pears, hollowing out the centers of each half.

2 In a large bowl combine the fruit halves, 1 tablespoon of the brown sugar, and 1 tablespoon of the melted butter; toss gently to coat. Set aside. For nut filling, in a small bowl combine the remaining 1 tablespoon brown sugar, remaining 1 tablespoon butter, the walnuts, raisins, finely crushed gingersnaps, and orange peel; set aside.

3 For charcoal grill, arrange medium-hot coals around a drip pan. Test for medium heat above the pan. Place fruit, cut sides down, on grill rack over drip pan. Cover and grill for 20 minutes. Turn fruit; spoon the nut filling into hollowed-out centers. Cover and grill about 5 minutes more or until fruit is tender. (For a gas grill, preheat grill. Reduce heat to medium. Adjust for indirect cooking. Grill as above.) Serve warm.

NUTRITION FACTS PER SERVING: 258 cal., 11 g total fat (4 g sat. fat), 15 mg chol., 102 mg sodium, 41 g carbo., 4 g fiber, 2 g pro.

Banana-Chocolate Tiramisu

Tiramisu, an Italian dessert, literally means "pick me up" in Italian. It was meant to go with coffee for a midafternoon lift. This version will lift you to dessert heaven!

PREP: 20 MINUTES **CHILL:** 1 TO 8 HOURS **GRILL:** 6 MINUTES **MAKES:** 4 TO 6 SERVINGS

1 **8-ounce carton mascarpone cheese or one 8-ounce tub cream cheese, softened**

½ **cup sifted powdered sugar**

⅓ **cup unsweetened cocoa powder**

1 **teaspoon vanilla**

3 **tablespoons milk**

1 **cup whipping cream, whipped**

4 **medium ripe, yet firm, bananas**

2 **tablespoons butter or margarine, melted**

1 **cup crushed amaretti cookies**

   Chocolate curls (optional)

1 For chocolate cream, in a medium bowl combine mascarpone cheese or cream cheese, powdered sugar, cocoa powder, and vanilla; beat with an electric mixer on low speed until combined. Gradually add milk, beating until smooth. By hand, fold in whipped cream. Cover and chill for at least 1 hour or up to 8 hours.

2 Brush peeled bananas with melted butter. For a charcoal grill, grill bananas on the rack of an uncovered grill directly over medium coals for 6 to 8 minutes or until lightly browned, turning once halfway through grilling. (For a gas grill, preheat grill. Reduce heat to medium. Place bananas on grill rack over heat. Cover and grill as above.)

3 To serve, slice bananas. Layer banana slices, crushed cookies, and chocolate cream in 4 to 6 dessert dishes. If desired, sprinkle with chocolate curls.

NUTRITION FACTS PER SERVING: 766 cal., 57 g total fat (32 g sat. fat), 169 mg chol., 136 mg sodium, 61 g carbo., 2 g fiber, 17 g pro.

Bananas Suzette over Grilled Pound Cake

Here is all the drama of crêpes suzette without the labor—and no chafing dish is required! This elegant dessert is made easily in a skillet right on your grill.

PREP: 10 MINUTES **GRILL:** 2 MINUTES + 1 MINUTE + 4 MINUTES + 1 MINUTE **MAKES:** 4 SERVINGS

2 medium ripe, yet firm, bananas

3 tablespoons sugar

2 tablespoons orange liqueur

2 tablespoons orange juice

1 tablespoon butter

⅛ teaspoon ground nutmeg

½ of a 10¾-ounce package frozen pound cake, thawed and cut into 4 slices

Shredded orange peel (optional)

Ground nutmeg (optional)

1 Bias-slice each banana into 8 pieces. For a charcoal grill, place an 8-inch skillet* on the rack of an uncovered grill directly over medium coals about 2 minutes or until hot. Add the sugar, liqueur, juice, and butter. Heat about 1 minute or until butter melts and sugar begins to dissolve. Add the bananas and heat about 4 minutes more or just until bananas are tender, stirring once. Stir in the ⅛ teaspoon nutmeg. Set skillet to the side of the grill rack. Grill pound cake slices directly over medium coals about 1 minute or until golden brown, turning once. (For a gas grill, preheat grill. Reduce heat to medium. Place skillet, then pound cake slices on grill rack over heat. Cover and grill as above.)

2 To serve, spoon bananas and sauce over pound cake slices. If desired, garnish with shredded orange peel and additional nutmeg.

NUTRITION FACTS PER SERVING: 292 cal., 12 g total fat (7 g sat. fat), 67 mg chol., 139 mg sodium, 42 g carbo., 1 g fiber, 3 g pro.

*NOTE: The heat from the grill will blacken the outside of the skillet, so use a cast-iron or old skillet.

Peanut Butter S'mores

Though you may not own up to it, this variation on the s'mores theme could become one of those private pleasures. No one will ever have to know your secret obsession.

PREP: 15 MINUTES **GRILL:** 7 MINUTES **MAKES:** 8 SERVINGS

¾ **cup peanut butter**

4 **9- to 10-inch flour tortillas (burrito size)**

1 **cup tiny marshmallows**

½ **cup miniature semisweet chocolate pieces**

1 **medium ripe, yet firm, banana, thinly sliced**

1 Spread about 3 tablespoons of the peanut butter over one half of each tortilla. Top each with some of the marshmallows, chocolate pieces, and banana slices. Fold tortillas in half, pressing gently to flatten and seal slightly.

2 For a charcoal grill, grill filled tortillas on the rack of an uncovered grill directly over medium coals for 7 to 9 minutes or until tortillas are golden and chocolate is melted, turning once halfway through grilling. (For a gas grill, preheat grill. Reduce heat to medium. Place filled tortillas on grill rack over heat. Cover and grill as above.)

3 To serve, cut each filled tortilla into 4 wedges.

NUTRITION FACTS PER SERVING: 290 cal., 17 g total fat (3 g sat. fat), 0 mg chol., 207 mg sodium, 31 g carbo., 2 g fiber, 8 g pro.

Mango Blossoms

A mango is ripe when the skin is bright in color and the fruit yields very slightly to touch and has a strong floral aroma.

PREP: 30 MINUTES **GRILL:** 2 MINUTES + 4 MINUTES **MAKES:** 8 SERVINGS

4 mangoes

4 kiwifruit, peeled

½ of a 15-ounce purchased angel food cake

¼ cup butter or margarine, melted

3 tablespoons mild-flavored molasses or honey

Vanilla ice cream (optional)

1 Using a sharp knife, cut each mango lengthwise down both flat sides, keeping the blade about ¼ inch from the seed. Discard seeds. Score mango pieces, making cuts through the fruit just to the peel in a crosshatch fashion. Set aside.

2 Carefully remove and discard the peel remaining around the mango seeds. Cut away as much of the fruit remaining around each mango seed as you can; discard seeds. Place the removed fruit portion in a food processor bowl or blender container. Cover and process or blend fruit pieces until smooth. Transfer pureed fruit to a small covered container or a clean squeeze bottle. Chill until ready to use.

3 Rinse the food processor bowl or blender container. Place peeled kiwifruit in bowl or container. Cover and process or blend until smooth. If desired, strain the kiwifruit puree through a sieve to remove seeds. Transfer to a small covered container or squeeze bottle. Chill until ready to use.

4 Cut angel food cake in half horizontally (forming 2 half-rings). Brush all sides of the cake with half of the melted butter. For a charcoal grill, grill cake on rack of an uncovered grill directly over medium coals for 2 to 3 minutes or until lightly browned, turning once. Cut angel food cake into large, irregular-shape croutons.

5 Brush fruit side of reserved mango pieces with molasses or honey and remaining melted butter. Grill mangoes, cut sides down, over medium coals for 4 to 6 minutes or until brown around the edges and heated through. (For a gas grill, preheat grill. Reduce heat to medium. Place cake, then mangoes on grill rack over heat. Cover and grill as above.)

6 To serve, spoon or drizzle mango and kiwifruit sauces on the bottom of 8 chilled, shallow dessert bowls. Carefully bend the peel back on each mango half, pushing the inside up and out until the mango cubes pop up and separate. Place each mango "blossom" on sauces in dessert bowl. Surround with several cake croutons. If desired, serve with vanilla ice cream.

NUTRITION FACTS PER SERVING: 215 cal., 4 g total fat (3 g sat. fat), 15 mg chol., 249 mg sodium, 45 g carbo., 2 g fiber, 3 g pro.

Nectarine-Raspberry Crisp

Chock-full of juicy nectarines and jewel-tone raspberries, this juicy crisp takes full advantage of the best of summer's sweet fruits. If you're pressed for time, assemble it up to 6 hours ahead, then chill until it's time to put it on the grill.

PREP: 15 MINUTES GRILL: 20 MINUTES MAKES: 6 SERVINGS

⅓ **cup granulated sugar**

5 **tablespoons all-purpose flour**

1 **tablespoon lemon juice**

1¼ **teaspoons apple pie spice or ground nutmeg**

6 **medium nectarines (about 2 pounds total), pitted and cut into 1-inch chunks**

1 **cup fresh raspberries**

¼ **cup packed brown sugar**

¼ **cup rolled oats**

¼ **cup cold butter**

⅓ **cup pecans, coarsely chopped**

Vanilla ice cream (optional)

❶ In a large bowl combine granulated sugar, 2 tablespoons of the flour, the lemon juice, and ¼ teaspoon of the apple pie spice. Gently stir in nectarines and raspberries. Transfer mixture to an 8½×1½-inch round disposable foil baking pan.

❷ For the topping, combine the remaining 3 tablespoons flour, the remaining 1 teaspoon apple pie spice, the brown sugar, and rolled oats. Using a pastry blender, cut in butter until mixture resembles coarse crumbs. Stir in nuts. Sprinkle topping evenly over fruit mixture.

❸ For a charcoal grill, arrange medium coals in bottom of grill with a cover in a donut-shape, leaving a 9-inch circle in the center without coals. Test for medium-low heat in center (not over coals). Place crisp in pan on center of grill rack (not over coals). Cover and grill for 20 to 25 minutes or until fruit mixture is bubbly in the center. (For a gas grill, preheat grill. Reduce heat to medium-low. Adjust for indirect cooking. Grill as above.) Serve warm. If desired, serve with ice cream.

NUTRITION FACTS PER SERVING: 291 cal., 13 g total fat (5 g sat. fat), 20 mg chol., 80 mg sodium, 45 g carbo., 4 g fiber, 3 g pro.

Peaches with Quick Cherry Sauce

Don't tell anyone you're making this or they'll insist on starting the meal with dessert.

PREP: 15 MINUTES GRILL: 6 MINUTES MAKES: 6 SERVINGS

3   **medium peaches or nectarines, pitted and quartered**

3   **tablespoons orange juice**

1½   **cups fresh or thawed frozen unsweetened pitted dark sweet cherries**

½   **cup cherry jam**

3   **cups vanilla ice cream**

2   **tablespoons coconut or almonds, toasted**

❶ Brush peaches or nectarines with 1 tablespoon of the orange juice. Thread peaches or nectarines onto 2 long metal skewers. For sauce, in a small saucepan combine the remaining 2 tablespoons orange juice, the cherries, and cherry jam. Bring to boiling over medium heat, stirring frequently; reduce heat. Simmer, uncovered, for 3 minutes. Set aside.

❷ For a charcoal grill, grill skewers on the rack of an uncovered grill directly over medium coals for 6 to 8 minutes or until heated through, turning once halfway through grilling. If desired, add sauce in saucepan* to grill beside peaches to keep warm. (For a gas grill, preheat grill. Reduce heat to medium. Place skewers, then sauce in saucepan [if desired] on grill rack over heat. Cover and grill as above.)

❸ To serve, spoon peaches or nectarines and sauce over scoops of vanilla ice cream. Sprinkle with coconut or almonds.

NUTRITION FACTS PER SERVING: 273 cal., 8 g total fat (5 g sat. fat), 29 mg chol., 56 mg sodium, 50 g carbo., 2 g fiber, 3 g pro.

*NOTE: The heat from the grill will blacken the outside of the saucepan, so use an old saucepan.

Grilled Fruit Kabobs with Lime-Yogurt Sauce

When you want a little something sweet after a hearty meal, these light and refreshing fruit kabobs are a natural choice. Save the leftovers—if there are any—for a breakfast treat with muffins or cereal the next morning.

PREP: 15 MINUTES SOAK: 30 MINUTES GRILL: 8 MINUTES MAKES: 6 SERVINGS

6   6-to 8-inch wooden skewers

1   8-ounce carton vanilla low-fat yogurt

1   teaspoon grated lime peel

1   tablespoon lime juice

¼   teaspoon ground cinnamon

1   small fresh pineapple, peeled and cored

2   large ripe, yet firm, nectarines or peeled peaches

2   medium ripe, yet firm, bananas

1   tablespoon butter or margarine, melted

2   teaspoons lime juice

1 Soak the skewers in enough warm water to cover for 30 minutes; drain before using. Meanwhile, for sauce, in a small bowl combine the yogurt, lime peel, the 1 tablespoon lime juice, and the cinnamon. Cover and chill until serving time.

2 For the kabobs, cut pineapple into 1-inch-thick slices; quarter slices. Cut nectarines or peeled peaches into wedges. Cut bananas into chunks. On the soaked skewers, alternately thread pineapple, nectarines or peaches, and bananas. In a small bowl combine melted butter and the 2 teaspoons lime juice. Brush over kabobs.

3 For a charcoal grill, grill kabobs on the rack of an uncovered grill directly over medium coals for 8 to 10 minutes, turning once or twice and brushing often with remaining butter mixture. (For a gas grill, preheat grill. Reduce heat to medium. Place kabobs on grill rack over heat. Cover and grill as above.) Serve kabobs with the sauce.

NUTRITION FACTS PER SERVING: 161 cal., 3 g total fat (2 g sat. fat), 7 mg chol., 43 mg sodium, 33 g carbo., 2 g fiber, 3 g pro.

Pineapple with Sugared Wontons

Juicy, rum-glazed, grilled pineapple is sprinkled with a touch of coconut and a whimsical embellishment: wonton skins crisped on the grill and sprinkled with sugar.

PREP: 10 MINUTES **GRILL:** 6 MINUTES + 2 MINUTES + 2 MINUTES **MAKES:** 4 SERVINGS

6	¾-inch-thick slices peeled and cored fresh pineapple, quartered
¼	cup packed brown sugar
2	tablespoons rice vinegar or seasoned rice vinegar
2	tablespoons rum
4	teaspoons lime juice
6	wonton wrappers, halved diagonally
1	tablespoon butter, melted
3	tablespoons shredded coconut
1	tablespoon granulated sugar

1 Place pineapple in a single layer in a shallow dish. In a small bowl combine brown sugar, vinegar, rum, and lime juice, stirring until brown sugar dissolves. Pour brown sugar mixture over the pineapple; set aside. Place a sheet of waxed paper on a cookie sheet. Lay wonton wrappers on waxed paper. Brush both sides of each wonton wrapper with melted butter. Put coconut in a disposable foil pie pan or on a double thickness of heavy foil; set aside.

2 Drain pineapple, reserving brown sugar mixture. For a charcoal grill, grill pineapple on the rack of an uncovered grill directly over medium coals for 6 to 8 minutes, turning once and brushing occasionally with some of the reserved brown sugar mixture. (For a gas grill, preheat grill. Reduce heat to medium. Place pineapple on grill rack over heat. Cover and grill as above.) Transfer pineapple to serving bowls.

3 Place the wonton wrappers directly on the grill rack over medium coals; grill for 2 to 4 minutes or until browned, using tongs to turn once. Return the grilled wontons to the cookie sheet; immediately sprinkle with the granulated sugar. Transfer the pie pan or foil with the coconut to the grill. Using a pair of tongs, shake pan or foil back and forth about 2 minutes or until coconut is lightly toasted. Drizzle the remaining brown sugar mixture over pineapple; sprinkle with coconut and serve with sugared wontons.

NUTRITION FACTS PER SERVING: 204 cal., 5 g total fat (3 g sat. fat), 9 mg chol., 103 mg sodium, 38 g carbo., 2 g fiber, 2 g pro.

Hot-Off-the-Grill Tropical Treat

Looking for an informal yet special summer dish? You'll surprise your guests when you serve this sweet grilled fruit. Fresh pineapple slices get brushed with a nicely spiced lime and honey sauce while they grill to perfection.

PREP: 20 MINUTES **GRILL:** 8 MINUTES **MAKES:** 6 SERVINGS

1 large fresh pineapple, peeled and cored

¼ cup butter or margarine

1 teaspoon finely shredded lime peel

2 tablespoons lime juice

2 tablespoons honey

1 tablespoon cornstarch

¼ teaspoon ground ginger

1 Cut pineapple crosswise into 6 slices. In a small saucepan melt butter over medium heat. In a small bowl stir together lime peel, lime juice, honey, cornstarch, and ginger. Stir into the melted butter. Cook and stir until mixture is thickened and bubbly. Cook and stir for 2 minutes more. Remove from heat.

2 For a charcoal grill, grill pineapple slices on the rack of an uncovered grill directly over medium coals for 8 to 10 minutes or until heated through, turning once halfway through grilling and brushing frequently with lime–butter mixture. (For a gas grill, preheat grill. Reduce heat to medium. Place pineapple slices on grill rack over heat. Cover and grill as above.)

NUTRITION FACTS PER SERVING: 190 cal., 8 g total fat (5 g sat. fat), 22 mg chol., 91 mg sodium, 29 g carbo., 2 g fiber, 1 g pro.

Chocolate-Raspberry Burritos

Chocolate on the grill may sound like a mess, but when it's wrapped up in a tortilla with fresh raspberries, it's anything but. For an extra-special touch, top each serving with a scoop of vanilla ice cream.

PREP: 12 MINUTES   GRILL: 5 MINUTES + 3 MINUTES   MAKES: 4 SERVINGS

4   8- to 9-inch flour tortillas

1   cup semisweet chocolate pieces

1   cup fresh raspberries

2   tablespoons butter, melted

2   teaspoons sugar

½   teaspoon ground cinnamon

1 Stack the tortillas and wrap in a piece of heavy foil. For a charcoal grill, grill foil packet on rack of an uncovered grill directly over medium-low coals about 5 minutes or until tortillas are warm and pliable, turning packet once. (Or wrap the tortilla stack in microwave-safe paper towels instead of foil; microwave on 100% power [high] for 20 to 40 seconds or until tortillas are warm and pliable.)

2 Sprinkle ¼ cup each of the chocolate pieces and the raspberries in the center of each tortilla; fold in sides and roll up. Brush burritos with half of the melted butter. Grill burritos over medium-low coals about 3 minutes or until the tortillas begin to show grill marks and the chocolate is melted, turning once. (For a gas grill, preheat grill. Reduce heat to medium-low. Place foil packet, then burritos on grill rack over heat. Cover and grill as above.)

3 Transfer burritos to a serving platter. Brush burritos with remaining melted butter. In a small bowl combine the sugar and cinnamon; sprinkle over the burritos. Serve immediately.

NUTRITION FACTS PER SERVING: 361 cal., 20 g total fat (4 g sat. fat), 15 mg chol., 179 mg sodium, 49 g carbo., 2 g fiber, 4 g pro.

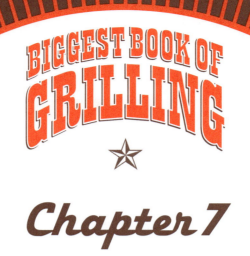

Chapter 7

SMOKE COOKING

Pepper-Crusted Beef Ribeye Roast

*Here's a beef lover's dream. A glorious ribeye roast, a pepper crust,
a good long smoke, and tomato chutney make for a great entrée.*

PREP: 15 MINUTES **SOAK:** 1 HOUR **SMOKE:** 3 HOURS **COOK:** 45 MINUTES
STAND: 15 MINUTES **MAKES:** 10 TO 12 SERVINGS

10	to 12 oak wood chunks
1	4- to 5-pound beef ribeye roast
1	to 2 tablespoons cracked black pepper
1	teaspoon bottled minced garlic (2 cloves)
4	ripe tomatoes, chopped (about 3 cups)
1	to 1¼ cups packed brown sugar
1	large onion, chopped
1	cup raisins
½	cup balsamic vinegar or red wine vinegar
2	to 3 tablespoons chopped crystallized ginger
1	to 2 fresh jalapeño chile peppers, finely chopped*
½	to 1 teaspoon dry mustard
	Salt (optional)
	Ground black pepper (optional)

1. At least 1 hour before smoke cooking, soak wood chunks in enough water to cover. Drain before using.

2. Trim fat from meat. For rub, in a small bowl combine cracked black pepper and garlic. Sprinkle rub evenly over meat; rub in with your fingers.

3. In a smoker arrange preheated coals, half of the drained wood chunks, and water pan according to the manufacturer's directions. Pour water into pan. Place meat, fat side up, on grill rack over water pan. Cover and smoke for 3 to 4 hours or until medium-rare doneness (135°F). Add coals, wood chunks, and water as needed. Remove meat from smoker. Cover with foil; let stand for 15 minutes before carving. The meat's temperature after standing should be 145°F.

4. Meanwhile, for chutney, in a small saucepan combine tomatoes, brown sugar, onion, raisins, vinegar, ginger, jalapeño peppers, and mustard. Bring to boiling; reduce heat. Simmer, uncovered, about 45 minutes or until desired consistency. If desired, cover and chill until ready to serve.

5. If desired, season meat with salt and ground black pepper. Serve meat with warm or chilled chutney.

NUTRITION FACTS PER SERVING: 458 cal., 19 g total fat (8 g sat. fat), 107 mg chol., 113 mg sodium, 36 g carbo., 2 g fiber, 37 g pro.

*NOTE: Because chile peppers contain volatile oils that can burn your skin and eyes, avoid direct contact with them as much as possible. When working with chile peppers, wear plastic or rubber gloves. If your bare hands do touch the chile peppers, wash your hands and nails well with soap and warm water.

Beer-Sauced Beef Brisket

A savory rub and a beer-vinegar sauce give the beef brisket exceptional flavor.

PREP: 10 MINUTES SOAK: 1 HOUR GRILL: 2 HOURS MAKES: 15 SERVINGS

4 cups mesquite or hickory wood chips

2 tablespoons sugar

1 tablespoon garlic salt or seasoned salt

1 tablespoon paprika

1½ teaspoons chili powder

1½ teaspoons ground black pepper

⅛ teaspoon cayenne pepper

⅛ teaspoon celery seeds

Dash ground cloves

1 3- to 4-pound fresh beef brisket

½ cup beer

1 tablespoon cider vinegar

1 tablespoon olive oil

1 tablespoon Worcestershire sauce

1 tablespoon bottled barbecue sauce

½ teaspoon seasoned salt

¼ teaspoon celery seeds

1 At least 1 hour before grilling, soak wood chips in enough water to cover. Drain before using.

2 For rub, in a small bowl combine sugar, the 1 tablespoon garlic salt or seasoned salt, the paprika, chili powder, ground black pepper, cayenne pepper, the ⅛ teaspoon celery seeds, and the cloves. Trim fat from brisket. Sprinkle rub evenly over meat; rub in with your fingers.

3 For mop sauce, in a medium bowl combine beer, vinegar, oil, Worcestershire sauce, barbecue sauce, the ½ teaspoon seasoned salt, and the ¼ teaspoon celery seeds. Set aside.

4 For a charcoal grill, arrange medium-hot coals around a drip pan. Test for medium heat above the pan. Sprinkle half of the drained wood chips over the coals. Place brisket on grill rack over drip pan. Cover and grill for 2 to 2½ hours or until meat is tender. Add remaining wood chips as needed and additional coals as necessary to maintain heat. Brush once or twice with mop sauce during the last hour of grilling. (For a gas grill, preheat grill. Reduce heat to medium. Adjust for indirect cooking. Add drained wood chips according to manufacturer's directions. Place meat on a rack in a roasting pan, place on grill rack, and grill as above.) Discard any remaining mop sauce. To serve, thinly slice meat across the grain.

NUTRITION FACTS PER SERVING: 262 cal., 20 g total fat (7 g sat. fat), 61 mg chol., 436 mg sodium, 3 g carbo., 0 g fiber, 16 g pro.

Texans' Beef Brisket

Texans get mighty finicky about their barbecue.
This brisket—with a mopping sauce, dry rub, and passing sauce—covers all the bases.

PREP: 15 MINUTES SOAK: 1 HOUR SMOKE: 5 HOURS MAKES: 12 SERVINGS

15	to 20 mesquite, hickory, or pecan wood chunks
1	3- to 3½-pound fresh beef brisket
2	teaspoons seasoned salt
1	teaspoon paprika
1	teaspoon chili powder
1	teaspoon garlic pepper
½	teaspoon ground cumin
1	recipe Vinegar Mop Sauce
1	recipe Spicy Beer Sauce

1 At least 1 hour before smoke cooking, soak wood chunks in enough water to cover. Drain before using.

2 Trim fat from meat. For rub, in a small bowl combine seasoned salt, paprika, chili powder, garlic pepper, and cumin. Sprinkle rub evenly over meat; rub in with your fingers.

3 In a smoker arrange preheated coals, about one-fourth of the drained wood chunks, and the water pan according to the manufacturer's directions. Pour water into pan. Place meat on grill rack over pan. Cover and smoke for 5 to 6 hours or until meat is tender, brushing occasionally with Vinegar Mop Sauce during the last hour of smoking. Add coals, wood chunks, and water as needed.

4 To serve, thinly slice meat across the grain. Serve meat with Spicy Beer Sauce.

Vinegar Mop Sauce: In a small bowl stir together ¼ cup beer, 4 teaspoons Worcestershire sauce, 1 tablespoon cooking oil, 1 tablespoon vinegar, ½ teaspoon jalapeño mustard or other hot-style mustard, and a few dashes bottled hot pepper sauce.

Spicy Beer Sauce: In a medium saucepan melt 2 tablespoons butter or margarine. Add 1 large peeled, seeded, and chopped tomato (¾ cup); ½ cup chopped onion; and ½ cup chopped green sweet pepper. Cook about 5 minutes or until onion is tender, stirring occasionally. Stir in 1 cup bottled chili sauce, ½ cup beer, ½ cup cider vinegar, 2 tablespoons brown sugar, 1 to 2 tablespoons chopped canned chipotle chile peppers in adobo sauce,* 1¼ teaspoons ground black pepper, and ½ teaspoon salt. Bring to boiling; reduce heat. Boil gently, uncovered, about 10 minutes or until reduced to about 2¼ cups.

NUTRITION FACTS PER SERVING: 277 cal., 14 g total fat (5 g sat. fat), 83 mg chol., 689 mg sodium, 11 g carbo., 1 g fiber, 26 g pro.

*NOTE: Because chile peppers contain volatile oils that can burn your skin and eyes, avoid direct contact with them as much as possible. When working with chile peppers, wear plastic or rubber gloves. If your bare hands do touch the chile peppers, wash your hands and nails well with soap and warm water.

Sirloin with Horseradish Sauce

*Give your guests the royal treatment with succulent smoked sirloin
and a side of creamy horseradish sauce.*

PREP: 15 MINUTES **MARINATE:** 1 TO 4 HOURS **SOAK:** 1 HOUR
GRILL: 32 MINUTES **MAKES:** 6 SERVINGS

- **1** 2- to 2½-pound beef top sirloin steak, cut 1½ inches thick
- **2** teaspoons bottled minced garlic (4 cloves)
- **¾** teaspoon ground cumin
- **½** teaspoon cracked black pepper
- **¼** teaspoon salt
- **3** cups oak or hickory wood chips
- **⅓** cup dairy sour cream
- **2** tablespoons Dijon-style mustard
- **1** tablespoon snipped fresh chives
- **2** teaspoons prepared horseradish
- **¼** cup whipping cream, whipped

1 Trim fat from steak. For rub, in a small bowl stir together garlic, cumin, pepper, and salt. Sprinkle rub evenly over one side of steak; rub in with your fingers. Cover and chill in the refrigerator for at least 1 hour or up to 4 hours.

2 At least 1 hour before grilling, soak wood chips in enough water to cover. Drain before using.

3 For a charcoal grill, arrange medium-hot coals around a drip pan. Test for medium heat above pan. Sprinkle the drained wood chips over the coals. Place steak, seasoned side up, on grill rack over drip pan. Cover and grill until desired doneness. Allow 32 to 36 minutes for medium-rare doneness (145°F) or 36 to 40 minutes for medium doneness (160°F). (For a gas grill, preheat grill. Add drained wood chips according to manufacturer's directions. Reduce heat to medium. Add drained wood chips according to manufacturer's directions. Adjust for indirect cooking. Place steak on the grill rack. Cover and grill as above.)

4 Meanwhile, for sauce, in a small bowl stir together sour cream, mustard, chives, and horseradish. Fold in the whipped cream. To serve, thinly slice steak across the grain. Pass sauce.

NUTRITION FACTS PER SERVING: 255 cal., 11 g total fat (6 g sat. fat), 90 mg chol., 308 mg sodium, 2 g carbo., 0 g fiber, 33 g pro.

Smoky Fajitas

The vegetables and tortillas grill alongside the
flank steak in this meal-on-the-grill.

PREP: 30 MINUTES **MARINATE:** 6 TO 24 HOURS **SOAK:** 1 HOUR
GRILL: 23 MINUTES **MAKES:** 4 TO 6 SERVINGS

1 1- to 1¼-pound beef flank steak

1 cup beer

½ cup lime juice

½ cup chopped onion

3 tablespoons cooking oil

2 tablespoons bottled steak sauce

1 tablespoon chili powder

1 teaspoon ground cumin

2 teaspoons bottled minced garlic (4 cloves)

2 cups oak or hickory wood chips

3 red, yellow, and/or green sweet peppers, cut into thin strips

1 medium onion, thinly sliced

8 7-inch flour or corn tortillas

1 recipe Pico de Gallo

1 Score both sides of steak in a diamond pattern by making shallow diagonal cuts at 1-inch intervals. Place steak in a resealable plastic bag set in a shallow dish. For marinade, in a medium bowl combine beer, lime juice, chopped onion, oil, steak sauce, chili powder, cumin, and garlic. Pour over steak. Seal bag; turn to coat steak. Marinate in the refrigerator for at least 6 hours or up to 24 hours, turning bag occasionally.

2 At least 1 hour before grilling, soak wood chips in enough water to cover. Drain before using.

3 Fold a 24×18-inch piece of heavy foil in half to make an 18×12-inch rectangle. Place pepper strips and sliced onion in center of foil. Bring up 2 opposite edges of the foil and seal with a double fold. Fold remaining ends to completely enclose vegetables, leaving space for steam to build. Wrap tortillas in heavy foil.

4 For a charcoal grill, arrange medium-hot coals around a drip pan. Test for medium heat above pan. Sprinkle drained wood chips over the coals. Drain steak, discarding marinade. Place steak on the grill rack directly over the drip pan. Place pepper packet on the grill rack directly over coals. Cover and grill for 23 to 28 minutes or until steak is medium doneness (160°F) and vegetables are tender. Place tortilla packet on grill rack directly over coals for the last 10 minutes of grilling. (For a gas grill, preheat grill. Reduce heat to medium. Add drained wood chips according to manufacturer's directions. Adjust for indirect cooking. Place the steak and pepper packet, then tortilla packet on grill rack and grill as above.)

5 To serve, thinly slice steak diagonally across the grain. Divide steak and pepper mixture among the tortillas. Roll up and serve with Pico de Gallo.

Pico de Gallo: In a medium bowl gently stir together 2 plum tomatoes, chopped; 2 green onions, sliced; 1 fresh serrano chile pepper, seeded and chopped (see Note, page 334); ¼ of a medium cucumber, seeded and chopped; 2 tablespoons snipped fresh cilantro; and ⅛ teaspoon salt. Cover and chill in the refrigerator for up to 24 hours.

NUTRITION FACTS PER SERVING: 425 cal., 15 g total fat (5 g sat. fat), 46 mg chol., 405 mg sodium, 42 g carbo., 4 g fiber, 31 g pro.

Red-Rub BBQ Ribs

Keep these succulent ribs cookin' low and slow for the better part of an afternoon—more than 2 hours. You'll be rewarded with smoke-infused slabs of heaven, slathered in wickedly good Mutha Sauce.

PREP: 10 MINUTES SOAK: 1 HOUR GRILL: 2½ HOURS MAKES: 6 SERVINGS

1 recipe Red Rub

6 pounds (2 racks) beef back ribs

3 to 4 cups hickory wood chips

1 recipe Mutha Sauce (see recipe, page 286) or 2 cups bottled barbecue sauce

1 Sprinkle Red Rub evenly over ribs; rub in with your fingers. If desired, cover rubbed ribs and refrigerate up to 48 hours.

2 At least 1 hour before grilling, soak hickory chips in enough water to cover. Drain before using.

3 For a charcoal grill, arrange medium coals around a drip pan. Test for medium-low heat above the pan. Divide drained wood chips into 3 equal portions; wrap each portion in foil. Poke holes in the foil packets. Place 1 foil packet on hot coals. Place ribs, bone sides down, on lightly greased grill rack over drip pan. (Or place ribs in a lightly greased rib rack; place on grill rack over drip pan.) Cover and grill for 2½ to 3 hours or until meat is tender, basting occasionally with Mutha Sauce after 1 hour of grilling. Add remaining foil packets as needed and additional coals as necessary to maintain heat. (For a gas grill, preheat grill. Reduce heat to medium-low. Adjust for indirect cooking. Place 1 foil packet on hot side of grill. Place ribs on a rack in a roasting pan, place on grill rack, and grill as above.) Reheat remaining sauce until bubbly; serve with ribs.

Red Rub: In a small bowl combine 1 tablespoon paprika, 1 tablespoon garlic powder, 1 tablespoon brown sugar, 1 tablespoon onion powder, 2 teaspoons chili powder, 1 teaspoon coarse salt, ½ teaspoon ground black pepper, ⅛ teaspoon ground cumin, and ⅛ teaspoon cayenne pepper. Rub ingredients together with your fingers.

NUTRITION FACTS PER SERVING: 372 cal., 18 g total fat (7 g sat. fat), 88 mg chol., 667 mg sodium, 15 g carbo., 1 g fiber, 38 g pro.

Hickory-Smoked Pork Loin

The barbecue kings of the Deep South wouldn't think of using any wood but hickory. It's fine for beef, but it really shines with all kinds of pork.

PREP: 15 MINUTES SOAK: 1 HOUR MARINATE: 30 MINUTES SMOKE: 1¾ HOURS
STAND: 10 MINUTES MAKES: 6 TO 8 SERVINGS

10	to 12 hickory wood chunks
1	2- to 2½-pound boneless pork top loin roast (single loin)
2	tablespoons light brown sugar
1	tablespoon finely shredded orange peel
1	teaspoon ground coriander
1	teaspoon paprika
½	teaspoon ground ginger
½	teaspoon salt
¼	teaspoon ground black pepper

1 At least 1 hour before smoke cooking, soak wood chunks in enough water to cover. Drain before using.

2 Meanwhile, trim fat from meat. Place meat in a shallow dish. For rub, in a small bowl stir together brown sugar, orange peel, coriander, paprika, ginger, salt, and pepper. Sprinkle rub evenly over meat; rub in with your fingers. Cover and let stand at room temperature for 30 minutes or chill in the refrigerator for 2 hours.

3 In a smoker arrange preheated coals, half of the drained wood chunks, and the water pan according to the manufacturer's directions. Pour water into pan. Place meat on grill rack over pan. Cover and smoke for 1¾ to 2 hours or until meat juices run clear (155°F). Add coals, wood chunks, and water as needed.

4 Remove meat from smoker. Cover meat with foil; let stand for 10 minutes before carving. The meat's temperature after standing should be 160°F.

NUTRITION FACTS PER SERVING: 199 cal., 10 g total fat (3 g sat. fat), 68 mg chol., 231 mg sodium, 5 g carbo., 0 g fiber, 22 g pro.

Rosemary and Garlic Smoked Pork Roast

For a simple but luscious pork dish, rub pork loin with rosemary and oil before grilling, then drizzle with lemon or lime juice before serving.

PREP: 15 MINUTES SOAK: 1 HOUR GRILL: 1 HOUR
STAND: 10 MINUTES MAKES: 8 TO 10 SERVINGS

4 cups apple or hickory wood chips

1 2- to 3-pound boneless pork top loin roast (single loin)

2 tablespoons snipped fresh rosemary

1 tablespoon olive oil

2 teaspoons bottled minced garlic (4 cloves)

½ teaspoon ground black pepper

¼ teaspoon salt

4 sprigs fresh rosemary

½ of a lemon or lime

1 At least 1 hour before grilling, soak wood chips in enough water to cover. Drain before using.

2 Trim fat from meat. For rub, combine the snipped rosemary, oil, garlic, pepper, and salt. Sprinkle rub evenly over meat; rub in with your fingers.

3 For a charcoal grill, arrange medium coals around a drip pan. Pour 1 inch of water into drip pan. Test for medium-low heat above the pan. Sprinkle half of the drained wood chips over the coals; sprinkle rosemary sprigs over chips. Place meat on grill rack over drip pan. Cover and grill for 1 to 1½ hours or until meat juices run clear (155°F). Add remaining wood chips as needed and additional coals as necessary to maintain heat. (For a gas grill, preheat grill. Reduce heat to medium-low. Adjust for indirect cooking. Add drained wood chips according to manufacturer's directions. Place meat on a rack in a roasting pan, place on grill rack, and grill as above.)

4 Remove meat from grill. Squeeze juice from lemon or lime over meat. Cover with foil; let stand for 10 minutes before carving. The meat's temperature after standing should be 160°F.

NUTRITION FACTS PER SERVING: 154 cal., 9 g total fat (3 g sat. fat), 51 mg chol., 106 mg sodium, 1 g carbo., 0 g fiber, 16 g pro.

Coastal Carolina Pulled Pork BBQ

The Carolinas may well offer more variations on barbecue than anywhere else in the country. These shredded pork sandwiches get dressed up with slaw and a simple vinegar sauce.

PREP: 15 MINUTES **SOAK:** 1 HOUR **SMOKE:** 4 HOURS **STAND:** 15 MINUTES **MAKES:** 12 SERVINGS

10   to 12 oak or hickory wood chunks

1   4½- to 5-pound boneless pork shoulder roast

1½   teaspoons salt

1½   teaspoons ground black pepper

2   cups cider vinegar

3   tablespoons brown sugar (optional)

1   tablespoon salt

1   tablespoon crushed red pepper

12   hamburger buns, split and toasted

Coleslaw (optional)

Bottled hot pepper sauce (optional)

1 At least 1 hour before smoke cooking, soak wood chunks in enough water to cover. Drain before using.

2 Trim fat from meat. For rub, in a small bowl combine the 1½ teaspoons salt and the ground black pepper. Sprinkle rub evenly over meat; rub in with your fingers. For sauce, in a medium bowl combine vinegar, brown sugar (if desired), the 1 tablespoon salt, and the red pepper. Set aside.

3 In a smoker arrange preheated coals, half of the drained wood chunks, and the water pan according to the manufacturer's directions. Pour water into pan. Place meat on the grill rack over pan. Cover and smoke for 4 to 5 hours or until meat is very tender. Add coals, wood chunks, and water as needed. Remove meat from smoker.

4 Cover with foil; let stand for 15 minutes. Using 2 forks, gently shred the meat into long, thin strands. Add enough of the sauce to the meat to moisten.

5 Place shredded meat on toasted buns. If desired, top meat with coleslaw. Pass remaining sauce and, if desired, hot pepper sauce.

NUTRITION FACTS PER SERVING: 314 cal., 11 g total fat (3 g sat. fat), 64 mg chol., 1,096 mg sodium, 24 g carbo., 1 g fiber, 31 g pro.

Memphis-Style Smoked Pork with Bourbon Sauce

*Tennessee is famed for its bourbon and its barbecue,
so isn't it time to put the two together?*

**PREP: 25 MINUTES MARINATE: 24 HOURS SOAK: 1 HOUR
SMOKE: 4 HOURS STAND: 15 MINUTES MAKES: 12 SERVINGS**

1	8-ounce can tomato sauce
1	cup chopped onion
1	cup vinegar
½	cup bourbon or beef broth
¼	cup Worcestershire sauce
2	tablespoons brown sugar
¼	teaspoon ground black pepper
	Dash bottled hot pepper sauce
1	4½- to 5-pound boneless pork shoulder roast
8	to 10 hickory wood chunks

1 For sauce, in a medium saucepan combine tomato sauce, onion, ½ cup of the vinegar, the bourbon or beef broth, Worcestershire sauce, brown sugar, ground black pepper, and hot pepper sauce. Bring to boiling; reduce heat. Cover and simmer for 15 minutes; cool. Reserve 1 cup of the sauce. Cover reserved sauce and chill until ready to serve.

2 Meanwhile, trim fat from meat. Place meat in a resealable plastic bag set in a shallow dish. For marinade, combine the remaining sauce and the remaining ½ cup vinegar. Pour over meat. Seal bag; turn to coat meat. Marinate in the refrigerator for 24 hours, turning bag occasionally.

3 At least 1 hour before smoke cooking, soak wood chunks in enough water to cover. Drain before using.

4 Drain meat, reserving marinade. In a smoker arrange preheated coals, half of the drained wood chunks, and the water pan according to the manufacturer's directions. Pour water into pan. Place meat on grill rack over water pan. Cover and smoke for 4 to 5 hours or until meat juices run clear (155°F), basting occasionally with the reserved marinade during the first 3 hours of smoking. Discard any remaining marinade. Add coals, wood chunks, and water as needed.

5 Remove meat from smoker. Cover meat with foil; let stand for 15 minutes before carving. The meat's temperature after standing should be 160°F. Meanwhile, in a small saucepan cook the reserved 1 cup sauce over medium heat until heated through. Slice meat. Serve meat with sauce.

NUTRITION FACTS PER SERVING: 324 cal., 17 g total fat (6 g sat. fat), 112 mg chol., 253 mg sodium, 6 g carbo., 0 g fiber, 30 g pro.

Mesquite Mixed Grill

A savory blend of mustard, vinegar, and tarragon serves as the dipping sauce for grilled chops, Polish sausage, and leeks.

PREP: 20 MINUTES **SOAK:** 1 HOUR **GRILL:** 12 MINUTES **MAKES:** 4 SERVINGS

2 cups mesquite wood chips

4 boneless pork top loin chops, cut ¾ inch thick (about 1 pound total)

4 small leeks or 1 medium red sweet pepper, seeded and cut into 1-inch pieces

¼ teaspoon ground black pepper

⅛ teaspoon garlic salt

8 ounces cooked turkey kielbasa or Polish sausage, cut into 4 pieces

⅓ cup whole-grain mustard

2 teaspoons white wine vinegar or cider vinegar

1 teaspoon snipped fresh tarragon

1 At least 1 hour before grilling, soak wood chips in enough water to cover. Drain before using.

2 Trim fat from pork chops. If using leeks, rinse well, trim root ends, and cut 3 to 4 inches off each top and discard. Sprinkle pepper and garlic salt evenly over chops and leeks or sweet pepper.

3 For a charcoal grill, arrange medium coals in bottom of a grill with a cover. Sprinkle drained wood chips on coals. Cover and heat about 10 minutes or until chips begin to smoke. Place the chops and leeks or sweet pepper on grill rack directly over coals. Cover and grill for 5 minutes. Turn chops; add the sausage pieces to grill. Cover and grill for 7 to 10 minutes more or until the chops are done and juices run clear (160°F) and sausage is heated through, turning sausage once. (For a gas grill, preheat grill. Reduce heat to medium. Add drained wood chips according to manufacturer's directions. Place chops and leeks or sweet peppers, then sausage pieces on grill and grill as above.)

4 Meanwhile, in a small bowl combine mustard, vinegar, and tarragon. Serve as a dipping sauce with chops, sausage, and leeks or sweet pepper.

NUTRITION FACTS PER SERVING: 282 cal., 12 g total fat (3 g sat. fat), 86 mg chol., 880 mg sodium, 12 g carbo., 4 g fiber, 27 g pro.

342

Pecan-Smoked Pork Chops

Though milder than other woods, pecan wood punches up these thick chops with plenty of flavor. Rubbed-on allspice comes alive when it meets the cherry relish.

PREP: 25 MINUTES SOAK: 1 HOUR SMOKE: 1¾ HOURS MAKES: 4 SERVINGS

- **6** to 8 pecan wood chunks
- **4** pork loin chops, cut 1½ inches thick
- **1** tablespoon brown sugar
- **½** teaspoon salt
- **½** teaspoon paprika
- **¼** teaspoon ground allspice
- **¼** teaspoon ground black pepper
- **1** tablespoon cider vinegar
- **1** recipe Apple-Cherry Relish

1 At least 1 hour before smoke cooking, soak wood chunks in enough water to cover. Drain before using.

2 Trim fat from chops. For rub, in a small bowl stir together brown sugar, salt, paprika, allspice, and pepper. Brush the chops with vinegar. Sprinkle rub evenly over chops; rub in with your fingers.

3 In a smoker arrange preheated coals, half of the drained wood chunks, and water pan according to the manufacturer's directions. Pour water into pan. Place chops on grill rack over water pan. Cover and smoke for 1¾ to 2¼ hours or until meat juices run clear (160°F). Add coals, wood chunks, and water as needed. Serve chops with Apple-Cherry Relish.

Apple-Cherry Relish: In a small saucepan combine 1 cup chopped, peeled apple; ½ cup dried tart cherries; and 3 tablespoons water. Bring to boiling; reduce heat. Cover and simmer about 5 minutes or until apple is tender. In a small bowl combine 2 tablespoons brown sugar, 2 tablespoons vinegar, 1 teaspoon cornstarch, and ¼ teaspoon ground allspice. Stir into apple mixture. Cook and stir until thickened and bubbly. Cook and stir for 2 minutes more. Just before serving, stir in ¼ cup chopped pecans, toasted.

NUTRITION FACTS PER SERVING: 417 cal., 19 g total fat (5 g sat. fat), 102 mg chol., 348 mg sodium, 27 g carbo., 2 g fiber, 33 g pro.

Smoked Iowa Pork Chops

Thick, bone-in pork top loin chops may be labeled Iowa chops. If you prefer boneless chops, use thick-cut ones, which are sometimes sold as America's cut chops. You can almost squeeze two servings out of each chop.

PREP: 10 MINUTES **SOAK:** 1 HOUR **GRILL:** 35 MINUTES **MAKES:** 4 SERVINGS

2 cups oak or pecan wood chips

1 tablespoon dry mustard

1½ teaspoons salt

1½ teaspoons paprika

1½ teaspoons dried basil, crushed

1 to 1½ teaspoons freshly ground black pepper

½ teaspoon garlic powder

4 pork loin or rib chops, cut 1¼ inches thick (about 3 pounds total)

1 At least 1 hour before grilling, soak wood chips in enough water to cover. Drain before using.

2 For rub, in a small bowl stir together the dry mustard, salt, paprika, basil, pepper, and garlic powder. Trim fat from chops. Sprinkle rub evenly over chops; rub in with your fingers.

3 For a charcoal grill, arrange medium-hot coals around a drip pan. Test for medium heat above the pan. Sprinkle drained wood chips over the coals. Place chops on grill rack over drip pan. Cover and grill for 35 to 40 minutes or until meat juices run clear (160°F). (For a gas grill, preheat grill. Reduce heat to medium. Adjust for indirect cooking. Add the drained wood chips according to manufacturer's directions. Place pork chops on grill rack. Grill as above.)

NUTRITION FACTS PER SERVING: 356 cal., 14 g total fat (5 g sat. fat), 139 mg chol., 975 mg sodium, 1 g carbo., 0 g fiber, 52 g pro.

SMOKER DIRECTIONS: Prepare as above through step 2, except use 8 to 10 oak or pecan wood chunks. In a smoker arrange preheated coals, half of the drained wood chunks, and the water pan according to the manufacturer's directions. Pour water into pan. Place chops on the grill rack over pan. Cover and smoke for 1¾ to 2¼ hours or until meat juices run clear (160°F). Add coals, wood chunks, and water as needed.

344

Memphis-Style Ribs

Dry rubs, such as this slightly sweet, slightly spicy one, are typical of Memphis-style barbecue.

PREP: 5 MINUTES CHILL: 4 TO 24 HOURS SOAK: 1 HOUR

SMOKE: 3 HOURS MAKES: 4 SERVINGS

4 pounds pork loin back ribs or meaty spareribs

3 tablespoons brown sugar

3 tablespoons paprika

2 tablespoons chili powder

1 tablespoon ground cumin

1 tablespoon garlic pepper

1 teaspoon seasoned salt

½ to 1 teaspoon cayenne pepper

8 to 10 hickory wood chunks

1 Trim fat from ribs. Place ribs in a shallow dish. For rub, in a small bowl combine the brown sugar, paprika, chili powder, cumin, garlic pepper, seasoned salt, and cayenne pepper. If desired, reserve 2 tablespoons of the rub to sprinkle on ribs near the end of smoking. Sprinkle the remaining rub evenly over ribs; rub in with your fingers. Cover and chill in the refrigerator for at least 4 hours or up to 24 hours.

2 At least 1 hour before smoke cooking, soak wood chunks in enough water to cover. Drain before using.

3 In a smoker arrange preheated coals, half of the drained wood chunks, and the water pan according to the manufacturer's directions. Pour water into pan. Place ribs on grill rack over pan. (Or place ribs in a rib rack; place on grill rack.) Cover and smoke for 3 to 4 hours or until ribs are tender. Add coals, wood chunks, and water as needed. If desired, sprinkle ribs with the reserved rub during the last 15 minutes of smoking.

NUTRITION FACTS PER SERVING: 509 cal., 27 g total fat (9 g sat. fat), 118 mg chol., 163 mg sodium, 15 g carbo., 1 g fiber, 51 g pro.

Summer Breeze Ribs

A coating of yellow mustard—a trick borrowed from barbecue champions—helps the spice rub stay on and gives the meat a distinctive flavor.

PREP: 20 MINUTES **CHILL:** 6 TO 24 HOURS **SOAK:** 1 HOUR
GRILL: 1½ HOURS + 5 MINUTES **MAKES:** 6 SERVINGS

¼   cup packed brown sugar

2   teaspoons seasoned salt

2   teaspoons chili powder

4   pounds pork loin back ribs or pork spareribs

¼   cup yellow mustard

4   cups hickory or fruitwood chips

¼   cup bottled barbecue sauce

   Bottled barbecue sauce

1 In a small bowl combine brown sugar, seasoned salt, and chili powder. Trim fat from ribs. Brush ribs with mustard. Sprinkle brown sugar mixture onto ribs. Cover and refrigerate for at least 6 hours or up to 24 hours.

2 At least 1 hour before grilling, soak wood chips in enough water to cover. Drain before using.

3 For a charcoal grill, arrange medium-hot coals around a drip pan. Test for medium heat above the pan. Sprinkle half of the drained wood chips over the coals. Pour 1 inch of water into the drip pan. Place ribs, bone sides down, on grill rack over drip pan. (Or place ribs in a rib rack; place on grill rack over drip pan.) Cover and grill for 1½ to 1¾ hours or until ribs are tender. Add remaining wood chips as needed and additional coals as necessary to maintain heat. (For a gas grill, preheat grill. Reduce heat to medium. Adjust for indirect cooking. Add drained wood chips according to manufacturer's directions. Place ribs on a rack in a roasting pan, place on grill rack, and grill as above.)

4 Brush with the ¼ cup barbecue sauce. Grill ribs for 5 minutes more. Serve with additional bottled barbecue sauce.

NUTRITION FACTS PER SERVING: 244 cal., 9 g total fat (3 g sat. fat), 57 mg chol., 810 mg sodium, 11 g carbo., 1 g fiber, 27 g pro.

Sweet-and-Spicy Pork Ribs

Slather on your favorite barbecue sauce for the perfect finish to these flavorful ribs.

PREP: 20 MINUTES **CHILL:** 8 TO 24 HOURS **SOAK:** 1 HOUR
GRILL: 1½ HOURS **MAKES:** 6 SERVINGS

⅓ **cup sugar**

2 **tablespoons paprika**

1 **tablespoon seasoned salt**

1 **tablespoon hickory-flavored salt**

2 **teaspoons garlic powder**

2 **teaspoons ground black pepper**

4 **pounds pork loin back ribs**

4 **cups hickory wood chips**

1 **cup bottled barbecue sauce**

1 For rub, in a small bowl combine sugar, paprika, seasoned salt, hickory-flavored salt, garlic powder, and pepper. Remove ¼ cup of the rub. (Store remaining rub in a tightly covered container for up to 3 months.)

2 Pull membrane off the back of the ribs; trim fat from ribs. Sprinkle the ¼ cup rub evenly over both sides of ribs; rub in with your fingers. Wrap ribs tightly in plastic wrap; refrigerate for at least 8 hours or up to 24 hours.

3 At least 1 hour before grilling, soak wood chips in enough water to cover. Drain before using.

4 For a charcoal grill, arrange medium-hot coals around a drip pan. Test for medium heat above the pan. Sprinkle half of the drained wood chips over the coals. Place ribs, bone sides down, on grill rack over drip pan. (Or place ribs in a rib rack; place on grill rack.) Cover and grill for 1½ to 1¾ hours or until ribs are tender, brushing once with barbecue sauce during the last 15 minutes of grilling. Add remaining wood chips as needed and additional coals as necessary to maintain heat. (For a gas grill, preheat grill. Reduce heat to medium. Adjust for indirect cooking. Add the drained wood chips according to manufacturer's directions. Place ribs on a rack in roasting pan, place on grill rack, and grill as above.)

5 To serve, heat remaining barbecue sauce until bubbly; pass with ribs.

NUTRITION FACTS PER SERVING: 365 cal., 19 g total fat (6 g sat. fat), 75 mg chol., 1,014 mg sodium, 10 g carbo., 1 g fiber, 37 g pro.

What-a-Back Ribs

This recipe offers another angle on East meets West. The hoisin, ginger, and sesame flavors come singing through, along with plenty of hearty smokiness.

PREP: 25 MINUTES **MARINATE:** 6 TO 24 HOURS **SOAK:** 1 HOUR
GRILL: 1½ HOURS **MAKES:** 6 SERVINGS

4 pounds pork loin back ribs

1 recipe Hidden Pleasures Hoisin-Ginger Glaze

3 cups hickory or apple wood chips

Whole fresh chile peppers (optional)

Lime wedges (optional)

Bok choy leaves (optional)

1 Trim fat from ribs. Place the ribs in a large resealable plastic bag set in a shallow dish. Cover and refrigerate ½ cup of the Hidden Pleasures Hoisin-Ginger Glaze. Pour the remaining glaze over the ribs. Seal bag; turn to coat meat. Marinate in the refrigerator for at least 6 hours or up to 24 hours, turning bag occasionally.

2 At least 1 hour before grilling, soak wood chips in enough water to cover. Drain before using.

3 Drain ribs, discarding marinade. For a charcoal grill, arrange medium-hot coals around a drip pan. Test for medium heat above the pan. Sprinkle half of the drained wood chips over the coals. Place ribs, bone sides down, on grill rack over drip pan. (Or place ribs in a rib rack; place on grill rack over the drip pan.) Cover and grill for 1½ to 1¾ hours or until ribs are tender, brushing occasionally with the ½ cup reserved glaze during the last 15 minutes of grilling. Add remaining wood chips as needed and additional coals as necessary to maintain heat. (For a gas grill, preheat grill. Reduce heat to medium. Adjust for indirect cooking. Add drained wood chips according to manufacturer's directions. Place ribs on a rack in a roasting pan, place on grill rack, and grill as above.) To serve, if desired, garnish with whole chile peppers, lime wedges, and bok choy.

Hidden Pleasures Hoisin-Ginger Glaze: In a medium bowl combine ½ cup bottled hoisin sauce; ¼ cup bottled plum sauce; ¼ cup reduced-sodium soy sauce; 2 tablespoons dry sherry; 2 tablespoons toasted sesame oil; 2 tablespoons honey; 1 tablespoon grated fresh ginger; 2½ teaspoons bottled minced garlic (5 cloves); and ½ teaspoon ground black pepper.

NUTRITION FACTS PER SERVING: 447 cal., 19 g total fat (5 g sat. fat), 90 mg chol., 750 mg sodium, 21 g carbo., 0 g fiber, 43 g pro.

Kansas City Pork Spareribs

In this recipe from a classic barbecue city, Kansas City
genius and wood smoke combine for unforgettable baby back ribs.

PREP: 10 MINUTES **SOAK:** 1 HOUR **GRILL:** 1½ HOURS **MAKES:** 4 SERVINGS

4   cups hickory, oak, or apple wood chips
4   pounds meaty pork spareribs or loin back ribs
1   tablespoon brown sugar
1   tablespoon garlic pepper
1   tablespoon paprika
1½ teaspoons chili powder
1   teaspoon salt
½   teaspoon celery seeds
¼   cup cider vinegar
1   recipe Kansas City Barbecue Sauce

1 At least 1 hour before grilling, soak wood chips in enough water to cover. Drain before using.

2 Trim fat from ribs. For rub, in a small bowl combine brown sugar, garlic pepper, paprika, chili powder, salt, and celery seeds. Brush ribs with vinegar. Sprinkle rub evenly over ribs; rub in with your fingers.

3 For a charcoal grill, arrange medium-hot coals around a drip pan. Test for medium heat above the pan. Sprinkle half of the drained wood chips over the coals. Place ribs, bone side down, on grill rack over drip pan. (Or place ribs in a rib rack; place on grill rack.) Cover and grill for 1½ to 1¾ hours or until ribs are tender. Add remaining wood chips as needed and additional coals as necessary to maintain heat. (For a gas grill, preheat grill. Reduce heat to medium. Adjust for indirect cooking. Add drained wood chips according to manufacturer's directions. Place ribs on rack in a roasting pan, place on grill rack, and grill as above.)

4 Meanwhile, prepare Kansas City Barbecue Sauce; serve sauce with ribs.

Kansas City Barbecue Sauce: In a medium saucepan cook ½ cup finely chopped onion and 1 teaspoon bottled minced garlic (2 cloves) in 1 tablespoon hot olive oil until onion is tender. Stir in ¾ cup apple juice, ½ of a 6-ounce can tomato paste (⅓ cup), ¼ cup vinegar, 2 tablespoons brown sugar, 2 tablespoons molasses, 1 tablespoon paprika, 1 tablespoon prepared horseradish, 1 tablespoon Worcestershire sauce, 1 teaspoon salt, and ½ teaspoon ground black pepper. Bring to boiling; reduce heat. Simmer, uncovered, about 30 minutes or until desired consistency, stirring occasionally.

NUTRITION FACTS PER SERVING: 688 cal., 42 g total fat (14 g sat. fat), 176 mg chol., 1,470 mg sodium, 34 g carbo., 2 g fiber, 46 g pro.

Texas Beer-Smoked Ribs

For extra flair, add dried chile peppers to the smoker's water pan.

PREP: 10 MINUTES **MARINATE:** 24 HOURS **SOAK:** 1 HOUR
SMOKE: 3 HOURS **MAKES:** 6 SERVINGS

6 pounds meaty pork spareribs or pork loin back ribs

1 12-ounce bottle beer

2 tablespoons chili powder

2 tablespoons lime juice

1½ teaspoons bottled minced garlic (3 cloves)

1 teaspoon ground cumin

¾ teaspoon salt

4 to 6 mesquite or hickory wood chunks

3 dried ancho or other dried large chile peppers (optional)

❶ Trim fat from ribs. Cut ribs into 8-rib portions. Place ribs in a large resealable plastic bag set in a large shallow dish. For marinade, in a medium bowl combine beer, chili powder, lime juice, garlic, cumin, and salt. Pour marinade over ribs. Seal bag; turn to coat meat. Marinate in the refrigerator for 24 hours, turning bag occasionally.

❷ At least 1 hour before smoke cooking, soak wood chunks in enough water to cover. Drain before using.

❸ Drain ribs, reserving marinade. In the smoker arrange preheated coals, half of the drained wood chunks, and the water pan according to the manufacturer's directions. Pour the reserved marinade into pan; add the dried peppers (if desired). Place ribs on grill rack over pan. Cover and smoke for 3 to 4 hours or until ribs are tender. Add coals, wood chunks, and water as needed.

NUTRITION FACTS PER SERVING: 580 cal., 43 g total fat (17 g sat. fat), 133 mg chol., 232 mg sodium, 1 g carbo., 0 g fiber, 43 g pro.

Moroccan-Style Lamb Chops

These seasoned lamb chops are flavored with a profusion of spices found in abundance at the open-air markets of North Africa. Cool the fire with a creamy yogurt sauce.

PREP: 15 MINUTES **CHILL:** 6 TO 24 HOURS **SOAK:** 1 HOUR

SMOKE: 55 MINUTES **MAKES:** 4 SERVINGS

8	lamb loin chops, cut 1¼ to 1½ inches thick
2	tablespoons sliced green onion
1½	teaspoons ground coriander
½	teaspoon salt
½	teaspoon ground cumin
½	teaspoon ground cardamom
¼	teaspoon ground cinnamon
¼	teaspoon ground cloves
¼	teaspoon ground ginger
4	cherry or alder wood chunks
1	medium cucumber, seeded and chopped
1	medium tomato, seeded and chopped
½	cup plain low-fat yogurt
⅓	cup chopped onion
⅛	teaspoon salt
	Hot cooked couscous or rice (optional)

1 Trim fat from chops. Place chops in a single layer in a shallow dish. For rub, in a small bowl combine the green onion, coriander, the ½ teaspoon salt, the cumin, cardamom, cinnamon, cloves, and ginger. Sprinkle mixture evenly over chops; rub in with your fingers. Cover and chill in the refrigerator for at least 6 hours or up to 24 hours.

2 At least 1 hour before smoke cooking, soak wood chunks in enough water to cover. Drain before using.

3 In a smoker arrange preheated coals, half of the drained wood chunks, and water pan according to the manufacturer's directions. Pour water into pan. Place chops on the grill rack over water pan. Cover and smoke until chops are desired doneness. Allow 55 to 65 minutes for medium-rare doneness (145°F) or 65 to 75 minutes for medium doneness (160°F). Add coals, wood chunks, and water as needed.

4 About 30 minutes before serving, prepare sauce. In a medium bowl combine cucumber, tomato, yogurt, onion, and the ⅛ teaspoon salt. Cover and refrigerate until ready to serve. If desired, serve chops with hot cooked couscous or rice. Pass the sauce with chops.

NUTRITION FACTS PER SERVING: 466 cal., 30 g total fat (13 g sat. fat), 142 mg chol., 501 mg sodium, 7 g carbo., 2 g fiber, 40 g pro.

Tangy Barbecued Chicken

Red wine vinegar and Worcestershire sauce provide a pleasant tanginess.

PREP: 15 MINUTES **MARINATE:** 2 TO 4 HOURS **SOAK:** 1 HOUR
GRILL: 50 MINUTES **MAKES:** 4 SERVINGS

1	3- to 3½-pound broiler-fryer chicken, quartered
1	cup red wine vinegar
½	cup Worcestershire sauce
½	cup packed brown sugar
2	tablespoons liquid smoke
1	teaspoon seasoned salt
½	teaspoon ground black pepper
3	cups hickory wood chips

1 Place chicken in a resealable plastic bag set in a shallow dish. For marinade, in a medium bowl stir together vinegar, Worcestershire sauce, brown sugar, liquid smoke, seasoned salt, and pepper. Pour marinade over chicken. Seal bag; turn to coat chicken. Marinate in the refrigerator for at least 2 hours or up to 4 hours, turning bag occasionally.

2 At least 1 hour before grilling, soak wood chips in enough water to cover. Drain before using.

3 Drain chicken, reserving marinade. For a charcoal grill, arrange medium-hot coals around a drip pan. Test for medium heat above the pan. Sprinkle the drained wood chips over the coals. Place chicken, bone sides down, on grill rack over drip pan. Cover and grill for 50 to 60 minutes or until chicken is tender and no longer pink (170°F for breast portions; 180°F for thigh and drumstick portions), turning and brushing once with the reserved marinade halfway through grilling. (For a gas grill, preheat grill. Reduce heat to medium. Adjust for indirect cooking. Add drained wood chips according to manufacturer's directions. Place chicken on grill rack. Grill as above.) Discard any remaining marinade.

NUTRITION FACTS PER SERVING: 521 cal., 33 g total fat (10 g sat. fat), 172 mg chol., 325 mg sodium, 9 g carbo., 0 g fiber, 43 g pro.

352

Green Tea and Ginger-Smoked Chicken

Green tea leaves and ginger are smoked in a foil pan to give this chicken an exotic flavor.

PREP: 20 MINUTES **MARINATE:** 4 TO 24 HOURS **GRILL:** 1¼ HOURS
STAND: 15 MINUTES **MAKES:** 4 SERVINGS

1   3- to 3½-pound whole broiler-fryer chicken
½   cup rice wine or dry sherry
2   tablespoons grated fresh ginger
2   tablespoons soy sauce
½   teaspoon ground black pepper
3   tablespoons honey
1   teaspoon soy sauce
1   ½-inch-thick slice peeled fresh ginger
½   cup green tea leaves
6   ¼-inch-thick slices peeled fresh ginger

1 Remove the neck and giblets from chicken. Skewer the neck skin to the back. Tie legs to tail. Twist wing tips under back. Place chicken in a resealable plastic bag set in a deep bowl.

2 For marinade, in a small bowl combine rice wine or dry sherry, the grated ginger, the 2 tablespoons soy sauce, and the pepper. Pour marinade over chicken. Seal bag; turn to coat chicken. Marinate in the refrigerator for at least 4 hours or up to 24 hours, turning bag occasionally.

3 For glaze, in a small saucepan combine honey, the 1 teaspoon soy sauce, and the 1 slice ginger. Bring to boiling; reduce heat. Simmer, uncovered, for 1 minute. Remove from heat. Discard ginger. Set aside.

4 Fold an 18×9-inch piece of heavy foil in half to make a 9-inch square. Fold up sides of foil, forming a pan. Place tea leaves and the 6 slices ginger in foil pan. Drain chicken, discarding marinade. Insert an oven-going meat thermometer in an inside thigh muscle, making sure bulb does not touch bone.

5 For a charcoal grill, arrange medium-hot coals around a drip pan. Test for medium heat above the pan. Place chicken, breast side up, on grill rack over drip pan. Place tea leaves and ginger in the foil pan on grill rack directly over coals. Cover and grill for 1¼ to 1½ hours or until thermometer registers 180°F. Add coals as necessary to maintain heat. (For a gas grill, preheat grill. Reduce heat to medium. Adjust for indirect cooking. Place chicken, breast side up, on a rack in a roasting pan and place on grill rack. Place tea leaves and ginger in the foil pan on grill rack directly over heat. Grill as above.)

6 Remove chicken from grill; discard tea leaves and ginger. Cover chicken with foil; let stand for 15 minutes before carving. To serve, drizzle chicken with glaze.

NUTRITION FACTS PER SERVING: 418 cal., 18 g total fat (5 g sat. fat), 118 mg chol., 712 mg sodium, 17 g carbo., 0 g fiber, 37 g pro.

Salt and Pepper Chickens

A simple rub made with four kinds of salt and two kinds of pepper dresses up these grilled birds.

PREP: 20 MINUTES SOAK: 1 HOUR CHILL: 1 HOUR
GRILL: 1¼ HOURS STAND: 10 MINUTES MAKES: 8 SERVINGS

4	cups hickory or mesquite wood chips
1	teaspoon salt
1	teaspoon onion salt
1	teaspoon garlic salt
1	teaspoon seasoned salt
1	teaspoon paprika
1	teaspoon ground black pepper
¼	teaspoon cayenne pepper (optional)
2	3- to 3½-pound whole broiler-fryer chickens
	Fresh fruit (optional)

1 At least 1 hour before grilling, soak wood chips in enough water to cover. Drain before using.

2 For rub, in a small bowl stir together salt, onion salt, garlic salt, seasoned salt, paprika, ground black pepper, and, if desired, cayenne pepper. Sprinkle rub evenly over chickens; rub in with your fingers. Skewer neck skin to backs. Tie legs to tails. Twist wing tips under backs. Cover and refrigerate for 1 hour.

3 Insert an oven-going meat thermometer in the center of an inside thigh muscle, making sure bulb does not touch bone.

4 For a charcoal grill, arrange medium-hot coals around a drip pan. Test for medium heat above the pan. Sprinkle half of the drained wood chips over the coals. Place chickens, breast sides up, on grill rack over drip pan. Cover and grill for 1¼ to 1½ hours or until thermometer registers 180°F. Add remaining wood chips as needed and additional coals as necessary to maintain heat. (For a gas grill, preheat grill. Reduce heat to medium. Adjust for indirect cooking. Add drained wood chips according to manufacturer's directions. Place chickens, breast sides up, on a rack in a roasting pan and place on grill rack. Grill as above.)

5 Remove chickens from grill. Cover with foil; let stand for 10 minutes before carving. If desired, garnish serving platter with fresh fruit.

NUTRITION FACTS PER SERVING: 323 cal., 18 g total fat (5 g sat. fat), 118 mg chol., 911 mg sodium, 0 g carbo., 0 g fiber, 37 g pro.

Gremolata Chicken

Gremolata—the garnish of garlic, lemon, and parsley that's traditionally sprinkled over osso buco—gives this smoked bird great flavor.

PREP: 20 MINUTES **SOAK:** 1 HOUR **SMOKE:** 3¼ HOURS
STAND: 15 MINUTES **MAKES:** 6 TO 8 SERVINGS

10 to 12 apple or cherry wood chunks

1 6- to 7-pound whole roasting chicken

2 to 3 tablespoons snipped fresh flat-leaf parsley

2 teaspoons finely shredded lemon peel

¼ teaspoon coarsely ground black pepper

1 bulb garlic

1 small lemon, cut into wedges

Salt (optional)

1 At least 1 hour before smoke cooking, soak wood chunks in enough water to cover. Drain before using.

2 Remove the neck and giblets from chicken. For rub, in a small bowl combine parsley, lemon peel, and pepper. Sprinkle rub evenly over chicken; rub in with your fingers. With a sharp knife, cut off the top ½ inch from garlic bulb to expose the ends of the individual cloves. Leaving garlic bulb whole, remove any loose, papery outer layers. Place the garlic bulb and lemon wedges in cavity of chicken. Skewer the neck skin to the back. Tie legs to tail. Twist wing tips under back. Insert an oven-going meat thermometer into the center of an inside thigh muscle, making sure bulb does not touch bone.

3 In a smoker arrange preheated coals, half of the drained wood chunks, and water pan according to the manufacturer's directions. Pour water into pan. Place chicken, breast side up, on grill rack over pan. Cover and smoke for 3¼ to 4 hours or until thermometer registers 180°F. Add coals, wood chunks, and water as needed.

4 Remove chicken from smoker. Cover with foil; let stand for 15 minutes before carving. Remove garlic and lemon wedges from chicken cavity. If desired, season chicken with salt.

NUTRITION FACTS PER SERVING: 363 cal., 20 g total fat (6 g sat. fat), 162 mg chol., 120 mg sodium, 2 g carbo., 0 g fiber, 41 g pro.

Smoked Chicken-Cabbage Salad

This is not your basic chicken salad. This one gets a flavor punch from smoke, fresh oranges, and a dressing of oil, vinegar, and hot Thai chile sauce.

PREP: 25 MINUTES SOAK: 1 HOUR SMOKE: 2½ HOURS MAKES: 4 TO 6 SERVINGS

6 to 8 apple or other fruit wood chunks

1 tablespoon olive oil or cooking oil

1 teaspoon bottled minced garlic (2 cloves)

½ teaspoon salt

¼ teaspoon ground black pepper

1 3- to 3½-pound whole broiler-fryer chicken

3 tablespoons olive oil

3 tablespoons balsamic vinegar

2 tablespoons bottled Thai chile sauce or chile sauce plus several dashes bottled hot pepper sauce

4 cups shredded cabbage

1 cup orange sections (about 3 oranges)

1 large tomato, chopped

2 green onions, chopped

1 At least 1 hour before smoke cooking, soak wood chunks in enough water to cover. Drain before using.

2 In a small bowl stir together the 1 tablespoon oil, the garlic, salt, and pepper. Twist wing tips under back. Starting at the neck on 1 side of the breast, slip your fingers between skin and meat, loosening the skin as you work toward the tail end. Repeat on the other side of the breast. Lift chicken skin and carefully rub the garlic mixture under skin directly on meat. Skewer the neck skin to the back. Tie legs to tail. Insert an oven-going meat thermometer into the center of an inside thigh muscle, making sure bulb does not touch bone.

3 In a smoker arrange preheated coals, half of the drained wood chunks, and water pan according to the manufacturer's directions. Pour water into pan. Place chicken, breast side up, on grill rack over pan. Cover and smoke for 2½ to 3 hours or until thermometer registers 180°F. Add coals, wood chunks, and water as needed.

4 Transfer chicken to a cutting board. Cool slightly. Remove skin from chicken; remove meat from bones. Discard skin and bones. Cut meat into bite-size pieces.

5 Meanwhile, for dressing, in a screw-top jar combine the 3 tablespoons oil, the balsamic vinegar, and chile sauce. Cover and shake well. In a large salad bowl combine cabbage, orange sections, tomato, and green onions. Add chicken; toss gently to combine. Pour dressing over chicken mixture; toss gently to coat.

NUTRITION FACTS PER SERVING: 379 cal., 24 g total fat (5 g sat. fat), 66 mg chol., 450 mg sodium, 19 g carbo., 3 g fiber, 23 g pro.

Mesquite-Grilled Chicken Sandwiches

A lime and mayonnaise mixture is the perfect partner to the flavor of these mesquite-kissed chicken sandwiches, which are special enough to serve the most regal of guests.

PREP: 25 MINUTES SOAK: 1 HOUR GRILL: 5 MINUTES MAKES: 4 SERVINGS

2 cups mesquite wood chips

¼ cup fat-free mayonnaise dressing or salad dressing

1 teaspoon white wine Worcestershire sauce

½ teaspoon finely shredded lime peel or lemon peel

4 skinless, boneless chicken breast halves (about 1¼ pounds total)

2 tablespoons white wine Worcestershire sauce

¼ to ½ teaspoon garlic pepper

⅛ teaspoon salt

½ cup shredded part-skim mozzarella cheese (2 ounces)

4 whole wheat hamburger buns, split and toasted

4 tomato slices

½ of a large avocado, seeded, peeled, and thinly sliced

1 At least 1 hour before grilling, soak wood chips in enough water to cover. Drain before using.

2 Meanwhile, in a small bowl combine mayonnaise dressing, the 1 teaspoon white wine Worcestershire sauce, and the lime or lemon peel. Cover and refrigerate until serving time.

3 Place each chicken breast half between two pieces of plastic wrap. Using the flat side of a meat mallet, lightly pound chicken into a rectangle about ½ inch thick. Brush chicken pieces with the 2 tablespoons white wine Worcestershire sauce; sprinkle with garlic pepper and salt.

4 For a charcoal grill, place medium coals in the bottom of grill. Sprinkle drained wood chips over coals. Cover and heat about 10 minutes or until chips begin to smoke. Grill chicken on the rack of an uncovered grill directly over medium coals for 5 to 7 minutes or until tender and juices run clear, turning once halfway through grilling. Sprinkle each piece of chicken with cheese. Continue grilling just until cheese melts. (For a gas grill, preheat grill. Reduce heat to medium. Add drained wood chips according to manufacturer's directions. Place chicken on grill rack over heat. Cover and grill as above.)

5 Serve chicken on toasted buns; top with mayonnaise dressing mixture, tomato slices, and avocado slices.

NUTRITION FACTS PER SERVING: 342 cal., 10 g total fat (3 g sat. fat), 81 mg chol., 695 mg sodium, 29 g carbo., 3 g fiber, 37 g pro.

Pineapple-Soy Chicken

The flavorful chicken quarters are equally delicious cooked in a smoker or on a grill over wood.

PREP: 15 MINUTES **MARINATE:** 4 HOURS **SOAK:** 1 HOUR
SMOKE: 1½ HOURS **MAKES:** 4 SERVINGS

1	3-pound whole broiler-fryer chicken, quartered
½	cup unsweetened pineapple juice
¼	cup vinegar
2	tablespoons cooking oil
1	tablespoon soy sauce
6	to 8 apple or hickory wood chunks
1½	teaspoons sugar
¾	teaspoon salt
¾	teaspoon paprika
¾	teaspoon ground sage
¼	to ½ teaspoon ground black pepper
¼	teaspoon chili powder
⅛	teaspoon onion powder

1 Place chicken pieces in a resealable plastic bag set in a shallow dish. For marinade, in a small bowl combine pineapple juice, vinegar, oil, and soy sauce. Pour marinade over chicken. Seal bag; turn to coat chicken. Marinate in the refrigerator for 4 hours, turning bag occasionally.

2 At least 1 hour before smoke cooking, soak wood chunks in enough water to cover. Drain before using.

3 For rub, in a small bowl stir together sugar, salt, paprika, sage, pepper, chili powder, and onion powder; set aside. Drain chicken, discarding marinade. Pat dry. Sprinkle rub evenly over chicken; rub in with your fingers.

4 In a smoker arrange preheated coals, half of the drained wood chunks, and the water pan according to the manufacturer's directions. Pour water into pan. Place chicken pieces, bone sides down, on the grill rack over pan. Cover and smoke for 1½ to 2 hours or until chicken is tender and juices run clear (170°F for breast portions; 180°F for thigh and drumstick portions). Add coals, wood chunks, and water as needed.

NUTRITION FACTS PER SERVING: 349 cal., 20 g total fat (5 g sat. fat), 118 mg chol., 590 mg sodium, 3 g carbo., 0 g fiber, 37 g pro.

GRILLING DIRECTIONS: Prepare as above through step 3, except use 2 cups apple or hickory chips. For a charcoal grill, arrange medium-hot coals around a drip pan. Test for medium heat above the pan. Sprinkle drained wood chips over the coals. Place chicken pieces, bone sides down, on grill rack over drip pan. Cover and grill for 50 to 60 minutes or until chicken is tender and juices run clear (170°F for breast portions; 180°F for thigh and drumstick portions). (For a gas grill, preheat grill. Reduce heat to medium. Adjust for indirect cooking. Add drained wood chips according to manufacturer's directions. Place chicken, bone sides down, on grill rack. Grill as above.)

Smokin' Jerk Chicken

Smoke coupled with a spicy mix of seasonings gives chicken the distinctive flavor of Jamaican jerk.

PREP: 15 MINUTES **MARINATE:** 1 TO 4 HOURS **SOAK:** 1 HOUR
SMOKE: 1½ HOURS **MAKES:** 6 SERVINGS

- **3** pounds meaty chicken pieces (breast halves, thighs, and drumsticks)
- **½** cup tomato juice
- **⅓** cup finely chopped onion
- **2** tablespoons water
- **2** tablespoons lime juice
- **1** tablespoon cooking oil
- **1** tablespoon Pickapeppa sauce* (optional)
- **2** teaspoons bottled minced garlic (4 cloves)
- **½** teaspoon salt
- **6** to 8 fruit wood chunks
- **1** to 2 tablespoons Jamaican jerk seasoning
  Lime wedges

1 If desired, skin chicken. Place chicken in a resealable plastic bag set in a deep dish. For marinade, in a small bowl combine tomato juice, onion, the water, lime juice, oil, Pickapeppa sauce (if desired), garlic, and salt. Pour marinade over chicken. Seal bag; turn to coat chicken. Marinate in the refrigerator for at least 1 hour or up to 4 hours, turning bag occasionally.

2 At least 1 hour before smoke cooking, soak wood chunks in enough water to cover. Drain before using.

3 Drain chicken, discarding marinade. Sprinkle jerk seasoning evenly over chicken; rub in with your fingers. In a smoker arrange preheated coals, half of the drained wood chunks, and the water pan according to the manufacturer's directions. Pour water into pan. Place chicken on the grill rack over pan. Cover and smoke for 1½ to 2 hours or until chicken is tender and juices run clear (170°F for breast pieces; 180°F for thighs and drumsticks). Add coals, wood chunks, and water as needed. Serve chicken with lime wedges.

NUTRITION FACTS PER SERVING: 283 cal., 14 g total fat (4 g sat. fat), 104 mg chol., 331 mg sodium, 3 g carbo., 0 g fiber, 34 g pro.

*NOTE: If Pickapeppa sauce is difficult to locate, substitute ⅓ cup Worcestershire sauce plus a generous dash of bottled hot pepper sauce.

Sweet 'n' Sticky Chicken

Tie a napkin around your neck and dig into this American barbecue classic.
Serve it with garden vegetable salad, whole wheat rolls, and fresh berries for dessert.

PREP: 5 MINUTES SOAK: 1 HOUR SMOKE: 1½ HOURS MAKES: 6 SERVINGS

6 to 8 maple or hickory wood chunks
6 whole chicken legs (drumstick and thigh pieces)
1½ teaspoons dried oregano, crushed
1½ teaspoons dried thyme, crushed
½ teaspoon garlic salt
¼ teaspoon onion powder
¼ teaspoon ground black pepper
1 recipe Sweet 'n' Sticky Barbecue Sauce

1 At least 1 hour before smoke cooking, soak wood chunks in enough water to cover. Drain before using.

2 If desired, skin chicken. For rub, in a small bowl stir together oregano, thyme, garlic salt, onion powder, and pepper. Sprinkle rub evenly over chicken; rub in with your fingers.

3 In a smoker arrange preheated coals, half of the drained wood chunks, and the water pan according to the manufacturer's directions. Pour water into pan. Place chicken on the grill rack over pan. Cover and smoke for 1½ to 2 hours or until chicken is tender and juices run clear (180°F). Add coals, wood chunks, and water as needed.

4 Remove chicken from smoker. Generously brush some of the warm Sweet 'n' Sticky Barbecue Sauce over smoked chicken. Pass remaining sauce.

Sweet 'n' Sticky Barbecue Sauce: In a small saucepan cook ½ cup finely chopped onion and 1 teaspoon bottled minced garlic (2 cloves) in 1 tablespoon hot olive oil until onion is tender. Stir in ¾ cup bottled chili sauce, ½ cup unsweetened pineapple juice, ¼ cup honey, 2 tablespoons Worcestershire sauce, and ½ teaspoon dry mustard. Bring to boiling; reduce heat. Simmer, uncovered, for 20 to 25 minutes or until desired consistency.

NUTRITION FACTS PER SERVING: 535 cal., 29 g total fat (8 g sat. fat), 186 mg chol., 725 mg sodium, 25 g carbo., 2 g fiber, 43 g pro.

Smoked Chicken Salad

The blend of spices in this dressing and rub—thyme, mustard, onion, and, of course, cayenne pepper—makes this chicken salad smokin'. Serve it with warm corn bread.

PREP: 20 MINUTES **SOAK:** 1 HOUR **SMOKE:** 45 MINUTES **MAKES:** 4 SERVINGS

- **4** cherry or apple wood chunks
- **2** tablespoons salad oil
- **2** tablespoons vinegar
- **1½** teaspoons sugar
- **1½** teaspoons snipped fresh thyme or ¼ teaspoon dried thyme, crushed
- **⅛** teaspoon dry mustard
- **1** tablespoon salad oil
- **1** teaspoon onion powder
- **½** teaspoon ground black pepper
- **¼** teaspoon salt
- **¼** teaspoon cayenne pepper
- **4** skinless, boneless chicken breast halves (about 1¼ pounds total)
- **6** cups torn mixed salad greens
- **1** small green or red sweet pepper, cut into thin bite-size strips
- **1** pear, cored and thinly sliced
- **1** medium carrot, shredded
- **1** green onion, sliced

1 At least 1 hour before smoke cooking, soak wood chunks in enough water to cover. Drain before using.

2 For dressing, in a screw-top jar combine the 2 tablespoons oil, the vinegar, sugar, thyme, and dry mustard. Cover and shake well. Refrigerate until ready to serve.

3 For rub, in a small bowl combine the 1 tablespoon oil, the onion powder, ground black pepper, salt, and cayenne pepper. Sprinkle mixture evenly over chicken; rub in with your fingers.

4 In a smoker arrange preheated coals, half of the drained wood chunks, and water pan according to the manufacturer's directions. Pour water into pan. Place chicken on the grill rack over pan. Cover and smoke for 45 to 60 minutes or until chicken is tender and juices run clear (170°F). Remove chicken from smoker.

5 In a large salad bowl combine salad greens, sweet pepper, pear, carrot, and green onion. Cut chicken diagonally into strips; add to greens mixture. Shake the dressing and pour over greens mixture; toss gently to coat.

NUTRITION FACTS PER SERVING: 304 cal., 12 g total fat (2 g sat. fat), 82 mg chol., 236 mg sodium, 14 g carbo., 3 g fiber, 35 g pro.

Greek Smoked Turkey

If you can't find Greek seasoning, opt for another seasoning blend, such as Italian or Cajun.

PREP: 15 MINUTES **SOAK:** 1 HOUR **GRILL:** 2½ HOURS
STAND: 15 MINUTES **MAKES:** 8 SERVINGS

1 8- to 12-pound fresh or frozen whole turkey

4 cups apple or hickory wood chips

1 teaspoon Greek seasoning or other seasoning blend

½ teaspoon salt

½ teaspoon garlic powder

¼ teaspoon ground black pepper

1 tablespoon olive oil or cooking oil

1 Thaw turkey, if frozen. At least 1 hour before grilling, soak wood chips in enough water to cover. Drain before using.

2 For rub, in a small bowl stir together the Greek seasoning or other seasoning blend, salt, garlic powder, and pepper; set aside.

3 Remove the neck and giblets from the turkey. Rinse the inside of the turkey; pat dry with paper towels. Skewer neck skin to the back. Tie legs to tail. Twist wing tips under the back. Insert an oven-going meat thermometer into the center of an inside thigh muscle, making sure bulb does not touch bone. Brush turkey with cooking oil. Sprinkle rub evenly over turkey; rub in with your fingers.

4 For a charcoal grill, arrange medium-hot coals around a drip pan. Fill the drip pan with 1 inch of water. Test for medium heat above the pan. Sprinkle half of the drained wood chips over the coals. Place turkey, breast side up, on grill rack over drip pan. Cover and grill for 2½ to 3½ hours or until meat thermometer registers 180°F (skin will be very dark). Add remaining wood chips as needed and additional coals as necessary to maintain heat. (For a gas grill, preheat grill. Reduce heat to medium. Adjust for indirect cooking. Add the drained wood chips according to manufacturer's directions. Place the turkey, breast side up, on a rack in a roasting pan and place on grill rack. Grill as above.)

5 Remove turkey from grill. Loosely cover with foil; let stand for 15 minutes before carving. (Turkey skin becomes quite dark when smoked.)

NUTRITION FACTS PER SERVING: 463 cal., 15 g total fat (4 g sat. fat), 275 mg chol., 303 mg sodium, 0 g carbo., 0 g fiber, 76 g pro.

Hickory-Smoked Turkey

Long, slow cooking in a smoker results in succulent turkey with a subtle hickory flavor.

PREP: 15 MINUTES **SOAK:** 1 HOUR **SMOKE:** 5 HOURS
STAND: 15 MINUTES **MAKES:** 12 TO 14 SERVINGS

1	10- to 12-pound fresh or frozen whole turkey
10	to 12 hickory wood chunks
2	tablespoons olive oil
1	teaspoon dried thyme, crushed
1	teaspoon dried sage, crushed
½	teaspoon salt
¼	teaspoon ground black pepper

1 Thaw turkey, if frozen. At least 1 hour before smoke cooking, soak wood chunks in enough water to cover. Drain before using.

2 Remove the neck and giblets from turkey. Rinse the inside of the turkey; pat dry with paper towels. Rub skin of turkey with olive oil. Sprinkle turkey inside and out with thyme, sage, salt, and pepper. Skewer the neck skin to the back. Tie legs to tail. Twist wing tips under back. Insert an oven-going meat thermometer into the center of an inside thigh muscle, making sure bulb does not touch bone.

3 In a smoker arrange preheated coals, half of the drained wood chunks, and the water pan according to the manufacturer's directions. Pour water into pan. Place turkey, breast side up, on grill rack over water pan. Cover and smoke about 5 hours or until meat thermometer registers 180°F. Add coals, wood chunks, and water as needed. Cut string between legs after about 3½ hours of smoke cooking.

4 Remove turkey from smoker. Cover with foil; let stand for 15 minutes before carving.

NUTRITION FACTS PER SERVING: 277 cal., 14 g total fat (4 g sat. fat), 120 mg chol., 173 mg sodium, 0 g carbo., 0 g fiber, 35 g pro.

Turkey with Raspberry Sauce

A double dose of fruit gives this all-white meat feature its appeal. Orange wood imparts the turkey breast with a citrusy-smoky taste and fresh raspberry sauce sweetens the deal.

PREP: 10 MINUTES **SOAK:** 1 HOUR **SMOKE:** 2 HOURS
STAND: 10 MINUTES **MAKES:** 4 OR 5 SERVINGS

8 to 10 orange, apple, or peach wood chunks
½ cup seedless raspberry jam
4 teaspoons Dijon-style mustard
1 teaspoon finely shredded orange peel
1 cup fresh or frozen (thawed) raspberries
1 2- to 2½-pound bone-in turkey breast half

1 At least 1 hour before smoke cooking, soak wood chunks in enough water to cover. Drain before using.

2 For sauce, in a small bowl stir together raspberry jam, mustard, and orange peel. Transfer ¼ cup of the sauce to another bowl for basting. Stir raspberries into the remaining sauce. Cover and refrigerate until ready to serve.

3 If desired, skin turkey. Insert an oven-going meat thermometer into the center of turkey breast half, making sure bulb does not touch bone.

4 In a smoker arrange preheated coals, half of the drained wood chunks, and the water pan according to the manufacturer's directions. Pour water into pan. Place turkey breast half, bone side down, on the grill rack over pan. Cover and smoke for 2 to 2½ hours or until meat thermometer registers 170°F, brushing once with the ¼ cup basting sauce during the last 15 minutes of cooking. Add coals, wood chunks, and water as needed. Discard any remaining basting sauce.

5 Remove turkey from smoker. Cover turkey with foil; let stand for 10 minutes before carving. Serve turkey with the chilled sauce.

NUTRITION FACTS PER SERVING: 220 cal., 7 g total fat (2 g sat. fat), 64 mg chol., 65 mg sodium, 16 g carbo., 1 g fiber, 22 g pro.

Chili-Rubbed Drumsticks

Free your inner barbarian—and feast on fun-to-eat turkey legs! Wisps of smoke and hot and spicy seasonings give the turkey a bonanza of lip-tingling flavor.

PREP: 5 MINUTES **SOAK:** 1 HOUR **SMOKE:** 2½ HOURS **MAKES:** 6 SERVINGS

8   to 10 hickory wood chunks

1   tablespoon chili powder

1   tablespoon finely shredded lime peel

1½   teaspoons ground cumin

½   teaspoon salt

6   turkey drumsticks (3 to 4½ pounds total)

    Bottled salsa or barbecue sauce (optional)

1 At least 1 hour before smoke cooking, soak wood chunks in enough water to cover. Drain before using.

2 For rub, in a small bowl combine chili powder, lime peel, cumin, and salt. Sprinkle mixture evenly over turkey; rub in with your fingers.

3 In a smoker arrange preheated coals, half of the drained wood chunks, and the water pan according to the manufacturer's directions. Pour water into pan. Place drumsticks on the grill rack over pan. Cover and smoke for 2½ to 3 hours or until turkey is tender and juices run clear (180°F). Add coals, wood chunks, and water as needed. If desired, serve the turkey with salsa or barbecue sauce.

NUTRITION FACTS PER SERVING: 178 cal., 9 g total fat (3 g sat. fat), 80 mg chol., 269 mg sodium, 1 g carbo., 1 g fiber, 22 g pro.

Duck with Honey-Thyme Sauce

The dark, moist flesh of duck lends itself beautifully to smoking.

PREP: 15 MINUTES **MARINATE:** 2 TO 24 HOURS **SOAK:** 1 HOUR
GRILL: 1 HOUR **MAKES:** 4 SERVINGS

2 skinless, boneless duck breast halves (about 1½ pounds total)

⅔ cup chicken broth

⅓ cup honey

1 shallot, finely chopped

1 tablespoon snipped fresh lemon thyme or regular thyme

1 teaspoon bottled minced garlic (2 cloves)

1 teaspoon white wine vinegar

¼ teaspoon salt

⅛ teaspoon ground black pepper

4 cups orange or apple wood chips

Fresh lemon thyme or regular thyme sprigs

1 Place duck in a resealable plastic bag set in a shallow dish. For marinade, in a small bowl combine chicken broth, honey, shallot, the snipped thyme, garlic, wine vinegar, salt, and pepper. Pour half of the marinade over duck. Seal bag; turn to coat duck. Marinate in the refrigerator for at least 2 hours or up to 24 hours, turning bag occasionally. Cover the remaining marinade and store in refrigerator to use as sauce.

2 At least 1 hour before grilling, soak wood chips in enough water to cover. Drain before using.

3 Drain duck, reserving marinade. For a charcoal grill, arrange medium-hot coals around a drip pan. Test for medium heat above the pan. Sprinkle half of the drained wood chips and the thyme sprigs over the coals. Place duck on the grill rack over drip pan. Cover and grill about 1 hour or until duck is tender and juices run clear (180°F), brushing once with reserved marinade halfway through grilling. Add remaining wood chips as needed and additional coals as necessary to maintain heat. (For a gas grill, preheat grill. Reduce heat to medium. Adjust for indirect cooking. Add drained wood chips according to manufacturer's directions. Place duck on grill rack and grill as above.) Discard any remaining marinade used as brush-on. Remove duck from grill.

4 Meanwhile, for sauce, in a small saucepan bring the chilled marinade to boiling; reduce heat. Simmer, uncovered, about 5 minutes or until reduced to ⅓ cup. Remove from heat. If desired, remove skin and fat from duck. Slice duck and serve with sauce.

NUTRITION FACTS PER SERVING: 144 cal., 3 g total fat (1 g sat. fat), 136 mg chol., 256 mg sodium, 2 g carbo., 0 g fiber, 27 g pro.

Smoked Duck Breast on Mixed Greens

Duck—with its moist and flavorful flesh—takes particularly well to grilling over wood chips. Here it highlights a Chinese-inspired salad of greens, mandarin oranges, mushrooms, and toasted almonds.

PREP: 25 MINUTES **SOAK:** 1 HOUR **GRILL:** 15 MINUTES **MAKES:** 4 SERVINGS

2	cups oak, apple, or pecan wood chips
⅓	cup rice wine vinegar or white wine vinegar
4	teaspoons soy sauce
1	teaspoon bottled minced garlic (2 cloves)
½	teaspoon toasted sesame oil
¼	cup cooking oil
4	5- to 6-ounce skinless, boneless duck breast halves
	Salt
	Ground black pepper
9	cups torn mixed salad greens
1	cup fresh shiitake mushrooms, stemmed and sliced
1	11-ounce can mandarin orange sections, drained
½	cup sliced almonds, toasted

1 At least 1 hour before grilling, soak wood chips in enough water to cover. Drain before using.

2 For dressing, in a food processor bowl or blender container combine wine vinegar, soy sauce, garlic, and sesame oil. With the machine running, slowly add cooking oil. Set aside.

3 For a charcoal grill, arrange medium-hot coals around a drip pan. Test for medium heat above the pan. Sprinkle drained wood chips over the coals. Cover and heat about 10 minutes or until chips begin to smoke. Sprinkle duck with salt and pepper. Place duck on grill rack over drip pan. Cover and grill for 15 to 18 minutes or until duck is tender and juices run clear (180°F). (For a gas grill, preheat grill. Reduce heat to medium. Adjust for indirect cooking. Add drained wood chips according to manufacturer's directions. Place duck on grill rack and grill as above.)

4 In a large bowl combine salad greens, mushrooms, oranges, and almonds. Stir dressing. Pour half of the dressing over greens mixture; toss gently to coat. Divide mixture among 4 dinner plates. Slice smoked duck and arrange on top of greens mixture. Pass the remaining dressing.

NUTRITION FACTS PER SERVING: 437 cal., 26 g total fat (3 g sat. fat), 122 mg chol., 487 mg sodium, 22 g carbo., 6 g fiber, 31 g pro.

Double-Smoked Salmon with Horseradish Cream

What makes this double smoked—and doubly good—is that the fresh salmon is stuffed with smoked salmon and then is smoked in your smoker.

PREP: 15 MINUTES   SOAK: 1 HOUR   SMOKE: 30 MINUTES   MAKES: 4 SERVINGS

4   hickory or apple wood chunks

4   6-ounce fresh or frozen salmon fillets (with skin), about 1 inch thick

4   slices smoked salmon (about 3 ounces total)

2   tablespoons snipped fresh dill

1   tablespoon lemon juice

    Salt

    Ground black pepper

½   cup dairy sour cream

4   teaspoons prepared horseradish

1   green onion, thinly sliced

1 At least 1 hour before smoke cooking, soak wood chunks in enough water to cover. Drain before using.

2 Thaw fish, if frozen. Rinse fish; pat dry with paper towels. Make a pocket in each fish fillet by cutting horizontally from one side almost through to the other side. Fill pockets with slices of smoked salmon and 2 teaspoons of the dill, folding salmon slices as necessary to fit. Brush fillets with lemon juice and top with another 2 teaspoons of the dill. Sprinkle with salt and pepper.

3 In a smoker arrange preheated coals, drained wood chunks, and the water pan according to the manufacturer's directions. Pour water into pan. Place fish, skin sides down, on the grill rack over pan. Cover and smoke about 30 minutes or until fish flakes easily when tested with a fork.

4 Meanwhile, for sauce, in a small bowl combine the remaining 2 teaspoons dill, the sour cream, horseradish, and green onion. Serve fish with the sauce.

NUTRITION FACTS PER SERVING: 245 cal., 13 g total fat (5 g sat. fat), 48 mg chol., 337 mg sodium, 2 g carbo., 0 g fiber, 29 g pro.

Planked Salmon with Cucumber-Dill Sauce

Native Americans in the Pacific Northwest nailed butterflied salmon to planks and set the planks vertically around a center fire to smoke the fish. You'll capture much of that wonderful smoky flavor in this recipe.

PREP: 10 MINUTES CHILL: 8 TO 24 HOURS GRILL: 18 MINUTES MAKES: 4 TO 6 SERVINGS

1 1½-pound fresh or frozen salmon fillet, about 1 inch thick

1 tablespoon brown sugar

1 teaspoon salt

¼ teaspoon ground black pepper

Cedar grill plank*

1 recipe Cucumber-Dill Sauce (see recipe, page 290)

1 Thaw salmon, if frozen. Rinse salmon; pat dry with paper towels. Place salmon, skin side down, in a shallow dish. For rub, in a small bowl stir together brown sugar, salt, and pepper. Sprinkle rub evenly over salmon (not on skin side); rub in with your fingers. Cover and chill in the refrigerator for at least 8 hours or up to 24 hours.

2 Wet both sides of a cedar grill plank under running water; set aside.

3 For a charcoal grill, arrange medium-hot coals in a circle around edge of grill. Place salmon, skin side down, on grill plank. Place plank in center of grill rack (not over coals). Cover and grill for 18 to 22 minutes or just until fish flakes easily when tested with a fork. (For a gas grill, preheat grill. Reduce heat to medium. Adjust for indirect cooking. Place plank with salmon on grill rack over unlit burner. Grill as above.)

4 To serve, cut salmon into 4 to 6 pieces. Slide a spatula between the fish and skin to release pieces from plank. Serve with Cucumber-Dill Sauce.

NUTRITION FACTS PER SERVING: 357 cal., 21 g total fat (4 g sat. fat), 109 mg chol., 715 mg sodium, 3 g carbo., 0 g fiber, 37 g pro.

*NOTE: Look for a cedar grill plank at a store that specializes in grilling supplies.

Salmon with Lemon-Dill Mayonnaise

Classic flavors for fish adorn this salmon entrée.
Dill, lemon, and mayonnaise combine for a dish that is simply the best.

PREP: 20 MINUTES **SOAK:** 1 HOUR **SMOKE:** 2½ HOURS **MAKES:** 4 TO 6 SERVINGS

1	3½- to 4-pound fresh or frozen dressed salmon
10	to 12 alder or apple wood chunks
¾	cup mayonnaise or salad dressing
2	tablespoons snipped fresh dill
1½	teaspoons finely shredded lemon peel
1	tablespoon lemon juice
¼	teaspoon lemon-pepper seasoning
8	sprigs fresh dill

1 Thaw fish, if frozen. Rinse fish; pat dry with paper towels. At least 1 hour before smoke cooking, soak wood chunks in enough water to cover. Drain before using.

2 Meanwhile, for sauce, in a small bowl combine mayonnaise, snipped dill, lemon peel, lemon juice, and lemon-pepper seasoning. Cover; chill until serving time.

3 Fill cavity of fish with fresh dill sprigs. Place salmon on an 18×12-inch piece of greased heavy foil.

4 In a smoker arrange preheated coals, drained wood chunks, and water pan according to manufacturer's directions. Pour water into pan. Place fish on foil on grill rack over water pan. Cover and smoke for 2½ to 3 hours or until fish flakes easily when tested with a fork. Add coals, wood chunks, and water as needed.

5 To serve, remove skin from one side of salmon; cut salmon into serving-size pieces. Serve fish with sauce.

NUTRITION FACTS PER SERVING: 661 cal., 46 g total fat (8 g sat. fat), 95 mg chol., 541 mg sodium, 2 g carbo., 0 g fiber, 57 g pro.

Halibut in Hazelnut Sauce

Nut butters (not the peanut butter variety, but toasted nuts in melted butter) are wonderful, simple accompaniments to grilled fish, smoked or not. Another time, try this recipe with pistachios.

PREP: 30 MINUTES **SOAK:** 1 HOUR **GRILL:** 14 MINUTES **MAKES:** 4 SERVINGS

4 6-ounce fresh or frozen halibut steaks, cut 1 inch thick

2 cups apple, pecan, or oak wood chips

3 cups apple juice or water

⅓ cup butter

⅓ cup blanched hazelnuts (filberts)

1 tablespoon apple juice or dry white wine

1 tablespoon snipped fresh parsley (optional)

1 Thaw fish, if frozen. Rinse fish; pat dry with paper towels. About 1 hour before smoking, soak wood chips in the 3 cups apple juice or water. Drain before using.

2 For a charcoal grill, arrange medium-hot coals around a drip pan. Test for medium heat above the pan. Sprinkle drained wood chips over the coals. Cover and heat about 10 minutes or until chips begin to smoke. Place fish on lightly greased grill rack over drip pan. Cover and grill for 14 to 18 minutes or just until fish flakes easily when tested with a fork. (For a gas grill, preheat grill. Reduce heat to medium. Adjust for indirect cooking. Add drained wood chips according to manufacturer's directions. Place fish on lightly greased grill rack. Grill as above.) Remove from grill; keep warm.

3 For sauce, in a small skillet melt butter over medium heat. Add hazelnuts and cook, stirring occasionally, until nuts are toasted and butter is browned but not burned. Remove from heat. Stir in the 1 tablespoon apple juice or wine. Serve immediately over grilled fish. If desired, garnish with parsley.

NUTRITION FACTS PER SERVING: 402 cal., 27 g total fat (11 g sat. fat), 98 mg chol., 257 mg sodium, 2 g carbo., 1 g fiber, 37 g pro.

Sweet and Salty Smoked Halibut

Using fruit wood imparts a slightly sweet, smoky flavor to the fish.

PREP: 10 MINUTES SOAK: 1 HOUR SMOKE: 1 HOUR MAKES: 4 SERVINGS

4 6-ounce fresh or frozen halibut steaks, cut 1 inch thick

4 apple or other fruit wood chunks

½ cup packed brown sugar

1 to 2 tablespoons balsamic vinegar

2 teaspoons kosher salt

1 tablespoon olive oil

1 Thaw fish, if frozen. Rinse fish; pat dry with paper towels. At least 1 hour before smoke cooking, soak wood chunks in enough water to cover. Drain before using.

2 In a small bowl combine brown sugar, vinegar, and kosher salt. Brush both sides of halibut with olive oil. Use your fingers to rub sugar and salt mixture into tops of fish steaks.

3 In a smoker arrange preheated coals, drained wood chunks, and the water pan according to manufacturer's directions. Pour water into pan. Place fish on grill rack over water pan. Cover and smoke about 1 hour or until fish flakes easily when tested with a fork.

NUTRITION FACTS PER SERVING: 323 cal., 7 g total fat (1 g sat. fat), 55 mg chol., 1,169 mg sodium, 28 g carbo., 0 g fiber, 35 g pro.

GRILLING DIRECTIONS: Prepare as directed through step 2, except use 2 cups apple or other fruit wood chips. For a charcoal grill, arrange medium-hot coals around a drip pan. Test for medium heat above the pan. Sprinkle drained wood chips over the coals. Cover and heat about 10 minutes or until chips begin to smoke. Place fish on grill rack over drip pan. Cover and grill for 14 to 18 minutes or just until fish flakes easily when tested with a fork. (For a gas grill, preheat grill. Reduce heat to medium. Adjust for indirect cooking. Add drained wood chips according to manufacturer's directions. Place fish on grill rack. Grill as above.)

Honeyed Smoked Trout

Trout welcomes a sweet kiss of honey in this dish. Smoking adds another dimension, and the cream sauce makes the finished fish magnificent.

PREP: 10 MINUTES **MARINATE:** 2 HOURS **SOAK:** 1 HOUR

SMOKE: 1½ HOURS **MAKES:** 4 SERVINGS

4 8- to 10-ounce fresh or frozen dressed, boned rainbow trout

¼ teaspoon salt

¼ teaspoon ground white pepper

3 tablespoons honey

2 tablespoons orange juice

4 hickory or apple wood chunks

⅓ cup whipping cream

2 tablespoons lemon juice

1 tablespoon prepared horseradish

Salt

Ground white pepper

Fresh dill sprigs (optional)

1 Thaw fish, if frozen. Rinse fish; pat dry with paper towels. In a large shallow dish spread the fish open, skin side down and overlapping as necessary. Sprinkle with the ¼ teaspoon salt and the ¼ teaspoon white pepper. In a small bowl stir together the honey and orange juice; spoon evenly over the fish. Cover and marinate in the refrigerator for 2 hours.

2 At least 1 hour before smoke cooking, soak wood chunks in enough water to cover. Drain before using.

3 Meanwhile, for sauce, in a medium bowl beat the whipping cream with an electric mixer on medium speed just until it starts to thicken. Stir in the lemon juice and horseradish. Season to taste with additional salt and white pepper. Cover and chill until serving time.

4 In a smoker arrange preheated coals, drained wood chunks, and water pan according to the manufacturer's directions. Pour water into pan. Fold the fish closed and place on grill rack over water pan. Cover and smoke for 1½ to 2 hours or until fish flakes easily when tested with a fork. Add coals, wood chunks, and water as needed.

5 Serve fish with the sauce. If desired, garnish with dill sprigs.

NUTRITION FACTS PER SERVING: 395 cal., 15 g total fat (6 g sat. fat), 157 mg chol., 277 mg sodium, 15 g carbo., 0 g fiber, 47 g pro.

Hot and Smokin' Nut Munch

This snack mix is positively irresistible with a cold drink.

PREP: 10 MINUTES SOAK: 1 HOUR GRILL: 25 MINUTES MAKES: 3 CUPS

2 cups mesquite or hickory chips

2 tablespoons Worcestershire sauce

4 teaspoons red chile powder (New Mexico-style or ground ancho chile peppers)

4 teaspoons soy sauce

1 tablespoon butter, melted

2 to 3 teaspoons bottled hot pepper sauce

1 tablespoon brown sugar

1 teaspoon bottled minced garlic (2 cloves)

¼ teaspoon ground cinnamon

3 cups pecan halves or assorted whole nuts

1 At least 1 hour before grilling, soak wood chips in enough water to cover. Drain before using.

2 In a large bowl stir together Worcestershire sauce, chile powder, soy sauce, melted butter, hot pepper sauce, brown sugar, garlic, and cinnamon; add nuts. Toss to coat evenly. Transfer to a 13×9×2-inch disposable foil pan.

3 For a charcoal grill, arrange low coals around edge of a grill with a cover. Test for very low heat in center of grill (not over coals). Sprinkle drained wood chips over the coals. Place pan of nuts on grill rack over center of grill (not over coals). Cover and grill for 25 to 30 minutes or until nuts are dry and crisp, stirring every 10 minutes (watch carefully the last 10 minutes of grilling because nuts burn easily). (For a gas grill, preheat grill. Reduce heat to very low. Adjust for indirect cooking. Add drained wood chips according to manufacturer's directions. Place pan of nuts on grill rack. Grill as above.) Remove from heat; cool. Store in an airtight container at room temperature for up to 3 days.

NUTRITION FACTS PER ¼-CUP SERVING: 198 cal., 19 g total fat (2 g sat. fat), 3 mg chol., 162 mg sodium, 7 g carbo., 2 g fiber, 2 g pro.

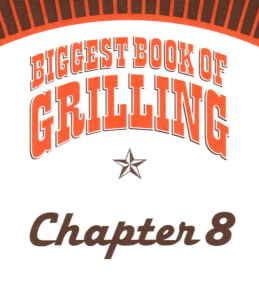

Chapter 8

INDOOR GRILLING

Adobo Steaks

Mexican adobo sauce is a power-packed red sauce made from ground chiles, vinegar, and herbs. This homemade version makes an outrageously good marinade.

PREP: 15 MINUTES MARINATE: 2 TO 24 HOURS
GRILL: 3 MINUTES (COVERED) OR 7 MINUTES (UNCOVERED) MAKES: 4 SERVINGS

4	6- to 8-ounce beef top loin steaks, cut ¾ inch thick
2	tablespoons brown sugar
2	tablespoons snipped fresh cilantro
2	tablespoons olive oil
2	tablespoons orange juice
1	tablespoon red wine vinegar or cider vinegar
2	teaspoons hot chili powder
1½	teaspoons bottled minced garlic (3 cloves)
1	teaspoon ground cumin
1	teaspoon dried oregano, crushed
½	teaspoon salt
¼	teaspoon cayenne pepper (optional)
¼	teaspoon ground cinnamon

1 Trim fat from steaks. Place steaks in a plastic bag set in a shallow dish. For marinade, in a small bowl combine brown sugar, cilantro, oil, orange juice, vinegar, chili powder, garlic, cumin, oregano, salt, cayenne pepper (if desired), and cinnamon. Pour marinade over steaks; seal bag. Marinate in the refrigerator for at least 2 hours or up to 24 hours, turning bag occasionally.

2 Preheat an indoor electric grill. Drain steaks, discarding marinade. Place steaks on the grill rack. (If grill is too small to hold all of the steaks at once, grill in 2 batches.) If using a covered grill, close lid. Grill until desired doneness. (For a covered grill, allow 3 to 5 minutes for medium-rare doneness [145°F] or 5 to 7 minutes for medium doneness [160°F]. For an uncovered grill, allow 7 to 11 minutes for medium-rare doneness [145°F] or 11 to 14 minutes for medium doneness [160°F], turning once halfway through grilling.)

NUTRITION FACTS PER SERVING: 336 cal., 19 g total fat (7 g sat. fat), 99 mg chol., 163 mg sodium, 3 g carbo., 0 g fiber, 37 g pro.

Southwest Steak

The salsa you use will dictate the amount of hotness the marinade imparts.

PREP: 20 MINUTES **MARINATE:** 8 TO 24 HOURS
GRILL: 5 MINUTES (COVERED) OR 12 MINUTES (UNCOVERED) **MAKES:** 4 TO 6 SERVINGS

1 pound boneless beef top sirloin steak, cut 1 inch thick

¼ cup lime juice

¼ cup bottled steak sauce

¼ cup bottled mild, medium, or hot salsa

1 tablespoon cooking oil

½ teaspoon bottled minced garlic (1 clove)

½ teaspoon coarsely ground black pepper

Flour tortillas, warmed

Bottled mild, medium, or hot salsa

1 Place steak in a resealable plastic bag set in a shallow dish. For marinade, in a small saucepan combine lime juice, steak sauce, the ¼ cup salsa, the oil, garlic, and pepper. Bring to boiling; reduce heat. Simmer, uncovered, for 5 minutes, stirring occasionally; cool.

2 Pour marinade over steak. Seal bag; turn to coat steak. Marinate in the refrigerator for at least 8 hours or up to 24 hours, turning bag occasionally.

3 Preheat indoor electric grill. Drain steak, discarding marinade. Place steak on the grill rack. If using a covered grill, close lid. Grill steak until desired doneness. (For a covered grill, allow 5 to 7 minutes for medium-rare doneness [145°F] or 7 to 9 minutes for medium doneness [160°F]. For an uncovered grill, allow 12 to 15 minutes for medium-rare doneness [145°F] or 15 to 18 minutes for medium doneness [160°F], turning once halfway through grilling.)

4 To serve, thinly slice meat across the grain. Serve with warmed tortillas and additional salsa.

NUTRITION FACTS PER SERVING: 243 cal., 7 g total fat (2 g sat. fat), 54 mg chol., 282 mg sodium, 16 g carbo., 1 g fiber, 26 g pro.

Honey-Mustard-Glazed Steaks

With both a marinade and a glaze,
these sweet pepper-topped steaks have double the flavor.

PREP: 20 MINUTES **MARINATE:** 30 MINUTES TO 6 HOURS
GRILL: 4 MINUTES (COVERED) OR 8 MINUTES (UNCOVERED) **MAKES:** 4 SERVINGS

4   boneless beef top loin steaks, cut 1 inch thick (about 2 pounds total)

    Salt

    Ground black pepper

⅓   cup lime juice

¼   cup cooking oil

1   teaspoon ground cinnamon

1   teaspoon bottled minced garlic (2 cloves)

½   of a 7-ounce jar roasted red sweet peppers (about ½ cup), finely chopped

2   tablespoons honey

2   tablespoons Dijon-style mustard

½   teaspoon bottled minced garlic (1 clove)

1 Sprinkle steaks with salt and black pepper. Place in a resealable plastic bag set in a deep bowl. For marinade, in a small bowl stir together lime juice, oil, cinnamon, and the 1 teaspoon garlic. Pour over steak. Seal bag; turn to coat steak. Marinate in the refrigerator for at least 30 minutes or up to 6 hours.

2 Preheat an indoor electric grill. Drain the steaks, discarding marinade. Place steaks on the grill rack. If using a covered grill, close lid. Grill until desired doneness. (For a covered grill, allow 4 to 6 minutes for medium-rare doneness [145°F] or 6 to 8 minutes for medium doneness [160°F]. For an uncovered grill, allow 8 to 12 minutes for medium-rare doneness [145°F] or 12 to 15 minutes for medium doneness [160°F], turning once halfway through grilling.)

3 Meanwhile, for glaze, in a small saucepan stir together roasted sweet peppers, honey, mustard, and the ½ teaspoon garlic. Cook over medium-low heat for 3 to 5 minutes or until heated through, stirring occasionally. Remove from heat. Brush steaks generously with glaze. Pass any remaining glaze.

NUTRITION FACTS PER SERVING: 420 cal., 18 g total fat (6 g sat. fat), 133 mg chol., 360 mg sodium, 11 g carbo., 1 g fiber, 49 g pro.

All-American Burgers

Here's a spiffed-up burger that's filled with savory seasonings.

PREP: 15 MINUTES

GRILL: 5 MINUTES (COVERED) OR 14 MINUTES (UNCOVERED) **MAKES:** 4 SERVINGS

1 slightly beaten egg

¼ cup fine dry bread crumbs

2 tablespoons finely chopped onion

1 tablespoon Worcestershire sauce

½ teaspoon garlic powder

¼ teaspoon salt

¼ teaspoon ground black pepper

1 pound lean ground beef

4 hamburger buns, split and toasted

Sliced tomatoes

Lettuce leaves

1 Preheat an indoor electric grill. In a large bowl combine egg, bread crumbs, onion, Worcestershire sauce, garlic powder, salt, and pepper. Add beef; mix well. Shape meat mixture into four ¾-inch-thick patties.

2 Place patties on the grill rack. If using a covered grill, close lid. Grill patties until meat is done (160°F).* (For a covered grill, allow 5 to 7 minutes. For an uncovered grill, allow 14 to 18 minutes, turning once halfway through grilling.)

3 Serve burgers on buns with sliced tomatoes and lettuce leaves.

NUTRITION FACTS PER SERVING: 359 cal., 15 g total fat (5 g sat. fat), 125 mg chol., 629 mg sodium, 29 g carbo., 2 g fiber, 27 g pro.

*NOTE: The internal color of a burger is not a reliable doneness indicator. A beef patty cooked to 160°F is safe, regardless of color. To measure the doneness of a patty, insert an instant-read thermometer through the side of the patty to a depth of 2 to 3 inches.

Beef Kabobs and Noodles

Japanese soba noodles, made with buckwheat, are a tasty serve-along for the sake and hoisin seasoned beef. If you can't find soba noodles, substitute spaghetti.

PREP: 30 MINUTES **MARINATE:** 1 TO 3 HOURS
GRILL: 4 MINUTES (COVERED) OR 8 MINUTES (UNCOVERED) **MAKES:** 4 SERVINGS

1   pound beef tenderloin

⅓   cup sake or dry white wine

3   tablespoons bottled hoisin sauce

2   tablespoons soy sauce

4   teaspoons sugar

1   teaspoon grated fresh ginger

⅛   teaspoon cayenne pepper

6   ounces dried soba (buckwheat noodles) or spaghetti

4   ounces fresh pea pods, halved

1   medium carrot, cut into thin strips

2   teaspoons toasted sesame oil

3   medium green onions, bias-sliced into ¼- to ½-inch-long pieces

1   tablespoon sesame seeds, toasted

1 Trim fat from meat. Cut meat into 1-inch cubes. Place meat cubes in a resealable plastic bag set in a shallow dish. In a small bowl whisk together the sake or dry white wine, hoisin sauce, soy sauce, sugar, ginger, and cayenne pepper.

2 Pour 3 tablespoons of the sake mixture over meat cubes. Seal bag; turn to coat meat cubes. Marinate in the refrigerator for at least 1 hour or up to 3 hours, turning bag occasionally. Cover and chill remaining sake mixture until serving time.

3 Meanwhile, lightly grease the rack of an indoor electric grill or lightly coat it with nonstick cooking spray. Preheat grill. Drain meat, discarding marinade. Thread meat onto eight 6- to 8-inch metal skewers. Place kabobs on the grill rack. (If grill is too small to hold all of the kabobs at once, grill in 2 batches.) If using a covered grill, close lid. Grill until desired doneness. (For a covered grill, allow 4 to 6 minutes for medium-rare doneness or 6 to 8 minutes for medium doneness. For an uncovered grill, allow 8 to 12 minutes for medium-rare doneness or 12 to 15 minutes for medium doneness, turning once halfway through grilling.)

4 Meanwhile, in a large saucepan cook soba noodles or spaghetti according to package directions until tender but still firm, adding pea pods and carrot for the last 2 minutes of cooking. Drain. Return noodle mixture to hot saucepan. Add chilled sake mixture and the sesame oil; toss gently to coat. Heat through.

5 Transfer soba mixture to a serving platter. Place kabobs on soba mixture. Sprinkle with green onions and sesame seeds.

NUTRITION FACTS PER SERVING: 443 cal., 12 g total fat (3 g sat. fat), 70 mg chol., 825 mg sodium, 46 g carbo., 4 g fiber, 33 g pro.

Pork Chops with Onion-Raisin Chutney

*Fans of the Asian classic sweet-and-sour pork will love this dish.
A homemade chutney provides the sweet yet sour bite that enhances the grilled pork.*

PREP: 30 MINUTES **MARINATE:** 4 TO 24 HOURS
GRILL: 6 MINUTES (COVERED) OR 12 MINUTES (UNCOVERED) **MAKES:** 4 SERVINGS

4	boneless pork top loin chops, cut ¾ inch thick
¾	cup bottled lemon-pepper marinade or herb-and-garlic marinade
1	medium onion, finely chopped
½	cup finely chopped red sweet pepper
¼	cup raisins
¼	teaspoon ground cloves
1	tablespoon butter or margarine
¼	cup red wine vinegar
2	tablespoons brown sugar
2	tablespoons finely chopped walnuts, toasted

1 Trim fat from chops. Place the chops in a resealable plastic bag set in a shallow dish. Pour marinade over chops; seal bag. Marinate in the refrigerator for at least 4 hours or up to 24 hours, turning bag occasionally.

2 For chutney, in a medium skillet cook and stir onion, sweet pepper, raisins, and cloves in hot butter over medium heat about 4 minutes or until onion is tender. Stir in red wine vinegar and brown sugar; reduce heat. Simmer, uncovered, about 8 minutes or until liquid is nearly evaporated. Stir in nuts. Remove from heat; cover and let stand for 10 minutes.

3 Meanwhile, preheat indoor electric grill. Drain chops, discarding marinade. Place chops on the grill rack. If using a covered grill, close lid. Grill until meat juices run clear (160°F). (For a covered grill, allow 6 to 8 minutes. For an uncovered grill, allow 12 to 15 minutes, turning once halfway through grilling.) If necessary and available, adjust heat if chops brown too quickly.

4 To serve, top pork chops with some of the chutney. Pass remaining chutney.

NUTRITION FACTS PER SERVING: 368 cal., 14 g total fat (5 g sat. fat), 101 mg chol., 506 mg sodium, 19 g carbo., 1 g fiber, 39 g pro.

Sweet Surprise Chops

The surprise in this pork chop recipe is that so few ingredients result in so much good flavor. The recipe no doubt will be asked back for many a repeat performance.

PREP: 15 MINUTES **MARINATE:** 4 TO 6 HOURS
GRILL: 10 MINUTES (UNCOVERED) **MAKES:** 4 SERVINGS

4 pork loin chops, cut ¾ inch thick*
1 medium onion, chopped
¼ cup soy sauce
2 tablespoons olive oil or cooking oil
2 tablespoons ketchup
½ teaspoon bottled minced garlic (1 clove)
Freshly ground black pepper

1 Trim fat from chops. Place chops in a plastic bag set in a shallow dish. For marinade, in a small bowl combine onion, soy sauce, oil, ketchup, and garlic. Pour marinade over chops; seal bag. Marinate in the refrigerator for at least 4 hours or up to 6 hours, turning bag occasionally.

2 Preheat an uncovered indoor electric grill. Drain chops, discarding marinade. Sprinkle chops with pepper. Place chops on the grill rack. Grill for 10 to 12 minutes or until meat juices run clear (160°F), turning once halfway through grilling.

NUTRITION FACTS PER SERVING: 248 cal., 11 g total fat (3 g sat. fat), 77 mg chol., 562 mg sodium, 2 g carbo., 0 g fiber, 33 g pro.

*NOTE: If you are using a covered indoor electric grill, substitute 4 boneless pork loin chops, cut ¾ inch thick, for the pork loin chops. Preheat grill. Place boneless chops on the grill rack; close lid. Grill for 6 to 8 minutes or until meat juices run clear (160°F).

Asian-Style Pork Chops

Fresh ginger and soy sauce accent these marinated pork chops.

PREP: 15 MINUTES **MARINATE:** 4 TO 24 HOURS
GRILL: 6 MINUTES (COVERED) OR 12 MINUTES (UNCOVERED) **MAKES:** 4 SERVINGS

4   boneless pork loin chops, cut ¾ inch thick (about 1½ pounds total)

¼   cup soy sauce

¼   cup dry red wine

¼   cup lemon juice

3   tablespoons dried minced onion

2   teaspoons grated fresh ginger

½   teaspoon bottled minced garlic (1 clove)

¼   teaspoon ground black pepper

1 Trim fat from chops. Place chops in a resealable plastic bag set in a shallow dish. For marinade, in a small bowl stir together soy sauce, red wine, lemon juice, dried minced onion, ginger, garlic, and pepper.

2 Pour marinade over chops. Seal bag; turn to coat chops. Marinate in the refrigerator for at least 4 hours or up to 24 hours, turning bag occasionally.

3 Preheat an indoor electric grill. Drain chops, discarding marinade. Place chops on the grill rack. If using a covered grill, close lid. Grill until meat juices run clear (160°F). (For a covered grill, allow 6 to 8 minutes. For an uncovered grill, allow 12 to 15 minutes, turning once halfway through grilling.)

NUTRITION FACTS PER SERVING: 262 cal., 9 g total fat (3 g sat. fat), 92 mg chol., 300 mg sodium, 3 g carbo., 0 g fiber, 38 g pro.

Sweet-and-Spicy Pork Patties

*Choose your favorite barbecue sauce for these easy-to-make pork patties.
Be sure to pass additional barbecue sauce for topping the burgers.*

PREP: 10 MINUTES

GRILL: 5 MINUTES (COVERED) OR 14 MINUTES (UNCOVERED) MAKES: 4 SERVINGS

1 pound lean ground pork

¼ cup bottled barbecue sauce

¼ cup fine dry bread crumbs

1 teaspoon seasoned pepper blend

4 hamburger buns or kaiser rolls, split and toasted

Leaf lettuce (optional)

Tomato slices (optional)

Onion slices (optional)

Bottled barbecue sauce

1 Lightly grease the rack of an indoor electric grill or lightly coat it with nonstick cooking spray. Preheat grill. In a large bowl combine ground pork, the ¼ cup barbecue sauce, bread crumbs, and seasoned pepper blend. Form the meat mixture into four ¾-inch-thick patties.

2 Place patties on the grill rack. If using a covered grill, close lid. Grill patties until meat is done (160°F).* (For a covered grill, allow 5 to 7 minutes. For an uncovered grill, allow 14 to 18 minutes, turning once halfway through grilling.)

3 Serve grilled patties on buns. If desired, top patties with lettuce, tomato, and onion. Pass additional barbecue sauce.

NUTRITION FACTS PER SERVING: 287 cal., 11 g total fat (4 g sat. fat), 53 mg chol., 543 mg sodium, 28 g carbo., 2 g fiber, 18 g pro.

*NOTE: The internal color of a burger is not a reliable doneness indicator. A pork patty cooked to 160°F is safe, regardless of color. To measure the doneness of a patty, insert an instant-read thermometer through the side of the patty to a depth of 2 to 3 inches.

Ham with Peach Salsa

Perk up your taste buds with this colorful salsa made from sweet, juicy tree-ripened peaches. It's the perfect sauce for a slice of grilled ham.

PREP: 20 MINUTES

GRILL: 4 MINUTES (COVERED) OR 8 MINUTES (UNCOVERED) MAKES: 4 SERVINGS

1   1-pound partially cooked center-cut ham slice, cut ½ inch thick

2   tablespoons honey mustard

1   medium peach or nectarine, peeled and chopped

1   medium fresh jalapeño pepper, seeded and finely chopped*

¼   cup chopped red sweet pepper

2   tablespoons snipped fresh cilantro

1   tablespoon orange juice

2   teaspoons lime juice

1 Lightly grease the rack of an indoor electric grill or lightly coat it with nonstick cooking spray. Preheat grill. Spread both sides of ham slice with honey mustard.

2 Place ham slice on the grill rack. If using a covered grill, close lid. Grill until meat is done (160°F). (For a covered grill, allow 4 to 6 minutes. For an uncovered grill, allow 8 to 11 minutes, turning once halfway through grilling.)

3 Meanwhile, for peach salsa, combine chopped peach or nectarine, jalapeño pepper, sweet pepper, cilantro, orange juice, and lime juice.

4 To serve, cut ham slice into serving-size pieces. Serve with the peach salsa.

NUTRITION FACTS PER SERVING: 231 cal., 12 g total fat (4 g sat. fat), 65 mg chol., 1,555 mg sodium, 9 g carbo., 1 g fiber, 20 g pro.

*NOTE: Because chile peppers contain volatile oils that can burn your skin and eyes, avoid direct contact with them as much as possible. When working with chile peppers, wear plastic or rubber gloves. If your bare hands do touch the chile peppers, wash your hands and nails well with soap and warm water.

Lamb Chops with Fruit Sauce

A simple sauce featuring orange juice, sage, and dried fruit bits complements succulent lamb.

PREP: 10 MINUTES

GRILL: 6 MINUTES (COVERED) OR 12 MINUTES (UNCOVERED) MAKES: 4 SERVINGS

2	teaspoons sugar
1½	teaspoons cornstarch
⅛	teaspoon salt
1	cup orange juice
1	teaspoon snipped fresh sage or ¼ teaspoon dried sage, crushed
½	cup tropical blend mixed dried fruit bits
8	lamb loin or rib chops, cut ¾ to 1 inch thick (about 2½ pounds total)
	Fresh sage sprigs (optional)

1 For sauce, in a small saucepan combine sugar, cornstarch, and salt. Stir in orange juice. Cook and stir over medium heat until slightly thickened and bubbly. Stir in snipped or dried sage. Cook and stir for 2 minutes more. Remove from heat. Remove and set aside 2 tablespoons of the sauce. For fruit sauce, stir fruit bits into remaining sauce; cover and keep warm.

2 Preheat indoor electric grill. Trim fat from chops. Place chops on the grill rack. If using a covered grill, close lid.* Grill until chops are medium doneness (160°F). (For a covered grill, allow 6 to 8 minutes. For an uncovered grill, allow 12 to 15 minutes, turning once halfway through grilling.)

3 To serve, brush the reserved 2 tablespoons sauce over chops. Serve chops with the fruit sauce. If desired, garnish with sage sprigs.

NUTRITION FACTS PER SERVING: 322 cal., 9 g total fat (3 g sat. fat), 100 mg chol., 187 mg sodium, 25 g carbo., 1 g fiber, 32 g pro.

*NOTE: When cooking in a covered indoor electric grill, it is important to use chops of the same thickness so the lid will sit evenly and close completely. If the lid does not fit tightly over the chops, you'll need to turn the chops once halfway through grilling.

Balsamic Chicken

For maximum flavor, let the chicken marinate for a full 24 hours.

PREP: 15 MINUTES **MARINATE:** 4 TO 24 HOURS
GRILL: 4 MINUTES (COVERED) OR 12 MINUTES (UNCOVERED) **MAKES:** 4 SERVINGS

4   **skinless, boneless chicken breast halves (about 1¼ pounds total)**

¼   **cup balsamic vinegar**

¼   **cup olive oil**

1½   **teaspoons bottled minced garlic (3 cloves)**

¼   **teaspoon crushed red pepper**

    Salt

    Ground black pepper

1 Place each chicken breast half between 2 pieces of plastic wrap. Pound each lightly with the flat side of a meat mallet to an even thickness (about ½ inch). Remove plastic wrap.

2 Place the chicken in a shallow dish. For marinade, in a small bowl combine balsamic vinegar, oil, garlic, and crushed red pepper; pour over chicken. Cover and marinate in the refrigerator for at least 4 hours or up to 24 hours.

3 Lightly grease the rack of an indoor electric grill or lightly coat it with nonstick cooking spray. Preheat grill. Drain chicken, discarding marinade. Sprinkle chicken with salt and pepper. Place chicken on the grill rack. If using a covered grill, close lid. Grill until chicken is tender and no longer pink (170°F). (For a covered grill, allow 4 to 6 minutes. For an uncovered grill, allow 12 to 15 minutes, turning once halfway through grilling.)

NUTRITION FACTS PER SERVING: 305 cal., 16 g total fat (2 g sat. fat), 82 mg chol., 153 mg sodium, 5 g carbo., 0 g fiber, 33 g pro.

Vietnamese Chicken Breasts

This is no ho-hum chicken sandwich. Spicy-sweet peanut sauce and crisp broccoli slaw lend an Asian accent to this out-of-the-ordinary grilled chicken.

PREP: 15 MINUTES

GRILL: 4 MINUTES (COVERED) OR 12 MINUTES (UNCOVERED) MAKES: 4 SERVINGS

2 teaspoons toasted sesame oil

½ teaspoon crushed red pepper

4 skinless, boneless chicken breast halves (about 1¼ pounds total)

2 tablespoons sugar

2 tablespoons peanut butter

2 tablespoons soy sauce

2 tablespoons water

1 tablespoon cooking oil

½ teaspoon bottled minced garlic (1 clove)

¾ cup packaged shredded broccoli (broccoli slaw mix)

4 French-style rolls, split and toasted

¼ cup chopped peanuts (optional)

❶ Lightly grease the rack of an indoor electric grill or lightly coat it with nonstick cooking spray. Preheat grill. Combine sesame oil and crushed red pepper; brush over chicken.

❷ For sauce, in a small saucepan whisk together sugar, peanut butter, soy sauce, the water, oil, and garlic. Cook and stir over medium heat until sugar is dissolved. Remove from heat; divide in half.

❸ Place chicken on the grill rack. If using a covered grill, close lid. Grill until chicken is tender and no longer pink (170°F). (For a covered grill, allow 4 to 6 minutes. For an uncovered grill, allow 12 to 15 minutes, turning once halfway through grilling.) For a covered grill, brush with half of the sauce the last minute of grilling; for an uncovered grill, brush with half of the sauce the last 2 minutes of grilling. Discard remainder of the sauce used as brush-on.

❹ Toss remaining half of the sauce with the packaged shredded broccoli.

❺ To serve, place grilled chicken breasts on bottom halves of rolls; top with broccoli slaw mixture, peanuts (if desired), and roll tops.

NUTRITION FACTS PER SERVING: 531 cal., 16 g total fat (3 g sat. fat), 82 mg chol., 1,097 mg sodium, 51 g carbo., 4 g fiber, 44 g pro.

Citrus-Herb Chicken

Keep this recipe in mind whenever you want to dress up chicken. Bottled hot pepper sauce and ground black pepper, coupled with ginger and other seasonings, add plenty of zip.

PREP: 20 MINUTES **MARINATE:** 2 TO 3 HOURS
GRILL: 4 MINUTES (COVERED) OR 12 MINUTES (UNCOVERED) **MAKES:** 4 SERVINGS

4	skinless, boneless chicken breast halves (about 1¼ pounds total)
¼	cup cooking oil
¼	cup lime juice
¼	cup water
2	tablespoons finely chopped onion
2	teaspoons dried tarragon, crushed
¾	teaspoon salt
½	teaspoon ground ginger
½	teaspoon bottled hot pepper sauce
¼	teaspoon garlic powder
¼	teaspoon ground black pepper

1 Place chicken in a resealable plastic bag set in a shallow dish. For marinade, in a screw-top jar combine oil, lime juice, the water, onion, tarragon, salt, ginger, hot pepper sauce, garlic powder, and black pepper. Cover and shake well.

2 Pour marinade over chicken. Seal bag; turn to coat chicken. Marinate in the refrigerator for at least 2 hours or up to 3 hours, turning bag occasionally.

3 Lightly grease the rack of an indoor electric grill or lightly coat it with nonstick cooking spray. Preheat grill. Drain chicken, discarding marinade. Place chicken on the grill rack. If using a covered grill, close lid. Grill until chicken is tender and no longer pink (170°F). (For a covered grill, allow 4 to 6 minutes. For an uncovered grill, allow 12 to 15 minutes, turning once halfway through grilling.)

NUTRITION FACTS PER SERVING: 204 cal., 7 g total fat (1 g sat. fat), 82 mg chol., 224 mg sodium, 1 g carbo., 0 g fiber, 33 g pro.

Tangy Lemon Chicken

Bottled Italian salad dressing combined with lemon juice and lemon peel makes a super-speedy marinade that's lip-smackin' delicious.

PREP: 10 MINUTES **MARINATE:** 2 TO 4 HOURS
GRILL: 4 MINUTES (COVERED) OR 12 MINUTES (UNCOVERED) **MAKES:** 4 SERVINGS

4 skinless, boneless chicken breast halves (about 1¼ pounds total)

½ cup bottled creamy Italian salad dressing

1 tablespoon finely shredded lemon peel

¼ cup lemon juice

Dash freshly ground black pepper

❶ Place chicken in a resealable plastic bag set in a shallow dish. For marinade, in a small bowl stir together salad dressing, lemon peel, lemon juice, and pepper. Pour marinade over chicken. Seal bag; turn to coat chicken. Marinate in the refrigerator for at least 2 hours or up to 4 hours, turning bag occasionally.

❷ Lightly grease the rack of an indoor electric grill or lightly coat it with nonstick cooking spray. Preheat grill. Drain chicken, discarding marinade.

❸ Place chicken on the grill rack. If using a covered grill, close the lid. Grill until chicken is tender and no longer pink (170°F). (For a covered grill, allow 4 to 6 minutes. For an uncovered grill, allow 12 to 15 minutes, turning once halfway through grilling.)

NUTRITION FACTS PER SERVING: 201 cal., 6 g total fat (1 g sat. fat), 82 mg chol., 240 mg sodium, 1 g carbo., 0 g fiber, 33 g pro.

Apple-Glazed Chicken Kabobs

Fruit, vegetables, and chicken soar under a sweet glaze.

PREP: 30 MINUTES

GRILL: 4 MINUTES (COVERED) OR 12 MINUTES (UNCOVERED) MAKES: 4 SERVINGS

1 cup apple jelly

2 tablespoons honey

2 tablespoons lemon juice

2 tablespoons butter or margarine

1 teaspoon ground cinnamon

¼ teaspoon ground cloves

1 pound skinless, boneless chicken breast halves, cut into 1-inch cubes

1 teaspoon garlic powder

½ teaspoon celery salt

½ to 1 teaspoon ground black pepper

1 large onion, cut into 8 wedges

1 large green sweet pepper, cut into 1-inch pieces

1 large red apple, cut into 8 wedges

1 tablespoon olive oil

1 For glaze, in a medium saucepan combine jelly, honey, lemon juice, butter, cinnamon, and cloves. Bring to boiling; reduce heat. Simmer, uncovered, for 6 to 8 minutes or until reduced to 1⅓ cups, whisking frequently. Set aside.

2 Sprinkle chicken with garlic powder, celery salt, and black pepper. On eight 6- to 8-inch metal skewers, alternately thread chicken, onion, sweet pepper, and apple, leaving ¼ inch space between pieces. Drizzle with oil.

3 Meanwhile, lightly grease the rack of an indoor electric grill or lightly coat it with nonstick cooking spray. Preheat grill. Place kabobs on the grill rack. (If grill is too small to hold all of the kabobs at once, grill in 2 batches.) If using a covered grill, close lid. Grill until chicken is no longer pink and vegetables are crisp-tender. (For a covered grill, allow 4 to 6 minutes. For an uncovered grill, allow 12 to 15 minutes, turning frequently.)

4 To serve, brush the kabobs generously with the glaze. Reheat and pass the remaining glaze.

NUTRITION FACTS PER SERVING: 510 cal., 12 g total fat (5 g sat. fat), 82 mg chol., 346 mg sodium, 76 g carbo., 4 g fiber, 28 g pro.

Savory Chicken Kabobs

Although the formula for fines herbes differs from brand to brand, chives, parsley, and tarragon are typically part of the mix.

PREP: 20 MINUTES **MARINATE:** 2 HOURS
GRILL: 4 MINUTES (COVERED) OR 12 MINUTES (UNCOVERED) **MAKES:** 4 SERVINGS

- **1** pound skinless, boneless chicken breast halves, cut into 1-inch pieces
- **¼** cup soy sauce
- **3** tablespoons dry white wine
- **2** tablespoons lemon juice
- **2** tablespoons cooking oil
- **¾** teaspoon dried fines herbes, crushed
- **½** teaspoon bottled minced garlic (1 clove)
- **½** teaspoon grated fresh ginger
- **¼** teaspoon onion powder
- Dash ground black pepper

1 Place chicken in a resealable plastic bag set in a deep bowl. For marinade, in a small bowl combine soy sauce, white wine, lemon juice, oil, fines herbes, garlic, ginger, onion powder, and pepper. Pour marinade over chicken. Seal bag; turn to coat chicken. Marinate in the refrigerator for 2 hours, turning bag occasionally.

2 Lightly grease the rack of an indoor electric grill or lightly coat it with nonstick cooking spray. Preheat grill. Drain chicken, discarding marinade. Thread chicken on eight 6- to 8-inch metal skewers, leaving ¼-inch space between pieces.

3 Place kabobs on the grill rack. (If grill is too small to hold all of the kabobs at once, grill in 2 batches.) If using a covered grill, close lid. Grill until chicken is no longer pink. (For a covered grill, allow 4 to 6 minutes. For an uncovered grill, allow 12 to 15 minutes, turning frequently.)

NUTRITION FACTS PER SERVING: 151 cal., 4 g total fat (1 g sat. fat), 66 mg chol., 292 mg sodium, 1 g carbo., 0 g fiber, 27 g pro.

Apple and Grilled Chicken Salad

A sweet–savory mixture of apple jelly and horseradish mustard is brushed on grilled chicken and tossed with mixed greens, chopped apples, and toasted walnuts.

PREP: 20 MINUTES

GRILL: 4 MINUTES (COVERED) OR 12 MINUTES (UNCOVERED) MAKES: 4 SERVINGS

⅓   cup apple jelly

3   tablespoons horseradish mustard

1   pound skinless, boneless chicken breast halves

4   cups mesclun or torn mixed salad greens

2   tart medium apples, cored and sliced

⅓   cup coarsely chopped walnuts, toasted

1   tablespoon cider vinegar

1   tablespoon salad oil

1 Lightly grease the rack of an indoor electric grill or lightly coat it with nonstick cooking spray. Preheat grill. In a small saucepan melt apple jelly over low heat. Remove from heat; stir in mustard. Set aside 2 tablespoons of the jelly mixture to brush on chicken. Reserve remaining jelly mixture for dressing.

2 Place chicken on the grill rack. If using a covered grill, close the lid. Grill until chicken is tender and no longer pink (170°F). (For a covered grill, allow 4 to 6 minutes. For an uncovered grill, allow 12 to 15 minutes, turning once halfway through grilling.) Brush chicken with the 2 tablespoons jelly mixture. Transfer chicken to a cutting board; cool slightly and bias-slice.

3 Meanwhile, toss the mesclun or mixed salad greens with the apples and walnuts. For dressing, stir together the reserved jelly mixture, the vinegar, and oil. Divide the greens mixture among 4 dinner plates. Arrange chicken on the greens; drizzle with the reserved jelly mixture.

NUTRITION FACTS PER SERVING: 345 cal., 13 g total fat (2 g sat. fat), 66 mg chol., 175 mg sodium, 30 g carbo., 3 g fiber, 29 g pro.

Jamaican Chicken Salad

Give taco and chef salads a rest for a while and try this light, refreshing possibility for a summer meal.

PREP: 20 MINUTES

GRILL: 4 MINUTES (COVERED) OR 12 MINUTES (UNCOVERED) MAKES: 4 SERVINGS

½ cup bottled honey-mustard salad dressing

½ teaspoon finely shredded lime peel

1¼ pounds skinless, boneless chicken breast halves

2 to 3 teaspoons Jamaican jerk seasoning*

6 cups torn mixed salad greens

2 medium peeled, sliced fresh mangoes or one 24-ounce jar chilled mango slices in light syrup, drained

1 For dressing, in a small bowl combine honey-mustard dressing and lime peel. Cover; chill until ready to serve or up to 24 hours.

2 Lightly grease the rack of an indoor electric grill or lightly coat it with nonstick cooking spray. Preheat grill. Sprinkle chicken with Jamaican jerk seasoning. Place chicken on the grill rack. If using a covered grill, close lid. Grill until chicken is tender and no longer pink (170°F). (For a covered grill, allow 4 to 6 minutes. For an uncovered grill, allow 12 to 15 minutes, turning once halfway through grilling.) Transfer chicken to a cutting board; cool slightly. Slice chicken diagonally across the grain.

3 Divide greens among 4 dinner plates. Top with chicken and mango slices; drizzle with dressing.

NUTRITION FACTS PER SERVING: 338 cal., 15 g total fat (3 g sat. fat), 82 mg chol., 397 mg sodium, 23 g carbo., 3 g fiber, 34 g pro.

*NOTE: If you can't find Jamaican jerk seasoning, make your own. In a small bowl combine 2 teaspoons onion powder; 1 teaspoon sugar; 1 teaspoon crushed red pepper; 1 teaspoon dried thyme, crushed; ½ teaspoon salt; ½ teaspoon ground cloves; and ½ teaspoon ground cinnamon. Store in a tightly covered container. Makes about 2 tablespoons.

Turkey with Ginger Salsa

Try a new twist on basic salsa. A hint of ginger supplies the refreshing difference.

PREP: 30 MINUTES **MARINATE:** 6 TO 24 HOURS
GRILL: 4 MINUTES (COVERED) OR 8 MINUTES (UNCOVERED) **MAKES:** 4 SERVINGS

1	pound turkey breast tenderloins
¼	cup vinegar
2	tablespoons dry sherry
2	tablespoons soy sauce
1	tablespoon grated fresh ginger
½	teaspoon crushed red pepper
½	teaspoon bottled minced garlic (1 clove)
1	medium tomato, peeled, seeded, and chopped
¼	cup chopped green sweet pepper
1	green onion, thinly sliced
1	tablespoon snipped fresh cilantro

1 Split each turkey breast tenderloin in half horizontally. Place turkey in a plastic bag set in a shallow dish. For marinade, in a small bowl combine vinegar, sherry, soy sauce, ginger, crushed red pepper, and garlic. Reserve 1 tablespoon of the marinade for the salsa. Pour the remaining marinade over turkey. Seal bag; turn to coat turkey. Marinate in the refrigerator for at least 6 hours or up to 24 hours, turning bag occasionally.

2 Meanwhile, for salsa, in a small bowl combine tomato, sweet pepper, green onion, cilantro, and the reserved 1 tablespoon marinade. Cover and refrigerate until ready to serve.

3 Lightly grease the rack of an indoor electric grill or lightly coat it with nonstick cooking spray. Preheat grill. Drain turkey, discarding marinade. Place turkey on the grill rack. If using a covered grill, close lid. Grill until turkey is tender and no longer pink (170°F). (For a covered grill, allow 4 to 6 minutes. For an uncovered grill, allow 8 to 12 minutes, turning once halfway through grilling.) Serve the turkey with the salsa.

NUTRITION FACTS PER SERVING: 145 cal., 2 g total fat (1 g sat. fat), 68 mg chol., 173 mg sodium, 3 g carbo., 1 g fiber, 27 g pro.

Caesar Turkey and Penne Salad

Tired of ordinary Caesar salad? Try this new spin on the classic.

PREP: 25 MINUTES

GRILL: 4 MINUTES (COVERED) OR 8 MINUTES (UNCOVERED) MAKES: 6 SERVINGS

6	ounces dried penne or gemelli pasta
1	pound turkey breast tenderloins
¾	cup bottled Caesar salad dressing
6	cups torn romaine
12	yellow and/or red cherry tomatoes, halved
¼	cup finely shredded Parmesan cheese (1 ounce)
	Cracked black pepper (optional)

1 Lightly grease the rack of an indoor electric grill or lightly coat it with nonstick cooking spray. Preheat grill. Cook pasta according to package directions; drain. Rinse with cold water; drain again.

2 Split each turkey breast tenderloin in half horizontally. Measure ¼ cup of the salad dressing; brush over turkey. Discard remainder of the salad dressing used as brush-on. Place turkey on the grill rack. If using a covered grill, close lid. Grill until turkey is tender and no longer pink (170°F). (For a covered grill, allow 4 to 6 minutes. For an uncovered grill, allow 8 to 12 minutes, turning once halfway through grilling.) Transfer turkey to a cutting board; cool slightly. Slice turkey diagonally across the grain.

3 In a large salad bowl combine cooked pasta, romaine, and tomatoes. Add the remaining ½ cup salad dressing; toss gently to coat. Arrange turkey on greens mixture. Sprinkle with Parmesan cheese and, if desired, cracked black pepper.

NUTRITION FACTS PER SERVING: 380 cal., 20 g total fat (4 g sat. fat), 49 mg chol., 451 mg sodium, 24 g carbo., 2 g fiber, 25 g pro.

396

Salmon with Apricot Sauce

Topping salmon or halibut with a fruity hot pepper sauce gives a happy burst of flavor.

PREP: 20 MINUTES

GRILL: 4 MINUTES (COVERED) OR 8 MINUTES (UNCOVERED) MAKES: 4 SERVINGS

4 4-ounce fresh or frozen salmon or halibut steaks, cut 1 inch thick

8 dried apricot halves, snipped

½ cup apricot nectar

⅓ cup apricot preserves

3 tablespoons sliced green onions

1½ teaspoons snipped fresh oregano or ½ teaspoon dried oregano, crushed

⅛ teaspoon salt

Few dashes bottled hot pepper sauce

Salt

Ground black pepper

1 Thaw fish, if frozen. Rinse fish; pat dry with paper towels. In a small bowl cover dried apricots with boiling water; let stand for 10 minutes. Drain well.

2 Meanwhile, in a small saucepan combine apricot nectar, apricot preserves, green onions, oregano, and the ⅛ teaspoon salt. Bring just to boiling, stirring frequently; reduce heat. Boil gently, uncovered, about 8 minutes or until preserves mixture thickens slightly. Remove from heat; reserve ¼ cup of the preserves mixture to brush on fish.

3 For sauce, in a small bowl combine remaining preserves mixture, drained apricots, and hot pepper sauce. Cover sauce and keep warm.

4 Lightly grease the rack of an indoor electric grill or lightly coat it with nonstick cooking spray. Preheat grill. Sprinkle fish lightly with additional salt and black pepper.

5 Place fish on grill rack. If using a covered grill, close lid. Grill until fish flakes easily when tested with a fork. (For a covered grill, allow 4 to 6 minutes. For an uncovered grill, allow 8 to 12 minutes, carefully turning once halfway through grilling.) For a covered grill, brush with reserved ¼ cup preserves mixture the last minute of grilling; for an uncovered grill, brush with reserved ¼ cup preserves mixture the last 2 minutes of grilling. To serve, spoon sauce over salmon.

NUTRITION FACTS PER SERVING: 279 cal., 8 g total fat (2 g sat. fat), 60 mg chol., 234 mg sodium, 30 g carbo., 2 g fiber, 24 g pro.

Spiced Grilled Salmon

Toasting the coriander, cumin, and mustard seeds before blending them enhances the flavor of the rub.

PREP: 20 MINUTES **CHILL:** 1 TO 2 HOURS

GRILL: 4 MINUTES (COVERED) OR 9 MINUTES (UNCOVERED) **MAKES:** 4 SERVINGS

2   12-ounce fresh or frozen salmon steaks, cut 1 inch thick

1   teaspoon coriander seeds

1   teaspoon cumin seeds

1   teaspoon mustard seeds

¼   teaspoon whole black peppercorns

1   tablespoon brown sugar

1 Thaw fish, if frozen. Rinse fish; pat dry with paper towels. Set aside.

2 For rub, in a small skillet toast coriander seeds, cumin seeds, and mustard seeds over medium-high heat for 1 to 2 minutes or until lightly toasted and fragrant, stirring often. Remove from heat. Stir in peppercorns; cool slightly. Transfer to a blender container. Cover; blend until finely ground (there will still be some shell pieces). Transfer to a small bowl. Stir in brown sugar.

3 Sprinkle rub evenly over both sides of each salmon steak; rub in with your fingers. Cover and refrigerate salmon for at least 1 hour or up to 2 hours.

4 Lightly grease the rack of an indoor electric grill or lightly coat it with nonstick cooking spray. Preheat grill. Place salmon steaks on the grill rack. If using a covered grill, close lid. Grill until fish flakes easily when tested with a fork. (For a covered grill, allow 4 to 6 minutes. For an uncovered grill, allow 9 to 13 minutes, carefully turning once halfway through grilling.) Cut each salmon steak in half to serve.

NUTRITION FACTS PER SERVING: 262 cal., 12 g total fat (3 g sat. fat), 90 mg chol., 118 mg sodium, 4 g carbo., 0 g fiber, 35 g pro.

Swordfish with Tomato Relish

The fresh tomato and basil relish is also great served with grilled chicken breast halves.

PREP: 20 MINUTES

GRILL: 4 MINUTES (COVERED) OR 8 MINUTES (UNCOVERED) MAKES: 4 SERVINGS

2 6-ounce fresh or frozen swordfish or halibut steaks, cut 1 inch thick

2 teaspoons olive oil

1 small leek or 2 green onions, chopped

1 cup chopped, seeded tomato

¼ cup snipped fresh basil

1 tablespoon drained capers

¼ teaspoon ground black pepper

⅛ teaspoon salt

2 teaspoons olive oil

1 Thaw fish, if frozen. Rinse fish; pat dry with paper towels. Lightly grease the rack of an indoor electric grill or lightly coat it with nonstick cooking spray. Preheat grill.

2 For tomato relish, in a small saucepan heat 2 teaspoons oil over medium heat. Add leek or green onions; cook and stir for 2 to 3 minutes or just until tender. Remove from heat. Stir in tomato, basil, capers, pepper, and salt. Set aside.

3 Brush 2 teaspoons oil over fish steaks. Place fish on the grill rack. If using a covered grill, close lid. Grill until fish flakes easily when tested with a fork. (For a covered grill, allow 4 to 6 minutes. For an uncovered grill, allow 8 to 12 minutes, carefully turning once halfway through grilling.) Serve with warm tomato relish. Cut each fish steak in half to serve.

NUTRITION FACTS PER SERVING: 155 cal., 8 g total fat (2 g sat. fat), 32 mg chol., 218 mg sodium, 3 g carbo., 1 g fiber, 17 g pro.

Grilled-Shrimp Cocktail

Dinner guests coming? Dazzle them with this impressive meal starter.

PREP: 20 MINUTES **MARINATE:** 30 TO 45 MINUTES
GRILL: 2½ MINUTES (COVERED) OR 6 MINUTES (UNCOVERED)
MAKES: 4 APPETIZER SERVINGS OR 2 MAIN-DISH SERVINGS

12	fresh or frozen extra-large shrimp in shells (about 8 ounces total)
1	large tomato, seeded and coarsely chopped
2	tablespoons coarsely snipped fresh tarragon leaves
2	tablespoons lemon juice
1½	teaspoons bottled minced garlic (3 cloves)
⅛	teaspoon salt
⅛	teaspoon ground black pepper

1 Thaw shrimp, if frozen. Peel and devein shrimp, leaving tails intact. Rinse shrimp; pat dry with paper towels. Set aside.

2 In a small food processor bowl or a blender container combine tomato, tarragon, lemon juice, garlic, salt, and pepper. Cover and process or blend with several on/off turns until mixture is coarsely chopped. Remove half of the mixture (about ⅓ cup) to a small bowl and set aside. Process or blend remaining mixture until nearly smooth.

3 In a resealable plastic bag combine shrimp and the smooth tomato mixture. Seal bag; turn to coat shrimp. Marinate in the refrigerator for at least 30 minutes or up to 45 minutes.

4 Lightly grease the rack of an indoor electric grill or lightly coat it with nonstick cooking spray. Preheat grill. Thread shrimp onto four 6- to 8-inch metal skewers, leaving ¼ inch space between pieces.

5 Place skewers on the grill rack. If using a covered grill, close lid. Grill until shrimp turn opaque. (For a covered grill, allow 2½ to 4 minutes. For an uncovered grill, allow 6 to 8 minutes, turning occasionally to cook evenly.) Remove shrimp from skewers and place in a large bowl. Toss shrimp with the reserved coarsely chopped tomato mixture. Serve in individual cocktail glasses.

NUTRITION FACTS PER SERVING: 54 cal., 1 g total fat (0 g sat. fat), 59 mg chol., 135 mg sodium, 3 g carbo., 1 g fiber, 8 g pro.

INDEX

411

I N D E X

414

METRIC INFORMATION

The charts on this page provide a guide for converting measurements from the U.S. customary system, which is used throughout this book, to the metric system.

Product Differences

Most of the ingredients called for in the recipes in this book are available in most countries. However, some are known by different names. Here are some common American ingredients and their possible counterparts:

- Sugar (white) is granulated, fine granulated, or castor sugar.
- Powdered sugar is icing sugar.
- All-purpose flour is enriched, bleached or unbleached white household flour. When self-rising flour is used in place of all-purpose flour in a recipe that calls for leavening, omit the leavening agent (baking soda or baking powder) and salt.
- Light-color corn syrup is golden syrup.
- Cornstarch is cornflour.
- Baking soda is bicarbonate of soda.
- Vanilla or vanilla extract is vanilla essence.
- Green, red, or yellow sweet peppers are capsicums or bell peppers.
- Golden raisins are sultanas.

Volume and Weight

The United States traditionally uses cup measures for liquid and solid ingredients. The chart below shows the approximate imperial and metric equivalents. If you are accustomed to weighing solid ingredients, the following approximate equivalents will be helpful.

- 1 cup butter, castor sugar, or rice = 8 ounces = ½ pound = 250 grams
- 1 cup flour = 4 ounces = ¼ pound = 125 grams
- 1 cup icing sugar = 5 ounces = 150 grams

Canadian and U.S. volume for a cup measure is 8 fluid ounces (237 ml), but the standard metric equivalent is 250 ml.

1 British imperial cup is 10 fluid ounces.

In Australia, 1 tablespoon equals 20 ml, and there are 4 teaspoons in the Australian tablespoon.

Spoon measures are used for smaller amounts of ingredients. Although the size of the tablespoon varies slightly in different countries, for practical purposes and for recipes in this book, a straight substitution is all that's necessary. Measurements made using cups or spoons always should be level unless stated otherwise.

Common Weight Range Replacements

Imperial / U.S.	Metric
½ ounce	15 g
1 ounce	25 g or 30 g
4 ounces (¼ pound)	115 g or 125 g
8 ounces (½ pound)	225 g or 250 g
16 ounces (1 pound)	450 g or 500 g
1¼ pounds	625 g
1½ pounds	750 g
2 pounds or 2¼ pounds	1,000 g or 1 Kg

Oven Temperature Equivalents

Fahrenheit Setting	Celsius Setting*	Gas Setting
300°F	150°C	Gas Mark 2 (very low)
325°F	160°C	Gas Mark 3 (low)
350°F	180°C	Gas Mark 4 (moderate)
375°F	190°C	Gas Mark 5 (moderate)
400°F	200°C	Gas Mark 6 (hot)
425°F	220°C	Gas Mark 7 (hot)
450°F	230°C	Gas Mark 8 (very hot)
475°F	240°C	Gas Mark 9 (very hot)
500°F	260°C	Gas Mark 10 (extremely hot)
Broil	Broil	Grill

*Electric and gas ovens may be calibrated using celsius. However, for an electric oven, increase celsius setting 10 to 20 degrees when cooking above 160°C. For convection or forced air ovens (gas or electric) lower the temperature setting 25°F/10°C when cooking at all heat levels.

Baking Pan Sizes

Imperial / U.S.	Metric
9×1½-inch round cake pan	22- or 23×4-cm (1.5 L)
9×1½-inch pie plate	22- or 23×4-cm (1 L)
8×8×2-inch square cake pan	20×5-cm (2 L)
9×9×2-inch square cake pan	22- or 23×4.5-cm (2.5 L)
11×7×1½-inch baking pan	28×17×4-cm (2 L)
2-quart rectangular baking pan	30×19×4.5-cm (3 L)
13×9×2-inch baking pan	34×22×4.5-cm (3.5 L)
15×10×1-inch jelly roll pan	40×25×2-cm
9×5×3-inch loaf pan	23×13×8-cm (2 L)
2-quart casserole	2 L

U.S. / Standard Metric Equivalents

⅛ teaspoon = 0.5 ml	
¼ teaspoon = 1 ml	
½ teaspoon = 2 ml	
1 teaspoon = 5 ml	
1 tablespoon = 15 ml	
2 tablespoons = 25 ml	
¼ cup = 2 fluid ounces = 50 ml	
⅓ cup = 3 fluid ounces = 75 ml	
½ cup = 4 fluid ounces = 125 ml	
⅔ cup = 5 fluid ounces = 150 ml	
¾ cup = 6 fluid ounces = 175 ml	
1 cup = 8 fluid ounces = 250 ml	
2 cups = 1 pint = 500 ml	
1 quart = 1 litre	